SUICIDE

of a

SUPERPOWER

SUICIDE
of a
SUPERPOWER

Will America Survive to 2025?

PATRICK J. BUCHANAN

Thomas Dunne Books
St. Martin's Press ♏ New York

To the Old Right

THOMAS DUNNE BOOKS.

An imprint of St. Martin's Press.

SUICIDE OF A SUPERPOWER. Copyright © 2011 by Patrick J. Buchanan. All rights reserved. Printed in the United States of America. For information, address St. Martin's Press, 175 Fifth Avenue, New York, N.Y. 10010.

www.thomasdunnebooks.com

www.stmartins.com

Library of Congress Cataloging-in-Publication Data

Buchanan, Patrick J. (Patrick Joseph), 1938–
    Suicide of a superpower : will America survive to 2025? / Patrick J. Buchanan.—1st ed.
        p. cm.
    Includes bibliographical references.
    ISBN 978-0-312-57997-5
    1. United States—Civilization—21st century.   2. United States—Politics and government—21st century.   3. United States—Social conditions—21st century.   4. United States—Religion—21st century.   5. Christianity—United States—21st century.   I. Title.
    E169.12.B7818 2011
    973.932—dc23   2011024811

First Edition: October 2011

10   9   8   7   6   5   4   3   2   1

Contents

Preface

"What happened to the country we grew up in?"

Like *Death of the West*, a decade ago, this book seeks to answer that question. But *Suicide of a Superpower* is being published in another time in another America. When *Death of the West* came out on New Year's, 2002, the nation was united and resolved. America had just swept to a bloodless victory over the Taliban and a triumphant George W. Bush had the approval of nine in ten of his countrymen. In his State of the Union address that same month, the president informed the "axis-of-evil" nations we were coming for them, and, in his second inaugural address, he would call Americans to a great crusade to "end tyranny in our world." Hubristic times.

This book is published after ten years of war in Afghanistan, eight in Iraq, the worst recession and debt crisis America has faced since the 1930s, with the nation divided and seemingly everywhere in retreat. We have entered an era of austerity and retrenchment unlike any this generation has ever known. But not only is it in the realm of economics and politics that America appears in a downward spiral. Socially, culturally, morally, America has taken on the aspect of a decadent society and a declining nation.

When the faith dies, the culture dies, the civilization dies, the people die. That is the progression. And as the faith that gave birth to the West is dying in the West, peoples of European descent from the steppes of Russia to the coast of California have begun to die out, as the Third World treks north to claim the estate. The last decade provided corroborating if not conclusive proof that we are in the Indian summer of our civilization. Historian Arnold Toynbee wrote, "Civilizations die from suicide, not by murder." And so it is. We are the Prodigal Sons who squandered their inheritance; but, unlike the Prodigal Son, we can't go home again.

Introduction

DISINTEGRATING NATION

Pity the nation divided into fragments,
each fragment deeming itself a nation.[1]
—Kahlil Gibran, 1934
The Garden of the Prophet

I think the country is coming apart...[2]
—George Kennan, 2000

The centrifugal forces have become dominant.[3]
—Lee Hamilton, 2010

Will the Soviet Union Survive Until 1984?" was the title of a 1970 essay by Russian dissident Andrei Amalrik. Forced into exile, Amalrik died in a car crash in Spain in 1980. Few had taken him seriously. Yet, nine years after his death, the Soviet Empire had collapsed and the Soviet Union disintegrated.

What has this to do with us? More than we might imagine.

As did the Soviet Union, America commands an empire of allies, bases, and troops. America, too, is engaged in a seemingly endless war in Afghanistan. America, too, is an ideological nation. America, too, is a land of many races, tribes, cultures, creeds, and languages. America, too, has reached imperial overstretch.

Many will reflexively reject the comparison. Where the Soviet empire was a prison house of nations whose Marxist ideology had been imposed by force and terror, America is a democracy whose allies have freely sought her protection.

Yet the similarities should alarm us.

For ethnonationalism, the force that tore the Soviet Union apart, that relentless drive of peoples to separate that translates into tribalism within a country, is not only pulling our world apart, it is tearing at the seams of American union. And the ideals that once defined us as a people—freedom, equality, democracy—have been corrupted into concepts more reminiscent of Marxist revolutions than of the American Revolution.

For what is a nation?

Is it not a people of a common ancestry, culture, and language who worship the same God, revere the same heroes, cherish the same history, celebrate the same holidays, share the same music, poetry, art, literature, held together, in Lincoln's words, by "bonds of affection. . . . mystic chords of memory, stretching from every battle-field, and patriot grave, to every living heart and hearth-stone"?

If that is what a nation is, can we truly say America is still a nation?

The European and Christian core of our country is shrinking. The birthrate of our native born has been below replacement level for decades. By 2020, deaths among white Americans will exceed births, while mass immigration is altering forever the face of America. The *Atlantic* titled its January/February 2009 cover story "The End of White America?" *Newsweek*'s 2009 Easter cover was "The Decline and Fall of Christian America." The statistics bear these stories out.

And for the United States, as for any nation, the death of its cradle faith brings social disintegration, an end to moral community, and culture war. Meanwhile, globalization dissolves the bonds of economic dependency that held us together as a people, as the cacophony of multiculturalism drowns out the old culture.

Is America coming apart? This book's answer is yes.

Our nation is disintegrating, ethnically, culturally, morally, politically. Not only do we not love one another, as Christ's teaching commands, we seem to detest each other in ways as deep as Southerners detested a mercantile North and Northerners detested an agrarian slaveholding South.

Half of America views abortion as the killing of the unborn meriting the wrath of God. The other half regards right-to-life as a reactionary movement and repressive ideology. In 2009, George Tiller became the fourth abortionist to be assassinated, while James Pouillon was shot and killed outside Owosso High School in Michigan while staging an anti-abortion protest.[4] Advocates of gay marriage see adversaries as homophobic bigots; opponents see advocates as seeking to elevate unnatural acts to the moral and legal status of sacred matrimony. Where one half of America sees progress, the other half sees decadence. The common moral ground on which we once stood united is gone.

Christmas and Easter, the holy days of Christendom, once united us in joy. Now we fight over whether they may be mentioned in public schools. Half of America regards her history as glorious; the other half reviles it as racist. Old heroes like Columbus and Robert E. Lee may be replaced on calendars by Martin Luther King and Cesar Chavez, but the old holidays and heroes endure as the new put down only the shallowest of roots in middle America. Mexican Americans may celebrate Cinco de Mayo, but to most Americans that was the date of a skirmish in a war about which they know little and care nothing, that took place in the year of the bloodiest battle ever fought on American soil: Antietam.

Our twenty-four-hour cable news networks have chosen sides in the culture and political wars. Even our music seems designed to divide us. Where we once had classical, pop, country and western, and jazz, now we have countless varieties tailored to separate and exclude races, generations, and ethnic groups.

We are seceding from one another not only on matters of morality, politics, and culture, but race. When President Obama was inaugurated, there was talk and hope of a new "postracial America." But three weeks into Obama's administration, Attorney General Eric Holder began Black History Month by calling us a "nation of cowards" for not discussing the subject of race more openly. Conservatives who opposed Justice Sonia Sotomayor and stood with Sergeant James Crowley in his confrontation with Harvard professor Henry Louis Gates Jr. were denounced as racists. They threw the same ugly word back in the face of their accusers and Barack Obama.

In August 2009, when crowds turned out for town hall meetings to oppose health care reform, Majority Leader Harry Reid called them "evilmongers" and Speaker Nancy Pelosi called their conduct "un-American."[5] Yet, by year's end, Americans had a more favorable view of the Tea Party than of the Democratic Party.

When Congressman Joe Wilson shouted "You lie!" at Obama during an address to a joint session of Congress, his apology was accepted by the president, but that did not satisfy the Congressional Black Caucus, which demanded a roll call vote to rub Wilson's nose in it. One Black Caucus member, Congressman Hank Johnson, said Wilson had "instigated" racism and must be rebuked or we will "have folks putting on white hoods and white robes again, riding through the countryside intimidating people."[6]

In "Inside the Mind of Joe Wilson," Rich Benjamin, the author of *Searching for Whitopia: An Improbable Journey to the Heart of White America,* said that the congressman's outburst "exposes a virulent racism and paranoia against undocumented workers."[7] Jimmy Carter said Wilson's shout had been "based on racism.... There is an inherent feeling among many in this country that an African-American should not be president."[8] Carter returned to his theme the following day:

> I think an overwhelming portion of the intensely demonstrated animosity toward President Barack Obama is based on the fact that he is a black man, that he's African-American....
>
> I live in the South, and I've seen the South come a long way, and I've seen the rest of the country that shares the South's attitude toward minority groups at that time, particularly African-Americans.[9]

How did Carter know what was in Joe Wilson's heart?

How did Carter know an "overwhelming portion" of those who had turned out for town hall meetings were motivated by "the fact that [Obama] is a black man, that he's African-American"?

That same week in September 2009, Kanye West stomped onto the stage at the MTV Music Video Awards to grab the microphone from country music singer Taylor Swift and tell her she did not deserve her best female video award for "You Belong with Me." And that the award should have gone to Beyoncé.[10]

Race consciousness is rising. Indeed, the first year of the Obama presidency seems to have radicalized much of white America. Ron Brownstein wrote of a startling survey done by the *National Journal:*

> Whites are not only more anxious, but also more alienated. Big majorities of whites say the past year's turmoil has diminished their confidence in government, corporations, and the financial industry.... Asked which institution they trust most to make economic decisions in their interest, a plurality of whites older than 30 pick "none"—a grim statement.[11]

By fall 2009, a majority told a USA Network polling firm that we Americans are "too divided" over race and religion, while three-fourths said we are "too divided" over politics and economics. A majority believe our divisions have worsened in the new century. Only one in four saw racial and religious diversity as a national strength.[12]

Consider but a few of the issues over which we have fought, often for decades: prayer and the Ten Commandments in public schools, crosses in public parks, evolution, the death penalty, abortion, assisted suicide, embryonic stem cell research, affirmative action, quotas, busing, the Confederate battle flag, the Duke rape case, letting Terri Schiavo die, amnesty, torture, the war in Iraq. Now it is "death panels," global warming, gay marriage, socialism, history books, and whether Barack Obama is really a citizen of the United States. If a married couple fought as bitterly as we Americans do over such basic beliefs, the couple would have divorced and gone their separate ways long ago.

The crudeness of our public debate is matched by its incivility. In politics it is insufficient to defeat an opponent. One must demonize, disgrace, and destroy him. The tradition of political foes being social friends when the sun goes down, maintained by Speaker of the House Sam Rayburn when he invited Republicans to his "Board of Education" meetings in his office after hours, is passé. Today, we criminalize politics and go for the throat.

In January 2011, when a crazed gunman nursing a grudge against Congresswoman Gabrielle Giffords shot her in Tucson, killed six others, including a nine-year-old girl and a federal judge, and wounded a dozen more, Markos Moulitsas of *Daily Kos* instantly tweeted: "Mission Accomplished, Sarah Palin."[13] This began a week-long campaign to indict Palin and conservative commentators as moral accomplices who had set the table for mass murder by having created a "climate of hate" in which the killer acted. Rather than bring the nation together in mourning, the massacre drove a new wedge between us.

In February, when Governor Scott Walker proposed requiring Wisconsin state employees to contribute more than a pittance to their generous health and pension benefits and restricting collective bargaining to wage increases no higher than the rate of inflation, the state capitol was invaded by scores of thousands of enraged and raucous demonstrators. Wildcat strikes by teachers followed with Democratic state senators fleeing to Illinois to prevent a quorum from voting on the proposal.

Yet, it is not only the rancor of our politics pulling us apart. We have gone through such periods before: the Truman-McCarthy era, Vietnam, and Watergate. But those turbulent periods were followed by eras of good feeling: Eisenhower-JFK, and the Reagan decade that saw a rebirth of national confidence crowned in 1989 by a peaceful end to a Cold War that had lasted a half-century.

Something is different today. The America we grew up in is gone. The unity and common purpose we had when we could together pledge allegiance to a flag that stood for "one nation, under God, indivisible" is gone.

In America today, the secession that is taking place is a secession from one another, a secession of the heart.

"E pluribus unum"—out of many, one—was the national motto the men of 1776 settled upon. Today, one sees the *pluribus*; but where is the *unum*?

"What happened to the center?" asked retired congressman Lee Hamilton, a Democrat, as he returned to Indiana. "The question at Gettysburg"—will America remain one nation?—is "the operative question of today."[14]

President Carter echoed Hamilton:

> This country has become so polarized that it's almost astonishing....Not only with the red and blue states... President Obama suffers from the most polarized situation in Washington that we have ever seen—even maybe than the time of Abraham Lincoln and the initiation of the war between the states.[15]

Six months after his comeback victory in 2010, Governor Jerry Brown of California was echoing his old rival Jimmy Carter: "We are at a point of civil discord, and I would not minimize the risk to our country and our state....We are facing...a regime crisis. The legitimacy of our very democratic institutions [is] in question."[16]

Barack Obama did not disagree. He had begun his presidency in what seemed a new Era of Good Feeling, when even Fred Barnes of the *Weekly Standard* christened him the "bearer of moral authority as our first African-American president."[17] By Labor Day 2010, Obama was ruefully relating to an audience in Wisconsin, "They talk about me like a dog."[18]

This, then, is the thesis of this book. America is disintegrating. The centrifugal forces pulling us apart are growing inexorably. What once united us is dissolving. And this is true of Western civilization. "There is no room in this country for hyphenated Americanism," Theodore Roosevelt warned the Knights of Columbus in 1915. "The one absolutely certain way of bringing this nation to ruin, of preventing all possibility of its continuing to be a nation at all, would be to permit it to become a tangle of squabbling nationalities."[19]

What Roosevelt warned us against, we have become.

Meanwhile, the state is failing in its most fundamental duties. It is no longer able to defend our borders, balance our budgets, or win our wars.

As the bonds of brotherhood are corroded, a crisis of democracy impends. America is running the third consecutive deficit of 10 percent of our gross domestic product (GDP). Unfunded liabilities of the federal government run into the scores of trillions. By Herbert Stein's Law, if something cannot go on forever, it will stop. By the middle of this decade, if it does not roll back the welfare-warfare state, the United States will face monetary and fiscal collapse. Already, Standard & Poor's has begun the process of down-grading U.S. debt and global creditors are signaling that the United States may be forced to default or float its way out of this crisis with a Weimar-style inflation that destroys the dollar. In 2010, only a debt crisis in Greece and Ireland threatening the euro sent panicked investors running back to the dollar.

On the news of Burgoyne's defeat at Saratoga in 1777, which portended the loss of the North American colonies, John Sinclair wrote to Adam Smith in despair that Britain was headed for ruin.

"There is a great deal of ruin in a nation," replied Smith.[20]

We are severely testing Smith's proposition.

1

THE PASSING OF A SUPERPOWER

America is in unprecedented decline.[1]
—ROBERT PAPE, 2008
The National Interest

The United States is declining as a nation and a world power,
with mostly sighs and shrugs to mark this seismic event.[2]
—LESLIE H. GELB, 2009
President Emeritus, Council on Foreign Relations

At no time in human history has a nation of diminished economic vitality
maintained its military and political primacy.[3]
—BARACK OBAMA, 2010

I f money isn't loosened up, this sucker is going to go down," said the
president of the United States.[4]

The place was the cabinet room. The occasion: the September
2008 meeting of Bush and the congressional leadership—to persuade
recalcitrant Republicans to approve a $700 billion bailout of America's
imperiled banks to prevent a panic after Treasury Secretary Henry Paulson let Lehman Brothers collapse.

The "sucker" that was going down was the global financial system.

Nine months earlier, CNBC's Lawrence Kudlow, in a column titled, "Bush Boom Continues," had rhapsodized about the Bush economy: "You can call it Goldilocks 2.0."[5] A few months can make quite a
difference.

LOST DECADE

This generation of Americans has been witness to one of the most stunning declines of a great power in the history of the world.

In 2000, the United States ran a surplus. In 2009, it ran a deficit of $1.4 trillion—10 percent of the economy. The 2010 deficit was almost equal, and the 2011 deficit is projected to be even higher. The national debt is surging to 100 percent of GDP, portending an eventual run on the dollar, a default, or Weimar-like inflation. The greatest creditor nation in history is now the world's greatest debtor.

In 2010, Republican Senator Judd Gregg, the fiscal conservative Obama wanted in his cabinet, went home to New Hampshire with a warning: "This nation is on a course where if we don't ... get ... fiscal policy [under control], we're Greece":

> The Tea Party is in the mainstream of where political thought is right now. We've had a radical explosion in the size of government in the last two years: You've gone from 20 percent of GDP to 24 percent of GDP headed toward 28 percent of GDP. That has to be brought under control or ... we're going to bankrupt the country.[6]

According to the International Monetary Fund, America's GDP has fallen from 32 percent of world product in 2001 to 24 percent.[7] As Leslie Gelb, president emeritus of the Council on Foreign Relations, has written, "[N]o nation with a massive debt has ever remained a great power":

> [U.S.] heavy industry has largely disappeared, having moved to foreign competitors, which has cut deeply into its ability to be independent in times of peril. Its public-school students trail their peers in other industrialized countries in math and science. They cannot compete in the global economy. Generations of Americans, shockingly, read at a grade-

school level and know almost no history, not to mention no geography.[8]

Even the establishment has begun to get the message.

Political science professor Robert Pape, of the University of Chicago, echoes Gelb:

> The self-inflicted wounds of the Iraq war, growing government debt, increasingly negative current-account balances and other internal economic weaknesses have cost the United States real power in today's world of rapidly spreading knowledge and technology. If present trends continue, we will look back at the Bush administration years as the death knell of American hegemony.[9]

When Pape correlated the rise of the nineteenth-century powers with the growth in their shares of world product, he found America's decline in the Bush years to be almost without precedent:

> America's relative decline since 2000 of some 30 percent represents a far greater loss of relative power in a shorter time than any power shift among European great powers from roughly the end of the Napoleonic Wars to World War II.... Indeed, in size, it is clearly surpassed by only one other greatpower decline, the unexpected internal collapse of the Soviet Union in 1991.[10]

In the first decade of what was to be the Second American Century, a net of zero new jobs was created. Average households were earning less in real dollars at the end of the decade than at the beginning. The net worth of the American family, in stocks, bonds, savings, home values, receded 4 percent.[11] Fifty thousand plants and factories shut down.[12] As a source of jobs, manufacturing fell below health care and education in

2001, below retail sales in 2002, below local government in 2006, below leisure and hospitality (restaurants and bars) in 2008—all for the first time.[13] Be it shoes, clothes, cars, furniture, radios, TVs, appliances, bicycles, toys, cameras, computers, we buy from abroad what we used to make here. Our economic independence is history. In April 2010, three of every four Americans, 74 percent, said the country is weaker than a decade ago, and 57 percent said life in America will be worse for the next generation than it is today.[14]

Who did this to us? We did it to ourselves.

We abandoned economic nationalism for globalism. We cast aside fiscal prudence for partisan bidding for voting blocs. We ballooned our welfare state to rival the socialist states of Europe. We invited the world to come and partake of the feast. And we launched a crusade for democracy that has us tied down in two decade-long wars.

WHAT GLOBALIZATION WROUGHT

In 2009, Paul Volcker, former chairman of the Federal Reserve, told Congress the cause of the financial crisis was trade-related imbalances. Pressed by Senator Chris Dodd, Volcker added, "Go back to the imbalances in the economy. The United States has been consuming more than it has been producing for many years."[15]

Starting in the 1980s and accelerating with NAFTA and GATT, the United States set out to meld its economy with those of Europe and Japan and create a global economy. We decided to create the interdependent world envisioned by such nineteenth-century dreamers as David Ricardo, Richard Cobden, Frédéric Bastiat, and John Stuart Mill.

That experiment did not work out well for the free-trade British in the nineteenth century, who were shouldered aside in the struggle for world primacy by America. But our generation would make it work for the world.

What happened was predictable and was, in fact, predicted. With the abolition of tariffs and with U.S. guarantees that goods made in foreign countries would enter America free of charge, manufacturers began to shut plants here and move production abroad to countries where U.S. wage-and-hour laws and health, safety, and environmental regulations did not apply, countries where there were no unions and workers' wages were below the U.S. minimum wage. Competitors who stayed in America were undercut and run out of business, or forced to join the stampede abroad.

After Japan and Europe had carted off their shares of the U.S. market, the Tigers of Asia queued up: South Korea, Taiwan, Malaysia, and Singapore. But the big winner was Beijing. In 1994, China made a brilliant strategic move. She devalued her currency 45 percent, cutting in half the already cheap cost of labor for companies relocating to China, and doubling the price of U.S. goods entering China. The result? Those "imbalances" to which Volcker referred.

For decades, Japan's trade surplus with the United States was the largest on earth. In the 21st century, China's trade surplus with the United States began to dwarf Japan's. In 2008, China exported five times the dollar volume of goods to America as she imported and her trade surplus with America set a world record between any two nations—$266 billion.[16] In August 2010, China's trade surplus with the United States set a new all-time monthly record of $28 billion, and was headed for a new annual record.[17]

Nor was the trade surplus all in toys and textiles. In critical items that the Commerce Department defines as advanced technology products (ATPs), the U.S. trade deficit with China in 2010 hit a record $95 billion. During President Bush's eight years, total trade deficits with China in ATPs exceeded $300 billion.[18] China today has the trade profile of an industrial and technological power while the manifest of U.S. exports to China, aircraft excepted, reads like the exports of the Jamestown Colony back to the Mother Country.

What was the impact of this tsunami of imports on employment? During the first decade of the twenty-first century, U.S. semiconductors and electronic component producers lost 42 percent of their jobs; communications equipment producers lost 48 percent of their jobs; textile and apparel producers lost, respectively, 63 percent and 61 percent of their jobs.[19]

In that same first decade of the twenty-first century, the United States issued 10,300,000 green cards inviting foreigners to come compete for the remaining jobs of U.S. workers. In fiscal year 2009 alone, the first full year of massive layoffs and soaring unemployment in the Great Recession, 1,130,000 green cards were issued, with 808,000 going to permanent immigrants of working age.[20]

What in the name of patriotism are we doing to our own people?

At every election, politicians decry America's deepening dependence on foreign oil. But the U.S. trade deficit in manufacturing, $440 billion in 2008, was $89 billion larger than the U.S. deficit in crude oil. Why is our dependence on the oil of Canada, Mexico, Venezuela, Nigeria, Saudi Arabia, and the Gulf states a greater concern than our dependence on computers and vital components of our high-tech industries and weapons systems produced by a rival power run by a Communist politburo? As Auggie Tantillo, executive director of the American Manufacturing Trade Action Committee, argues:

> Running a trade deficit for natural resources that the United States lacks is something that cannot be helped, but running a massive trade deficit in man-made products that America easily could produce itself is a choice—a poor choice that is bankrupting the country and responsible for the loss of millions of jobs.[21]

What have been the consequences for our country of these trade "imbalances"?

The deindustrialization of America. A growing dependence on China for the necessities of our national life and the loans to pay for them. A loss of millions of the best jobs Americans ever had. A median wage and family income that have been stagnant for a decade. A steep decline in the global purchasing power of the dollar. A loss of national dynamism. A debt bomb that went off in our face in September 2008.

And permanent peril to our national security. As South Carolina's "Fritz" Hollings, the economic patriot of the Senate for four decades, writes:

> The defense industry has been off-shored. We had to wait months to get flat panel displays from Japan before we launched Desert Storm. Boeing can't build a fighter plane except for the parts from India. Sikorsky can't build a helicopter except for the tail motor from Turkey. Today, we can't go to war except for the favor of a foreign country.[22]

FRUITS OF FREE TRADE

Though Bush 41 and Bush 43 often disagreed, one issue united them and Bill Clinton: protectionism. Globalists all, they rejected any measure to protect America's manufacturing base or the wages of U.S. workers. They enacted NAFTA, created the World Trade Organization, abolished tariffs, and granted China unrestricted access to the U.S. market.

Charles W. McMillion, of MBG Information Services, has compiled the results of two decades of this Bush-Clinton-Bush embrace of globalism. His compilation might be entitled "An Index of the Decline and Fall of Industrial America."[23]

- From December 2000 through December 2010, U.S. industrial production fell for the first time since the Depression, and America lost over 3 million private sector jobs, the worst record since 1928 to 1938.
- In that same decade, 5.5 million U.S. manufacturing jobs, one of every three we had, disappeared. Manufacturing, 27 percent of the U.S. economy in 1950, is down to 11 percent and accounts for only 9 percent of the non–farm labor force.[24]

- In traded goods, we ran up $6.2 trillion in deficits, $3.8 trillion of that in manufactured goods.
- The Bush II era was the first in U.S. history in which government began to employ more workers than manufacturing.
- U.S. trade surpluses in advanced technology products ended in Bush's first term. From 2007 through 2010, the United States ran trade deficits in ATP totaling $300 billion with China alone.
- The cumulative U.S. trade deficit with China in manufactured goods was $2 trillion. China now holds the mortgage on America.
- From December 2000 to December 2010, New York and Ohio lost 38 percent of their manufacturing jobs. Over the same period, New Jersey lost 39 percent, and Michigan lost 48 percent.
- The cumulative current account deficit of the United States from 2000 through the third quarter of 2010 exceeded $6 trillion. To finance it, we had to borrow $1.5 billion abroad every day for ten years.

Stephen Moore contrasts the America of 2011 with a country some of us still remember:

> Today in America there are nearly twice as many people working for the government (22.5 million) than in all of manufacturing (11.5 million). This is an almost exact reversal of the situation in 1960, when there were 15 million workers in manufacturing and 8.7 million collecting a paycheck from the government.[25]

"More Americans work for the government," writes Moore, "than work in construction, farming, fishing, forestry, manufacturing, mining and utilities combined. We have moved decisively from a nation of makers to a nation of takers."

This is our reward for turning our backs on the economic national-ism of the men who made America, and embracing the free-trade ideol-ogy of economists and academics who never made anything.

In early 2010 it was reported that Detroit, forge and furnace of the Arsenal of Democracy in World War II, was considering razing a fourth of the city and turning it into pastureland. Did that $1.2 trillion trade deficit we ran in autos and auto parts in the Bush 43 decade help to kill Detroit?

If our purpose in negotiating NAFTA was to assist Mexico, consider this: textile and apparel imports from China are now five times the dol-lar value of those same imports from Mexico and Canada combined.

America's trade deficits are "selling the nation out from under us," said Warren Buffett back in 2003.[26] U.S. trade deficits that have averaged $500 to $600 billion a year for ten years represent the single greatest wealth transfer in history and the single greatest factor raising China up and pulling America down. As astonishing as these indices of Amer-ican decline is the feckless indifference of our political class. How to explain it?

Ignorance of history is surely one answer. Every nation that rose to world power did so by protecting and nurturing its manufacturing base—from Great Britain under the Acts of Navigation, to the United States from the Civil War to the Roaring Twenties, to Bismarck's Germany before World War I, to postwar Japan, to China today. No nation rose to world power on free trade. From Britain after 1860 to America after 1960, free trade has been the policy of powers that put consumption before production, today before tomorrow.

The historical record is clear. Nations rise on economic nationalism. They descend on free trade.

Ideology is another explanation. Even a (Milton) Friedmanite free trader should be able to see the disaster around us and ask: What benefit did our country receive from these mountains of imported goods, and was that benefit great enough to justify the terrible damage done to our economic independence and vitality? Can not the free-trade ideologues see the direct correlation between trade deficits and national decline?

"Free trade! Free trade!" mocked Henry Clay, architect of the American System, in the great tariff debate of 1832–33. To Clay, the benefits of free trade were illusory: "The call for free trade is as unavailing as the cry of a spoiled child, in its nurse's arms, for the moon or stars that glitter in the firmament of heaven. It never existed. It never will exist." Instead of liberating America, free trade would, said Clay, place us "under the commercial domination of Great Britain."[27]

We have spurned the economic patriotism of Hamilton, Jackson, Clay, Lincoln, Teddy Roosevelt, and Coolidge to embrace free trade. And so it is that we now find ourselves under the commercial domination of the People's Republic of China.

NINETEENTH-CENTURY AMERICANS

"Thank you, Hu Jintao, and thank you, China," said Hugo Chávez, as he announced a $20 billion loan from Beijing—to be repaid in oil.[28]

The Chinese had thrown Chávez a life preserver. Venezuela was reeling from 25 percent inflation, government-induced blackouts to cope with energy shortages, and an economy that shrank by 3.3 percent in 2009.

Where did China get that $20 billion? From consumers at Walmart and all of us who purchase goods made in China. That $20 billion is just 1 percent of the $2 trillion in trade surpluses Beijing has run up with the United States over two decades. And Beijing is using its trillions of dollars in cash reserves to cut deals to lock up strategic resources for the coming struggle with America for global hegemony. China has struck multibillion-dollar deals with Sudan, Brazil, Kazakhstan, Russia, Iran, and Australia to secure a steady supply of oil, gas, and minerals to maintain the 10 to 12 percent growth China has been racking up since Deng Xiaoping dispensed with Maoism and launched China on the road to capitalism.

America has not built a nuclear power plant in thirty years. China has dozens under way. America built Hoover Dam and Grand Coulee Dam in Franklin Delano Roosevelt's first two terms. China just completed Three Gorges Dam, the largest power source on earth. China used its stimulus money to tie the nation together with light rail, bullet trains, and highways in infrastructure projects. America used much of her stimulus money to save government jobs. The United States has retired the space shuttle and her astronauts will hitchhike to a U.S.-built space station aboard Russian rockets. China is headed for the moon.

Even before the Gulf of Mexico oil spill in mile-deep waters, we had declared vast swaths of our country and continental shelf closed to drilling and declared war on fossil fuels to save the planet. Given the power of the environmental lobby to tie up projects in seemingly endless litigation, America could never today build the Interstate Highway System, the TVA, or the Union Pacific railroad.

China puts savings ahead of spending, capital investment ahead of consumption, and manufacturing ahead of finance. Before the collapse of 2008, the U.S. savings rate stood at zero percent of income. In China the savings rate ranges from 35 to 50 percent. In two decades, China has grown from a vast undeveloped country into the second largest economy on earth, ahead of Japan, and the world's leading exporter, ahead of Germany. China is now the factory to the world and the banker to America.

Since the Cold War, America has been playing empire—punishing evil-doers and advancing democracy—in Panama, Somalia, Haiti, Bosnia, Kosovo, Kuwait, Iraq, Afghanistan, and Libya. China has fought no one but built up her military power and developed ties to an expanding number of nations at odds with America, from Russia to Iran to Sudan to Venezuela.

The Chinese today call to mind nineteenth-century Americans who shoved aside Mexicans, Indians, and Spanish to populate a continent, build a mighty nation, challenge the superpower of the day, the British Empire, and sweep past her to become the most powerful nation on earth. Men were as awed by America then as they are awed by China today.

During the Cold War, China was in the grip of a millenarian Maoist ideology that blinded her to her true national interests. Today, it is

America that is the captive of an ideology that is becoming perilous to the republic.

The people sense this danger, and the politicians are responding. The election of 2010 featured a series of inflammatory political ads that reflected the nation's anxiety about high unemployment and painted China as profiting from America's pain. In late October, the *Washington Post* reported:

> On the campaign trail, both Democrats and Republicans are slinging mud at China. Currently, 250 ads targeting China are being aired in just under half of the 100 competitive districts, such as the battle for the Senate seat in Pennsylvania between Republican Pat Toomey and Democrat Joe Sestak. Sestak's ads come equipped with a gong and this line: "Pat Toomey— he's fighting for jobs . . . in China. Maybe he ought to run for Senate . . . in China."
>
> At a news conference in October 2010, Democrat Alexi Giannoulias accused Republican Mark Kirk—with whom he was locked in a tight race in Illinois for President Obama's old Senate seat—of "economic treason" for raising money from American businessmen based in China.

Said Evan Tracey, president of the Campaign Media Analysis Group, "political ads are the leading indicator of the next set of policies."[29]

HOW CHINA FIGHTS—AND WINS

At the Walmart in Albany, Georgia, tires made in China were selling for less than tires made at the Cooper Tire plant just down the road. Unable to compete, Cooper Tire shut down its Albany plant, and 2,100 Georgians lost their jobs. How could tires made on the other side of the world, shipped to the USA, then moved by rail or truck to Albany, Georgia, be sold for less than tires made in Albany, Georgia? The *Washington Post*'s Peter Whoriskey solves the mystery: at Cooper, the wages were $18 to $21 per hour; in China, a fraction of that. The Albany factory was subject to U.S. health-and-safety, wage-and-hour, and civil rights laws, from which Chinese plants are exempt. At the Cooper plant, environmental standards had to be met or the factory would be shut down. China's factories are notorious polluters.

China won the competition because the Fourteenth Amendment's "equal protection of the laws" does not apply to the People's Republic. China can pay its workers little, force them to work longer, and operate plants whose health, safety, and environmental standards would have their U.S. competitors shut down as public nuisances. Beijing also undervalues its currency to keep export prices low and import prices high. Thus did China, between 2004 and 2008, triple her share of the U.S. tire market from 5 percent to 17 percent, and put Cooper Tire of Albany out of business.

Having seen the future, Cooper Tire is now opening and acquiring tire plants in China and sending its former Albany workers over to train the Chinese who took their jobs. Welcome to twenty-first-century America, where globalism has become the civil religion of our political and corporate elite.[30]

WHO BUILT THE DEBT BOMB?

Neither a borrower nor a lender be, said Shakespeare's Polonius. But when the Greatest Generation passed the torch to the baby boomers, we became both.

Auto loans were made at zero interest for sixty months by the lending arms of GM, Ford, and Chrysler, to people who could not afford what they drove off the lot. Student loans were lavished on high school graduates with little prospect of finishing college. Unsolicited credit cards were sent to college seniors. States strapped for cash issued bonds to cover current expenditures. Under Bush II, the U.S. government ran up $2.5 trillion in deficits to finance tax cuts, two wars, Medicare drug benefits, No Child Left Behind, and what Fred Barnes celebrated, two decades ago, as "big government conservatism."

But it was the housing bubble that burst on Bush's watch and brought down the stock and bond markets and almost took down the U.S. economy with it. The housing bubble began with an innovation called the subprime mortgage. These mortgages were blessed and given impetus by George W. Bush after he discovered a new inequality in society. To address it he called a White House Conference on Increasing Minority Homeownership and, on October 15, 2002, at George Washington University, Bush, in echo of JFK pledging to put a man on the moon by decade's end, announced a new national goal:

> We have a problem here in America because fewer than half of the Hispanics and half the African Americans own their home. That's a home ownership gap . . . we've got to work together to close for the good of our country, for the sake of a more hopeful future.
>
> We've got to work to knock down the barriers that have created a home ownership gap.
>
> I set an ambitious goal . . . that by the end of this decade we'll increase the number of minority homeowners by at least 5.5 million families. (*Applause.*) . . . And it's going to require a strong commitment from those of you involved in the housing industry.[31]

What was wrong with this plan?

First, it was based on a superficial analysis. While Hispanics had a homeownership rate of 47 percent to whites' 75 percent, the difference was only 5 percent if one compared white Americans and native-born Hispanics. Immigrants have traditionally had a lower rate of home ownership. And as columnist Larry Elder points out, "The 1990 Census . . .

found Chinese immigrants approximately 20 percent more likely than whites to own their own home in San Francisco, Los Angeles, and New York."[32] Were banks discriminating against whites in favor of Chinese?

As to those "barriers" to black homeownership, writes Elder:

> Bush failed to address the primary reason that some blacks fail to qualify for homes—poor credit records. *U.S. News & World Report* found that the Fed's own Freddie Mac released a report in 1999 showing that 48 percent of blacks are likely to have bad credit histories—almost *twice* the 27 percent rate of whites. That same year, the *Washington Post* found that the credit rating for blacks earning between $65,000 and $75,000 stood lower than that of whites earning $25,000 a year or less. Even National Urban League president Hugh Price said, "If people have bad credit, they'll be denied loans, end of story."[33]

Ignoring the real causes of racial disparity in home ownership—age, income, length of residency, and the credit ratings of mortgage applicants—the Bush administration plowed ahead in the same suicidal direction the Congress had set out on years before with the Community Reinvestment Act. Local banks were pressured to make mortgages to home-buyers who could not qualify under standards set from decades of experience. Millions of these sub-prime mortgages were then sold by the banks that made them to Fannie Mae and Freddie Mac. The banks thus had fresh money to go out and make more risky mortgages and sell those to Fannie and Freddie. The mortgages were then bundled into securities and sold to Wall Street banks anxious to have on their balance sheets income-producing paper backed by real property in America's booming housing market. As *Bloomberg*'s Betty Liu and Matthew Leising reported:

> The debt of Fannie Mae, Freddie Mac and the Federal Home Loan Banks grew an average of $184 billion annually from 1998 to 2008, helping fuel a bubble that drove home prices up

by 107 percent between 2000 and mid-2006, according to the
S&P/Case-Shiller Home-Price Index.[34]

By mid-2006, not yet four years after Bush's speech, minority home ownership had grown by 2.7 million, trumpeted the *Weekly Standard*, in "Closing the Gap: The Quiet Success of the Bush Administration's Push for
Home Ownership."[35]

New York-based AIG, among the world's largest financial and insurance institutions, launched a program to insure the banks against losses
should the housing market crash. As the risk seemed minuscule, so were
the premiums. But payouts, should it come to that, were far beyond the
capacity of AIG. In its financial products division in Connecticut and
London, young wizards were at work creating credit default swaps to
guarantee against losses.

The Federal Reserve kept the game going by keeping interest rates
low and money gushing, creating a bubble that saw home prices surging
annually at 10, 15, and 20 percent.

As the economy began to heat up, the Fed began to apply the brakes.
Money became tighter, mortgage terms tougher. Housing prices stabi-
lized, then began to fall. Homeowners with subprime mortgages found
they could not "flip," or sell, their houses and had to start paying down
principal. People began to walk away from homes. The bubble popped.
Folks awoke to the reality that housing prices can fall, as well as rise, and
word went out that all that mortgage-backed paper that had been bought
by banks all over the world was overvalued and that a good bit of it was
worthless. As housing prices began to fall below the face value of mortgages, more and more homeowners mailed the keys back to the bank. And
so the crash came and the panic ensued.

Who is to blame for the greatest crash since 1929–1933?

Their name is legion. The banks that made the subprime mortgages.
The politicians who pushed them to make loans they would never have
made without threats, promises of political favor, or the ability to offload
the paper onto Fannie Mae and Freddie Mac. Fannie and Freddie, who

bought up the subprime paper, massaged the politicians with campaign contributions, and walked away from the wreckage leaving taxpayers with a bill of hundreds of billions of dollars.

Then there are the Wall Street bankers who bought up the securities backed by subprime mortgages and were too ignorant, indolent, or just plain greedy to inspect the paper. There are the ratings agencies like Moody's and Standard & Poor's who gazed at the paper and graded it AAA prime. In short, the political and financial elite of a generation revealed itself to be unfit to lead a great nation. We have a system failure rooted in a societal failure. For behind the disaster lay greed, stupidity, and incompetence on a colossal scale. "Avarice, ambition," warned John Adams, will "break the strongest cords of our Constitution as a whale goes through a net. Our Constitution was made only for a moral and religious people. It is wholly inadequate to the government of any other."[36]

FAT CITY IN LEAN TIMES

"It's time to stop worrying about the deficit—and start panicking about the debt," the *Washington Post* editorial warned. "The fiscal situation was serious before the recession. It is now dire":

> In the space of a single fiscal year, 2009, the debt soared from 41 percent of the gross domestic product to 53 percent. This sum, which does not include what the government has borrowed from its own trust funds, is on track to rise to a crushing 85 percent of the economy by 2018.[37]

Focusing on the "public debt"—the debt held by citizens, corporations, pension funds, and foreign governments—understates the true national debt, which is well over $14 trillion. But even that figure does not reflect the "structural deficit" the nation faces from legislated commitments to Social Security, Medicare, and government and military pensions. According to David Walker, former head of the General Accounting Office, these unfunded liabilities total $62 trillion.[38] With the first wave of baby boomers reaching eligibility for full Social Security benefits in 2011, and the entire boomer generation moving onto the rolls by 2029, an Everest of debt will become visible to the world. What are the risks of the exploding U.S. public debt?

Chinese, Japanese, and Persian Gulf governments and sovereign wealth funds will come to suspect, as some already do, that they are holding U.S. paper on which America will one day default or cheapen by inflation. As their fears rise, our creditors will either stop buying and start selling U.S. debt or demand a higher rate of interest commensurate with their rising risk. The Fed will have to raise rates to attract borrowers, and this increase in rates will push the economy into recession. Once the vicious cycle begins, warns Walker, interest on the U.S. debt will become the largest item in the federal budget.

Is Congress aware of the peril? In 2009, Congress was surely not. The lead story in the December 14 edition of the *Washington Post* began thus: "The Senate cleared for President Obama's signature on Sunday a $447 billion omnibus spending bill that contains thousands of earmarks and double-digit increases for several Cabinet agencies." The total cost of the Senate bill was enormous—"$1.1 trillion, including average spending increases of 10 percent for dozens of federal agencies."[39]

That last figure bears repeating. Staring at trillion-dollar deficits to the horizon, a Congress dominated by Democrats, the Party of Government, had voted all federal agencies an average budget increase of 10 percent. Bad times for America are the best of times for D.C.

Democrats claimed the gusher of money was needed to make up for the neglect of the Bush years. But the Bush years had been the fattest years for federal spending since LBJ's Great Society and Bush had added his trillion-dollar wars and trillion-dollar tax cuts. By the end of his presidency, conservatives were calling Bush our first Great Society Republican.

Yet Senator Dick Durbin said in 2009 that more spending was needed "to keep cops on the street.... so that families feel secure.... Money spent to help our first responders, firefighters and policemen is a critical investment."[40] But are not cops, firemen and first responders a state and local responsibility?

"It is business as usual, spending money like a drunken sailor," said John McCain.[41] But when sailors get drunk on shore leave they spend their own money. When they get back aboard ship, they sober up. Congressmen never stop spending. It is what they do. But the money they are spending now must be paid back by future generations.

The Democrats were following rule one of White House chief of staff Rahm Emanuel: "Never allow a crisis to go to waste. They are opportunities to do big things."[42] Small things, too. According to Taxpayers for Common Sense, there were 5,200 earmarks in that Senate bill, which averages out to twelve projects for every House member and fifty for every senator.[43]

The Party of Government exploited the crisis of 2008–2009 to grow the government. Between the passage of Obama's stimulus bill in 2009 and September 2010, millions of private sector jobs disappeared but 416,000 new government jobs were created.[44] "Although 85 percent of Americans work for private employers, the administration's own Recovery Act database reveals that four of every five jobs 'created or saved' were in government."[45] As a matter of political self-interest this made sense, for the vast majority of bureaucrats vote Democratic as do the vast majority of beneficiaries of government programs. The same week the *Post* editorial ran, Dennis Cauchon's lead story on page one of *USA Today* reported:

> Federal employees making salaries of $100,000 or more jumped from 14% to 19% of civil servants during the recession's first 18 months—and that is before overtime pay and bonuses are counted.
>
> Federal workers are enjoying an extraordinary boom time— in pay and hiring—during a recession that has cost 7.3 million jobs in the private sector.[46]

When the recession began, the Department of Defense had 1,868 civilian employees earning $150,000. By December 2009, Defense had 10,100 employees earning $150,000 or more. When the recession began, the Department of Transportation had one person earning $170,000. By 2010, Transportation had 1,690 employees earning above $170,000.[47]

Between 2005 and 2010, the number of federal workers earning more than $150,000 soared tenfold, and it doubled in the first two years of the Obama administration, during "the worst recession since the Great Depression."[48]

The three congressional districts north and west of the District of Columbia, Maryland's Eighth, and Virginia's Eleventh and Eighth, are among the ten most affluent congressional districts in America. And of the ten major metropolitan areas in the nation, the D.C. metro area ranks first in per capita income.[49]

The financial crisis was the work of Washington and Wall Street, but Washington never saw better days. As *USA Today* reported in August 2010, in the first decade of the twenty-first century U.S. government workers left their fellow Americans in the dust.

> Federal workers have been awarded bigger average pay and benefit increases than private employees for nine years in a row. The compensation gap between federal and private workers has doubled in the past decade.
>
> Federal civil servants earned average pay and benefits of $123,049 in 2009 while private workers made $61,051 in total compensation.... The federal compensation advantage has grown from $30,415 in 2000 to $61,998 last year.[50]

Remarkable. U.S. government workers, who enjoy the greatest job security of any Americans, receive twice as much in annual pay and benefits as the average American. This is not the D.C. some of us grew up in.

Is this the kind of government our fathers envisioned, or the kind of government they took up arms to overthrow?

After his "shellacking" in 2010, Obama, reacting to public rage over federal pay, proposed a two-year freeze. But as *USA Today* reported, this freeze involved the use of smoke and mirrors. Across-the-board pay hikes would be frozen, but "many federal workers will receive other pay hikes—longevity increases (called steps), promotions in grade, bonuses, overtime and other cash payments":

> Most federal employees are ranked at a general schedule (GS) grade from 1 to 15, and each grade has 10 steps within it. Step raises are largely automatic, based on longevity, but merit can hasten a step pay raise or even move a worker up multiple steps. Not every worker gets a step raise every year, but the raises average about 2% per year for workers as a group.[51]

SOCIALIST AMERICA

Like Sandburg's "Fog," socialism came in on little cat feet.

In his 1938 "The Revolution Was," Garet Garrett, who had spent his life fighting federal encroachments, began, "There are those who still think they are holding the pass against a revolution that may be coming up the road. But they are gazing in the wrong direction. The revolution is behind them. It went by in the Night of Depression, singing songs to freedom."[52]

Garrett wrote of a revolution within the form. To the world, America seemed the same country. But within, he argued, an irreversible revolution had taken place. One need only glance at where we were before the New Deal, to where we are today, to where we are headed to see how far we are off the course set by the Founding Fathers.

Taxes drove the American Revolution, for we were a taxaphobic people who believed in severely limited government. That government governs best that governs least is an American axiom. When Coolidge left the White House in March 1929, the U.S. government was spending 3 percent of the gross national product.

And today? Obama's first budget consumed one-fourth of the gross domestic product. The deficit was 10 percent of GDP. Fiscal year 2010 produced a deficit of nearly equal magnitude. Obama sought to repeal the Bush tax cuts on the top two percent of earners and raise the top rate to nearly 40 percent. This does not include state and local income taxes which, in California and New York, can take another 10 or 12 percent. Nor does it include payroll taxes for Social Security and Medicare, which add up to 15.3 percent on most wages and salaries, half of it coming out of workers' pay. The Tax Foundation estimates that New Yorkers could face a combined income tax rate of 60 percent. Added to this are sales taxes that can run to 8 percent, property taxes, gasoline taxes, excise taxes, and "sin taxes" on booze, beer, cigarettes, and, soon, hamburgers, hot dogs, and soft drinks.

"Tax Refugees Staging Escape From New York," ran the headline on a *New York Post* story that revealed that 1.5 million people had left New York State between 2000 and 2008, "the biggest out-of-state migration in the country." Those departing Manhattan earned, on average, over $93,000 a year while those arriving earned less than $73,000.[53]

A 2011 Marist poll found that 36 percent of all New Yorkers under thirty planned to leave the city within five years. Two-thirds gave high taxes as a principal reason.[54]

In the Declaration of Independence, Jefferson indicted George III as a tyrant for having "erected a multitude of New Offices, and sent hither Swarms of Officers to harass our people and eat out their substance." What did King George do with his Stamp Act or tea tax to compare with what America's rulers are doing to Americans today?

After receiving the IRS figures for 2007, the Tax Foundation did an analysis of who pays the U.S. income tax—and who does not.[55]

Taxpayers	Share of Income Tax Paid
Top 1 percent	44.42%
Top 10 percent	71.22%
Top 25 percent	86.59%
Top 50 percent	97.11%
Bottom 50 Percent	2.89%

The hardest-working and most productive Americans are being bled, and Obama plans to increase the number of free riders. In 2007, not only did one-third of all wage earners carry none of the federal income tax load, 25 million got an Earned Income Tax Credit from the Treasury. Half the states are now sending out checks to people who pay no income taxes.[56]

How large is the EITC program? Writes Edwin Rubenstein, an economic analyst formerly with *Forbes* and *National Review:*

> Since the Earned Income Tax Credit (EITC) became part of the income tax code in 1975, it has quietly become the largest cash transfer program in the United States.... EITC spending dwarfs that of the traditional welfare program...and food stamps combined....
>
> From 1985 to 2006, EITC payments grew from $2.1 billion to $44.4 billion, or by an eye-popping 2,014 percent.... [T]he number of returns claiming the EITC rose from 6.4 million to 23.0 million.[57]

Tax credits, paid in cash to people who pay no taxes, are welfare.

The EITC helps explain a startling discovery. According to the Tax Policy Center, 47 percent of all wage earners in the United States would "pay no federal income taxes at all for 2009. Either their incomes were too low, or they qualified for enough credits, deductions and exemptions to eliminate their liability."[58] In May 2011, Congress's Joint Committee on Taxation revised that figure—upward. Fully 51 percent of all households in the United States in 2009 had paid no federal income taxes.[59] More than half the nation was now free-riding on the taxes of the other half.

The free society has become the Entitlement Nation. Everyone is entitled to health care, housing assistance, food stamps, welfare, earned income tax credits, and a free education, from kindergarten through grade 12. And soon, college, with Obama's promise "to put a college education within reach of every American."[60]

The whole world is coming to feast at the banquet table.

More than a million immigrants, legal and illegal, arrive each year. They come with less education and fewer skills than U.S. citizens and consume three times as much in benefits as they pay in taxes. As most immigrants are people of color, they and their children quickly qualify for racial and ethnic preferences in hiring, promotions, and admissions.

And as America's richest states, California and New York, are buckling and breaking under this burden, so, too, must the United States.

FOOD STAMP NATION

"The lessons of history ... show conclusively that continued dependence upon relief induces a spiritual and moral disintegration fundamentally destructive to the national fibre. To dole out relief in this way is to administer a narcotic, a subtle destroyer of the human spirit."[61]

These words about Depression-era welfare are from President Roosevelt's 1935 State of the Union address. FDR feared that formerly self-reliant Americans might come to depend permanently upon government for the necessities of their daily lives. And, as with narcotics, such a dependency would destroy individuals'—and the nation's—fiber and spirit.

Seventy-five years later in 2010 came news that 41.8 million Americans were on food stamps and the White House was predicting that the number would grow to 43 million in 2011. It did: by February 2011, 44.2 million Americans, one in seven, were on food stamps. In Washington, D.C., more than a fifth of the population was receiving food stamps.[62]

To chart America's decline, the explosion in the food stamp program is a good place to begin. A harbinger of the Great Society, the Food Stamp Act was signed into law in 1964 by LBJ. Initially, $75 million was appropriated for 350,000 individuals in forty counties and three cities. Ironically, the Food Stamp Act became law half a decade after John Kenneth Galbraith in his best-seller of the same name had declared America to be the world's "affluent society."

However, no one was starving in the 1960s. There had been no starvation since Jamestown, with such exceptions as the Donner Party, who were caught in the Sierra Nevada mountains in the winter of 1846–47 and who took to eating their dead.

In May 1968, however, CBS ran "Hunger in America," narrated by Charles Kuralt, who held up an emaciated baby, dead of starvation. Senator George McGovern was jolted and began hearings. In *The Manipulators: America in the Media Age,* Robert Sobel would charge CBS with deceiving the nation and exploiting a baby that had died after being born prematurely. But the documentary had given real impetus to the Great Society program. When Nixon took office in 1969, three million Americans were receiving food stamps at a cost of $270 million a year. When he left in 1974, the program was feeding sixteen million people at a cost of $4 billion a year.

Fast forward to 2011. The cost to taxpayers of the U.S. food stamp program hit $77 billion, more than doubling in four years. First among the reasons is family disintegration. Forty-one percent of America's children are born out of wedlock. Among black Americans it is 71 percent. Food stamps feed children abandoned by their fathers. Taxpayers are taking up slack for millions of deadbeat dads.

Have food stamps made us healthier? Consider New York City: there, 1.7 million people, one in every five in the city, rely on food stamps for daily sustenance. Forty percent of the kids in the city's public schools from kindergarten through eighth grade are overweight or obese. Among the poor who depend on food stamps, the percentage of obese children is even higher. Mothers in poverty use food stamps to buy their kids sugar-heavy soda pop, candy, and junk food. When Mayor Michael Bloomberg proposed to the U.S. Department of Agriculture that recipients not be allowed to use food stamps to buy sugar-rich soft drinks, however, he ran into resistance.

"The world might be better... if people limited their purchases of sugared beverages," said George Hacker, of the Center for Science in the Public Interest. "However, there are a great many ethical reasons to consider why one would not stigmatize people on food stamps." In 2004, the Department of Agriculture denied a request by Minnesota that would have prevented the use of food stamps to buy junk food. To grant the request, said the department, would "perpetuate the myth" that food stamp users make poor shopping decisions.[64] Is that a myth or the simple truth?

What a changed country we have become. A less affluent America survived a Depression and world war without anything like 99 weeks of unemployment insurance, welfare payments, earned income tax credits, food stamps, rent supplements, government day care, school lunches, and Medicaid.

In the past, public or private charity were thought to be necessary but were viewed as temporary fixes until the breadwinner could find work or the family could get back on its feet. The expectation was that almost everyone, with hard work and perseverance, could make his or her own way and support a family.

This expectation has changed radically. Today we have accepted the existence of a permanent underclass of scores of millions who cannot cope and must be carried by society—fed, clothed, housed, tutored, and medicated at taxpayer's expense their entire lives. We have a dependent nation the size of Spain in our independent America. We have a new division in our country, those who pay a double or triple fare, and those who ride forever free.

There has been a precipitous decline in the character of our people. We are not the people our parents were. We are not even the people *we* used to be. FDR was right about what would happen if we did not get off the narcotic of welfare. Our country has undergone a "spiritual and moral disintegration, fundamentally destructive to the national fiber."

In 2010, The Education Trust gave us a glimpse into how far our young have fallen. Because they are physically unfit, have a criminal record, or have failed to complete high school, 75 percent of America's young, ages seventeen to twenty-four, do not even qualify to take the exam to enter the army. Of recent high school graduates who do take the test, nearly one-fourth fail to get the minimum score needed to join a branch of the military, though the questions "are often basic such as, 'If 2 plus x equals 4, what is the value of x?' "[64]

HOW GOVERNMENTS STEAL

In his *The Economic Consequences of the Peace,* written after the Paris conference of 1919 that produced the Treaty of Versailles, John Maynard Keynes wrote, "Lenin is said to have declared that the best way to destroy the capitalist system was to debauch the currency. By a continuing process of inflation, governments can confiscate, secretly and unobserved, an important part of the wealth of their citizens." Keynes agreed:

> Lenin was certainly right. There is no subtler, no surer means
> of overturning the existing basis of society than to debauch
> the currency. The process engages all the hidden forces of
> economic law on the side of destruction, and does it in a man-
> ner which not one man in a million is able to diagnose.[65]

Thinking back on what a nickel could buy years ago, and what a dollar buys today, calls to mind the insight of Lenin and Keynes. In 1952, a Coke cost a nickel as did a candy bar. Movies cost 25 cents, as did a gallon of gas or a pack of cigarettes, though you could pick up a carton for two dollars. On the Internet, a Kentucky-based retailer recently offered smokers a bargain: "Cut your smoking costs by as much as 60 percent. On an annual basis the savings are enormous. Premium Brand Name cigarettes like Camel and Marlboro as low as $43.99 per carton."[66]

Even at a 60 percent discount, cigarettes cost twenty times what they did in the 1950s. Cokes and candy bars cost ten times as much, movies thirty or forty times. Today's four-dollar gallon of gas costs sixteen times as much. While the prices have soared and taxes help explain the cost of cigarettes and gas, what has happened is the debauching of the dollar, which has lost more than 90 percent of its purchasing power. In 1947, this writer's father, an accountant, became a senior partner in his firm and bought a new Cadillac—for $3,200. The same car today would cost over $50,000.

Who is guilty of this debauching of the dollar? Well, who has had custody of the currency since 1913?

Many have felt the lash of public anger for the financial crisis that wiped out trillions in wealth and dumped us into the deepest recession since the 1930s. The Bush Republicans and Barney Frank Democrats who prodded banks into making subprime mortgages to people who could not afford the houses they were buying. Fannie and Freddie. The Wall Street banks. The AIG geniuses. Yet, the Federal Reserve, though it controls the money, and every financial crisis is a monetary crisis, has escaped indictment.

"[T]he very people who devised the policies that produced the mess are now posing as the wise public servants who will show us the way out," writes Thomas E. Woods Jr., whose *Meltdown* traced the Fed's role in every financial crisis since the creature was spawned at a meeting on Jekyll Island, off the coast of Georgia.[67]

The "forgotten depression" of 1920–21 was brought on by the Fed's printing of money for Woodrow Wilson's war. When, at war's end, the Fed tightened its monetary policy, production fell 20 percent between mid-1920 and mid-1921. Why is that depression so little known? Because President Harding refused to intervene. He let businesses and banks fail and prices fall. The fever broke, and America, after slashing Wilson's wartime tax rates, took off into the Roaring Twenties.

Then, as Milton Friedman related in *A Monetary History of the United States,* which contributed to his Nobel Prize, the Fed began to expand the money supply in the mid-1920s. Cash poured into equity markets where stocks could be bought on 10 percent margin. The market soared. When the market stalled and stocks began to fall, margin calls went out. Americans ran to the banks to get their savings. Panic ensued. Banks closed by the thousands. Stock prices fell by almost 90 percent. A third of the money supply was wiped out. Thus did the Federal Reserve cause the Depression. Smoot and Hawley were framed.

Though myth attributes the Great Depression to the innate conservatism of President Herbert Hoover, the man was no economic conservative. He abandoned laissez-faire, raised taxes, launched public works, extended emergency loans to failing businesses, and lent money to states for relief programs. Hoover did what Obama did eight decades later.

During the 1932 campaign, Roosevelt accused Hoover of presiding over the "greatest spending administration in peacetime in all of history." FDR's running mate, "Cactus Jack" Garner, claimed Hoover was "leading the country down the path to socialism."[68] On taking office, however, FDR, terrified of falling prices, ordered crops destroyed, pigs slaughtered, and business cartels created to cut production and fix prices. Roosevelt mistook the consequences of depression, falling prices, for its cause. But prices were merely returning to where they belonged in a free market. The drop in prices was really the first step to a lasting cure.

Of the Depression, Paul Krugman wrote: "What saved the economy, and the New Deal, was the enormous public works project known as World War II, which finally provided a fiscal stimulus adequate to the economy's needs."[69]

Krugman may have a Nobel Prize, writes Woods in *Meltdown*, but his analysis is a "stupefying and bizarre misunderstanding of what actually happened."[70] Obviously, with 29 percent of the labor force conscripted into the armed forces, their jobs taken by older men, by women, and by teenagers, unemployment will fall. But how could the economy be growing 13 percent a year, as economists claim it did, when there was rationing, declining product quality, an inability to buy homes and cars, a longer work week—and shortages everywhere? How can the economy be booming when the cream of the labor force is in boot camp, on military bases, aboard ships, storming beaches, or flying planes over enemy territory?

Ironically, it was 1946, a year the economists predicted would bring on a postwar depression because federal spending fell by two-thirds, that proved to be the biggest boom year in U.S. history. Why? The real economy was producing what people really wanted: cars, TVs, and homes. Businesses were responding to consumer desires, not to a government run by dollar-a-year men who wanted tanks, guns, ships, and planes to blow things up.

Backing Woods up, author Robert Dell wrote in 2011:

> Between 1945 and 1947, federal spending was cut from 41.9 percent of GDP to 14.7 percent. Yet the unemployment rate over that period stayed below 3.6 percent and real GDP grew by 9.6 percent. According to [economist David] Henderson, "The postwar bust that so many Keynesians expected to happen never did."[71]

Of the financial collapse that brought on the recession of 2008–2010, Woods writes, "The Fed was the greatest single contributor.... more dollars were created between 2000 and 2007 than in the rest of the republic's history."[72] When the Fed tightened, that bubble burst. Many argue that were it not for the independence and vision of Fed Chairman Ben Bernanke, the economy might have gone into the abyss after the Lehman Brothers collapse. But who brought us to the edge of the abyss?

"In questions of power ... let no more be heard of confidence in man, but bind him down from mischief by the chains of the Constitution," wrote Jefferson.[73] A century ago, we forgot Jefferson's warning when Congress and Wilson ceded to a Federal Reserve of anointed bankers the power to control the supply of America's money. That year, 1913, a twenty-dollar bill had the same value and purchasing power as a twenty-dollar gold piece. The twenty-dollar gold piece is today worth 75 twenty-dollar bills. The dollar has lost 98 to 99 percent of its purchasing power while in the custody of a Federal Reserve whose sworn duty it is to protect the purchasing power of the dollar.

For four generations, Americans have been subtly and systematically robbed of their savings by a Federal Reserve that has steadily inflated the money supply to accommodate politicians who wished to wage wars and win applause by an endless expansion of government that now consumes a fourth of the economy and taxes and regulates people in ways George III never dreamed of. "The first panacea for a mismanaged nation is inflation of the currency; the second is war," said Ernest Hemingway. "Both bring a temporary prosperity; both bring a permanent ruin. But both are the refuge of political and economic opportunists."[74]

In late 2009, Bernanke, frustrated by fourteen months of unemployment above 9.5 percent, terrified of deflation, even though gold and commodity prices were hitting record highs, signaled that the Fed would start printing money, because inflation was "too low."[75]

A DEADLOCK OF DEMOCRACY

We were blindsided. We never saw it coming.

So said Goldman Sachs's Lloyd Blankfein of the financial crisis of 2008, likening the probability of such a collapse to the probability of four hurricanes hitting the East Coast in a single season. Blankfein was reminded by the chairman of the Financial Crisis Inquiry Committee that hurricanes are "acts of God." But Blankfein was supported by Jamie Dimon, of JPMorgan Chase: "Somehow, we just missed...that home prices don't go up forever."[76]

The Wall Street titans conceded they did not foresee that the housing bubble might burst and that they never factored in the possibility of a collapse in value of the subprime mortgage securities they had piled up on their books. Backing Blankfein's plea of ignorance is this undeniable truth: the crisis that killed Lehman Brothers would have killed them all, had not the Treasury and Federal Reserve given America's "too big to fail" financial institutions cash transfusions of hundreds of billions in bailout money.

Yet, before the crisis, there were Americans who warned that a housing bubble was being created. Some predicted that what William Bonner called the *Empire of Debt* was coming down. Today we are hearing new warnings—that the United States, with deficits running at 10 percent of GDP, is risking a run on the dollar or default on the national debt.

Among those cautioning us to beware the consequences of huge deficits are Rudolph Penner, former head of the Congressional Budget Office, and David Walker, former comptroller general.

With the public debt—that share of the national debt held by citizens, corporations, pension funds, sovereign wealth funds, and governments—having risen by 2009 from 41 to 53 percent of GDP, Penner and Walker believe that it is imperative that we get the deficit under control. And to convince the world America is not Greece writ large, America must soon produce a credible plan for closing that deficit. There are three ways to do it. The first is through rapid economic growth that increases tax revenue and reduces outlays for safety-net programs such as unemployment insurance. But growth comes slowly and can take us only so far. To close a deficit of 10 percent of GDP, major cuts in federal spending and tax hikes seem unavoidable.

Now, consider the politics. The five largest items in the federal budget are Social Security, Medicare, Medicaid, defense spending, and interest on the debt. But with trillion-dollar deficits projected through the Obama years, even if he serves two terms, interest on the debt, which must be paid, must go up.

And with seniors angry over Medicare cuts to finance health coverage for the uninsured, it would seem suicidal for the Democrats to cut Medicare again. The same holds for Medicaid. Are Democrats, defeated in the congressional election of 2010, going to cut health benefits for the people who stood loyally by their party in defeat? Are Democrats going to grab the third rail of American politics and cut Social Security?

Any significant cuts in major entitlement programs by House Republicans would require the acquiescence of Harry Reid's Democrat-controlled Senate and Barack Obama's White House. And how likely is that?

As for defense, Obama has himself deepened America's involvement in Afghanistan, doubling troop presence to 100,000. The Pentagon has to replace weaponry and machines destroyed or depreciated in a decade of war. And any major defense cuts would meet with ferocious Republican resistance.

Where, then, are the big budget cuts to come from?

Will Congress or the White House slash spending for homeland security, the FBI, or CIA, after the near disaster over Detroit on Christmas Day 2009, and the failed bombing of Times Square? Will Democrats and Republicans come together to cut veterans' benefits, spending for our crumbling infrastructure of roads and bridges, or for education, when Obama is promising every child a chance at a college degree?

Will Reid's Senate approve of cuts in food stamps, unemployment insurance, or the Earned Income Tax Credit when joblessness is still near nine percent? Will a Senate that increased the budget of each department by an average of 10 percent for 2010 agree to take a knife to federal agencies or salaries when federal bureaucrats and the beneficiaries of federal programs are the most loyal and reliable voting blocs in the Democratic coalition?

Not only has Obama promised not to raise taxes on the middle class, any broad-based tax increase would be poison for him and his party and never be approved by a Republican House. Obama is caught in a dilemma from which there appears to be no escape. Democrats are the Party of Government. They feed it and it feeds them. The larger government becomes, the more agencies established, the more bureaucrats hired, the more citizens receiving benefits or checks, the more deeply entrenched is the Party of Government.

For eighty years, this has been the Democratic formula for success. "Tax and tax, spend and spend, elect and elect" was the pithy depiction of that policy attributed to FDR aide Harry Hopkins. And herein lies Obama's dilemma. How does the leader of the Party of Government preside over an era of austerity, in which federal employees and federal benefits are radically reduced, to avert a default on the national debt? How can the leader of the Party of Government shrink the government?

Republicans, too, have drawn a line from which they cannot retreat. They will not vote to raise taxes. Not only would that violate a commitment almost all Republicans have made to the people who elected them, it would seem suicidal. Republicans who sign on to tax hikes cannot go home again. For allied to the party today are Tea Party irregulars who shoot deserters in Washington's tax battles and budget wars.

Republicans are not going to cross these people, for they have before them examples of what happens to those who do. Senator Arlen Specter of Pennsylvania voted for the Obama stimulus and faced an instant primary challenge from former Representative Pat Toomey. Toomey took a twenty-point lead, forcing Specter to switch parties to keep his candidacy alive. Specter is gone and Toomey now serves in the Senate. Tea Party people are not schooled in the Gerald Ford politics of compromise and consensus.

Former Senator Alan Simpson, co-chairman of President Obama's National Commission on Fiscal Responsibility, has challenged the patriotism of fellow Republicans who plant their feet in concrete on tax increases:

> There isn't a single sitting member of Congress—not one— that doesn't know exactly where we're headed.... And to use the politics of fear and division and hate on each other—we're at a point right now where it doesn't make a damn [bit of difference] whether you're a Democrat or a Republican, if you've forgotten you're an American.[77]

Republicans did go along with Bush's spending for trillion-dollar tax cuts and trillion-dollar wars, and for prescription drug benefits for seniors and No Child Left Behind. But Simpson was wrong in implying that "fear and hate" are behind conservative opposition to tax increases.

History and principle are the drivers of conservative opposition to raising taxes. Ronald Reagan, who consented to tax increases in the 1982 Tax Equity and Fiscal Responsibility Act, told this writer he had been lied to by Congress. Promised three dollars in spending cuts for each dollar in tax increases, he got the opposite. George H. W. Bush won in 1988 by telling the nation, "Read my lips! No new taxes!" His breach of faith on that pledge left his loyal followers disheartened and deceived and cost him the presidency in 1992.

Conservatives are resisting tax hikes because they believe government has grown too immense for the good of the nation. If that means putting the beast on a starvation diet—no new tax revenue—so be it. Indeed, many prefer to run the risk of a debt default rather than transfer more wealth from the people and the private institutions that produce that wealth to a ravenous government that cannot control its appetite.

Where does that leave President Obama—and us?

If tax cuts are off the table, defense and war costs are rising, and cuts in Social Security, Medicare, Medicaid, and other entitlement programs are political poison, how do we reduce a deficit of $1.5 trillion? How do we stop the public debt from surging to 100 percent of GDP and beyond? America is facing not just a gridlock in government, but a deadlock of democracy, a crisis of the system and of the state itself.

On November 2, 2010, for the third time in four years, Americans voted to be rid of a ruling regime. The nation is taking on the aspect of the French Fourth Republic, which shifted from one party and premier to another until the call went out from an exasperated nation to General Charles de Gaulle to come and take charge of affairs. Now both parties have lost the mandate of heaven. America is in uncharted waters. The country is up for grabs.

Ours is the world's oldest constitutional republic, the model for all that followed. But if our elected leaders are incapable of imposing the sacrifices needed to pull the nation back from devaluation or default, is democracy really the future of mankind? Or is the model for the future the state capitalism of a China that weathered the storm better, spent its stimulus money more wisely, and has returned to double-digit annual growth?

How do we get off this highway to default?

America's fiscal crisis is a test of whether democracy is sustainable. John Adams, like other Founding Fathers, did not think a democracy could be long-lived. "Remember, that democracy never lasts long. It soon wastes, exhausts, and murders itself. There never was a democracy yet that did not commit suicide."[78]

WHAT HAPPENED TO US?

How did the republic that came through a Depression to win World War II, rebuild Europe and Japan, put a man on the moon, lead the world into an age of prosperity, and triumph over the Soviet Empire after a half century of Cold War come to this?

Where did we make the wrong turn? How did we lose our way?

How, in a generation, did we reach a point where a majority of our people believe America is headed in the wrong direction, that our children will not know the good life their parents had, that the American Dream may never become reality for scores of millions of our countrymen?

The answer: the failure of our system is rooted in a societal failure.

We are not ruled by the same ideas nor do we possess the same moral character as our parents did. Today, freedom takes a back seat to equality. "One nation, under God, indivisible" has become an antique concept in an age that celebrates diversity and multiculturalism. Our intellectual and cultural elites reject the God our parents believed in and the moral code they lived by.

Our fathers warned that, should this happen, the republic would fall. "Virtue, morality, and religion," said Patrick Henry, "this is the armor, my friend, and this alone that renders us invincible.... If we lose these, we are conquered, fallen indeed."[79]

"'Tis substantially true," said Washington, "that virtue or morality is a necessary spring of popular government." And the source of virtue and morality, Washington believed, was religion:

> Let us with caution indulge the supposition that morality can be maintained without religion.... Of all the dispositions and habits which lead to political prosperity, Religion and Morality are indispensable supports. In vain would that man claim the tribute of patriotism, who should labor to subvert these

great pillars of human happiness, these firmest props of the duties of man and citizens.[80]

Tocqueville found that Americans, half a century later, still shared Washington's conviction that religion was the pillar of the republic.

> I do not know whether all Americans have a sincere faith in their religion—for who can search the human heart?—but I am certain that they hold it to be indispensable for the maintenance of republican institutions. This opinion is not peculiar to a class of citizens or a party, but it belongs to the whole nation and every rank of society.[81]

"[O]ur ancestors," said Daniel Webster in his famous Plymouth Rock speech of 1820, "established their system of government on morality and religious sentiment. Moral habits, they believed, cannot safely be on any other foundation than religious principle, nor any government be secure which is not supported by moral habits."[82]

Religion is the foundation of morality and only a moral people can sustain a free republic, these men were asserting. Without religion, morality withers and dies, the community disintegrates, the nation falls. Our fathers' insight goes far toward explaining the current crisis of the republic, for America has ceased to be the Christian country they and we grew up in.

2

THE DEATH OF
CHRISTIAN AMERICA

America was born a Christian nation.[1]
—WOODROW WILSON

This is a Christian nation.[2]
—HARRY TRUMAN, 1947

...we do not consider ourselves a Christian nation...[3]
—BARACK OBAMA, 2009

At the 2009 inaugural, the official prayer was offered by Rick Warren, pastor of Saddleback Church, in Orange County, California, and author of *The Purpose Driven Life,* which had sold thirty million copies.

Warren, who had been attacked for his support of California's Proposition 8, a constitutional amendment that outlawed same-sex marriage, closed his prayer thusly: "I humbly ask this in the name of the one who changed my life, Yeshua, Isa, Jesus [Spanish pronunciation], Jesus, who taught us to pray, 'Our father who art in Heaven...'"[4]

Many Christians were startled that Pastor Warren did not identify Jesus as the Son of God but did identify him by his Muslim name, Isa. For Islam teaches that God had no son, that Isa was not God but a prophet superseded by Muhammad. Warren seemed to be implying that Islam's view of Jesus, a view that denies His divinity, was acceptable to him.

President Obama followed Warren and repudiated the notion that America is a Christian nation: "We are a nation of Christians and Muslims, Jews and Hindus, and non-believers."[5] For the first time, a president had denied the primacy of Christianity in America. The Supreme Court had declared in 1892, "This is a Christian nation."[6] The President was now declaring in his inaugural that we had ceased to be so.

The age of Obama marks the advent of post-Christian America.

In his inaugural benediction, Rev. Joseph Lowery sustained the theme of inclusiveness and extended it from every religion to every race.

> Lord ... we ask you to help us work for that day when black will not be asked to get in back, when brown can stick around, when yellow will be mellow, when the red man can get ahead, man; and when white will embrace what is right.[7]

The next morning, Rev. Dr. Sharon Watkins, general president of the Christian Church (Disciples of Christ), a member of the central committee of the World Council of Churches, strode to the pulpit of Washington National Cathedral as the first woman ever to deliver the homily at the National Prayer Service.

Determined to be ecumenical, Watkins began with an old Cherokee tale about wolves and wisdom, then pivoted to the Old Testament, saying: "In the later chapters of Isaiah, in the 500's BCE, the prophet speaks..."[8]

BCE?

The initials are used by those who wish to be rid of BC, "before Christ." For centuries, the civilized world has divided history into BC and AD, *anno domini,* "in the year of the Lord."

BCE stands for "before the common era," "before the current era," or "before the Christian era." Secularists seek to replace BC with BCE and AD with CE, for "Common Era," in all historical references—thus eliminating Christ and Christianity as the pivot of world history.

After relating the Cherokee tale of the good wolf and the fearful wolf, Rev. Watkins proceeded to ask:

So how do we go about loving God? Well, according to Isaiah, summed up by Jesus, affirmed by a worldwide community of Muslim scholars and many others, it is by facing hard times with a generous heart: by reaching out toward each other rather than by turning our backs on each other. As Mahatma Gandhi once said, "people can be so poor that the only way they see God is in a piece of bread."[9]

This was the sole mention of Jesus. Jesus was not identified as the Son of God or the redeemer of mankind, but as the fellow who had "summed up" Isaiah.

Rev. Watkin's sermon, "Harmonies of Liberty," went on to cite Emma Lazarus, Martin Luther King, Obama, and Katharine Lee Bates, author of "America the Beautiful," who had lived controversially for twenty-five years with fellow Wellesley professor Dr. Katharine Coman. She closed by reciting the final verses of James Weldon Johnson's "Lift Every Voice and Sing," which has been called "The Negro National Anthem."[10]

To Christians, Christ is the Son of God. Through Him alone can we come to the Father and attain salvation. Yet, Rev. Watkins all but excluded her Lord and his message of salvation when she had a worldwide audience, preferring to take her parable from a Cherokee tale.

The Obama inauguration symbolized the dilution and decline of a once-muscular Christianity that had guided American public life for two centuries.

INDICES OF CHRISTIAN DECLINE

Since President Harry Truman's time, a day each year has been set aside as a National Day of Prayer and presidents have traditionally hosted an annual ecumenical service marking the day in the East Room. Obama abolished the service. White House press secretary Robert Gibbs explained: "Prayer is something the president does every day."[11]

Atheists had long objected to the National Day of Prayer and Obama, according to a *Los Angeles Times* commentary, "has shown an unusual sensitivity toward atheists, the first president to mention nonbelievers in an inaugural."[12]

Obama's White House thus enlisted in the long and successful campaign to expel Christianity from the public square, diminish its presence in our public life, and reduce its role to that of just another religion. Cultural power in America long ago passed to an anti-Christian elite that rules the academy, Hollywood, and the arts. Secularism is now America's state religion and the people sense it. That same May, the Gallup organization found that 76 percent of Americans polled believed that religion was losing its influence on American life.[13]

Consider the statistics of Christian decline. According to an American Religious Identification Survey of 54,500 Americans conducted over six months in 2008 by the Program on Public Values at Hartford's Trinity College:

- Sixteen percent of all adults and 20 percent of all men have no religious affiliation. Among Americans under thirty, 25 percent have none.[14] Thirty percent of all married couples did not have a religious wedding; 27 percent of Americans do not want a religious funeral.[15]
- The nonreligious were the only group that added to its numbers in every state since the 2001 survey.[16] Robert Putnam and David Campbell, authors of *American Grace: How Religion Divides and Unites Us,* found higher figures two years later, in 2010:

Today, 17 percent of Americans say they have no religion, and these new "nones" are very heavily concentrated among Americans who have come of age since 1990. Between 25 and 30 percent of twentysomethings today say they have no religious affiliation—roughly four times higher than in any previous generation.[17]

.   "[I]f more than one quarter of young people are setting off in adult life with no religious identification," Putnam and Campbell added, "the prospects for religious observance in coming decades are substantially diminished."[18]

- Northern New England has passed the Pacific Northwest as the region with the highest percentage of those unaffiliated with a church. The Vermont of socialist senator Bernie Sanders leads the nation, with 34 percent professing no religion.[19] Unsurprisingly, it is in New England that same-sex marriage has been most warmly received. As the ranks of the unaffiliated grow in New England, the ranks of those attached to traditional churches decline. "Thanks to immigration and the natural increase among Latinos, California now has a higher proportion of Catholics than New England," says Barry Kosmin, of the American Religious Identification Survey. "The decline of Catholicism in the Northeast is nothing short of stunning."[20]

"That really hit me hard," President R. Albert Mohler, of the Southern Baptist Theological Seminary, told Jon Meacham. America's Northeast, Mohler said, "was the foundation, the home base of American religion. To lose New England struck me as momentous."[21]

This decline in religious faith helps to explain the defection to the Democratic Party of these once rock-ribbed, Republican states. For it has become a truism of American politics: the less religious an electorate, the more Democratic. The more frequently one attends church, the more conservative one tends to be. Half of those who attend church weekly describe themselves as conservatives, only 12 percent identify as liberals. Putnam traces the political "God gap" to the Reagan decade when "the public face of religion turned sharply right."[22]

Yet, there is a glaring exception to this rule.

Three-fourths of all members of historically black churches are

Democrats. And black Christians are more likely than any other church group to say the Bible is the "literal word of God," more likely than any church group save Jehovah's Witnesses to say "religion is very important to their lives," and more likely than any except Mormons to believe in heaven and hell.[23]

Thirty-six percent of black Americans attend church weekly and 44 percent pray daily. Because of their faith, they would seem to be natural conservatives. African Americans also voted overwhelmingly to outlaw gay marriage in California. But in politics, race trumps religion, and African Americans are the most reliable ethnic bloc of Democratic voters.

- As a share of the U.S. adult population, Christians declined from 86 percent in 1990 to 76 percent in 2008.[24] The denominations suffering the greatest losses are Episcopalians, Methodists, Lutherans, and Presbyterians.

These mainline churches which profess moderate theologies and stress social justice and personal salvation made up the vast majority of Protestants in the eighteenth, nineteenth, and early twentieth century. With the explosion of evangelical Christianity, however, the mainline churches saw their membership fall from 50 percent of U.S. adults in 1958 to 13 percent today.[25]

Nondenominational "megachurches" like Rick Warren's, in Lake Forest, California, have grown at the expense of traditional mainline churches, surging from 200,000 adherents in 1990 to 2.5 million in 2000, to 8 million today.[26] Says Mark Silk, of the Public Values Program, "A generic form of evangelicalism is emerging as the normative form of non-Catholic Christianity in the United States."[27]

Mainline Protestants are now mostly Democrats. By more than two-to-one (64–27 percent) they oppose any further restrictions on women's access to abortions.[28] When one considers that it was not until 1930 that the Anglican Church at its Lambeth Conference began to lead the

Christian community to accept birth control, the dilution of traditional Christian doctrine has been dramatic.

- This decline in religious affiliation is not restricted to Christians. Jews who describe themselves as practicing fell from 3.1 million in 1990 to 2.7 million in 2008—from 1.8 percent of the adult population to 1.2 percent.[29] Religiously observant Jews are no more numerous now than are adherents of the new religions such as Scientology, Wicca, and Santería. Writes Michael Felsen in the *Forward:*

> The JCC study notes that Jews score lower than Evangelicals, mainline Protestants and Roman Catholics on all available measures of religious belief. Compared to Christians, Jews are much less likely to say they believe in God, in the Bible as God's word, in life after death, in heaven or hell.[30]

Yet Jews made up 8.4 percent of Congress in 2010 and 13 percent of senators. Episcopalians were 7 percent of Congress.[31]

- Mormons have maintained their 1.4 percent share of the population.[32] The Pew Forum puts Mormons at 1.7 percent of a U.S. adult population that has grown to 228 million.[33] As of 2010, five senators and nine members of the House were Mormons. Writes Eric Kaufmann in "Breeding for God" in *Prospect*, "In the 1980s, the Mormon fertility rate was around three times that of American Jews. Today the Mormons, once a fringe sect, outnumber Jews among Americans under the age of 45."[34]
- Muslims have doubled their share of a growing U.S. population from 0.3 percent to 0.6 percent since 1990.[35] This growth rate would translate into fewer than 1.5 million Muslim adults, which seems too low. Speaking in Cairo, Obama

referred to "nearly 7 million American Muslims in our country today."[36] This is the highest figure this writer has seen. In an August 2009 story about the Washington, D.C., area Islamic population exploding to where Muslims were renting a synagogue for Friday prayers in the suburb of Reston, Virginia, the *Washington Post* conceded that estimates of Muslims in the United States are guesswork: "Nobody really knows how many Muslims are in America—estimates range from 2.35 million to 7 million—but researchers say the population is growing rapidly, driven by conversions, immigration and the tendency for Muslims to have larger families."[37] In August 2010, the *Wall Street Journal*'s Carl Bialik had similar difficulty in fixing the number of Muslims in the United States.[38]

The Pew Forum found that most Christians no longer believe their own faith is essential for salvation. Seven in ten of the religiously affiliated believe other religions can lead to eternal life and that there is more than one way to interpret the teachings of their faith. While 92 percent of Americans still believe in a God, only 60 percent believe in a personal God. Three in ten believe God to be an impersonal being.

THE EMERGING PROTESTANT MINORITY

The Trinity College survey closely tracks the U.S. Religious Landscape Survey by the Pew Forum on Religion and Public Life. After interviewing 35,000 Americans between May and August 2007, the Pew Forum found that:

- Forty-four percent of all adult Americans have lost their faith or changed religions.[39]
- While 99 percent percent of Americans were Protestants at the time of the Revolution, this figure had fallen to 51 percent

by 2007.[40] For the first time in our history, Protestants will soon be a minority in the United States.

- While 62 percent of those seventy and older are Protestants, the figure is 43 percent for those ages eighteen to twenty-nine.[41]

- While only 8 percent of Americans over seventy are unaffiliated with a church or religion, one-fourth of those under thirty have no religious affiliation.

"We are on the verge—within ten years—of a major collapse of evangelical Christianity," writes Michael Spencer,[42] who describes its progression:

The breakdown will follow the deterioration of the mainline Protestant world and it will fundamentally alter the religious and cultural environment in the West.

Within two generations, evangelicalism will be a house deserted of its occupants.... This collapse will herald the arrival of an anti-Christian chapter of the post-Christian West.[43]

Spencer lives and works in a Christian community in Kentucky and believes Evangelicals made a strategic blunder in tying their faith to political conservatism and the culture war.

The evangelical investment in moral, social, and political issues has depleted our resources and exposed our weaknesses. Being against gay marriage and being rhetorically pro-life will not make up for the fact that massive majorities of Evangelicals can't articulate the Gospel with any coherence. *We fell for the trap of believing in a cause more than a faith.*[44]

Spencer echoes Christ's admonition: "My kingdom is not of this world," and believes "consumer-driven megachurches" like Warren's Saddleback Church will be the beneficiaries of evangelical Christianity's collapse.[45]

In an essay, "God Still Isn't Dead," John Micklethwait and Adrian Wooldridge, authors of *God Is Back: How the Global Revival of Faith Is Changing the World,* agree with Spencer as to who will inherit the evangelical estate: it is the "pastorpreneurs":

> men like Bill Hybels of Willow Creek and Rick Warren of Saddleback. These are far more sober, thoughtful characters than the schlock-and-scandal televangelists of the 1970s, but they are not afraid to use modern business methods to get God's message across.
>
> Mr. Hybels's immaculately organized church employs several hundred staff, and the church has both its own mission statement and its own consulting arm.[46]

"The real strength of religious America is in its diversity," write Micklethwait and Wooldridge:

> There are more than 200 religious traditions in America, with 20 different sorts of Baptists alone.... There are services for bikers, gays, and dropouts (the Scum of the Earth Church in Denver); Bibles for cowboys, brides, soldiers and rap artists. ("Even though I walk through / The hood of death / I don't back down / Because you have my back") and even theme parks for every faith. This Holy Week you can visit the Golgotha Fun Park in Cave City, Ky.[47]

Is this a manifestation of the "real strength" of Christianity, or does it, instead, sound like disintegration, the loss of unity of the People of God?

"Are we witnessing the death of America's Christian denominations?" asks Russell D. Moore, dean of the School of Theology at the Southern Baptist Theological Seminary, and he answers his own question:

Studies by secular and Christian organizations indicate that we are. Fewer and fewer American Christians, especially Protestants, strongly identify with a particular religious community—Methodist, Baptist, Presbyterian, Pentecostal....

More and more Christians choose a church not on the basis of its denomination, but on the basis of more practical matters. Is the nursery easy to find? Do I like the music? Are there support groups for those grappling with addiction?[48]

Spencer believes it imperative that Evangelicals "shake loose the prosperity Gospel from its parasitical place on the evangelical body of Christ."[49]

Indeed, it sometimes seems that to counter liberation theology's First Church of Christ, Socialist, Christians preach a gospel of the First Church of Christ, Capitalist. Yet, in reading of the life and death of Christ and his apostles, it does not appear any were successful by the standards of the world, and surely not in the deaths they endured.

Atheism may be surging, but its hold on the heart appears weaker. Half of those raised in an atheist, agnostic, or nonreligious home have affiliated with a church.[50] Even in this secular age, the search for God and salvation captivates the heart. Many who lose their faith seek to rediscover God as they grow older, even if not in the church in which they were raised.

EPISCOPAL CRACK-UP

The decline and fall of mainstream Christianity is starkly reflected in the recent history of the Episcopal Church.

In the halcyon days of the Eastern Establishment, the Episcopal Church was known as "the Republican Party at prayer." Today, the Episcopal Church is divided and disintegrating, having lost a million members since 2000. It has been torn asunder over morality, the ordination of female and gay priests and bishops, and the legitimacy of same-sex unions. The church's share of the adult population has fallen to less than 1 percent.[51]

In Fairfax County, Virginia, nine parishes broke with the national Episcopal Church over the installation at Washington National Cathedral of Katharine Jefferts Schori as 26th Presiding Bishop. Schori had blessed same-sex unions and supported the consecration of Gene Robinson as bishop of New Hampshire, who had left his wife and daughters and entered a homosexual union.

Seven of 111 Episcopal dioceses refused to accept Schori's elevation. Their defection, and that of the Fairfax parishes, however, produced mockery and mirth from *Washington Post* columnist Harold Meyerson.

"Whether it was the thought of a woman presiding over God's own country club or gays snuggling under its eaves, it was all too much" for the "Fairfax Phobics," wrote Meyerson.[52] This is, he continued, "just the latest chapter in the global revolt against modernism and equality and, more specifically, in the formation of the Orthodox International."[53]

And what is the Orthodox International?

> The OI unites frequently fundamentalist believers of often opposed faiths in common fear and loathing of challenges to ancient tribal norms.... The OI's founding father was Pope John Paul II, who ... sought to build his church in nations of the developing world where traditional morality and bigotry, most especially on matters sexual, were ... more in sync with the Catholic Church's inimitable backwardness. Now America's schismatic Episcopalians are following in [John Paul's] footsteps—traditionalists of the two great Western hierarchical Christian churches searching the globe for sufficiently benighted bishops.[54]

"Fundamentalists," "phobics," "tribal," "bigotry," "backwardness," "benighted." Meyerson's vocabulary is that of the Christian-baiter who has come out of the closet and runs rampant on the op-ed pages of the mainstream media. Yet Meyerson is not wrong about which way the wind is blowing. Modernism does indeed appear triumphant, and traditionalism in retreat.

Still, in rejecting the authority of Bishop Schori and refusing to bless same-sex unions, the dissenters may yet prevail, for three reasons.

First, they have Scripture on their side. Did not Christ say to the Pharisees: "Have ye not read that He who made man at the beginning 'made them male and female'? And He said, 'For this cause shall a man leave his father and mother, and shall cleave to his wife, and they two shall be in one flesh.'" Second, it is the accommodationist faiths that are the dying faiths.

Third, dissenters have the country on their side. Thirty-one states have voted "No" to homosexual marriage. Not one has voted to approve. When the Washington, D.C., city council voted to recognize same-sex marriages from other states, the Board of Elections and Ethics refused to submit the issue to a referendum.[55] Voters have no right to authorize discrimination, said the board. The real fear is that, as in California, black churches would turn out their flocks and reverse the city council's decision.

All the efforts by mainstream churches to accommodate modernity have gone hand in hand with what *Newsweek* sees as the decline and fall of Christianity in the United States.[56] Now ranked fifteenth in congregants, the Episcopal Church is losing members more rapidly than are the Presbyterians, Lutherans, or Methodists.[57] The rising churches are the rigorous churches. The Church of Jesus Christ of Latter-Day Saints is now ranked fourth, with close to six million faithful, three times as many Mormons as Episcopalians.[58] Other rising churches are the Assemblies of God and Jehovah's Witnesses.[59]

Globally, writes sociologist Rodney Stark, it is "high-tension" religions "with the clearest boundaries and the highest demands of members that flourish."[60] Low-tension religions like Unitarians tend to be "dissolved into the cauldron of secularism."[61]

Columnist William Murchison explains the phenomenon:

> [T]he Mainline churches—not fully understanding their job description, which is basically to connect members with the God who created them—fare less and less well in the 21st century. Methodists, Presbyterians, Episcopalians, Lutherans—all have declined sharply in membership over these past few wonderful decades of liberalism. The Episcopal Church, my own shop, has fewer adherents than the Mormons—not least because whatever it is Mormons believe, they really believe it.[62]

"Sweet tolerance and gentle affirmation are the hallmarks of today's mainliners," Murchison muses. The Episcopal elite, "especially the baby-boom bishops, priests and theologians who run the national show—don't merely move the theological goalposts; they depict goalposts as unmodern, what with their rigor and fixity. Just kick, they admonish—it's fine with the Lord."[63]

The revised teachings of the Episcopal Church on what were once biblical truths and settled matters of morality call into question its credibility and that of the other mainstream churches. For if these Christian churches have been teaching falsely in condemning abortion and homosexuality as justifying damnation for five centuries, why should anyone believe the new catechism? If they were wrong for five hundred years, why are they right now?

What is happening to the Episcopal Church has been happening to the Protestant world since the Reformation. Having rebelled against Rome over papal authority, how do Protestant churches deny dissident factions the right to rebel and break away from them? If Rome has no authority to command obedience or teach infallibly, whence comes theirs?

Protestantism, some historians argue, must inexorably lead to where it is arriving at—a place where each faction, indeed, each individual, decides what is moral law and biblical truth: the privatization of morality.

But if the atomization of Protestantism is the future, that must lead to the atomization of America. For America was born a Protestant nation.

The Christian crack-up proceeds. In 2009, conservatives split from the 4.7 million-member Evangelical Lutheran Church in America after that church voted to "ordain partnered gay clergy."[64] And if the consecration of the gay bishop in New Hampshire proved traumatic for the Episcopal Church, no less did it do so for the bishop himself. At sixty-three, Bishop Robinson announced his resignation, to take effect in 2013, telling his annual diocesan convention, "Death threats, and the now worldwide controversy surrounding your election of me as bishop, have been a constant strain, not just on me, but on my beloved husband Mark," and on Episcopalians across the state.[65]

IS RELIGION NECESSARY?

The end of Christianity has long been sought by men both famous and infamous. Karl Marx called religion "the opiate of the masses." Winston Churchill, after reading Winwood Reade's exuberantly anti-Christian *Martyrdom of Man* in Bangalore as a twenty-one-year-old subaltern, wrote his mother:

> One of these days the cold bright light of science & reason will shine through the cathedral windows & we shall go out into the fields to seek God for ourselves. The great laws of Nature will be understood—our destiny and our past will be clear. We shall then be able to dispense with the religious toys that have agreeably fostered the development of mankind.[66]

Less respectful of these "religious toys" was Friedrich Nietzsche: "I regard Christianity as the most fatal, seductive lie that has ever existed."[67] His admirer Adolf Hitler agreed, "The heaviest blow that ever struck humanity was the coming of Christianity."[68] As Eugene G. Windchy relates, in *The End of Darwinism:*

[Hitler] thought it would have been better for the world if the Muslims had won the eighth century battle of Tours, which stopped the Arab advance into France. Had the Christians lost, [Hitler] reasoned, the Germanic peoples would have acquired a more warlike creed and, because of their natural superiority, would have become the leaders of an Islamic empire.[69]

In *Inside the Third Reich*, the memoir of his years as Hitler's architect, Albert Speer wrote that Hitler would often say:

You see, it's been our misfortune to have the wrong religion. Why didn't we have the religion of the Japanese, who regard sacrifice for the Fatherland as the highest good? The Mohammedan religion too would have been much more compatible to us than Christianity. Why did it have to be Christianity with its meekness and flabbiness?[70]

Yet even those who loathe Christianity often admit that mankind cannot do without religion. Though he detested the Christianity of the Sermon on the Mount, Hitler conceded in *Mein Kampf* what writer-historians Hilaire Belloc and Christopher Dawson would contend: religion is indispensable to society:

This human world of ours would be inconceivable without the practical existence of religious belief. The great masses of a nation are not composed of philosophers. For the masses of the people, especially faith is absolutely the only basis of a moral outlook on life. The various substitutes that have been offered have not shown any results that might warrant us in thinking that they might usefully replace the existing denominations.[71]

As for his Nazi elite, with its Darwinian pagan ideology, Hitler added: "There may be a few hundreds of thousands of superior men who can live wisely and intelligently without depending on the general standards which prevail in everyday life, but the millions of others cannot do so."[72]

Stalin, who had sought to eradicate Christianity, recognized its hold on the Russian people. In the Great Patriotic War, he opened cathedrals and churches, released bishops and clergy from prison, and called on her sons to fight, not for party or politburo, but for "Mother Russia." Stalin understood that the Russian masses were not Marxists, but God-and-country Christians.

By 1938, as he concluded that Europe was losing its faith to skepticism, agnosticism, and atheism, Belloc wrote that the West had embarked on a voyage certain to end on the reef of civilizational ruin.

> [T]he skeptical attitude upon transcendental things cannot, for masses of men, endure. It has been the despair of many that this should be so. They deplore the despicable weakness of mankind which compels the acceptance of some philosophy or some religion in order to carry on at all. But we have here a matter of positive and universal experience.[73]

Every nation, every culture has to be inspired by a body of morals. Behind that body of morals must be a doctrine we call religion. Throughout history, Belloc was saying, the death of a religion meant the death of the culture and the civilization to which it gave birth. Once Christianity had triumphed in the Roman Empire, the pagan gods were dethroned, the empire passed into history, and Christendom was born and began its ascendancy.

"Human society cannot carry on without some creed, because a code and a character are the product of a creed," Belloc wrote. Individuals may carry on with "a minimum of certitude or habit about transcendental things," but "an organic human mass cannot so carry on."[74] Belloc echoes the belief of Washington and John Adams that religion and morality were interdependent and indispensable to the survival of a free society and a virtuous republic.

SOCIAL DECOMPOSITION

If God is dead, said Dostoevsky's Ivan Karamazov, is not everything permitted? So it seems today. For what are the social consequences of what former *Newsweek* editor Meacham calls "The End of Christian America."[75] Since 1960,

- The U.S. illegitimacy rate has rocketed from 5 percent of all births to 41 percent.[76]
- Among African Americans the share of births out of wedlock is 71 percent, up from 23 percent in 1960.[77]
- The percentage of households that were married-couple families with children under eighteen had plummeted by 2006 to just 21.6 percent.[78]
- Since *Roe v. Wade* fifty million abortions have been performed.
- Between 1960 and 1990, the teenage suicide rate tripled. Though the number then fell, as of 2006 suicide was the third leading cause of death of young adults and adolescents aged fifteen to twenty-four, just behind homicides.[79]
- Cheating in sports, scholastics, business, and marriage is pandemic.
- Between 1960 and 1992, violent crime—murder, rape, assault—soared 550 percent.[80] The subsequent decline is due to the passing of the baby boomers out of the high-crime ages (sixteen to thirty-six), the birth dearth, and a 700 percent increase in the prison population, which today stands at 2.3 million Americans, with 5 million more on probation or parole.[81]

"Traditional America is dying," writes Jeffrey Kuhner, of the Edmund Burke Institute for American Renewal, who attributes its passing to "individualistic hedonism," the Playboy philosophy, and the "MTV morality" dominant in Hollywood and society.[82]

. . .

Rather than ushering in a new utopia, the abandonment of traditional morality has unleashed a sea of misery. Our culture has become coarsened, cheapening the value and dignity of human life. Legalized abortion has led to the murder of nearly fifty million unborn babies. Sexually transmitted diseases, such as AIDS, have resulted in the death of millions. Divorce has skyrocketed. The family has broken down. Pornography is ubiquitous, especially on the Internet. Out-of-wedlock births and teenage illegitimacy rates have soared. Drugs and gang violence plague our inner cities—and are spreading into our suburbs.[83]

Grim reading, but is it not all palpably true?

Cultural degeneration and social decomposition travel together. So T. S. Eliot predicted eighty years ago: "The World is trying the experiment of attempting to form a civilized but non-Christian mentality. The experiment will fail; but we must be very patient in awaiting its collapse."[84]

In his 1987 address at West Point, "The Meaning of Freedom," writer Tom Wolfe described the four phases of freedom America has known. First was freedom from foreign tyranny won in the Revolution. Second was freedom from the aristocratic British system of privilege and class. Third was freedom to pursue one's dreams and better one's station in life realized after the Civil War. We entered the fourth phase in the late twentieth century. It is "freedom *from* religion," said Wolfe—that is, freedom from the moral and ethical constraints of religion and the manners, customs, and conduct religion prescribes. Social decomposition is what this fourth phase of freedom has produced. "I believe there is something Nietzschean," said Wolfe, "about a country that has taken freedom to the point of getting rid of the constraints of the most ordinary rules."[85]

Russian writer Aleksandr Solzhenitsyn saw freedom from religion and the moral constraints it imposes as "destructive and irresponsible," a corruption of the idea that the Founding Fathers had believed in and fought for:

> All individual human rights are granted because man is God's creature. That is, freedom was given to the individual conditionally, in the assumption of his constant religious responsibility.... Two hundred or even fifty years ago, it would have seemed quite impossible, in America, that an individual could be granted boundless freedom simply for the satisfaction of his instincts or whims.[86]

Indeed, in that time of the Founding Fathers, Yale President Timothy Dwight wrote, "Without religion we may possibly retain the freedom of savages, bears and wolves, but not the freedom of New England."[87]

Can a nation survive freedom from religion? We are about to find out.

Chronicles editor Tom Piatak writes of a similar disintegration in a once-conservative Britain where 7 percent of the population attends church on Sunday. In his "Argument Against Abolishing Christianity," Jonathan Swift, the eighteenth-century satirist and Anglican minister, predicted that social disintegration would follow the death of Christian belief. He wrote of how a villager, hearing an argument against the Trinity, "most logically concluded" that "if it be as you say, I may safely whore and drink on, and defy the parson."[88]

"The moral collapse of post-Christian Britain is evident from statistics as well as anecdotes," writes Piatak. "The illegitimacy rate among white Britons is 46 percent, double the rate among American whites, and the crime rate is 40 percent higher in Britain." The United Nations Children's Fund calls Britain "the worst country in the Western world in which to be a child."[90]

British children have the earliest and highest consumption of cocaine of any young people in Europe; they are ten times more likely to sniff solvents than are Greek children; and they are six to seven times more likely to smoke pot than are Swedish children. Almost a third of British young aged 11, 13, and 15 say they have been drunk at least twice.[91]

Theodore Dalrymple, author of *Not with a Bang but a Whimper: The Politics of Culture and Decline*, writes that, "absent a transcendent purpose, material affluence...may lead to boredom, perversity and self-destruction."[92] In Britain, Dalrymple adds:

> The privatization of morality is so complete that no code of conduct is generally accepted, save that you should do what you can get away with: sufficient unto the day is the pleasure thereof. Nowhere in the civilized world has civilization gone so fast and so far into reverse, as in Britain.[93]

Dalrymple sees Anthony Burgess's novel *A Clockwork Orange*, about a future dystopia in Britain, as "socially prophetic."[94] British poet, essayist, and playwright T. S. Eliot had a similar vision earlier in the twentieth century. Asked by poet Stephen Spender what he saw ahead for our civilization, Eliot replied, "Internecine warfare...people killing one another in the streets."[95]

One recalls the observation of Edmund Burke, eighteenth-century British philosopher and statesman:

> Men are qualified for civil liberty in exact proportion to their disposition to put moral chains on their own appetites....Society cannot exist unless a controlling power upon will and appetite be placed somewhere, and the less of it there is within, the more there must be without. It is ordained in the eternal constitution of things, that men of intemperate minds cannot be free. Their passions forge their fetters.[96]

In his 1933 book *Enquiries into Religion and Culture*, Christopher Dawson emphasized that religion is the tap root of culture and the source of ethics. If that root is cut, society will disintegrate and the culture will die, no matter how prosperous the people.

> The central conviction which has dominated my mind ever since I began to write is the conviction that the society or culture which has lost its spiritual roots is a dying culture, however prosperous it may appear externally. Consequently, the problem of social survival is not only a political or economic problem; it is above all things religious, since it is in religion that the ultimate spiritual roots both of society and the individual are to be found.[97]

If Dawson is correct, the drive to de-Christianize America, to purge Christianity from the public square, from public schools, and from public life, will prove culturally and socially suicidal for the nation.

Giorgio Vasari, the sixteenth-century Italian painter, architect, and historian who studied the works of the Roman High Renaissance, believed that society was organic and biological, that once it passed its prime, decay and death were inevitable: "[o]nce human affairs start to deteriorate, improvement is impossible until the nadir has been reached."[98] As one looks back to what the West produced over the centuries, and what the West produces today, in painting, sculpture, music, literature, film, and governance, do we not appear to be a civilization closer to its nadir than its height of perfection?

In a *New York Times* review of a biography of Nietzsche, American scholar and author Francis Fukuyama writes that the most serious issue raised in any study of Nietzsche "concerns the nature of his politico-cultural program, the 'transvaluation of all values' that was to take place in the wake of the death of Christianity."[99]

> Acknowledgement of the death of God is a bomb that blows up many things, not just oppressive traditionalism, but also

values like compassion and the equality of human dignity on which support for a tolerant liberal political order is based. This then is the Nietzschean dead end from which Western philosophy has still not emerged.[100]

The death of God has blown up our decent and civil society.

GRAMSCI'S TRIUMPH

Today's social decomposition is the first consequence of the collapse of Christianity and the moral order it sustained. This is the triumph of Antonio Gramsci and the cultural revolution of the 1960s. Where the violent victories of Lenin and Mao were eventually reversed, Gramsci, an Italian communist theoretician who died in the 1930s after years in a fascist prison, proved to be the more perceptive Marxist.

On a visit to the Russia of Lenin and Stalin, Gramsci saw that, while the Bolsheviks had succeeded in seizing total power, they had not won over the people. The people obeyed, but hated their rulers and loathed the system. Their love and loyalty went not to the party or the state, but to family, faith, and Mother Russia.

Gramsci concluded that Christianity had immunized the West against Communism. The Russian people had lived for a thousand years with the Christian faith and cultural traditions that caused them instinctively to recoil from Marxism as immoral and unpatriotic and to reject the new Communist order as illegitimate, godless, and evil. Until Christianity was seared out of the soul of Western man, Gramsci concluded, Communism could never take root.

Therefore, Marxists must conduct a "long march through the institutions," religious, cultural, and educational, of the West, uprooting Christianity and its teachings about God, man, and morality, to create a new people who would not reflexively reject Marxism. Gramsci was a diagnostician of society and the cultural Marxism he preached triumphed in the West while the revolutions of Lenin, Stalin, and Mao ultimately failed in the East.

For two millennia, Christianity provided the immune system of Western man. And when an immune system breaks down in a society, just as it does in a man, opportunistic infections enter and kill the organism. And no cocktail of drugs can fend off the inevitable. *Souls in Transition,* by University of Notre Dame sociologist Christian Smith, seems to confirm the point. Smith sifted through data from the National Study of Youth and Religion, and Naomi Schaefer Riley summarizes the stark differences that Smith found in the social outlook and attitudes of religious and nonreligious youth:

> Not only does religion concentrate the mind and help young people to think about moral questions, it also leads to positive social outcomes. Religious young people are more likely to give to charity, do volunteer work and become involved with social institutions.... They are less likely to smoke, drink and use drugs. They have a higher age of first sexual encounter and are less likely to feel depressed or to be overweight. They are less concerned with material possessions and more likely to go to college.[101]

Young adults today, Riley wrote, are "'the least religious adults in the United States.' Only about 20 percent attend religious services at least once a week."[102] And these young people are almost deaf to the call of community and common decency. "Any notion of the responsibilities of a common humanity, a transcendent call to protect the life and dignity of one's neighbor or a moral responsibility to seek the common good, was almost entirely absent among the respondents."[103]

Smith is describing a generation of moral barbarians—"trousered apes," in the depiction of C. S. Lewis's *The Abolition of Man.*

CULTURE WAR WITHOUT END

A second consequence of the death of faith is a loss of social unity, an unraveling of the moral community, and culture wars without end. For all cultures originate in a religious faith, as social critic and historian Russell Kirk writes:

> From what source did humankind's many cultures arise? Why, from cults. A cult is a joining together for worship— that is, the attempt of people to commune with a transcendent power. It is from association in the cult, the body of worshipers, that human community grows.[104]

Christopher Dawson, too, warned that should the West lose its Christian faith, its culture would fragment and its civilization would disintegrate:

> It is the religious impulse which supplies the cohesive force which unifies a culture and civilization. The great civilizations of the world do not produce the great religions as a kind of cultural by-product... the great religions are the foundations on which the great civilizations rest. A society which has lost its religion becomes sooner or later a society which has lost its culture.[105]

For centuries, Christianity offered the peoples of the West and the world common ground on which to stand. For this is a faith that accepts all men and women of all races, countries, and continents and all walks of life without regard to lineage, language, culture, color, or past conduct. Acting on their beliefs, Christians abolished human sacrifice in the Americas, ended the Atlantic slave trade, and halted the Indian practice of suttee: burning widows on the funeral pyres of dead husbands. The abolition of slavery and the promotion of civil rights were the causes of Christian pastors who demanded that their flocks live up to Christ's teaching as enunciated in the Sermon on the Mount about how they ought to treat their fellow man. Christianity is a universal faith. Its death leaves a nation bereft of a unifying system of beliefs. In the absence of Christianity, individuals seek community in attachments like race, tribe, party, and ideology that must inevitably separate us.

With the rejection of Christianity and its moral code by hundreds of millions in the West and scores of millions in America, we have no common moral ground on which to stand. The matters on which we clash multiply. Now we fight not only over politics and economics but over abortion, embryonic stem cell research, homosexuality, assisted suicide, public displays of religious symbols, the teaching of evolution, and what children should and should not be taught about God and morality in public schools.

Culture wars are rooted in irreconcilable beliefs about what is right and wrong, moral and immoral. Among American atheists, agnostics, secularists, Reform and Conservative Jews, Buddhists, Unitarians, Episcopalians, New Age adherents, and the religiously unaffiliated, 70 to 80 percent and higher believe homosexuality is acceptable behavior. Only 12 percent of Jehovah's Witnesses, 24 percent of Mormons, 26 percent of Evangelicals, and 27 percent of Muslims agree. Among atheists, agnostics, and the religiously unaffiliated, 70 percent believe abortion should be legal in most cases. Only 33 percent of Evangelicals agree.[106]

If we no longer agree on what is right and wrong, we can never be one people again. Traditionalists are already seceding from a culture they see as steeped in immorality in its movies, magazines, music, books, and television shows—retreating into cultural enclaves. Our poets and seers saw it coming. Eight years after Charles Darwin's *Origin of Species* appeared, Matthew Arnold, in "Dover Beach," saw the faith that had created Europe inexorably receding.

The Sea of Faith
Was once, too, at the full, and round earth's shore
Lay like the folds of a bright girdle furled.

But now I only hear
Its melancholy, long, withdrawing roar,
Retreating... [107]

Writing on the eve of World War I, Spanish-born Harvard professor
George Santayana expressed the seismic cultural shift this way:

> The present age is a critical one and interesting to live in. The
> civilization characteristic of Christendom has not disappeared,
> yet another civilization has begun to take its place. We still
> understand the value of religious faith.... On the other hand, the
> shell of Christendom is broken. The unconquerable mind of the
> East, the pagan past, the industrial socialist future confront it
> with equal authority. Our whole life and mind is saturated with
> the slow upward filtration of a new spirit—that of an emanci-
> pated, atheistic, international democracy. [108]

Irish poet William Butler Yeats saw Christianity as a magnetic force
that held our world together. But by 1920, he sensed the West had gone
deaf to the call of its God, writing, in "The Second Coming":

> *Turning and turning in the widening gyre*
> *The falcon cannot hear the falconer;*
> *Things fall apart; the centre cannot hold;*
> *Mere anarchy is loosed upon the world.* [109]

Was not the falconer God? Was not the "centre" Christianity? Has not
"anarchy" been "loosed upon the world"? Yeats ends his poem with a
premonition: "And what rough beast, its hour come round at last, /
Slouches towards Bethlehem to be born?"

Is not the rough beast the new barbarism?

Christianity is the mother tongue of Europe, said Johann Wolfgang
Goethe well over a century ago. In the closing lines of *Europe and the*

Faith, published in 1920, the same year as Yeats's "Second Coming," Belloc wrote, "Europe will return to the Faith, or she will perish. The Faith is Europe. And Europe is the Faith."[110]

Two decades later, Belloc concluded that Europe had lost the Faith and the West would begin to disintegrate.

> Cultures spring from religions... the decay of a religion involves the decay of the culture corresponding to it—we see that most clearly in the breakdown of Christendom today. The bad work begun at the Reformation is bearing its final fruit in the dissolution of our ancient doctrines—the very structure of our society is dissolving.[111]

Before his arrest by the Gestapo in 1943, Dietrich Bonhoeffer, the Lutheran theologian and pastor later executed at Flossenbürg nine days before the Americans liberated the camp, echoed Belloc: "The unity of the West is not an idea but a historical reality, of which the sole foundation is Christ."[112]

UNRAVELING OF A CIVILIZATION

While the Christian peoples of Old Europe often fought, they united when the faith was imperiled. Charles Martel, the "Hammer of the Franks," who stopped the Muslim invasion at Tours in 732, was a hero to all of Christendom. When Pope Urban II preached the First Crusade in 1095 and called for an end to the persecution of Christian pilgrims by liberating Jerusalem and the Holy Land from Seljuk Turks, Christian knights from all over Europe enlisted and fought nine crusades until the fall of Acre in 1291. That Crusader defeat left the land where Jesus walked under the rule of Islam until British General Edmund Allenby strode into Jerusalem on December 11, 1917.

When Aragon and Castille united to expel the Moors in 1492, all of Europe rejoiced. When Suleiman laid siege to Vienna in 1529, Spanish and Austrian soldiers, aided by German mercenaries, halted Islam's advance up the Danube into the heart of Christian Europe.

At Lepanto in 1571, a galley fleet of the Holy League—a coalition of Spain, which ruled Naples, Sicily and Sardinia; the republics of Venice and Genoa; the Papacy; the Duchy of Savoy; and the Knights Hospitaller, under Don Juan of Austria, the illegitimate son of Charles V—sailed out of Messina to crush the main fleet of Ottoman war galleys in one of the decisive battles of history. Rome was secured from Turkish invasion. And Christian power displaced Ottoman power in the Mediterranean.

In September 1683, with the Turks again besieging Vienna, it was Germans, Austrians, and Poles under King John Sobieski who saved the city. The Battle of Vienna marked the beginning of the long retreat of Islam from Central Europe and the Balkans.

When did the struggle between Christianity and secularism begin? Solzhenitsyn traced it to the Renaissance when man displaced God at the center of all things, and to an Enlightenment that saw the Church as the arch-enemy and oppressor of mankind, whom the new philosophers had come to liberate.

"Men will never be free until the last king is strangled with the entrails of the last priest," said Diderot.[113] "Écrasez l'Infâme!" echoed Voltaire, "Crush the infamous thing!"—the Catholic Church.[114] Neither Voltaire nor Diderot lived to see what they had wrought. But they would get their wish. Within a decade of Diderot's death, Louis XVI had been guillotined and the September Massacres would begin with the priests.

Solzhenitsyn as well as Dostoevsky believed that every true "revolution" since 1789 had sought the extirpation of Christianity as essential to lasting victory:

"It was Dostoevsky ... who drew from the French Revolution and its seeming hatred of the Church the lesson that, 'revolution must necessarily begin with atheism.' That is absolutely true."[115] Solzhenitsyn saw a hatred of God as the dynamo powering the ideology that had seized his country by the throat:

[T]he world had never before known a godlessness as organized, militarized and tenaciously malevolent as that practiced by Marxism. Within the philosophical system of Marx
and Lenin, and at the heart of their psychology, hatred of
God is the principal driving force, more fundamental than all
their political and economic pretensions. Militant atheism is
not merely incidental or marginal to Communist policy; it is
not a side effect, but the central pivot.[116]

In his Templeton Prize lecture Solzhenitsyn reflected on the century and
agreed with Yeats: "Men have forgotten God; and that is why all this has
happened."[117] He saw World War I as the cataclysmic blow "when Europe,
bursting with health and abundance, fell into a rage of self-mutilation
which could not but sap its strength for a century or more, and perhaps
forever."[118]

What had caused the cataclysm? Solzhenitsyn offers this answer:

The only possible explanation...is a mental eclipse among
the leaders of Europe due to their lost awareness of a Supreme
Power above them. Only a godless embitterment could have
moved ostensibly Christian states to employ poison gas, a
weapon so obviously beyond the limits of humanity.[119]

Only rulers in whose hearts Christianity had died, Solzhenitzyn felt,
could commit such atrocities against fellow Christians, which exceeded
by many times the magnitude the horrors of the religious wars of the
sixteenth and seventeenth centuries and the Napoleonic Wars. The
Spanish Civil War (1936–39), in which Stalinists and Trotskyists sought
to create a Leninist state on the Iberian peninsula, would feature the
massacre of priests, the rape of nuns, the desecration of cathedrals, and
the destruction of churches.

The West, said Solzhenitsyn, "is experiencing a drying up of religious
consciousness. It, too, has witnessed racking schisms, bloody religious

wars, and rancor, to say nothing of the tide of secularism that, from the late Middle Ages, has progressively inundated the West."[120]

While the struggle between militant secularism and Christianity remains nonviolent, the fate of the West hangs upon its outcome.

In its millennium edition, the *Economist* declared the struggle over, publishing an obituary of God, observing that "the Almighty recently passed into history."[121] But while Christianity is indeed dying in Europe, Christianity's passing is not yet a fait accompli in America. British journalist Geoffrey Wheatcroft sees the Atlantic divide over religion and its value as a primary cause of "one of the great political developments— and great challenges—of the past generation, the growing gulf between the United States and Western Europe."[122]

> Mitt Romney was quite right when…he spoke of Europe's empty cathedrals. This is an extraordinary story…. [R]eligious observance in Europe has collapsed, Lutheran Sweden and Calvinist Holland followed by Roman Catholic Spain and Ireland. England has a national church "by law established," whose Supreme Governor, the Queen, is crowned by the Archbishop of Canterbury; and services of this Church of England are now attended regularly by less than 2 percent of the English population. France is the land of Joan of Arc and Bishop Bossuet, once a Catholic heartland ruled by the Most Christian Kings; today barely one French citizen of ten goes to church even once a year. The conversion of Europe from paganism to Christianity…was a seminal historical event; a book needs to be written on the re-paganization of Europe since the nineteenth century.[123]

This "re-paganization of Europe" raises a profound issue. If Europe is becoming non-Christian or anti-Christian, what are we defending? Why should America commit in perpetuity to fight and die for a re-paganized Europe that has become antireligious and even Christophobic?

Comes the reply: Europe is democratic and we are the defenders of democracy. But India is a democracy. Should we fight for India? Comes the reply: Europeans are the people from whence we come. But that will cease to be true when a majority of Americans trace their ancestry to Asia, Africa, and Latin America. Moreover, unlike democratic solidarity, ethnic solidarity is regarded as illegitimate if not irrational in today's West. Is that not why we abandoned Ian Smith's Rhodesia and Botha's South Africa?

At the August 1941 Atlantic Conference at Placentia Bay, off the coast of Newfoundland, Churchill and FDR sang "Onward Christian Soldiers" with British and American sailors to show their countrymen that the war Britain was fighting and America would soon enter was God's cause in which Christians must enlist. On the evening of D-day, June 6, 1944, FDR said that our men had crossed the Channel in "a struggle to preserve our Republic, our religion and our civilization."

Anti-interventionist Catholics of the 1930s, who had sought to keep America out of Europe's war, enlisted in the Cold War because they saw Bolshevism as mortal enemy. For wherever Communism had advanced—in Russia, Mexico, Spain, Poland, and China—priests went to the wall, nuns were raped, churches and cathedrals desecrated, and the faithful massacred, as were hundreds of thousands of Catholics in the Vendée during the French Revolution's Reign of Terror.

Liberals snickered at denunciations of "godless Communism" and "atheistic Communism." But it was this aspect—that Communists hated God and martyred Christians—that made Christians militant cold warriors. For Catholics, loyal to a hierarchical church ruled by an infallible Pope, the Cold War was never about democracy and free markets. It was about resisting a satanic ideology that had seized Russia by the throat and was hell-bent on the eradication of our church and faith as well as our country.

But if Christianity is dead in Europe and the continent has embraced what Pope John Paul II called the "culture of death," and has become what Pope Benedict XVI described as a "desert of godlessness," what is

America defending in Europe?[124] Why should American Christians be forever committed to fight for godless socialism or godless capitalism on the other side of the Atlantic? Why should American Catholics fight again for a Britain that *Financial Times* columnist Chris Caldwell calls "the anti-Catholic country par excellence" that gave Pope Benedict the "most hostile [reception] he has received in his half decade of papal travel?"[125] British intellectuals, some of whom demanded the Pope's arrest, cast "Catholic opinions and doctrines, many of them widely shared by non-Catholics—as crimes."[126]

The sundering of the West is another consequence of our dying faith.

THE GODS OF MODERNITY

"When we cease to worship God, we do not then worship nothing, we worship anything" is an insight attributed to British author G. K. Chesterton.[127]

A third consequence when Christianity dies in the soul is that people seek a new god to worship, a new explanation for life, a new reason for living, a new cause to believe in, live for, die for. When faith dies, something else will come to occupy the empty place in the heart. As nature abhors a vacuum, so, too, does the heart of man.

"All men need the gods," said the ancient Greek poet Homer.[128] And if the God of Sinai and God of Calvary is dead, men will find new gods, or create them, as Hebrews wandering in the desert created a golden calf and fell down to worship it. We saw the results of that search in the last century. "If you will not have God (and he is a jealous God)," wrote T. S. Eliot, "you should pay your respects to Hitler or Stalin."[129] Tens of millions did.

Whittaker Chambers, the American Communist who spied for the Soviet Union, and then recanted and converted to Christianity, explained in his 1952 book *Witness* Marxism's appeal to the educated young of the Depression. It was the appeal of the "second oldest faith":

> Its promise was whispered in the first days of the Creation
> under the Tree of the Knowledge of Good and Evil: "Ye shall

be as gods." It is the great alternative faith of mankind. Like all great faiths, its force derives from a simple vision.... The Communist Vision is the vision of Man without God.[130]

Writing of Chambers's insight about the "second oldest faith," author Wayne Allensworth lists other gods that have captured souls in our time:

Chambers captured the spiritual roots of what was made manifest in one form as communism, in others as the hydra of radicalism that has haunted mankind since the expulsion from Eden, whether as the sexual obsession of the libertines, feminists, and militant homosexuals, the growing power of Leviathan and bureaucracy, or the ruthlessness of global capitalism and self-absorbed consumerism.[131]

Ideology came first to capture the souls in which Christianity had died. As Europe lost the old faith, new faiths arose: Communism, and Nazism to combat it. In Britain, the religion to counter Nazism was nationalism, the religion of patriotism. But while nationalism unites countrymen, it divides countries. And the wars these secular religions produced proved more terrible than the Christian wars of the sixteenth and seventeenth centuries. These were the false Gods that failed an apostate Europe when she lost the faith that had given her birth, and it was when we learned the truth of Psalm 96: "[A]ll the gods of the Gentiles are devils."[132]

Dawson saw in democracy, socialism, and nationalism secular man's search to rediscover his lost sense of the sacred.

Democracy bases its appeal on the sacredness of the People— the consecration of Folk; socialism on the sacredness of Labour—the consecration of work; and nationalism on the sacredness of the Fatherland—the consecration of place. These concepts still arouse a genuine religious emotion, though the emotion has no basis in transcendent religious values or sanctions. It is a religious emotion divorced from religious belief.[133]

Neoconservatism, which shares attributes with the Trotskyism that is one of its roots, is one of the new ideologies to have seized the imagination of those seeking a cause, with its "belief in struggle, the utopian notion of a moral society at the 'end of history' ... and, most importantly, a Romantic belief in the power of ideas and morality to change the world."[134] The conversion of George W. Bush to neoconservatism was not without consequence.

Conservative scholar Robert Nisbet identified yet another new religion.

> It is entirely possible that when the history of the twentieth century is finally written, the single most important social movement of the period will be judged to be environmentalism.... Environmentalism is now well on its way to becoming the third great wave of redemptive struggle in Western history, the first being Christianity, the second modern socialism.[135]

By sacrificing to save our planet, Mother Earth, Gaia, millions believe, we redeem ourselves and save our souls. This effort to recover a lost sense of the sacred is truly "religious emotion divorced from religious belief."

Other new faiths have lately appeared: New Age, Wicca, Santería, Scientology. The occult is making a comeback. Young people flock to books and films about ghosts, vampires, and creatures from other planets in a seemingly endless search for the transcendent. Others seek community and a cause to believe in by joining with those of the same sexual orientation. In the eighteenth century, Samuel Johnson called patriotism the last refuge of a scoundrel. It is also the first refuge of many without faith. This, too, must ultimately prove futile for, as Belloc said, "self-worship is not enough."[136] Yet, the self, too, has become a deity, for, more than anything else today, individualism, hedonism, and materialism move Western man.

At the Oscar ceremony in 2009, comedian and atheist Bill Maher jibed that "our silly gods cost the world too greatly."[137]

"He's absolutely right," replied columnist Rod Dreher, "our silly gods *have* cost the world too greatly."[138]

> The God of Hedonism and Sexual Indulgence . . . has given us a world of broken marriages, shattered families, the destruction of the traditional family, miserable deaths from AIDS, epidemic teen pregnancy, fatherless children and the social (even criminal) dysfunction that accompanies such, and a younger generation unmoored from sexual sanity.
>
> The God of Money, which rules Wall Street and Washington, has delivered the world to a present and future calamity that will cause suffering not seen in at least a century.[139]

"The truth Maher may never recognize," wrote Dreher, "is not that God has failed us, but that we have failed Him."[140]

Time's 1966 Easter cover raised the question, "Is God Dead?" Yet, the search for God never ends, and when traditional faiths fail to satisfy the searchers, new cults arise. Nine hundred cult members perished in the mass suicide in Jonestown, Guyana, where charismatic pastor Jim Jones had moved his flock from San Francisco. In the 1990s, members of the Heaven's Gate cult in San Diego committed collective suicide to seek God in outer space. In 1993, two dozen children and scores of adult followers of David Koresh's Branch Davidian sect perished or were murdered in the inferno that erupted when FBI agents ended their siege and attacked the compound outside Waco, Texas. However, the greatest rival to a fading Christianity may be an ancient rival.

In the year of Munich, 1938, while the world was preoccupied with a potential world war between fascism, Bolshevism, and democracy, Belloc, with startling clarity of vision, looked to a somnolent south and saw an ancient adversary stirring again. "It has always seemed to me possible, and even probable, that there would be a resurrection of Islam and that our sons or our grandsons would see the renewal of that tremendous struggle between the Christian culture and what has been for more than a thousand years its greatest opponent."[141]

But how could a quiescent Islamic world imperil Western civilization? What did that backwater world have that modern Europe did not?

The tenacity of its belief in God.

> In Islam there has been no such dissolution of ancestral doctrine . . . nothing corresponding to the universal breakup of religion in Europe. The whole spiritual strength of Islam is still present in the masses of Syria and Anatolia, of the East Asian mountains, of Arabia, Egypt and North Africa.
>
> The final fruit of this tenacity, the second period of Islamic power, may be delayed, but I doubt whether it can be permanently postponed.[142]

These prophetic words were written seventy years ago, when most of the Islamic world was under the boot of Europe. Islam, said Belloc, is "the most formidable and persistent enemy which our civilization has had, and may at any moment become as large a menace in the future as it has been in the past."[143]

Half a century after Belloc wrote, Harvard's Samuel Huntington would be credited by Fouad Ajami with "remarkable prescience" for seeing in his *Clash of Civilizations* what Belloc saw in 1938:

> The relations between Islam and Christianity . . . have often been stormy. Each has been the other's Other. The twentieth-century conflict between liberal democracy and Marxist-Leninism is only a fleeting and superficial historical phenomenon compared to the continuing and deeply conflictual relation between Islam and Christianity.[144]

THE ISLAMIC ALTERNATIVE

As Belloc predicted, a hegemonic challenge to the secular West has arisen from a resurgent Islam that, with 1.57 billion adherents, has displaced Catholicism as the world's largest religion.[145] Islam is the majority faith of forty-eight nations, a fourth of all the member states of the United Nations. Muslims now constitute 5 percent of the total population of the European Union and an even higher share of the population of Britain, Spain, and Holland.[146]

It is myth that most Muslims are Arabs. Sixty percent of Muslims live in Asia. India's Muslims, 150 million, comprise one-seventh of the nation's population and are double the number of Muslims in Iran. Germany has more Muslims than does Lebanon. China, with 26 million, has more Muslims than Syria. Russia has more than Jordan and Libya combined. An increasingly Islamic world is inevitable.[147]

What makes Islam a candidate to reshape and replace the West?

First, with a more robust birth rate, its population is growing, while that of the West is declining. Second, immigration is bringing Islam back to Europe, five hundred years after its expulsion from Spain and three centuries after the retreat from the Balkans began. Millions have come to fill spaces left empty by aging, dying, and aborted Europeans. Third, as there was once a church militant, there is today a mosque militant.

Fourth, Islam gives its believers clear, cogent, and coherent answers to the great questions: Who created me? Why am I here? How do I live righteously? Has my God prepared a place for me? Islam's "insistence on personal immortality, on the Unity and Infinite Majesty of God, on His Justice and Mercy, its insistence on the equality of human souls in the sight of their Creator—these are its strength," wrote Belloc.[148] Islam gives men a reason to live and a cause to die for. It is a fighting faith. What will secular, hedonistic Western man, who believes this is the only life he has, give his life up for? Where are the martyrs of materialism?

The Muslim world, like what is left of the Christian, is repelled by and recoils from a sybaritic West. Writes columnist Jeffrey Kuhner, "the greatest source of global anti-American hatred is our decadent popular culture."[149] Many Western writers and thinkers have shared Islam's savage judgment of Western secular culture. Anglo-American culture, wrote English journalist Malcolm Muggeridge, is "nihilistic in purpose, ethically and spiritually vacuous, and Gadarene in destination."[150]

Lastly, Islam is a universal religion which claims it alone has the path to salvation and is destined to become the religion of all mankind. Islam divides the world into the lost and the elect, the Dar al-Harb and the Dar al-Islam. Missionaries who preach the Gospel in the Dar al-Islam and Muslims who convert to Christianity face a death sentence imposed by the state, clerical command, or the mob. To Muslims, all religions are not equal and it is blasphemy and apostasy to treat them equally. In the secular West, intolerance is a grievous sin—but it is also the mark of a rising faith.

When Abdul Rahman, 41, an Afghan who converted to Catholicism, tried to reclaim his daughters from the grandparents raising them, he was arrested and charged with apostasy. Rahman refused to recant. The prosecutor then demanded his death and the Afghan people supported that demand. Only by fleeing to Italy did Rahman survive.[151] This was in the sixth year after the United States had liberated Afghanistan from the Taliban.

While the Islamic presence is growing in Europe, populist parties are mushrooming to halt immigration from the Islamic world and demand that Western values remain dominant. In November 2009, the Swiss voted a ban on the building of minarets and prayer towers in mosques.[152] In 2010, surveys found that French president Nicolas Sarkozy's proposed ban on the burka, the full body garment that some Muslim women wear, was supported by 70 percent of the French and majorities in Germany, Britain, Holland, and Italy.[153]

Yet among Europe's elites there is a disposition to appease. Rowan Williams, the Archbishop of Canterbury, says it "seems unavoidable" that Britain will have to "face up to the fact" that millions of Muslims do not relate to the British legal system. An approach that says, "there's one law for everybody and that's all there is to be said, that's a bit of a danger."[154]

British law should accommodate Sharia, Islamic religious law, beginning with the laws on marriage and finance, Archbishop Williams is saying, or Britain will face an endless culture war with its Muslims. "What we don't want...is...a stand-off, where the law squares up to people's consciences," said Williams, "There's a place for finding what would be a constructive accommodation with some aspects of Muslim law."[155] Muslims must not be forced to choose between "the stark alternatives of cultural loyalty or state loyalty."[156]

Considering the ferocious resistance of secularists to accommodating Christians, the archbishop's receptivity to accepting aspects of Islamic law into Britain tells us whom it is that the West truly fears, and understandably so. The fatwa issued by the Ayatollah Khomeini against novelist Salman Rushdie for *The Satanic Verses* and the riots around the world and bomb plots that followed publication of the Danish cartoons mocking Muhammad have concentrated the mind of Europe, as did the ritual murder of filmmaker Theo van Gogh by a Muslim. The enraged murderer shot van Gogh twice, sat on him, cut his throat, then plunged a knife into his chest attached to a page of Koranic verses. In the new world we have entered, insulting Muslims is a more serious matter than insulting Christians.

Van Gogh, writes Flemish historian Paul Belien, "was a foul-mouthed, ugly man," who "particularly liked to upset religious people. He began with insulting Christians, but as this was not considered particularly shocking in the tolerant Holland of the late 20th century he soon moved on to insulting Jews."[157]

> By the end of the century, having shocked enough Jews, van Gogh went after the new "sacred cow"of the multicultural elite: the Muslims.
>
> When asked, after the murder of his friend Pim Fortuyn by an animal rights activist, whether he was afraid of being killed

as well, van Gogh said, "No. Who would want to kill the village idiot?" As it turned out, his big mistake was that, unlike
Christians and Jews, Muslims do not seem to be very tolerant
of village idiots.[158]

DEAD FAITH AND DEAD PEOPLE

The last consequence of a dying Christianity is a dying people. Not one
post-Christian nation has a birth rate sufficient to keep it alive. While
there is a correlation between rising affluence and a falling birth rate, it
is not absolute. Mormons have a robust birth rate, yet are among the
most affluent Americans. But the correlation between a dying faith and
a dying people seems to be absolute. Orthodox Jews have a high birth
rate. Secular Jews are a vanishing tribe. Whites in California do not re-
produce themselves. Whites in the Bible Belt have a healthy birth rate.
Utah has the highest birth rate in the nation.

The death of European Christianity means the disappearance of the
European tribe, a prospect visible in the demographic statistics of every
Western nation. "A nation that kills its own children is a nation without
hope," said John Paul II.[159] While all of Europe, save Ireland, Poland, and
Portugal, have laws guaranteeing abortion on demand, Africa and the Islamic world protect the unborn.[160] Europeans do not seem to understand
what is happening to them and why, but editorialist Richard Miniter sees
a causal connection between a dead faith and a dying continent.

> The loss of faith in Europe is like an unseen black star that
> still has a tremendous gravitational pull.... They don't under-
> stand why their culture is failing. They don't understand why
> divorce rates and suicide rates are so high. They don't under-
> stand why so few European women have more than one child,
> and why on most European streets, you see more dogs than
> children. This is the impact of the death of real Christian be-
> lief in Europe.[161]

German philosopher Jürgen Habermas, a secular nonbeliever, wrote in 2004: "Christianity, and nothing else, is the ultimate foundation of liberty, conscience, human rights and democracy, the benchmarks of Western civilization.... Everything else is idle postmodern chatter."[162]

In *Victory of Reason,* sociologist of religion Rodney Stark concurred. Europe, he said, owes everything—culture, freedom, science, wealth—to Christianity. He sees the crisis of the dying continent resolving itself. "Europe is going to get more religious than it is either because of a revival of Christianity or because they go Muslim.... you can't sit there with no babies forever."[163]

In his review of Huntington's *Clash of Civilizations and the Remaking of World Order,* Fr. John McCloskey restates the author's closing question: "Is Western civilization a new species, in a class by itself, incomparably different from all other civilizations that have ever existed?"[164] He answers "yes" with the caveat "that the civilization remains firmly rooted in a true supernatural Faith whence it originated."[165]

> If the West, however, has become a hedonistic de-populating civilization exporting its "values" of consumerism throughout the world, it will cave in and collapse like many civilizations before it and darkness will descend. The Faith cannot fail, but we can.[166]

The cycle is inescapable: when the faith dies, the culture dies, the civilization dies, and the people die. This appears less a bold prediction of what may happen than a depiction of what is happening now.

3

THE CRISIS OF CATHOLICISM

Bare ruin'd choirs, where late the sweet birds sang.
—Shakespeare, Sonnet 73

[O]n the French coast the light
Gleams and is gone.
—Matthew Arnold
"Dover Beach"

For if the trumpet give an uncertain sound,
who shall prepare himself for the battle?
—St. Paul, 1 Corinthians 14:8

No institution has been more ravaged by the revolution that has swept over America since the 1960s than has the Catholic Church. Under Pope Pius XII (1939–1958), the Church had made historic strides. The number of Catholics and priests doubled. Parochial schools, high schools, and churches could not be built fast enough to accommodate the faithful whose numbers were growing from the Catholic baby boom and conversions in the aftermath of World War II.

The 1950s were America's Catholic moment. The moral authority of the Pope and America's bishops was never higher. Long lines formed outside confessionals on Saturdays. It was standing room only at Sunday Mass. Fr. Patrick Peyton's Rosary Crusade ("The family that prays together stays together") drew huge crowds. The most visible prelate was Msgr. Fulton J. Sheen, whose television ratings bested those of Milton Berle. "He's got better writers than I do," quipped Berle. Notre Dame's legendary gridiron teams had millions of "subway alumni." Four out of five Catholics cast their votes in 1960 for John F. Kennedy, who became our first Catholic president. We were a people then.

Pope John XXIII, successor to Pius XII, thus startled faithful when he began his papacy by calling Vatican II, the first Church council since 1870, when Vatican I defined papal infallibility. With Catholic unity and vitality never greater, the Church's prestige and moral authority never higher, many felt that calling a council to modernize was unnecessary and unwise. Why call a convention if your party's in good shape, JFK mused to fellow Catholic Eugene McCarthy.

In his opening address to the council, Pope John chided the skeptics. "We feel we must disagree with those prophets of gloom, who are always forecasting disaster, as though the end of the world were at hand."[1]

May good Pope John rest in peace. But the end of the Catholic world was at hand.

AN INDEX OF CATHOLIC DECLINE

Half a century on, the disaster is manifest. The robust and confident Church of 1958 no longer exists. Catholic colleges and universities remain Catholic in name only. Parochial schools are closing as rapidly as they opened in the 1950s. The numbers of nuns, priests, and seminarians have fallen dramatically. Mass attendance is a third of what it was. From the former Speaker of the House Nancy Pelosi to vice president Joe Biden, Catholic politicians openly support abortion on demand.

Four decades after Vatican II, a quarter century into the pontificate of John Paul II, Kenneth C. Jones of St. Louis pulled together a slim volume of statistics demonstrating that the fears of traditionalists who warned that the council was courting catastrophe had been justified.[2] And they exposed as naive those who insisted that the council would revitalize the faith, reconcile Catholicism with modernity, and make the Church more appealing to our secular world. Here are Jones's statistics on the decline and fall.[3]

- **Clergy.** While the number of priests in the United States more than doubled to 58,000 between 1930 and 1965, between 1965 and 2002 that number fell to 45,000 and is on course to sink to 31,000 in 2020, when more than half of all Catholic priests will be over the age of seventy.
- **Ordinations.** In 1965, 1,575 priests were ordained. In 2002, the figure was 450.
- **Parishes.** In 1965, only 1 percent of parishes were without a priest. In 2002, 15 percent, or 3,000 parishes, were without priests.
- **Seminarians.** Between 1965 and 2002, the number of seminarians fell from 49,000 to 4,700, a decline of more than 90 percent. Two-thirds of the 600 seminaries operating at the end of Vatican II have closed.
- **Nuns.** In 1965, there were 180,000 Catholic nuns. By 2002, that number was down to 75,000 and their average age was 68. By 2009, their numbers had fallen to 60,000, a loss of two-thirds in four and a half decades.[4]
- **Teaching Nuns.** In 1965, there were 104,000 teaching nuns. Today, there are 8,200.
- **Jesuits.** In 1965, 3,559 young men were studying to become Jesuit priests. In 2000, the figure was 389.
- **Christian Brothers.** The situation here is even more dire. Their ranks have shrunk by two-thirds, while the number of seminarians has fallen by 99 percent. In 1965, there were 912 seminarians in the Christian Brothers. In 2000, there were seven.
- **Religious Orders.** The number of young men studying to become Franciscan and Redemptorist priests fell from 3,379 in 1965 to 84 in 2000. For many religious orders in America the end is in sight.
- **Diocesan High Schools.** Almost half of these high schools operating in the United States in 1965 had closed by 2002, and student enrollment had fallen from 700,000 to 386,000.

- **Parochial Schools**. In 1965, there were 4.5 million children in parish grammar schools. By 2000, the number had plunged to 1.9 million. In the first decade of this century, the number dropped again, to 1.5 million, a loss of two-thirds of Catholic parochial school enrollment since Vatican II—in a country whose population grew in that period by over 100 million.[5]

In 2007, after interviewing 35,000 people for its U.S. Religious Landscape Survey, the Pew Forum confirmed what Jones had reported. Since Vatican II, the Catholic Church in America had undergone a decline to rival what happened in some northern European countries during the Reformation. By 2007:

- One in three Catholics reared in the faith had left the Church.[6]
- One in ten American adults was a fallen-away Catholic.[7]
- Catholics remained 24 percent of the U.S. population only because of immigration. Forty-six percent of all immigrants are Catholics. As Irish, German, Italian, and Polish Catholics leave the Church or die, the pews fill up with Mexicans, Central Americans, Filipinos, and Vietnamese. Were it not for immigrants, Catholics would have fallen from a fourth of the population to 18.4 percent, or less than one fifth.[8] "Every week, I bury a Lithuanian or a Polish Catholic and baptize two Latino babies," one Chicago priest remarked.

Catholic losses have been "staggering," writes Fr. Joseph Sirba, "if one excludes immigrants and converts from the calculations, the Catholic Church has lost to other religions or to no religion at all 35.4 percent—or more than one-third—of the 64,131,750 of its native-born members."[9]

- Latinos comprise 29 percent of U.S. Catholics and 45 percent of Catholics aged eighteen to twenty-nine. According to the Conference of Catholic Bishops, by 2020, Hispanics may account for half of all U.S. Catholics.[10] This explains the hierarchy's support for immigration and amnesty for illegal aliens. The higher Hispanic birth rate and immigration represent the Church's last hope of retaining or expanding its one-quarter share of the U.S. population. It is no accident that the new archbishop of Los Angeles, who replaces Cardinal Roger Mahony, is Jose Gomez, who is destined to become the first Hispanic cardinal of the American Catholic Church. On appointment, Gomez expressed his joy that Los Angeles, "like no other city in the world, has the global face of the Catholic Church."[11]

Yet, there is a cultural divide among U.S. Catholics. Fifty-six percent of Hispanic Catholics prefer to hear Mass in Spanish. Only 8 percent prefer English. In the churches Hispanics attend, 91 percent offer Spanish language services, 82 percent have Hispanic clergy, 79 percent hold worship with a largely Hispanic congregation.[12] The adage that Sunday mornings are the most segregated hours in America applies to the Catholic Church.

AGE OF DISBELIEF

The Catholics who remain in the Church are not nearly as firm in the faith or devout as their parents were. The institutional shrinkage mirrors a spreading disbelief in doctrines that define the faith.

- Catholic marriages have fallen by a third since 1965, while annual annulments soared from 338 in 1968 to 50,000 in 2002.[13]
- Where a 1958 Gallup poll revealed that three of every four Catholics attended Mass on Sundays, a recent study by the University of Notre Dame found that one in four Catholics attend Sunday Mass today.[14]

Lay teachers have replaced nuns in the instruction of children and young adults in the faith, but they are nothing like the nuns of the 1940s and 1950s.

- Only 10 percent of lay teachers accept church teaching on contraception.[15]
- Fifty-three percent of lay teachers believe a woman can have an abortion and remain a good Catholic, even though participation in an abortion means automatic excommunication.[16]
- Sixty-five percent of lay teachers believe Catholics may divorce and remarry.
- Seventy-seven percent believe one can be a good Catholic without going to Sunday Mass.

Millions of Catholic children are being taught their faith by heretics. In April 2008, a survey of 1,000 Catholics, commissioned by the bishops and carried out by Georgetown University's Center for Applied Research in the Apostolate (CARA), found:

- Only 23 percent of Catholics say they attend Sunday Mass every week. Thirty-one percent attend Mass sometime during the month.[17]
- While 26 percent said they went to confession once a year or more often, 30 percent of Catholics said they went to confession less than once a year, *and 45 percent had never made a sacramental confession.*[18]

According to one *New York Times* poll, 70 percent of all Catholics 18–44 believed the Eucharist is but a "symbolic reminder" of Jesus, and nearly two-thirds of all Catholics agreed.[19]

Through the papacy of Pius XII, Catholicism remained the Church of the deeply traditionalist Council of Trent, which that redefined Catholic doctrine during the upheaval of the Protestant Reformation, refusing to modify its teachings to accommodate the age. After Vatican II, the Church came out to meet the world. The statistics give us the results of the encounter.

While the papacy of Pius XII was a period of explosive growth, the papacies of Paul VI and John Paul II were periods of unprecedented decline. Although he was charismatic and played a critical role in bringing down Communism, John Paul II failed to stop the hemorrhaging. But what caused the crisis?

WAS IT VATICAN II?

At the opening of Vatican II, the reformers were the young lions who were to lead the Church out of the Catholic ghettos by modernizing the liturgy, making the Bible more reader friendly, conducting Mass in vernacular languages, discarding old traditions, and engaging the world. They were called the *periti:* Hans Küng, Edward Schillebeeckx, the U.S. Jesuit John Courtney Murray. One wag warned that the Church would come down with peritonitis. And so it did. As former Jesuit Malachi Martin wrote:

> Some day, some historian of Second Vatican Council affairs will have access to all the relevant documents—the correspondence between the *periti,* the private position papers drawn up, the policy outlines—and establish beyond doubt that the Council of John XXIII was the object of a concerted and, as it turned out, successful attack by the Modernist leaders among Roman Catholics.[20]

Four decades of devastation followed the "ecumenical moment," with the final disgrace being bishops who lacked the moral courage shown by the Boy Scouts to keep perverts and predators out of seminaries and to throw them out of the rectories. "If gold rust, what shall iron do?" asked Chaucer, "For if a priest be foul, in whom we trust,/ No wonder is a lewd man to rust."[21]

In April 2011, the Christian Brothers of North America had to declare bankruptcy to protect the order from lawsuits arising from the abuse of boys at schools and orphanages in the Seattle area.

Not since the Reformation has the Church suffered so devastating a blow. Belated exposure revealed that, over decades, many priests had preyed on teenagers and altar boys, and the shepherds Christ had entrusted with his flock had been the enablers of wolves and secret wolves themselves. The revelations were disgusting and disheartening.

Result: The Church lost much of its moral authority and was forced to spend billions in legal fees and in damages to victims, accelerating the closing of Catholic schools, hospitals, and churches that had served the faithful all their lives. Not least of the losses were the broken hearts of the faithful at the shame and disgrace visited upon the Church they loved. For those responsible, the words of the Savior come to mind: "[W]hoso shall offend one of these little ones which believe in me, it were better for him that a millstone were hanged about his neck and that he were drowned in the depth of the sea."[22]

Defenders of Vatican II say that to blame the reforms for the decline in vocations and devotion is a classic case of the logical fallacy *"Post hoc ergo propter hoc."* After this, therefore, because of this. That the precipitous decline followed Vatican II does not prove Vatican II caused the decline. After all, all the mainstream Protestant churches—Episcopalian, Methodist, Presbyterian, Lutheran—suffered commensurate losses of faithful and, in some cases, greater turmoil and decline. Can Vatican II explain that?

Yet if one measures what Vatican II promised against what the Council produced, the Council failed. Neither Paul VI nor John Paul II was able to arrest the ensuing epidemic of heresy, defections, and disbelief. Paul VI once ruefully observed that when Pope John threw open the windows, the smoke of hell entered the vestibule of the Church.

Catholics must cease deluding themselves about the strength and vitality of their Church, says Archbishop Charles Chaput of Denver: "We need to stop over-counting our numbers, our influence, our institutions, and our resources, because they're not real. We can't talk about following

St. Paul and converting our culture until we sober up and get honest about what we've allowed ourselves to become."[23] The Catholic Church of 2010 is a hollow army. Though her numbers, 65 millions, are as large as they have ever been, the Church is an institution whose moral precepts are ignored even by Catholic politicians. And though Catholics represent nearly a fourth of the nation and almost a third of the Congress, they have gotten only crumbs from that table.[24] Republican platforms and presidents promised tuition tax credits for parochial schools but they were never enacted. And now the schools are dying. The right-to-life movement, representing millions, has been unable to effect protections for the unborn, fifty million of whom have died in the womb since the Supreme Court ruled in *Roe. v. Wade* in 1973 that the right to an abortion was now a constitutional right. Among the reasons abortion on demand endures— the support of Catholics in Congress.

Catholic politicians' failure to promote a Catholic agenda is their own collective fault. Divided on every issue, including life, rarely do they act in unison to advance Catholic interests. With the exception of the Hispanics, Catholic ethnic groups rarely act as such, though Polish and Lithuanian Catholics did push for and succeed in having the umbrella of the NATO alliance spread over Eastern Europe.

"THE DEEPEST BIAS"

"Anti-Catholicism is the anti-Semitism of the intellectual," said Peter Viereck.[25] Arthur Schlesinger called it the "deepest bias in the history of the American people."[26] And as the Church has weakened, anti-Catholicism has come out of the closet and is now rampant in the culture.

In 2007, the New York Philharmonic performed Paul Hindemith's 1921 opera *Sancta Susanna* in Avery Fisher Hall at Lincoln Center. In the opera, Sisters Klementia and Susanna are chatting in chapel and Klementia tells Susanna of having seen a nun strip naked and embrace Christ on the cross. Susanna disrobes and proceeds to the crucifix, as other nuns enter the chapel to condemn her as "Satana," a devil.[27]

That same year, an anatomically correct sculpture of a naked Jesus, made of chocolate and created by Cosimo Cavallaro, was scheduled for display during Holy Week at the art gallery of the Roger Smith Hotel. The Jesus statue was placed at street level, visible through the hotel windows to a passing public. After a Catholic League protest, with warnings of boycotts, the hotel canceled the "Chocolate Jesus" exhibit, but not before the gallery's creative director accused the League of conducting a "fatwa" against the hotel.[28]

In 2008, television's Comedy Central reran an episode of *South Park* that features a statue of the Virgin Mary spraying blood on people out of her backside.[29] Desecration of Christian icons has been going on for years. Insulting and blasphemous art, from the "Piss Christ" statue in a vat of urine to the Madonna smeared with elephant dung and surrounded by female genitalia at the Brooklyn Museum, from films like *The Last Temptation of Christ* to *The Da Vinci Code,* is defended as freedom of expression. Catholics who object are told, "You just don't understand the First Amendment."

In an October 2009 episode of HBO's *Curb Your Enthusiasm,* Larry David inadvertently urinates on a painting of Jesus in a Catholic home. The woman who discovers it believes these are the tears of Jesus, that the painting is weeping. She rushes off to church to report the miracle.[30] When the Catholic League expressed outrage over making a joke out of urinating on a picture of the face of Jesus, HBO said this was just another example of the "always playful...never malicious" Larry David.[31] Deal Hudson, publisher of InsideCatholic.com, asked, "Why is it that people are allowed to publicly show that level of disrespect for Christian symbols? If the same thing was done to a symbol of any other religions— Jewish or Muslim—there'd be a huge outcry."[32]

When Loveland Museum in Colorado hosted a 2010 exhibit featuring Stanford professor Enrique Chagoya's artwork depicting a man preforming oral sex on a naked Jesus, Kathleen Folden, a Montana truck driver, took a crowbar to the Plexiglas case housing the piece, then ripped it to pieces. Observed Bill Donahue of the Catholic League: Had that artwork depicted a man performing oral sex on a naked Muhammad, "the museum may have been blown up by now. So it is lucky that Ms. Folden is a Christian."[33]

Indeed, trendy artists would not dare put a naked chocolate statue of Muhammad in a show window, or urinate on the face of the Prophet in a television comedy. In 2010, *South Park* introduced a character named Muhammad in a bear costume. A warning of violence against creators Matt Stone and Trey Parker by a New York group called Revolution Muslim resulted in heavy censorship of the next episode by Comedy Central.[34]

Mocking Catholics, their religion, symbols, and beliefs, however, is considered innocent fun by a Hollywood that would regard reruns of *Amos 'n' Andy* as a hate crime. Historian John Higham's insight remains valid: anti-Catholicism "is the most luxuriant, tenacious tradition of paranoiac agitation in American history."[35]

The gay rights movement contains a coterie of Catholic-haters who do not shrink from what would be regarded as hate crimes, were they done to another religion. When Proposition 8, overturning California's law legalizing gay marriage, passed, swastikas were painted on Holy Redeemer Church in San Francisco. The words "Ratzinger" (Pope Benedict) and "Niederauer" (archbishop of San Francisco) were painted beside the Nazi symbol.[36] Crucifixes are sold in the city as sex toys and homosexual men dress up as nuns and show up at Mass.

From the 1930s to the 1950s, the Legion of Decency, with backing from the pulpit and threats of boycotts, could compel Hollywood to show respect for the faith. Now Hollywood revels in mockeries of Catholic beliefs and symbols—the Vatican, bishops, priests, nuns.

But Tinseltown is a coward when it comes to Islam. When *The Message,* starring Anthony Quinn as the Prophet, was released in 1976, there were threats to firebomb theaters. Message received. The film was pulled. Hollywood does not mess with Muhammad.

Director Roland Emmerich's *2012* depicts the Vatican and the statue of Christ the Redeemer on the mountaintop above Rio de Janeiro being blown up during the end of the world. Asked why he did not show the destruction of the Kaaba, the building inside the Grand Mosque in Mecca, the most sacred site in Islam, Emmerich, a self-described enemy of all religions, replied, "I wanted to do that. I have to admit.... You can actually let Christian symbols fall apart, but if you would do this with [an] Arab symbol you would have ... a fatwa."[37]

In November 2010, the Conservative News Service created a cultural storm with an arresting story about a staid old Washington museum:

> The federally funded National Portrait Gallery, one of the museums of the Smithsonian Institution, is currently showing an exhibition that features images of an ant-covered Jesus, male genitalia, naked brothers kissing, men in chains, Ellen DeGeneres grabbing her breasts, and a painting the Smithsonian itself describes in the show's catalog as "homoerotic."[38]

The film of ants crawling on the figure of a crucified Christ was from "A Fire in My Belly" (1987), a video by David Wojnarowicz, who died of AIDS-related complications in 1992. His video was created to express his rage and anguish at the death of a lover, Peter Hujar, who died of complications from AIDS the year the video was created.

The Christmas season exhibit came to the attention of the Catholic League, which called the image of Jesus covered by ants "hate speech" and demanded its removal. The rest of the four-minute video, wrote Penny Starr, of CNS News, portrays "the bloody mouth of a man being sewn shut ... a man undressing a man's genitals, a bowl of blood and mummified humans."[39]

The *Washington Post* rose to the defense of the exhibit, denouncing as censors any who would demand the removal of such art. But the National Portrait Gallery, hearing rumbles from the new Republican House about budget cuts, pulled the video. It was then acquired by the

Museum of Modern Art in New York, which began to exhibit it in January 2011.

As New York Archbishop Timothy Dolan writes, Catholic bashing has become "a national pastime," and manifestations of the classic bigotry "in the so-called entertainment media" are "so prevalent they seem almost routine and obligatory."[40] That, apart from Bill Donahue's Catholic League, Catholics have not made more effective protests against vile and blasphemous assaults upon Christ, the Mother of God, and Catholic teachings and beliefs, and that Catholics grin and bear it, is an unmistakable sign of a declining faith.

IS NOTRE DAME STILL CATHOLIC?

Revealing that their religious beliefs meant less to them than their political beliefs, a majority of Catholics in 2008 voted for a man who captured the endorsement of the National Abortion Rights Action League in a race against Hillary Clinton.

Obama supported partial-birth abortion, in which the baby's skull is sliced open with scissors in the birth canal and the brains sucked out to ease its passage, a procedure the late Senator Pat Moynihan said "comes as close to infanticide as anything I have seen in our judiciary." In the Illinois legislature, Obama blocked the proposed Born Alive Infant Protection Act, a bill to protect infants who survive abortion. He promised supporters he would sign a "Freedom of Choice Act" to repeal all legislated restrictions on abortion, state or federal. Taking office, he opened the door to federal funding of embryonic stem cell research and, by executive order, repealed the Reagan-Bush prohibition against using tax dollars to fund agencies abroad that perform abortions.

Yet, this perfect record of support for abortion did not inhibit Notre Dame from inviting Obama to deliver the 2009 commencement address and receive an honorary degree from that university whose name is synonymous with Catholicism. Said the late Ralph McInerny, a professor of philosophy at Notre Dame since 1955:

> By inviting Barack Obama to be the 2009 commencement speaker, Notre Dame has forfeited its right to call itself a Catholic University.... [T]his is a deliberate thumbing of the collective nose at the Roman Catholic Church to which Notre Dame purports to be faithful.
>
> Faithful? Tell it to Julian the Apostate.[41]

Julian was the emperor after Constantine who had died trying to return Rome to her old pagan gods.

McInerny called the invitation worse than the "usual effort of the university to get into warm contact with the power figures of the day. It is an unequivocal abandonment of any pretense at being a Catholic university."[42]

An honorary degree from a Catholic university, said George Weigel, biographer of John Paul II, is a statement that "This is a life worth emulating according to our understanding of the true, the good and the beautiful...It is beyond my imagining how Notre Dame can say that."[43] Indeed, how can a Catholic university celebrate the life and work of a politician who is publicly committed to nominating Supreme Court justices who will ensure that killing one's unborn child in America remains forever a Constitutional right.

Because of Obama's support of embryonic stem cell research, Bishop John D'Arcy of Fort Wayne-South Bend informed Notre Dame he would not attend the commencement. "While claiming to separate politics from science," said Bishop D'Arcy, Obama has "separated science from ethics and has brought the American government, for the first time in history, into supporting direct destruction of innocent human life."[44] Despite protests from Catholics across America, Obama spoke at the commencement and was awarded a doctorate of laws *honoris causa.*

The Reverend John Jenkins, Notre Dame's president, not only polarized the nation's Catholics, he raised a question for the Church: What does it mean to be a Catholic university? Are there truths about faith and morals that are closed to debate at Notre Dame? Or is a Catholic university an open forum for moral discourse, like London's Hyde Park, where all ideas and all advocates are welcome?

To Catholics, abortion is the killing of an unborn child, a breach of the commandment "Thou shalt not kill." Case closed. All who participate in an abortion are subject to automatic excommunication. Catholic politicians who support "choice" have been denied communion.

How can Notre Dame credibly teach that all innocent life is sacred, and then honor a president committed to ensuring that a woman's right to end the life of her innocent child must remain sacrosanct? Could Fr. Jenkins not see what others saw: the inherent contradiction that renders Notre Dame morally incoherent?

Any appeal to academic freedom by a Catholic institution "to justify positions that contradict the faith and teaching of the Church," said Benedict XVI, "would obstruct or even betray the university's identity and mission."[45] Did not honoring America's most visible advocate of abortion on demand "betray the identity and mission" of Notre Dame?

Fr. Jenkins said the invitation "should not be taken as condoning or endorsing [Obama's] positions on specific issues regarding the protection of human life."[46] Still, what Notre Dame said with its invitation is that the president's unwavering support for policies that have brought death to three thousand unborn babies every day for thirty-six years is no disqualification to being honored by a university named for Our Lady who carried to term the Son of God.

Is Notre Dame still Catholic? That question arose again in the fall, when the university, using fees collected from students, paid to send five members of the Notre Dame Progressive Student Alliance to D.C. to march from the White House to the Capitol for gay rights, although the Church teaches that homosexual acts are unnatural and immoral and homosexual desires are "disordered."

William Dempsey, a 1952 graduate who heads Project Sycamore, which represents ten thousand "fighting Irish" alumni, said his members are "tearing their hair out" over what is going on in South Bend. "What happens to Notre Dame is crucial in terms of what happens to all religious colleges in the country," said Dempsey. "We wonder if it's going to turn into another Georgetown."[47]

Good question.

"DESERT OF GODLESSNESS"

That same week (the first week of Lent) that Obama received his honorary degree from Notre Dame, Georgetown University hosted Sex Positive Week, funded by the Student Activities Commission and sponsored by the feminist and gay student clubs such as GU Pride. Monday's session offered a speaker whose organization "provides a forum" for fetishism, cross-dressing, and bondage. On Ash Wednesday, the university offered "Torn About Porn?" a discussion of "alternative forms of pornography that are not supposed to be exploitative." The first Saturday in Lent was set aside for a talk by a pornographic filmmaker about "Relationships Beyond Monogamy."[48]

Do not assume Catholic doctrine about human sexuality is being taught at Georgetown, said political science professor Patrick Deneen. "It is not. The university feebly attempts to pretend to be concerned about matters of sexuality, but addresses them in terms of 'health.' The only orthodoxy on campus is sexual liberation."[49]

Georgetown University has an established Lesbian, Gay, Bisexual, Transgender, and Questioning Resource Center, but no comparable campus center dedicated to Catholic teachings on human sexuality. Said Deneen:

> [W]hat is the message being sent to today's students? Sex, like everything else, is a matter of preference, choice, personal liberty and utilitarian pleasure. It is largely consequence-free recreation. We should recognize that the same moral climate that contributed to the devastation of the worldwide economy is the same moral climate that informs "Sex Positive Week."[50]

The Church of Vatican II was going to Christianize the culture. But the culture has de-Christianized Catholic institutions. "Rather than taking a part in attempting to shape, even change that culture, Georgetown is shaped in its image," concluded Deneen.[51]

Yet, though discussions of alternative sexual lifestyles are welcome at Georgetown, alternative Christian messages are apparently not. Three years before Sex Positive Week came to Georgetown, six evangelical Christian groups were kicked off campus and told to have no "activity or presence" there, be it worship services, retreats, or even helping students move into their dorms. The evangelicals were pro-life and opposed homosexual marriage.[52]

"Our job as educators and as priests is not to bring God to people, or even to bring people to God," says Fr. Ryan Maher, SJ, associate dean and director of Catholic studies at Georgetown. "Our job ... is to ask the right questions, and to help young people ask those questions."[53]

When this writer attended Georgetown half a century ago, the Jesuits taught us that the answers to those questions could be found in our faith.

What happened to the Catholic Church in America? The culture war against Christianity, once confined to dissenters and closet disbelievers, caught fire with the arrival of the baby boomers on the campuses in 1964. Their moral and social revolution spread swiftly to the media, Hollywood, the arts. Through museums, movies, magazines, music, books, and television, secularism converted much of the nation and changed the beliefs of millions about right and wrong and good and evil. Embedded in that least democratic of government institutions, the judiciary—where appointed judges and justices serve for life and answer to no electorate—secularism began to uproot and outlaw all symbols and expressions of Christianity from American public life and make its own tenets the basis of law. Thus, gay marriage is imposed by one state court after another, even as the people, in one referendum after another, reject it.

"I hate to inform Pat Buchanan," wrote Irving Kristol in 1992, "that those [culture] wars are over and the left has won."[54] Irving may have been right. But, if so, that is momentous. For, in *Christianity and Culture,*

T. S. Eliot, describing himself as a "student of social biology," warned what would come, should the culture collapse because the religion that gave it life had died.

> If Christianity goes, the whole of our culture goes. Then you must start painfully again, and you cannot put on a new culture ready made. You must wait for the grass to grow to feed the sheep to give the wool out of which your new coat will be made. You must pass through many centuries of barbarism. We should not live to see the new culture, nor would our great-great-great grandchildren; and if we did, not one of us would be happy in it.[55]

But Notre Dame and Georgetown have many imitators.

According to the Cardinal Newman Society, during that same Lenten season of 2009, at Loyola of Chicago, the Student Diversity and Cultural Affairs Office presented a film about a homosexual African American who is transported back in time to "cavort" with the supposedly homosexual writer Langston Hughes. The movie was part of a semester-long Color of Queer Film Series sponsored by Loyola. Another movie in the series concerns a twelve-year-old boy who falls in love with a male police officer.[56]

At Catholic Seattle University, the Office of Multicultural Affairs and the student Trans and Allies Club was sponsoring Transgender Awareness Week, which included a session on transgender heroes and heroines in the Bible. Also featured was Criss-Cross Day, when students were encouraged to "come dressed for the day in your best gender-bending outfit."[57]

"That Catholic universities would permit these events on their campuses at any time of the year is unthinkable, but to do so during the holy season of Lent is unconscionable," said Cardinal Newman Society president Patrick J. Reilly, adding that the "saddest part of this story is that there is no indication that these universities are ashamed or embarrassed by what is taking place on their Catholic campuses."[58]

But are these universities still Catholic? In the culture wars of the late twentieth and early twenty-first centuries, have they not gone over to the revolution?

On Good Friday 2009, Benedict XVI, speaking during the Way of the Cross procession at the Colosseum in Rome, deplored the secularization of Western society, saying "religious sentiments" were being held up to scorn and ridicule as the "unwelcome leftovers of antiquity."[59] Stopping at the seventh Station of the Cross, "Jesus falls the second time," where the Savior is made an "object of fun" as he is being led to his death, the Pope declared,

> We are shocked to see to what levels of brutality human beings can sink. Jesus is humiliated in new ways even today....
>
> Everything in public life risks being desacralised: persons, places, pledges, prayers, practices, words, sacred writings, religious formulae, symbols, ceremonies.
>
> Our life together is being increasingly secularized.... Values and norms that held societies together and drew people to higher ideals are laughed at and thrown overboard. Jesus continues to be ridiculed![60]

"Allow us not to drift into the desert of godlessness," the Pope prayed.[61]

In the fall of 2009, Pope Benedict undertook a mission to Prague, a city the *New York Times* described as "what many religious observers...consider ground zero of religious apathy in Europe." The Pope had hoped to "foment a spiritual revolt against what [he] labeled...as 'atheist ideology,' 'hedonistic consumerism,' and 'a growing drift toward ethical and cultural relativism.'" Fr. Tomas Halik, who had been secretly ordained under the Communist regime that snuffed out the Prague Spring of 1968, was philosophical about the Pope's prospects. Czechs inhabit a "spiritual desert," Fr. Halik said. "The reanimation of the Catholic Church is a long-term goal....And even the Pope can't work miracles that quickly."[62]

Jaroslav Plesl, lapsed Catholic and editor of a leading Czech daily, reflected the cold indifference of his countrymen to the Pope's visit: "If the Pope wants to create a religious revival in Europe, there is no worse place he could come to than the Czech Republic, where no one believes in anything.... Add to that the fact that the Pope is German and socially conservative and he might as well be an alien here."[63]

Plessl would seem to have a point. A 2011 report on the emerging extinction of religion in the West found that in the Czech Republic 60 percent of the people profess no religious affiliation, highest percentage of the nine nations studied.[64]

What happened to the Catholic Church in America happened to America. Catholicism and the country together went through the cultural revolution that altered the most basic beliefs of men and women. Both came out changed. What Nietzsche called a "transvaluation of all values" occurred. What was immoral and scandalous in 1960—promiscuity, abortion, homosexuality—is normal now. Were a Supreme Court nominee today to echo John Paul II on human life, Catholic senators would filibuster the nomination to death.

As for same-sex marriage, an ABC-*Washington Post* poll in 2011 found 63 percent of white Catholics now supporting its legalization, a leap of 23 points in five years.[65] What was a *National Review* jibe about a papal encyclical in 1961, "Mater si, magistra, no!" has become the belief of two-thirds of all Catholics when it comes to Church doctrine that marriage is between a man and a woman.

NADIR, 2009

How did an effort by Pope Benedict, to effect a reconciliation with the traditionalist Society of St. Pius X, cause a firestorm that blazed for weeks across Europe?

The tempest began January 24, the day the Holy Father lifted the excommunication of the four bishops of the Society of Saint Pius X (SSPX). The four had been severed from communion with Rome in 1988, when aging Archbishop Marcel Lefebvre, a severe critic of Vatican

II, consecrated them, against the direct instructions of Pope John Paul II. The Pope had authorized only one bishop to carry on Archbishop Lefebvre's work.

Quiet progress, however, had been made to bring the SSPX and its hundreds of thousands of Catholic followers back to full communion. But how did this internal church matter come to outrage secular Europe?

British-born Bishop Richard Williamson, one of the four, had long held some extreme views. He was said to believe 9/11 was an inside job and that Catholic women should not be sent to universities. More controversial were his views on the Holocaust. In 2008, the bishop had said in Stockholm, "I believe that the historical evidence is strongly against—is hugely against—6 million Jews having been deliberately gassed in gas chambers as a deliberate policy of Adolf Hitler. . . . I believe there were no gas chambers."[66]

Thus no sooner was the excommunication of Williamson lifted than his Holocaust views were broadcast worldwide and an assault on the Pope began, accusing him of "rehabilitating" a Holocaust denier. The charge was false. Williamson's excommunication had nothing to do with his views on the Holocaust, and Pope Benedict had been wholly unaware of them. The Pope immediately renounced Williamson's views and declared his "full and indisputable solidarity" with the Jewish people, especially those who had perished.[67] The SSPX ordered Bishop Williamson to cease broadcasting his views. The bishop sent a letter of personal apology to the Vatican.

But this did not end the matter. The issue was seized upon to berate Pope Benedict and demand he reexcommunicate Williamson until Williamson renounced beliefs that had nothing to do with matters of faith. A campaign was mounted, abetted by Peter Steinfels, then religion editor of the *New York Times,* to goad U.S. bishops into denouncing the Pope.[68] None collaborated. But in Germany the campaign met with some success. Cardinal Walter Kasper, who had overseen Catholic-Jewish relations for the Vatican, did not cease to protest. Theologian Hermann

Haering demanded the Pope resign. Austria's Cardinal Christoph Schönborn, still considered *papabile*, a potential Pope, declared that no Holocaust denier can be restored to communion with the Church.[69]

German chancellor Angela Merkel decided to intervene. "This should not be allowed to pass without consequences," she said. "The Pope and the Vatican should clarify unambiguously that there can be no denial and that there must be positive relations with the Jewish community overall."[70]

While searing to the Pope and wounding to Catholics, the episode was instructive. Many Catholics awoke to the realization that they were deluding themselves in assuming their church's critics were acting in good faith.

There is a cultural conflict in the West between Christianity and secularism. At issue is who has moral authority in the modern world. Secularists seek out clashes with the Church in which they can claim the moral high ground and force Rome repeatedly to capitulate. They look upon such Church troubles as Williamson's views as opportunities to force Rome into one apology after another until the Church's moral authority is wholly eroded. Georg Ratzinger, the Pope's brother, who came to his defense and called Merkel a theological ignoramus, had the correct instinct.

The Pope and the Vatican, having done all they could do, declared the matter closed. Yet when Benedict visited Israel and Jerusalem's Yad Vashem, the nation's memorial to the victims of the Holocaust, he was subjected to a barrage from rabbis and politicians for not apologizing for the Church's role in or for Pius XII's alleged complicity in the Holocaust, even though both Catholic and Jewish scholars have declared these accusations to be malicious lies.

RETURN OF A CHURCH MILITANT?

By late 2009, U.S. bishops decided things had gone so far in the culture and politics that appeasement had to yield to confrontation on moral precepts. When the House debate on health care was at its hottest, the

Catholic bishops issued a stunning ultimatum: impose an absolute ban on tax funding for abortions, or we will call for the defeat of the entire Pelosi-Obama health care bill.

Message received. The Stupak amendment, named for Representative Bart Stupak of Michigan, outlawing all federal funding, direct or indirect, for abortions, was passed with the support of sixty House Democrats, to the astonished rage of the pro-choice caucus. Said Stupak: "The Catholic Church used their power—their clout, if you will—to influence this issue. They had to. It's a basic teaching of the religion."[71]

No Democratic member was more upset than Patrick Kennedy of Rhode Island, the son of Edward Kennedy and nephew of JFK, who proceeded to bash the Church for imperiling the greatest advance for human rights in a generation.

Rhode Island Bishop Thomas Tobin responded, accusing Kennedy of an unprovoked attack on the Church and demanding an apology. Kennedy retorted that Bishop Tobin had already told him not to receive communion at Mass and ordered diocesan priests not to give him communion.[72]

"False!" the bishop fired back.

Bishop Tobin said he had sent Kennedy a private letter in February 2007 indicating that he ought not receive communion, as he was scandalizing the Church, but he had not instructed priests to deny him communion.

As Rhode Island is the nation's most Catholic state, Kennedy fell silent, but received a parting shot from Bishop Tobin: "Your position is unacceptable to the Church and scandalous to many of our members. It absolutely diminishes your Communion with the Church."[73]

The clash made national news. And Bishop Tobin's public chastisement of a Catholic politician who carries the most famous name in U.S. politics was made more significant because it seemed to reflect a new militancy in a hierarchy that had been largely AWOL from the political arena for decades. Soon after, Kennedy, facing a tough reelection, announced he would not run again.

Other bishops have begun to challenge our Lords Temporal. Archbishop Donald Wuerl informed the Washington, D.C., city council that rather than have Catholic social institutions recognize same-sex marriages and grant gay unions the rights and benefits of married couples, he would shut these institutions down and let the city take them over. When the law passed, Catholic Charities of D.C. ended its foster care program to avoid placing children with same-sex couples.

Archbishop Dolan sent an op-ed to the *New York Times* charging the paper with anti-Catholic bigotry and using a double standard in judging the Church. Commenting on the "horrible" scandal of priests abusing children, said the archbishop, the *Times* demanded the "release of names of abusers, rollback of the statute of limitations, external investigations, release of all records, and total transparency."[74]

When the *Times* "exposed the sad extent of child sexual abuses in Brooklyn's Orthodox Jewish Community . . . forty cases of such abuses in this tiny community last year alone," the district attorney swept the scandal under the rug while the *Times* held up the carpet. Archbishop Dolan singled out a "scurrilous . . . *Times* diatribe" by columnist Maureen Dowd "that rightly never would have passed muster with the editors had she so criticized an Islamic, Jewish or African-American" faith. Dowd, he wrote, "digs deep into the nativist handbook to use every Catholic caricature possible, from the Inquisition to the Holocaust, condoms, obsession with sex, pedophile priests, and oppression of women, all the while slashing Pope Benedict XVI for his shoes, his forced conscription . . . into the German army, his outreach to former Catholics and his recent welcome to Anglicans."[75]

Dowd's column reads like something out of the *Menace,* the anti-Catholic Know Nothing newspaper of a century ago, said the archbishop. The *Times* refused to publish Archbishop Dolan's stinging rebuke.

Nor are these the only signs of a new Catholic militancy that was first manifest when scores of bishops denounced Notre Dame for inviting Obama to speak at the 2009 graduation and receive an honorary degree.

In an address to the National Catholic Prayer Breakfast in 2009, Archbishop Raymond L. Burke, prefect of the Apostolic Signatura, the Vatican's highest court, said, "In a culture which embraces an agenda of death, Catholics and Catholic institutions are necessarily counter-cultural."[76]

Exactly. Catholicism is necessarily an adversary culture in an America where secularism has captured the culture, from Hollywood to the media, the arts and the academy, and relishes nothing more than mockery of the Church of Rome. In a sign of Vatican approval of their defense of the Church and Faith, in October 2010, Archbishops Burke and Wuerl were elevated to the College of Cardinals.

In November 2010, Archbishop Dolan was elected president of the U.S. Conference of Catholic Bishops, the voice and face of the Church in America. In the balloting for vice president, Archbishop Chaput was runner-up to Archbishop Joseph Kurtz of Louisville, an outspoken adversary of same-sex marriage. Said the Reverend Thomas Reese of Woodstock Theological Center at Georgetown, "This is a signal that the conference wants to be a leader in the culture wars."[77]

QUO VADIS?

If Catholicism is losing faithful to other religions or to no religion, most Americans will ask: What has this to do with America or with us? Why is this not merely the Church's problem?

The issue Pope Benedict was raising on that Good Friday, warning against Europe becoming a "desert of godlessness," was this. If Europe has ceased to be a moral community and the "values and norms that held societies together and drew people to higher ideals" are being "laughed at and thrown overboard," what holds Europe together? What holds the West together?

In 1899, Pope Leo XIII condemned a heresy called Americanism. The Pope feared that, with the separation of church and state, the rise of liberalism and the celebration of individualism, Catholics would come to rely on secular ideas alone in building their new nation, and fail to incorporate the spiritual values and social teachings of Christ and his

Church. While Leo XIII admired America, and America's bishops, clergy and faithful were patriotic, the Pope feared where secularism might lead the great nation rising on the far side of the Atlantic. "At least since the time of Leo XIII," writes columnist Russ Shaw, "American Catholics have faced a choice between assimilation and counter-culturalism.... Notre Dame's invitation to Obama comes from the assimilationist heart of Catholic Americanism. The outrage it has produced is counter-culturalism's response... the argument will go on."[78]

However, as America cuts her Christian roots, at some point that argument ends and a secession of the Catholic heart from the culture and country begins to take place. For whatever the conflict between Catholicism and America a century ago, that conflict is becoming irreconcilable in the age of Obama. For, increasingly today, principled opposition to embryonic stem cell research, abortion on demand, gay marriage, euthanasia, and assisted suicide puts one outside the American mainstream. To traditionalist Catholics, this is not the country we grew up in. This is a different country. And given where America is headed morally and culturally, we are not far from a day when traditionalist Catholics will be saying, "This isn't my country anymore."

In November 2009, nine U.S. archbishops joined the Primate of the Orthodox Church in America and 135 Evangelical, Roman Catholic, and Orthodox Christian leaders in signing the Manhattan Declaration: A Call to Christian Conscience. We pledge, the signers said, that "no power on earth, be it cultural or political, will intimidate us into silence or acquiescence":

> We will not comply with any edict that purports to compel our institutions to participate in abortions, embryo-destructive research, assisted suicide and euthanasia, or any anti-life act; nor will we bend to any rule purporting to force us to bless immoral sexual partnerships, [or] treat them as marriages or the equivalent.[79]

"The dangers to religious liberty are very real," said Princeton's Dr. Robert George, a Catholic who, with Evangelical Charles Colson, coauthored the declaration.[80] Is an era of Christian civil disobedience ahead?

Catholicism remains a house divided. Secessions of the heart from our own country increase. In "This Blessed Land," the first chapter of his book *USA Today,* Reid Buckley, brother of William F., confesses, "I am obliged to make a public declaration that I cannot love my country.... We are Vile."[81]

To love one's country, one's country ought to be lovely, said Burke.

Can anyone say unequivocally that that is true today?

AN END OF CHRISTENDOM?

Before the Battle of Milvian Bridge in 312, in which Constantine was to engage the legions of the Emperor Maxentius, he saw a sign of the cross emblazoned in the sky. Above the cross were the words "*In Hoc Signo, Vinces,*" "In this sign thou shalt conquer." Constantine's victory ended three centuries of persecution. Confirmation that Christianity was the emergent faith of the empire came with the death of Julian the Apostate, Gibbon's hero, who had gone to war to restore the pagan gods. "Galilean, thou hast conquered!" said the mortally wounded Julian.

After the fall of the empire, Catholicism inherited the estate, united Europe, and gave the continent its culture and identity. For a thousand years Catholicism held Europe together as its Christian peoples resisted invasions which could have ended our civilization. The threats were legion. As Hilaire Belloc wrote:

> The Mohammedan came within three days march of Tours, the Mongol was seen from the walls of Tournos on the Saône in France. The Scandinavian savage poured into the mouths of all the rivers of Gaul, and almost overwhelmed the whole island of Britain. There was nothing left of Europe but a central core.[82]

The Christian core survived and in the last year of the eleventh century, crusaders marched into Jerusalem. The unity forged by the Church lasted another four centuries. Then came the great sundering of Christendom. Martin Luther, England's Henry VIII, and John Calvin introduced a Reformation that led to massacres and martyrdoms from St. Bartholomew's Day to the Thirty Years' War to Oliver Cromwell's slaughter of the Irish Catholic resisters at Wexford and Drogheda.

That Europe retained a Christian character as late as the twentieth century was seen in 1914, when British and German soldiers came out of their trenches to sing Christmas carols and exchange gifts in the No Man's Land. It would not happen in 1915 or 1916, the year of Verdun and the Somme. What Napoleon had said remained true. Every European war is a civil war.

The twentieth century produced more Christian martyrs than any other. Between 1917 and 1960, there was Lenin's Communist revolution and the rise of the fanatically anti-Christian Bolshevik state, the anti-Catholic Mexican revolution, Hitler's Reich, a Spanish civil war in which bishops, priests, and nuns were murdered by the Madrid regime, and the Chinese, Vietnamese, and Cuban revolutions, all of which sought to eradicate Catholicism and Christianity. When the Red Army poured into Central Europe to stay for a half-century, Catholics and Protestants suffered the same persecution as had the Orthodox in Russia.

With the collapse of Communism came an end to the persecutions of Christianity in Europe and a revival of Christianity in Russia. But in Islamic, Hindu, and Sinic cultures, the story is different. Though not so brutally as did Mao, China still persecutes Christians. In South Asia, it is not the governments that carry out the persecutions but the fanatics.

In August 2009, seven Christians in Gorja, Pakistan, were burned alive, their homes demolished by Muslim mobs seeking revenge for an alleged desecration of the Koran.[83] Christians, at three percent of Pakistan's population of 170 million, are the largest religious minority in the country.

Early in 2011, Shahbaz Bhatti, minister for religious minorities, the only

Christian in Pakistan's parliament, was dragged from his car and assassinated. For twenty-five years Bhatti had fought the country's blasphemy law, under which death is the prescribed punishment for insulting the Prophet.

Bhatti, a Catholic, had come to the defense of Asia Bibi, a Christian woman sentenced to death after farm hands accused her of blasphemy.

Shortly before his martyrdom, Bhatti had said, "These Taliban threaten me. But I want to share that I believe in Jesus Christ, who has given his own life for us. I know what is the meaning of [the] cross, and I am following the cross." Wrote columnist Michael Gerson, "[h]e followed all the way to the end."[84]

In September 2009, the *London Times* reported on the "worst anti-Christian violence" in India's history. In Orissa state, said local officials, "Hindu fanatics tried to poison water sources at relief camps holding at least 15,000 people displaced by mob violence." Mother Teresa's Missionaries of Christ were beaten as they took four orphans to an adoption center.

"The Catholic Church said that at least 35 people—many of them burnt alive—had been killed by Hindu extremists in Orissa since August 23."[85] By October, *Sky News* was reporting, "Tens of thousands of Christians have been made homeless after an orgy of violence by Hindu hardliners."[86]

> More than 300 villages have been destroyed and more than 4,000 homes in violent attacks, which have been going on since August and show no signs of stopping.... Nearly 60 people have been killed, 18,000 injured, and there are scores of reports about gang rapes, including of one nun. Fourteen districts in the area have been affected and more than 200 churches burned.[87]

This was a Hindu pogrom against Catholics. From the West, there was only silence.

Early in 2010, seven churches in Malaysia were vandalized or firebombed to protest a court decision allowing Christians to use the name of Allah when referring to God.[88] Muslims in Iraq have assassinated priests and bishops and bombed churches to drive out Christians whom they consider collaborators of the American "Crusaders." Half the Christians of Iraq, whose ancestors have lived in Mesopotamia almost since the time of Christ, have fled. In a story in the UK's *Catholic Herald* headlined "Middle East May Soon Be Empty of Christians," Beirut's Chaldean Bishop Michel Kassarji warned, "The Arab and Muslim countries have to make a serious move to stop the extermination of the Christian existence in Iraq."[89]

After midnight Mass in Naga Hamady, Egypt, forty miles from Luxor, on the eve of the Coptic Christmas, January 7, 2010, six Christians were machine-gunned to death and ten were wounded outside church. The massacre was revenge for an alleged rape of a Muslim child in November that had led to five days of rioting, arson, and destruction of Christian property.[90]

On the eve of All Saints, November 1, 2010, the faithful gathered at the Assyrian Catholic Church of Our Lady of Salvation in Baghdad. As Fr. Wassim Sabih finished Mass, eight gunmen stormed in and ordered the priest to the floor. As Fr. Sabih pleaded that his parishioners be spared, they executed him and began their mission of murder.[91]

When security forces broke in, the killers threw grenades to finish off the surviving Catholics and detonated explosive-laden vests. The toll was two priests and forty-six parishioners killed, and seventy-eight wounded, with many in critical condition after losing limbs. This was the worst massacre of Christians yet. For the Assyrian Catholics known as Chaldeans, whose ancestors were converted by St. Thomas the Apostle, the U.S. liberation has brought eight years of hell.

Forty-eight hours later, Al Qaeda in Mesopotamia issued a bulletin: "All Christian centers, organizations and institutions, leaders and followers are legitimate targets for the (holy warriors)."[92] In the following month, a dozen more Christians died. "By one estimate only 5,000 of the original 100,000 Christians who once lived in Mosul remain."[93]

After midnight Mass, New Year's Day, 2011, at Saints Church in

Alexandria, Egypt, 21 worshipers were blown to pieces and 97 wounded by a suicide bomber in the worst anti-Christian violence in a decade. Sherif Ibrahim saw the aftermath: "There were bodies on the streets. Hands, legs, stomachs. Girls, women and men.... We are going to die here. But our churches are here. Our lives are here. What will we do?"[94]

In March 2011 some ten thousand Christians in western Ethiopia were forced to flee when their homes were invaded and fifty churches burned by Muslims after a Christian allegedly desecrated a Koran. Federal police sent to the region were overwhelmed by mobs.

The Islamist group Kawarja was apparently behind the pogrom. "We believe there are elements of the Kawarja sect and other extremists who have been preaching religious intolerance in the area," said Prime Minister Meles Zenawi.[95] Attacks on Christians have been reported across Ethiopia, where Muslims now make up a third of the population.

On May 7, 2011, Salafi Muslims, claiming a Christian woman who wished to convert to Islam was being held against her will in St. Mina's Church in the Imbaba section of Cairo, attacked and burned the church in a battle with Christians that left a dozen dead and 200 wounded. The post-Mubarak cabinet called a meeting on Sunday, May 8, to deal with the crisis created by militant Salafis using their new freedom to attack the Copts.

Paul Marshall of the Hudson Institute's Center for Religious Freedom warns we may be experiencing another great wave of persecution, "as Christians flee the Palestinian areas, Lebanon, Turkey, and Egypt. In 2003 in Iraq, Christians were some 4 percent of the population, but they have since comprised 40 percent of the refugees."[96] From Egypt to Iran, the Vatican counts seventeen million Christians left.[97]

"Across the Middle East," writes Robert Fisk in the *Independent,* "it is the same story of despairing—sometimes frightened—Christian minorities, and of an exodus that reaches almost Biblical proportions."[98]

In an essay titled in Christ's words, "Whoever Loses His Life for My Sake...", Cato Institute's Doug Bandow writes:

Although Christians are no longer tossed to the lions in the Roman Colosseum, believers are routinely murdered, imprisoned, tortured and beaten. Churches, businesses, and homes are regularly destroyed. The opportunity to meet for worship and prayer is blocked. There is real persecution rather than the cultural hostility often denounced as "persecution" in America.[99]

What is behind this drive to persecute and purge Christians?

With the fall of the Ottoman and European empires and the rise of nationalism from the Maghreb to Malaysia, religious identity—Muslim, Hindu, Sunni, Shia—has become part of national identity. And since American Christian evangelicals back Israel in the Arab-Israeli conflict, and America is at war in Muslim lands, Christians, whose ancestors lived in the Middle East for centuries before Muhammad, are coming to be seen as collaborators and traitors, a fifth column of the crusaders and the Zionists.

The phenomenon is not new. Catholicism came to be seen as part of Spanish identity before the expulsion of the Moors in 1492, a part of Irish identity during the long struggle against Protestant England, and a part of Polish identity under Communism, which made the Polish Pope John Paul II so powerful a symbol. Across the Middle East, Muslim identity is now conflated with patriotism, as is Hindu identity in India. Pluralism, and tolerance for Christians in particular, is on the way out. We may be witnessing the annihilation of Christianity in its cradle.

What, then, is the future for Catholicism and Christianity worldwide?

Pope Benedict XVI calls Europe "a desert of godlessness" that has embraced the "culture of death." It is impossible to be sanguine about a Christian revival or even survival on the aging old continent. As Marshall writes, more people go to church in China than in Europe.[100] In France, the "eldest daughter of the Church," fewer than half the children are baptized and only one in eight Catholics practices the faith.[101]

Since the death of Pius XII in 1958, the Catholic Church in America has seen a half century of staggering decline. Latin America is less Catholic than it has been in centuries. In the Middle East, Near East, and South Asia, from Copts in Egypt to Chaldean Christians in Iraq to Catholics in Pakistan and India, communities of faithful are being martyred and persecuted by Islamic and Hindu fanatics. The once-Christian West seems less concerned with whether Christianity is martyred than whether elections will be held.

In *Future Church*, John Allen, Vatican correspondent for the *National Catholic Reporter*, sees a decisive shift coming in Catholicism's center of gravity. In the twentieth century, Africa's Catholic population exploded from 1.9 million to 130 million. From 2001 to 2006, reports the *Catholic Statistical Yearbook*, the Catholic population in Africa increased 16.7 percent, "with a 19.4 percent increase in priests and a 9.4 percent increase in graduate- or theological-level seminarians." The Catholic population increased 9.5 percent in Asia.

> Americans had eleven cardinals in the conclave that elected Benedict XVI...the same number as all of Africa, even though Africa has twice the Catholic population. Brazil, the largest Catholic country on earth, had only three votes, which works out to one cardinal-elector for every 6 million American Catholics and for every 32 million Catholics in Brazil.[102]

"This has to change, and it will, certainly before 2020," writes Penn State professor Philip Jenkins.[103] With the number of bishops and cardinals from Latin America, Africa, and Asia inevitably rising, Allen sees a Church that is more Third World, Pentecostal, and Charismatic, with an African Pope before 2050. That Church may be more orthodox on theological and moral issues, but it will be far less receptive to capitalism and Western concerns.

Allen regards the steady Islamization of Europe as "a trend of massive significance" for the Catholic Church: "A Church whose primary interreligious relationship for the last forty years has been with Judaism now finds itself struggling to come to terms with a newly assertive Islam, not just in the Middle East, Africa and Asia, but in its own European backyard."[104] With Muslims outnumbering Jews in Europe 15–1 and worldwide 100–1, the Catholic-Jewish dialogue will likely be superseded by a Catholic-Muslim dialogue between two faiths that make up 40 percent of mankind. Jenkins writes of possible Muslim demands for apologies for the crusades and for return of the mosques long ago converted into churches in southern Italy and Spain—in Toledo, Córdoba, Seville, Palermo.

As Jenkins writes,

Critical theological questions abound. Most fundamentally, is Islam a separate religion, as distinct from Christianity as Shinto or Hinduism, or are the two religions sisters separated at birth and raised in different family settings? Is Islam the offspring of the devil? Or is it a Christian heresy [as Belloc argued] that could somehow be brought back into the fold?[105]

On moral issues such as abortion and homosexuality, the Vatican, as did the Reagan White House, stood with Muslim countries in the UN, against a re-paganized Europe. And a growing number of Muslims from abroad are now studying at Catholic colleges and universities in the United States. In December 2010, the *Washington Post* reported,

In the past few years, enrollment of Muslim students ... has spiked at Catholic campuses across the country. Last year, Catholic colleges had an even higher percentage of Muslim students than the average four-year institution in the United States.... Some Catholic campuses are creating prayer rooms for new Muslim students and hiring Islamic chaplains to minister to them.[106]

Between 2006 and 2010, the number of self-identified Catholics on the campus of Catholic University in northeast Washington, D.C., fell, as the number of Muslims more than doubled, from 41 to 91. The largest group of international students by far comes from Saudi Arabia.

The same Georgetown University that ordered Evangelical groups off campus now has "a prayer room, student association and entire center devoted to Muslim-Christian understanding, and the school hired a full-time Muslim chaplain in 1990."[107]

In the last analysis, for the Church, too, demography is destiny. Europe, the United States, Canada, and Australia, which accounted for 29 percent of the world's population in 1950, will constitute only 10 to 12 percent in 2050. Latin America and Africa, which accounted for 13 percent of world population in 1950 will, by 2050, contain 29 percent of the Earth's people. The West and South will change places in a single century. Unless the West reconverts to its ancient faith, a reconversion nowhere in sight, Catholicism will become a Church with its Holy Father in Rome and the vast majority of its bishops, priests, and faithful living in Asia, Africa, and Latin America. Catholicism is well on the way to becoming a Third World religion.

4

THE END OF WHITE AMERICA

*The new America in the twenty-first century will be primarily
non-white, a place that George Washington would not recognize.*[1]
—JOHN HOPE FRANKLIN
African American Historian

*Obama's victory creates the prospect of a new "real" America....
It is no longer a "white" country...*[2]
—JOE KLEIN, NOV. 5, 2008

*Demographically, economically, and geopolitically
white America is in decline.*[3]
—*THE NATION*, 2009

Civilization's going to pieces.... I've gotten to be a terrible pessimist about things," said Tom Buchanan. "Have you read *The
Rise of the Colored Empires* by this man Goddard?"[4] Tom's friends
had not.

"Well, it's a fine book and everybody ought to read it. The idea is if
we don't look out the white race will be—will be utterly submerged. It's
all scientific stuff; it's been proved."[5]

This scene from Scott Fitzgerald's *Great Gatsby* introduces "The End
of White America?" a long essay in the *Atlantic Monthly* by music critic
and Vassar professor Hua Hsu. "This man Goddard" appears to be a
composite of Henry Goddard, Madison Grant, and Lothrop Stoddard.

Goddard was a eugenicist who translated the Binet intelligence test
into English, introduced the word "moron" to the field of intelligence

testing, and wrote the first law requiring that mentally challenged children be given special education. Grant authored *The Passing of the Great Race,* which separated Caucasians into Nordic, Alpine, and Mediterranean peoples, with the Nordic being the superior stock. As this raw passage reveals, Grant was deeply into eugenics:

> Mistaken regard for what are believed to be divine laws and a sentimental belief in the sanctity of human life tend to prevent both the elimination of defective infants and the sterilization of such adults as are themselves of no value in the community. The laws of nature require the obliteration of the unfit and human life is valuable only when it is of use to the community or race.[6]

Pure Social Darwinism.

Stoddard authored *The Rising Tide of Color Against White World-Supremacy,* which warned that the carnage of the "White Civil War" of 1914–1918 and the population explosion in Asia and Africa meant Europeans were facing racial inundation, the loss of world supremacy, and the death of their civilization. "Colored migration is a universal peril, menacing every part of the white world." Yet "*The Rising Tide of Color* is eerily serene, scholarly, and gentlemanly, its hatred rationalized and in [Tom] Buchanan's term 'scientific.'" Published by Scribners, the book was a "phenomenon."[7]

Ivy League-educated, Grant and Stoddard were respected in academic circles and belonged to an elite that supported the eugenics movement, Margaret Sanger, and sterilization laws. Stoddard, though unashamedly racialist, was something of a prophet. He predicted Japan's rise to power, its war with the United States, a second European war, the fall of the Western empires, mass migration of peoples of color to the West, and the rise of Islam as a threat to Western civilization.[8]

What Tom Buchanan and "Goddard" feared Professor Hsu welcomes: "The End of White America is a cultural and demographic inevitability."[9]

According to the 2010 Census white Americans will be a minority in 2041.[10] Among those under eighteen, whites will become a minority in 2019. Every American child born after 2001 belongs to a generation more Third World than European.[11] Questions about the future arise. If the end of white America is a cultural and demographic inevitability, "What will the new mainstream of America look like—and what ideas or values might it rally around? What will it mean to be white after 'whiteness' no longer defines the mainstream? Will anyone mourn the end of white America? Will anyone try to preserve it?"[12]

One reaction Professor Hsu reports is that, among cultural elites, some are shedding their white identity. "[I]f white America is 'losing control,' and if the future will belong to people who can successfully navigate a post-racial, multicultural landscape—then it's no surprise that many white Americans are eager to divest themselves of their whiteness entirely."[13] Indeed, who would want to be numbered among *Stupid White Men*, the title of Michael Moore's 2002 bestseller about a people oblivious to what is happening to them?

The day after Obama's inaugural, television host Larry King blurted out to an uneasy Bob Woodward a secret desire of his son. "My younger son Cannon . . . is eight. And he now says that he would like to be black. I'm not kidding. He said there's a lot of advantages. Black is in. Is this a turning of the tide?"[14]

"This is the decade of Tiger Woods and Barack Obama. . . . [of] race combinations," says U.S. Census Bureau head Robert Groves, who looked ahead with excitement to the 2010 figures. "I can't wait to see the pattern of responses on multiple races. That'll be a neat indicator to watch."[15]

Professor Hsu cites examples to make his case that in the popular culture it is now un-hip to be white, and artists are seeking to escape any white identity.

> Successful network-television shows like *Lost, Heroes,* and *Grey's Anatomy* feature wildly diverse casts, and an entire genre

of half-hour comedy, from the *Colbert Report* to *The Office,* seems dedicated to having fun with the persona of the clueless white male. The youth market is following the same pattern....

Pop culture today rallies around an ethic of multicultural inclusion that seems to value every identity—except whiteness. "It's becoming harder for the blond-haired, blue-eyed commercial actor," remarks Rochelle Newman-Carrasco of the Hispanic marketing firm Enlace.[16]

One gets the drift. But while the music man cites artists embarrassed by their white identity, he also sees the white working class seceding into social-cultural enclaves like Nashville and NASCAR. The "core grievance" of this emerging minority "has to do with cultural and socioeconomic dislocation—the sense that the system that used to guarantee the white working class some stability has gone off-kilter."[17]

Here the professor was dead on target. The Tea Party and town hall protests of 2009 were almost wholly white affairs. Mocking them, Rich Benjamin, author of *Searching for Whitopia: An Improbable Journey to the Heart of White America,* explains what these folks fear:

> By 2042, whites will no longer be the American majority. This demographic projection sounds a frightening alarm to the likes of...Joe Wilson. It heralds significant change to our nation's culture, electoral politics and distribution of resources.
>
> We must understand Wilson's outburst by exposing its past and future context—including what I call "The White People Deadline," 2042.[18]

Benjamin's book reads like a Baedeker to the bolt-holes to which whites are fleeing to huddle as multiracial America approaches.

During the Sergeant Crowley–Professor Gates dustup in Cambridge, Massachusetts, and Obama's subsequent "beer summit," *New York Times* columnist Frank Rich also cited the year 2042, noting the fears it had engendered:

> That reaction [to Gatesgate] is merely the latest example of how the inexorable transformation of America into a white-minority country in some thirty years—by 2042 in the latest Census Bureau estimates—is causing serious jitters, if not panic, in the white establishments.... [W]e're just at the start of what may be a 30-year struggle. Beer won't cool the fury of those who can't accept the reality that America's racial profile will no longer reflect their own.[19]

When Tea Party activists raucously protested outside the Capitol as Democrats passed Obama's health care bill, Rich saw visions of Kristall-nacht, the Nazi pogrom against the Jews in 1938—and race as the "real source of the over-the-top rage." By 2012, he wrote, "non-Hispanic white births will be in the minority. The Tea Party movement is virtu-ally all white.... Their anxieties about a rapidly changing America are well-grounded," for what is coming is a "national existential reordering" unseen since the Civil Rights Act of 1964 made "some Americans run off the rails."[20]

With the Tea Party triumph in 2010, Tim Wise of the *Daily Kos*, in "The Last Gasp of Aging White Power," wrote that this victory by white folks is but a battle won by a dying tribe in a lost war:

> For all y'all rich folks, enjoy that champagne, or whatever fancy ass Scotch you drink. And for y'all a bit lower on the economic scale, enjoy your Pabst Blue Ribbon, or whatever shitty ass beer you favor.
>
> Whatever the case, and whatever your economic station, know this. You need to drink up. And quickly. And heavily. Because your time is limited. Real damned limited. So party while you can, but mind the increasingly loud clock ticking

away in the corners of your consciousness. The clock that reminds you how little time you and yours have left.[21]

Listening to Larry King, and reading Rich Benjamin and Hua Hsu,
one is reminded of the comment of 1960s essayist James Baldwin of *The
Fire Next Time* fame: "As long as you think you're white, there's no hope
for you."[22]

On MSNBC's *Morning Joe* on inauguration day, Tom Brokaw saw in
Obama's triumph payback for white bigotry Brokaw had witnessed:
"Having been in the South in the '60s and Los Angeles, in Watts and
northern urban areas, when we were evolving as a country, I'm thinking
of all the bigots and the rednecks and all the people that I met along the
way. I'm saying to them, 'Take this.' "[23] Robert Reich seemed of a similar
cast of mind. When Obama's stimulus bill came before Congress, the
former secretary of labor, now a Berkeley professor, testified to his hopes
as to who should benefit and who should not: "I am concerned, as I'm
sure many of you are, that these jobs not simply go to high-skilled people who are already professionals or to white male construction workers.
I have nothing against white male construction workers, I'm just saying
there are other people who have needs as well."[24] Reich got his wish. By
mid-2009, unemployment among women had reached 8 percent, but
among men it was 10.5 percent, the largest gap ever recorded by the Bureau of Labor Statistics.[25] Among male construction workers, unemployment rose in the Great Recession to 19.7 percent, while illegal aliens
held 17 percent of all construction jobs, up from 10 percent in 2003.[26]

In October 2010, the *Washington Post* reported that from July 1, 2009,
to July 1, 2010, foreign-born Hispanics gained 98,000 construction jobs
while U.S.-born Hispanics lost 133,000. Black and white construction
workers lost 511,000 jobs that same year. In the second quarter of 2010,
foreign-born workers gained 656,000 jobs. Native-born workers lost 1.2
million jobs.[27]

Economist Mark Perry called it "The Great Man-Cession," a wiping out
of construction and manufacturing jobs, which have a high concentration of

blue-collar workers, mostly white men.[28] *Politico*'s David Paul Kuhn wrote, "Millions of white men who voted for Barack Obama are walking away from the Democratic Party, and it appears increasingly likely that they'll take the election in November with them."[29] Kuhn noted that blue-collar men had suffered 57 percent of all job losses in the recession. "And blue-collar white men, who make up only 11 percent of the workforce, constitute 36 percent of those who have lost jobs."[30]

Sensing their country slipping away and their abandonment by their own elites, middle- and working-class whites have turned to talk-show hosts and television commentators Rush Limbaugh and Glenn Beck, as well as Sarah Palin. But the demoralization is deep. Just nine months into Obama's presidency, a survey by the *National Journal* found that a plurality of white Americans over thirty not only had lost confidence in Wall Street and corporate America but in the U.S. Government.

In November 2010, the Democratic Party sustained its worst off-year defeat since before World War II, losing sixty-three seats and control of the House. Whites made up more than three-fourths of the electorate and voted 62–38 for the Republicans.[31] In the South, the white vote went Republican 73–27. There is now only one white Democratic Congressman left in South Carolina, Georgia, Alabama, Mississippi, and Louisiana. White Democrats from the Deep South are close to extinct.

In 2011, the *Washington Post* reported on the alienation and despair of the white worker in America. If there is "an epicenter of financial stress and frustration it is among whites without college degrees," said the *Post*. Only 14 percent of these Americans thought that Obama's policies were helping the economy; 56 percent said America's best days were behind her; 61 percent said it would be a long time before recovery came, and 64 percent blamed the government in Washington.[32]

NEW TRIBE RISING?

"Is white the new black?"

So asked Kelefa Sanneh in his *New Yorker* review of *Searching for Whitopia* and other works on white America. Sanneh concluded we may be witnessing "the slow birth of a people."[33]

It has happened before. In 1754, American colonists were South Carolinians, New Yorkers, Pennsylvanians, Virginians, all loyal subjects of the king. But after the contemptuous treatment of colonial soldiers in the French and Indian War, the Stamp Act, the Townshend duties, the Boston Massacre, the Tea Party, the Quartering Act, the Quebec Act, and the battles at Lexington and Concord, a new people had been born: the Americans. Virginia Cavaliers, Boston Puritans, Pennsylvania Quakers, and Appalachian Scots-Irish, who had all cordially detested one another, had begun to meld into a nation.

Adversity and abuse have historically created an awareness of a separate identity and accelerated the secession of peoples. And as Sanneh writes, the trashing of Tea Party America has taken on a racial cast.

> Why is it that, from Christian Lander to Jon Stewart, a diagnosis of whiteness is often delivered, and received, as a kind of accusation? The answer is that the diagnosis is often accompanied by an implicit or explicit charge of racism. It is becoming customary to suppose that a measure of discrimination is built into whiteness itself, a racial category that has often functioned as a purely negative designation.... [34]

The most common media label used to describe Glenn Beck's "Restoring Honor" rally that drew hundreds of thousands to the Lincoln Memorial and National Mall on the forty-seventh anniversary of Martin Luther King's famous 1963 speech was that it was "overwhelmingly white."[35]

Beck's speakers included Dr. King's niece Alveda King. Yet the AP, *Politico, Newsweek,* CBS, the *Washington Post,* the *Los Angeles Times, Salon,*

CNN, NPR, and *USA Today* all zeroed in on the racial composition of the crowd as "predominantly," "overwhelmingly," or "almost all white."[36] The media's unsubtle message: the Tea Party is a protest movement of, by, and for white people.

In 2004, when presidential candidate Howard Dean reached out to "guys with Confederate flags in their pick-up trucks," Shelby Steele wrote that this was "absolutely verboten. Racial identity is simply forbidden to whites in America"—because of their history and white guilt.[37]

Sanneh suggests this may be changing. While the Tea Partiers have been stung by accusations of racism—a popular sign at rallies reads, "It doesn't matter what this sign says/You'll call it racism anyway"—most have not been intimidated.[38] Why not? First, even the president does not believe the charge. As Robert Gibbs said after the 9/12 Tea Party rally in 2009, "I don't think the president believes that people are upset because of the color of his skin."[39]

Second, few harbor the guilt of country-club Republicans and all regard the accusation of racism as an unsupportable slander. While Tea Partiers are anti-Obama, they were also anti-Pelosi, anti–Harry Reid, anti–Martha Coakley, and anti–Charlie Crist, all of them white. In 2010, the Tea Party supported two Southern black GOP candidates, both of whom were elected to the House.

Yet in the summer of 2010, some two thousand delegates to the NAACP national convention unanimously passed a resolution demanding that the Tea Party renounce the racist leaders in its ranks. Said NAACP president Benjamin Todd Jealous, "What we take issue with is the Tea Party's continued tolerance for bigotry and bigoted statements. The time has come for them to accept the responsibility that comes with influence and make clear that there is no place for racism and anti-Semitism, homophobia and other forms of bigotry in their movement."[40] The NAACP suddenly found itself under attack and on the defensive.

White America is a house divided, and within its womb a new people is gestating and fighting to be born.

THE EMERGING WHITE MINORITY

A close look at the numbers from the Census Bureau fleshes out the picture. In 2004, the bureau said the crossover year when minorities that identified themselves as Hispanic, black, Asian, Indian, Native Hawaiian, and Pacific Islander would outnumber whites would come in 2050.

In 2008, the *New York Times* reported that the bureau was now projecting that whites would become a minority in 2042 and would fall to 46 percent of the population by 2050, comprising only 38 percent of U.S. population under 18.[41]

The 2010 census confirmed it: the end of white America comes in thirty years. "The Census Bureau has estimated that the non-Hispanic white population [will] drop to 50.8% by 2040—then drop to 46.3% by 2050. The demographic transformation—Latinos now account for one in four people under age 18—holds the potential to shift the political dynamics of the country."[42]

So it does. And what is coming appears inexorable.

In 2000, 15 percent of kids entering kindergarten were Hispanic. By 2010 it had risen to 25 percent. In that same decade the white share of the kindergarten population fell from 59 to 53 percent. "Nearly 92 percent of the nation's population growth over the past decade—25.1 million people—came from minorities."[43]

"It's basically over for Anglos" in Texas, says Steve Murdock, former director of the U.S. Census Bureau, noting that two of three Texas children today are non-Anglo and by 2040 only one in five will be white.[44]

As the education and income levels of Hispanics lag far behind, says Murdock, the future is bleak. Unless the trend line changes, 30 percent of the Texas labor force by 2040 will not have a high school diploma and average household income will be dramatically lower than in 2000. "It's a terrible situation that you are in," Murdock told the Texas legislature.[45]

What caused this historic decline of white America to minority status?

First, a white birth rate that has been below replacement level for decades. Second, a forty-year tidal wave of immigrants that was predicted (before the recession) to surge from 1.3 million a year to 2 million by 2050, almost all of it from Asia, Africa, and Latin America. In 2008, over one million immigrants became citizens. Of these, 461,000 were Hispanics; more than half the Hispanics came from Mexico.[46] Third, birth rates among Hispanics, especially those who have come illegally, that far exceed the birth rate of native-born Americans.

Yet, no matter how many immigrants come or from where they come, white America is an endangered species. Between 2000 and 2010, the number of white children fell by 4.3 million, or 10 percent, a rate of disappearance of 430,000 a year.[47] By 2020, whites over age sixty-five will outnumber those aged seventeen and under. Deaths will exceed births.[48] The white population will begin to shrink and, should present birth rates persist, slowly disappear. Hispanics already comprise 42 percent of New Mexico's population, 37 percent of California's, 38 percent of Texas's, and over half the population of Arizona under the age of twenty. Citing a 2008 study by the Pew Hispanic Center, Michael Gerson noted in 2010, "Hispanics make up 40 percent of the K–12 students in Arizona, 44 percent in Texas, 47 percent in California, 54 percent in New Mexico."[49] By 2011, the Texas Education Agency was reporting that Hispanics already constitute a majority, 50.2 percent, of all public school students.[50]

Mexico is moving north. Ethnically, linguistically, and culturally, the verdict of 1848 is being overturned. Will this Mexican nation within a nation advance the goals of the Constitution—to "insure domestic tranquility" and "make us a more perfect union"? Or has our passivity in the face of this invasion imperiled our union?

DOES IT MATTER?

In 1997 President Clinton said of the demographic transformation of our country, that it "will arguably be the third great revolution of America.... which will prove we literally can live ... without having a dominant European culture."[51] A year later, he painted a picture for the graduating class at Portland State University of the America their children and grandchildren would inhabit:

> In a little more than 50 years, there will be no majority race in the United States. No other nation in history has gone through demographic change of this magnitude in so short a time.... [These immigrants] are energizing our culture and broadening our vision of the world. They are renewing our most basic values and reminding us all of what it truly means to be American.[52]

This episode is astonishing. Here was a president of the United States telling a largely white student body the day is coming when their own kind will cease to be the majority in a country where the majority rules. Most peoples would sit in stunned silence at such a revelation, or rise in rage at the prospect. The Portland State students cheered the news of the coming minority status to which they and their children have been consigned by their government. Among our best and brightest, many anticipate with delight the day that white Americans become just another minority in the country their forefathers created "for ourselves and our posterity."

Ethnomasochism, the taking of pleasure in the dispossession of one's own ethnic group, is a disease of the heart that never afflicted the America of Andrew Jackson, Theodore Roosevelt, or Dwight Eisenhower. It comes out of what James Burnham called an "ideology of Western suicide," a belief system that provides a morphine drip for people who have come to accept the inevitability of their departure from history. The archetype of the ethnomasochist was Susan Sontag, who wrote, in *Partisan Review*, "The white race is the cancer of human history."[53]

Most peoples would greet the news that their own kind were becoming a minority with stunned silence, apprehension, or even dread. As Euripides wrote, what greater grief is there than the loss of one's native land? What explains our nonchalance? Whence comes the calm confidence that all will be well? Observing the world and his own nation, twenty years ago, Arthur Schlesinger wrote:

> Nationalism remains after two centuries the most vital politi-cal emotion in the world—far more vital than social ideolo-gies such as communism or fascism or even democracy.... Within nation states nationalism takes the form of ethnicity or tribalism.... The ethnic upsurge in America, far from be-ing unique, partakes of the global fever.[54]

That global fever has not broken. It is, if anything, more severe. In a re-view of historian Nell Irvin Painter's *History of White People,* Anthony Pagden takes pains to disassociate himself from what appears to him and to most intellectuals to be an odious idea: that race and ethnicity are matters of importance.

> Modern genetics has demonstrated conclusively that no such thing as race exists. Thanks to the mapping of the human ge-nome, we now know that each person shares 99.99 percent of his or her genetic material with everyone else. Similarly, skin color and physiognomy are now no longer regarded as the most obvious ways of classifying people by the scientific com-munity....
>
> Yet a concept of race lingers: America remains obsessed.[55]

This may be the conventional academic wisdom. Yet, conceding the truth of what the professor writes about genetics and what the "scientific community" holds, anyone who acts as though race is an irrelevancy would himself appear to be irrelevant. For this force tore down the West-ern empires in Africa and Asia and has torn apart nations. Ethnic nation-alism, as Schlesinger writes, is the "most vital political emotion" in our world.

"Likeness...is a cause of love," wrote Aquinas, and "two white men are one thing in whiteness. Hence the affections of one tend to the other, as being one with him; and he wishes good to him as to himself."[56]

Aquinas, the Angelic Doctor, is saying that the affinity of peoples of a race for each other is natural and normal. And if this is true for black Americans who rejoiced in the triumph of Obama, it is true also of white Americans. And white racial consciousness is rising and has begun to manifest itself in politics because, for tens of millions of Americans, this is no longer the country they grew up in.

Apprehension about America's future is rooted in the ethnic conflicts of our recent past and our present day. Anyone who believes America is a more unified nation today than she was fifty years ago, when our oldest president watched the youngest elected president take the oath, was not alive in 1960, or was not aware, or he deceives himself.

"MYTH OF THE REDEMPTIVE HISPANIC"

Beyond the dramatic change in racial demographics, the census statistics offer new details about the world our children and grandchildren will inherit. In 2007, the illegitimacy rate began to rise again. For black America, it went from 69.9 percent to 71.6 percent of all births. For Hispanics, it rose above 50 percent for the first time, and Hispanics now account for one in four U.S. births. For whites, the illegitimacy rate rose to 28 percent. While births to married women fell, births among the unmarried surged 12 percent.[57] Forty-one percent of all U.S. births are out of wedlock.

How alarmed should Americans be?

When Senator Daniel Patrick Moynihan published his explosive 1965 report *The Negro Family: The Case for National Action*, the illegitimacy rate among black Americans was 23.6 percent.[58] That is less than the white rate today, less than half the Hispanic rate today, and less than one-third of the black rate of illegitimacy today.

Why are these dramatic increases significant? Because the correlation between illegitimacy rates, dropout rates, crime rates, and incarceration rates is absolute. The more children born out of wedlock, the more who will never graduate from high school and will get into trouble before they are adults. The social scientist Charles Murray calls illegitimacy "the single most important social problem of our time—more important than crime, drugs, poverty, illiteracy, welfare or homelessness because it drives everything else."[59] As the conservative columnist Ann Coulter writes:

> A study cited in the far-left *Village Voice* found that children brought up in single-mother homes "are five times more likely to commit suicide, nine times more likely to drop out of high school, 10 times more likely to abuse chemical substances, 14 times more likely to commit rape (for the boys), 20 times more likely to end up in prison, and 32 times more likely to run away from home."[60]

Many had hoped that immigrants from the Catholic countries of Latin America might reinforce traditional values. That hope appears forlorn.

Traditional values have been dying in Latin America as they have in the United States. Though Mexico is nominally Catholic and restrictive on abortion, Mexican women now have more abortions than American women.[61] The myth of the "redemptive Hispanic," writes Heather Mac Donald, of the Manhattan Institute, has been demolished. She cites an *Economist* report on the "bad news from California. The vaunted Latino family is coming to resemble the black family."[62] Rutgers sociologist David Popenoe affirms this:

> Hispanics seem to have assimilated into the American culture of secular individualism more than the reverse. For example, the unwed birth percentage among Hispanics has jumped from 19 percent in 1980 to 48 percent in 2005 [to 51 percent today].... These trends contradict earlier expectations that Hispanics might bring this nation a new wave of family traditionalism.[63]

U.S.-born Hispanics are far more likely to smoke, drink, abuse drugs, and become obese than foreign-born Hispanics, and their life expectancy declines as they become Americanized. "As people become acculturated, they adopt American ways, become more sedentary and eat fast foods," says Dr. J. Mario Molina of Long Beach, whose patients are in the Hispanic community.[64]

Our corrosive culture seems to overwhelm any traditional values that Hispanics bring to America. "Hispanics overall are not nearly as socially conservative as many believe," says Ruy Teixeira of the Center for American Progress. A 2009 survey, he noted, "showed that Hispanics actually had the highest average score of all racial groups on a 10-point progressive cultural index.... And young Hispanics are typically more progressive than their older conterparts on social issues."[65] Yet, according to the 2010 census figures, there will be 130 million Hispanics here by 2050.

BUENAS NOCHES, USA

"Mexico does not end at its borders. Where there is a Mexican, there is Mexico," declared President Felipe Calderón, bringing his audience to its feet in his state of the nation address at the National Palace.[66]

Were this the America of a century ago, Calderón's claim that his country extends into our country would have produced a demand for clarification from the U.S. ambassador. Failing to receive it, he would have been recalled. America was a serious nation then.

But it has now become a tradition for Mexican presidents to claim extraterritorial rights in the United States. Repeatedly, they have instructed U.S. citizens of Mexican birth and ancestry that loyalty to Mexico comes before allegiance to the United States. In 1995, President Ernesto Zedillo told a Dallas audience of Mexican Americans, "You're Mexicans—Mexicans who live north of the border."[67] Zedillo brought a Chicago gathering of La Raza to its feet in 1997 by exclaiming, "I have proudly affirmed that the Mexican nation extends beyond the territory enclosed by its borders."[68]

In 1998, Mexico changed its constitution to restore citizenship to

Mexican Americans who have taken an oath of loyalty to the United States, an oath that requires the renunciation of loyalty to any other country. Mexico's goal: reknit the ties between Mexican Americans and their mother country and convince them to vote Mexico's interests in U.S. elections.

In June 2004, President Vicente Fox trod Zedillo's path to the Mexican American community in Chicago, where he declared, "We are Mexicans that live in our territories and we are Mexicans that live in other territories. In reality there are 120 million that live together and are working together to construct a nation."[69] Fox was saying that the construction of his nation, Mexico, is taking place inside our nation, the United States.

Is this not sedition?

The following year, Carlos González Gutiérrez, the director of Mexico's Institute for Mexicans Abroad, asserted, "the Mexican nation goes beyond the borders that contain Mexico."[70] These Mexicans reject the idea of America as a melting-pot nation that has created a new people: Americans. They are caught up in what Schlesinger called the "cult of ethnicity."

> The new ethnic gospel rejects the unifying vision of individuals from all nations melted into a new race. Its underlying philosophy is that America is not a nation of individuals at all but a nation of groups, that ethnicity is the defining experience for most Americans, that ethnic ties are permanent and indelible, and that division into ethnic communities establishes the basic structure of American society and the basic meaning of American history.[71]

Her rulers believe Mexico is a land of blood, soil, and history, and that loyalty to Mexico of people of Mexican blood, be they U.S. citizens or not, supersedes any loyalty to the United States. "I want the third generation, the seventh generation, I want them all to think 'Mexico First,'" said Juan Hernandez, the dual citizen who headed up Vicente Fox's presidential Office for Mexicans Abroad and then went to work for John McCain.[72]

Hernandez seems to be plagiarizing or channeling Il Duce. In 1929, Mussolini proclaimed, about Italians living in America, "My order is that an Italian citizen remain an Italian citizen, no matter in what land he lives, even to the seventh generation."[73]

Yet a majority of Mexicans agree with Hernandez. A Zogby International Poll found that 69 percent of the people in Mexico believe the first loyalty of U.S. citizens of Mexican descent should be to Mexico.[74] Blood ties trump any oath of loyalty to the United States.

At a Quebec summit with his NAFTA partners, George W. Bush ridiculed fears of a North American Union of Canada, Mexico, and the United States, with a single currency, modeled on the European Union, as a fantasy of conspiracy theorists. "It's quite comical actually, to realize the difference between reality and what some people on TV are talking about."[75]

Calderón, too, laughed. "I'd be happy with one foot in Mexicali and one in Tijuana."[76] But in his state of the nation address, Calderón was talking about one foot in Tijuana and one in L.A. One wonders if Bush was aware of what his friend Vicente Fox declared in Madrid to be the goal of Mexican state policy:

> Eventually our long-range objective is to establish with the United States...an ensemble of connections and institutions similar to those created by the European Union, with the goal of attending to future themes as important as...the freedom of movement of capital, goods, services and persons. This new framework we wish to construct is inspired in the example of the European Union.[77]

Fox was telling Europeans that Mexico's goal was to erase the U.S.-Mexican border and merge our two nations in a North American Union modeled on the EU. Whether Bush was aware no longer matters. Mexican presidents are open about the end game, for they sense America cannot prevent it, and the U.S. establishment appears unconcerned about American sovereignty.

Have we passed the point of no return?

Steven Camarota, of the Center for Immigration Studies, using Census Bureau figures of a net of 1.25 million legal and illegal immigrants entering and staying in the United States every year, projects a population of 468 million by 2060.[78] If immigration policy and law remain constant, the addition alone to the U.S. population in fifty years will equal the entire U.S. population when John F. Kennedy took office. Some 105 million of these will be immigrants and their children. That is roughly the population of Mexico today, the homeland of most of these immigrants.

When Arizona passed its law authorizing the police during "lawful contact" to determine the status of an individual if there were a "reasonable suspicion" he was here illegally, Calderón charged Arizona with opening the door "to intolerance, hate, discrimination and abuse in law enforcement."[79]

Within days, Calderón was in the Rose Garden with Obama, attacking the Arizona law. When the Mexican president went before the Congress to charge that the law—which specifically prohibits racial profiling— "introduces racial profiling as a basis for law enforcement," the Democratic side of the aisle that included Attorney General Eric Holder and Homeland Security Secretary Janet Napolitano rose to cheer Calderón's defamation of the state of Arizona.[80]

The Mexican government then filed an amicus brief supporting the Department of Justice complaint that the Arizona law will "interfere with vital foreign policy and national security interests by disrupting the United States' relationship with Mexico and other countries."[81] The U.S. State Department filed an amicus brief, citing the Mexican brief against our own state of Arizona. In striking down the Arizona law, Judge Richard Paez, an Hispanic who sits on the U.S. Court of Appeals for the Ninth Circuit, cited the Mexican brief and the denunciations of Arizona's law by almost a dozen countries of Latin America. Foreign opinion now counts in U.S. courts.

The mass immigration of the last four decades, legal and illegal, exceeds anything any nation has ever known. And these scores of millions come from cultures, countries, and civilizations whose people have never before been assimilated. Not only is our melting pot cracked, it has been repudiated in favor of multiculturalism. Immigrants are urged to keep their language, customs, traditions, culture, and national identity. And the largest cohort comes from a country, Mexico, with an historic grievance against the United States: 58 percent of Mexicans believe the American Southwest by right belongs to Mexico.[82]

Nor is assimilation proceeding as it did with the European immigrants. Only 3 percent of young Hispanic immigrants ages sixteen to twenty-five respond "American" when asked to identify themselves. Only 33 percent of second-generation Hispanics—U.S. citizens born here—identify themselves as Americans first. Not until the third generation do 50 percent identify themselves as American. Even then, half prefer to call themselves Latino or Hispanic, or identify themselves by the country that their grandparents came from.[83]

CALIFORNIA, HERE WE COME!

"California is a mess," writes John Judis, in the opening line of "End State: Is California Finished?" his *New Republic* essay on the Golden State he came to know as a student at Berkeley in 1962. After chronicling the disaster area California has become, Judis asks if it can recreate and renew itself. "I have my doubts," he concludes.[84]

Pessimism seems justified and portentous, for, as Judis writes, "California remains America's state, but it also registers the state of America."[85] We should look long and hard at the wreck of the Golden Land, for California is where we all are headed.

Anglos are down to 40 percent of the state population and their numbers are steadily sinking. Hispanics comprise 38 percent of the population and their numbers are rising. Only 27 percent of public school children in California are white.[86] In 2007, twice as many children were born to Latinas as to white women, the former rising in one year from 284,000 to 297,000, while the latter fell from 160,000 to 156,000.[87]

"Is California Dreaming Over?" ran the headline over a 2009 story by the Associated Press's Michael Blood. "Michael Reilly spent his lifetime chasing the California dream," the story began. "This year he's going to look for it in Colorado.... For him, years of rising taxes, dead-end schools, unchecked illegal immigration, and clogged traffic have robbed the Golden State of its allure." Reilly is not alone. Between July 2007 and July 2008, 144,000 more Californians left than came in for the fourth consecutive year, a larger loss than that of any state.[88]

Although California boasts the world's eighth largest economy, the state has taken on the aspect of a Third World nation. The Golden Land has the lowest bond rating of any state. The income tax rate has reached 10 percent. As of 2009 the sales tax was 8.25 percent, with counties and cities allowed to impose another 2 percent.[89] Reilly's property taxes in Colorado will not be a third of what they were in California. In a CNBC survey, California was ranked fiftieth among the states in "cost of business," and forty-ninth in "business friendliness."[90]

In the fall of 2010, David Brooks of the *New York Times* went to California and came away with the same impression as John Judis. California, he wrote, is "a state in crisis."

> Eighty-two percent of Californians say they believe their state is heading in the wrong direction.... State growth has lagged behind national growth. Unemployment is at 12.4 percent statewide and at catastrophic levels in the Central Valley. More people are leaving California for Oklahoma and Texas than came here during the Dust Bowl days of the 1930s. Tom Joad is giving up.[91]

In its 2010 survey of the best and worst states in which to do business, *Chief Executive* ranked California dead last, and asked a relevant question: "How is it that the nation's most populous state at 37 million, one that is the world's eighth largest economy... that had the highest growth rate in the 1950s and 1960s during the tenures of Democratic Governor Pat Brown and Republican Governors Earl Warren and Ronald Reagan, should become the Venezuela of North America?"[92]

The magazine offered this explanation:

> Californians pay among the highest income and sales taxes in the nation, the former exceeding 10 percent in the top brackets.... State politics seems concerned with how to divide a shrinking pie rather than how to expand it.... [U]nfunded pensions and health care liabilities for state workers top $500 billion.... When state employees reach a critical mass they tend to become a permanent lobby for continued growth in government.[93]

Bill Dormandy, CEO of San Francisco-based medical device maker ITC, says the "state's taxes are not survivable."[94] In 2009, when unemployment first rose above 12 percent, the highest since Dust Bowl and Depression days, Sacramento was issuing IOUs.

When five revenue-raising proposals were put on the ballot, Governor Arnold Schwarzenegger pleaded with Californians not to make their state "the poster child for dysfunction." But, "on May 18th they did exactly that," said the *Economist,* as voters "rejected all measures except one that freezes legislators' pay during budget-deficit years—a ritualised form of venting general anger."[95]

From 2000 to 2008, according to the Census Bureau, 1.4 million "domestic" migrants left California for other parts of the United States, while 1.8 million "international" migrants moved into California from foreign nations.[96] A large share of the foreign immigrants are tax consumers while a large share of those leaving California are taxpayers. Hispanics who pick fruit, wash cars, work in kitchens, carry bricks, and clean up buildings do not earn the wages or pay the same taxes as auto and aerospace workers. And as the cost of education, health care, housing assistance, police, and prisons surges, the Mike Reillys and the companies that employ them head back over the mountains whence their fathers came.

By 2010, one in six U.S. workers was foreign born. But, in California, immigrants accounted for 35 percent of all workers. Ten percent of all the jobs in California, a state with one of the highest unemployment rates in the nation, were held by illegal aliens.[97] The fiscal cost to California, local and state combined, has been estimated at close to $22 billion.[98]

In June 1998, Mario Obledo, a cofounder of the Mexican-American Legal Defense and Education Fund, said on a radio station, "California is going to be an Hispanic state. Anyone who doesn't like it should leave."[99] If whites don't like it, he added, "they should go back to Europe."[100]

Obledo was awarded the Medal of Freedom by Bill Clinton.

He was wrong about where departing Californians are going, but Obledo was not wrong about who inherits the Golden State. Two centuries after gold was discovered at Sutter's Mill and the Bear Flag Republic joined the Union, in 2042, Hispanics will outnumber whites, Asians, and African Americans combined, and will be an absolute and growing majority of all Californians.[101]

Nor will Hispanic immigration end in 2042. For if California is no longer the paradise over the mountains for Americans, it is a far, far better place for Mexicans than is Mexico. A third of those entering the country illegally head for California. As the Americans leave, Mexicans come. State bankruptcy and a debt default appear inevitable, with California ending up like those Third World nations that rely upon regular cash infusions from the IMF and the World Bank.

The National Immigration Survey is a huge federal study of the U.S. immigrant population. Poring over NIS data for his Harvard dissertation, Jason Richwine, a senior policy analyst at the Heritage Foundation, discovered that on the Wechsler tests, which measure basic knowledge, auditory recall, vocabulary, arithmetic skills, and comprehension, the children of Hispanic immigrants average a score of 82, seven points below the average score of Hispanic citizens.[102]

Now, an IQ test is no absolute predictor of whether one will succeed in life, but it is a reliable predictor of academic performance. And with an illiteracy rate of 23 percent among California's adults, the highest in the nation, and one third to one-half of its Hispanic high school students dropping out, and those that graduate reading and computing at seventh, eighth, and ninth grade levels, one cannot be wildly optimistic about the future of the Golden State.[103] Her schools, once among the nation's best, are now, measured by dropout rates and academic achievement, among the nation's worst. In late 2010 came news that Latinos, at 50.4 percent, had become a majority of all pupils and students in California public schools.[104]

Los Angeles, which is what most U.S. cities will look like in forty years, is the most diverse city on earth. Among its scores of thousands of gang members, a war of the underclass is under way. In 2005, the Supreme Court ordered California prisons to end thirty years of segregation. But in the jails and prisons of the City of Angels, where the Aryan Brotherhood, the Black Guerrilla Family, and the Mexican Mafia are at war over drugs and turf, integration kills. In August 2009, a riot lasting eleven hours erupted in the Chino correctional facility "along racial lines," wrote the *New York Times,* citing prison officials, "with black prison gangs fighting Latino gangs in hand-to-hand combat."[105] Some 250 prisoners were injured, and 55 hospitalized. Much of the prison was burned and destroyed.

In June 2008, Lee Baca, a Latino raised in East Los Angeles and the elected county sheriff for a decade, wrote an op-ed in the *Los Angeles Times* titled, "In L.A. Race Kills." "We have a serious interracial violence problem in this county involving blacks and Latinos," wrote Sheriff Baca:

> Some people deny it. They say that race is not a factor in
> L.A.'s gang crisis; the problem, they say, is not one of blacks
> versus Latinos and Latinos versus blacks but merely one of

gang members killing other gang members (and, yes, they acknowledge, sometimes the gangs are race-based).

But they're wrong. The truth is that, in many cases, race is at the heart of the problem. Latino gang members shoot blacks not because they are members of a rival gang but because they are black. Likewise, black gang members shoot Latinos because they are brown.[106]

Of the hate crimes committed in Los Angeles by Hispanics against blacks, fully 78 percent are said to be "gang-related," while 52 percent of those committed by blacks against Hispanics are considered gang-related.[107]

As there is no bad history, indeed, no history at all between blacks and Hispanics—no slavery or Jim Crow in Mexico, no African American role in the war that cost Mexicans half their country—what explains this mutual hatred other than race?

But if race explains gang killings by Hispanics of African Americans and the reverse, violence within minority groups, as between the Crips and Bloods of yesterday, is also burgeoning. In December 2009, the *New York Times* reported on the proliferation of gangs on Indian reservations.[108] The Navajo Nation has seen a tripling of gangs from 76 to 225 in twelve years. Among the Oglala Sioux on Pine Ridge reservation in South Dakota, 5000 young males are involved with 39 gangs. "Groups like Wild Boys, TBZ, Nomads and Indian Mafia draw children from broken, alcohol-ravaged homes … offering brotherhood, an identity drawn from urban gangsta rap and self-protection."[109]

Abandonment and fatherlessness, generating a lifelong search for family, community, identity, and protection, are behind the proliferation of gangs among minorities, including now young Asians whose parents remain the most law-abiding of U.S. citizens.

The Californians running away from communities and towns they grew up in have Arizona, Idaho, Colorado, Utah, and Nevada to run to. Where do their children run to, when the whole nation begins to resemble California?

POSTRACIAL AMERICA?

Tribal politics is not unusual, tribal politics is eternal. John F. Kennedy would not have gotten 78 percent of the Catholic vote had he not been Catholic. Hillary Clinton would not have rolled up those margins among New Hampshire women had she not been a sister in trouble. Mitt Romney would not have swept Utah and flamed out in Dixie were he not Mormon. Mike Huckabee would not have stormed through the Bible Belt were he not an evangelical Christian and Baptist preacher. The late city supervisor Harvey Milk did well in San Francisco's Castro because he was "one of us."

African Americans have voted 9–1 against Republican presidential nominees since Senator Barry Goldwater ran in 1964. But what, other than race, explains how Obama rolled up 9–1 margins among black voters running against the wife of the man Toni Morrison called "our first black president"? Even the *New York Times* seemed stunned by the solidarity of the black electorate and black radio. On *The Tom Joyner Morning Show, The Michael Baisden Show,* and *The Steve Harvey Morning Show,* which together may reach twenty million, wrote Jim Rutenberg, there is "little pretense of balance.... More often than not the Obama campaign is discussed as the home team."[110]

Black Entertainment Television announced it would carry Obama's acceptance speech to the Democratic convention live, but had no plans to carry McCain's speech to the Republican convention. Barack's speech "is an historic occasion," said BET chair Debra L. Lee, "so that demands some special treatment from us."[111]

And as the mainstream media have moved left, talk radio right, and cable TV has split on ideological lines, an ethnic Balkanization of the press has begun. On July 27, 2008, the final day of the quadrennial convention of UNITY: Journalists of Color, 6,800 were in attendance. Bush had been booed at the UNITY convention in 2004, while Democratic presidential candidate John Kerry had received a standing ovation. In 2008, McCain declined an invitation. The featured speaker: Barack Obama.

The major concern of the journalists who run UNITY was that their colleagues might lift the roof off McCormick Place convention center. Said Luis Villarreal, a producer of NBC's *Dateline*, "I don't think it's such a bad thing if for 15 minutes you take off your reporter hat and respond to [Obama] as a human being at an event where you're surrounded by people of color and you're here for a united cause."[112]

What cause united the ten thousand journalists who belonged to UNITY?

Advancement of journalists of color, based on color. For UNITY is composed of four groups, each created to advance journalists of a particular race or ethnic group: the Asian American Journalists Association, the Native American Journalists Association, the National Association of Hispanic Journalists, and the National Association of Black Journalists. Leaving no doubt as to what UNITY is about, its July 22, 2008, press release was titled: "Aim of New UNITY Initiative Is More Diversity in Top Media Management."[113]

"With more than fifty percent of the population projected to be people of color in less than a generation," said President Karen Lincoln Michel, "the nation's news organizations continue to generate dismal diversity numbers year after year.... 'Ten by 2010' is a significant step in the right direction."[114]

What was "Ten by 2010"?

UNITY was demanding that ten major U.S. news organizations, by mid-2010, elevate to senior management positions in the newsroom at least one journalist of color and provide "customized training to help prepare them."[115] The chosen journalist might be Asian, African American, Native American, or Hispanic, but could not be Irish, English, Polish, Italian, German, or Jewish.

With Obama's election, the spirit of UNITY came to the Federal Communications Commission in the person of "diversity czar" Mark Lloyd. Working at the Center for American Progress, Lloyd had hailed the "incredible revolution" of Hugo Chávez, praising his seizure of media outlets that opposed his Bolivarian revolution:

> The property owners and the folks who then controlled the media in Venezuela rebelled—worked, frankly, with folks here in the U.S. government—worked to oust him.... But he came back with another revolution, and then Chávez began to take very seriously the media in his country.[116]

By "taking very seriously the media in his country," Lloyd apparently meant Chávez's decision not to renew the license of RCTV, the nation's oldest television network, replacing it, writes columnist Amanda Carpenter, "with a state-run station that showed cartoons and old movies while protesters marched in the streets against the shutdown."[117]

Earlier, Lloyd had talked of how white journalists had to "step down" to open up positions of power for people of color.

> There's nothing more difficult than this because we have really truly, good white people in important positions, and... there are a limited number of those positions. And unless we are conscious of the need to have more people of color, gays, other people in those positions, we will not change the problem. But we're in a position where you have to say who is going to step down so someone else can have power.[118]

Lloyd added, "There are few things, I think, more frightening in the American mind than dark-skinned black men. Here I am."[119]

Half a century after Martin Luther King envisioned a day when his children would be judged "not by the color of their skin, but the content of their character," journalists of color are demanding the hiring and promotion of journalists based on the color of their skin. Jim Crow is back. Only the color of the beneficiaries and the color of the victims have been reversed.

TRIBAL POLITICS

Since the Home Rule Act of 1973 gave Washingtonians the right to elect their mayor, every mayor has been an African American. So, too, has every mayor of Detroit and Atlanta, since each city elected its first black mayor in 1973. The same is true of Memphis and Birmingham.

By 2006, every congressional district in America with a black majority had a black congressman. That year, however, Congressman Harold Ford chose to run for the U.S. Senate and state senator Steve Cohen won the Democratic primary in a field with twelve black candidates. Cohen went on to become the only white to represent a majority black district in the U.S. House and the first Jewish congressman ever from Tennessee.

Cohen went to Washington and became sole primary sponsor of a Congressional apology to black America, pledging the House to rectify "the lingering consequences of the misdeeds committed against African Americans under slavery and Jim Crow."[120] Cohen thus opened the door to reparations for slavery. And as he promised his constituents, he applied for membership in the Black Caucus. The door was slammed in Cohen's face.

"I think they're real happy I'm not going to join," said Cohen. "It's their caucus and they do things their way. You don't force your way in. You need to be invited."

But no white congressman has ever been invited. All who dared to apply, like Pete Stark of California, were rejected. As Representative William Clay Sr. said, it is "critical" that the Black Caucus remain "exclusively African-American." Clay's son and successor, Representative William Lacy Clay, affirmed the Black Caucus's restrictive covenant: "Mr. Cohen asked for admission, and he got his answer.... It's time to move on. It's an unwritten rule. It's understood. It's clear."[121]

Indeed it is. No whites need apply. Yet the Black Caucus conducts its business in federal offices on U.S. government grounds.

Running in the 2008 primary in his 60 percent black district against African American Nikki Tinker, Cohen was featured in a TV ad beside a hooded Klansman. The justification for this outrage? Cohen had opposed removing the gravesite, statue, and name of General Nathan Bedford Forrest from a Memphis park. The Confederate hero had later become a founder of the Klan. Another ad attacked Cohen for going into "our churches clapping his hands and tapping his feet," while being the only congressman who "thought our kids shouldn't be allowed to pray in school."[122] At a meeting of the Memphis Baptist Ministerial Association, Cohen was booed and jeered.[123]

"Anti-Semitic fliers—'Why Do Steve Cohen and the Jews Hate Jesus?' one asked—written by an African American minister from outside the district" were circulating in Memphis, said the *New York Times*.[124] The purpose of these fliers was to drive home the message to black voters that Cohen is a Jew, not "one of us." Had Republicans conducted such a campaign, there would have been a nationwide uproar. The *Lincoln Review*, published by conservative African American Jay Parker, detailed what has been done to Cohen and decried those who apply the double standard of former Representative Gus Savage of Illinois, who once said, "Racism constitutes actions or thoughts or expressions by white Americans against Afro-Americans.... racism is an attempt by powerful people to oppress less powerful people—Blacks don't have the power to oppress whites. Racism is white. There is no black racism."[125]

Although Cohen's resolution apologizing for slavery was passed by the House in 2008, Memphis Mayor Willie Herenton decided to run against him in 2009. Even though Herenton was under investigation by a federal grand jury, Rhodes College professor Marcus Pohlmann predicted the mayor could win: "One of the motivations may be that he or his supporters feel that a majority minority district should be held by a minority."[126]

Herenton was blunt about why Cohen ought to be dumped: his race. "[I]t remains a fact that the 9th Congressional District provides the only real opportunity to elect a qualified African-American to the all-white 11-member delegation representing Tennessee in Washington."[127]

"To know Steve Cohen is to know that he really does not think very much of African-Americans.... He's played the black community well," said Herenton, when he announced for the Cohen seat.[128] Herenton's campaign manager Sidney Chism added, "This seat was set aside for people who look like me.... It wasn't set aside for a Jew or a Christian. It was set aside so that blacks could have representation." Herenton, a former Golden Gloves boxer, promised, "This Congressional race" is "going to be about race, representation and power." Cohen's sheepish reply: "I vote like a black woman."[129]

This was the ugliest political race in America in 2010. So nasty did Herenton's attacks become that Obama himself stepped in to endorse Cohen, who then cruised to victory.

White congressman Chris Bell did not fare as well. After redistricting turned his district into a majority black district, a dozen Democratic colleagues of Bell's in the Black Caucus contributed to his black challenger, Al Green, who then crushed Bell in the primary.[130] For members of Congress to contribute to the defeat of a colleague on racial grounds is extraordinary.

What happened to Cohen and Bell is similar to what happened to Jewish leaders in the civil rights movement when blacks gained power, access to the media, and federal money. They were shoved aside. Black folks took over. Those who believe the rise to power of an Obama rainbow coalition of peoples of color means the whites who helped to engineer it will steer it are deluding themselves. The whites may discover what it is like to ride in the back of the bus.

"BLOOD RUNS THICKER"

Early in 2008, veteran Georgia Congressman John Lewis, a hero of Selma Bridge, was threatened with a primary challenge if he did not recant his endorsement of his old friend Hillary Clinton and switch his support to Barack Obama. Lewis got the message. As he abandoned Hillary to enlist with Obama, Lewis claimed a road-to-Damascus conversion: "Something's happening in America, something some of us did not see coming.... Barack Obama has tapped into something that is extraordinary.... It's a movement. It's a spiritual event.... It's amazing what's happening."[131]

During Obama's streak of a dozen straight primary victories, the late Geraldine Ferraro, a feminist icon since her nomination in 1984 as first woman to run for vice president on a major party ticket, expressed frustration at what was happening to Hillary: "If Obama was a white man he would not be in this position. And if he was a woman [of any color] he would not be in this position. He happens to be very lucky to be who he is. And the country is caught up with the concept."[132] Ferraro did not say race was the sole reason Obama was succeeding. She said that being black was as indispensable to Obama's success as being a woman had been to hers. Said Ferraro, "Had my name been Gerald rather than Geraldine, I would not have been on that '84 ticket."

Subjected to a forty-eight-hour barrage of allegations of racism by Obama's political and media allies, Ferraro resigned from the Clinton campaign. Yet what she said was transparently true. Was the fact that Obama was black irrelevant to the Democratic Party's decision to give the Chicago state senator the keynote address to the 2004 Democratic national convention? Did his being black have nothing to do with Barack's winning 91 percent of the black vote against Hillary in Mississippi the previous Tuesday?

Bill Clinton was charged with racism for saying Obama's claim to having been consistent on Iraq was a "fairy tale," and for implying that Barack's victory in South Carolina was no big deal because Jesse Jackson had carried the state twice. Yet both statements were relevant and both were true.

Harvard professor Orlando Patterson sniffed out racism in the Hillary ad that portrayed her picking up the red phone in the White House at 3:00 a.m. How so? None of the sleeping children in the ad were black. The red phone ad, said Patterson, reminded him of D. W. Griffith's 1915 film *Birth of a Nation,* which lionized the Ku Klux Klan.[133]

Two weeks before the election, Colin Powell, who had risen from army colonel to national security adviser, chairman of the Joint Chiefs of Staff and secretary of state under Republican Presidents Reagan, Bush I, and Bush II—the first African American to attain these heights—turned his back on his party's nominee and friend of twenty-five years, John McCain, and endorsed Obama. Thus did Powell embrace, over a fellow Republican and fellow Vietnam vet, a liberal Democrat who owed his nomination to his denunciation, as the worst blunder in American history, of the war Colin Powell had himself sold to the country.

Was race Powell's reason for defecting to Obama?

Powell did not deny it, contending only that race was not the only or decisive factor. "If I had only that fact in mind," he told Tom Brokaw, "I could have done this six, eight, ten months ago." Yet, in hailing Barack as a "transformational figure" whose victory would "not only electrify our country but electrify the world," Powell testified to the centrality of race to his decision.[134] For what else was there about this freshman senator with zero legislative accomplishments to transform American politics and electrify the world—other than that he would be the first black president?

Republicans were as intimidated by Obama's race as Powell was attracted. When North Carolina Republicans ran an ad linking Obama to the Reverend Jeremiah ("God-damn-America!") Wright, who had married Barack and Michelle and baptized Sasha and Malia, McCain asked the state party to pull it. In the fall, the GOP pummeled Obama for his association with the 1960s Weatherman Bill Ayers, but shied away from pounding Obama for his twenty-year close friendship with the race-baiting Wright, for fear of being accussed of "playing the race card."

Organizing a fund raiser for Democratic Governor Bill Richardson in 2007, fellow Hispanic Lionel Sosa of San Antonio, a strategist for Reagan, Bush I, and Bush II, said it all, "Blood runs thicker than politics."[135]

"AFFIRMATIVE ACTION BABY"

Affirmative action is becoming an increasingly onerous burden for white males in America. The reason, in Steve Sailer's phrase, is the changing "racial ratio." When the Philadelphia Plan was adopted in the Nixon era, imposing racial quotas on unions working on federally funded contracts, there were eight white Americans for every African American.[136] The burden of race preferences in hiring and promotions and admissions to colleges and graduate schools was correspondingly light.

However, the black community has since grown to where the ratio is five-to-one. More critically, Hispanics, though they never suffered slavery or endured Jim Crow, have been made beneficiaries of affirmative action. And there are now fifty million Hispanics. Add in Asians, Native Americans, and Pacific Islanders and there are fewer than two white Americans for every person of color. And, now, there is affirmative action for women. This leaves white males, a shrinking third of the nation, to bear almost the entire burden of reverse discrimination.

This is not a formula for social peace. It will lead to repeated conflicts like the New Haven firefighters case, in which Frank Ricci and fellow firemen were denied promotions they earned in competitive exams because they were white and no black firemen had done as well. Race preferences will either be abolished by state referenda or declared unconstitutional by the Supreme Court, or America will become another Malaysia or South Africa with an established and enduring regime of racial and ethnic entitlements.

The backlash has already arrived. In Michigan, California, and Washington, majorities have voted to abolish all racial, ethnic, and gender preferences. In 2010, Arizona followed suit with 60 percent of the electorate voting to outlaw affirmative action. Opposition to race, ethnic, and gender preferences was behind the thirty-one GOP Senate votes against Supreme Court nominee Sonia Sotomayor. On the only two previous court nominations by Democratic presidents in forty years, the Senate voted 87–9 for Stephen Breyer and 96–3 for Ruth Bader Ginsburg. To conservatives, the Sotomayor nomination was an Obama declaration that affirmative action is forever.

Judge Sotomayor was herself a lifetime beneficiary, who once called herself an "affirmative action baby." If she had gone through the "traditional numbers route" of Princeton and Yale Law, she said, "it would have been highly questionable if I would have been accepted.... [M]y test scores were not comparable to that of my classmates."[137]

Sonia Sotomayor, said the *New York Times,* "has championed the importance of considering race and ethnicity in admissions, hiring and even judicial selection at almost every stage of her career." As a student at Princeton, she filed a complaint with the Department of Health, Education, and Welfare demanding that the school be ordered to hire Hispanic teachers. At Yale, she co-chaired a coalition that demanded more Latino professors and administrators and "shared the alarm of others in the group when the Supreme Court prohibited the use of quotas in university admissions in the 1978 decision *Regents of the University of California v. Bakke.*"[138] Alan Bakke was an applicant to the University of California Medical School at Davis who was rejected, although his test scores were higher than almost all of the minority applicants admitted. Bakke was white.

Tribal politics has been a constant of Sotomayor's career. As a federal judge she ruled that the New York state law denying convicted felons the right to vote violated civil rights laws. There is a disproportionate number of blacks and Hispanics in prison, said Sotomayor. To deny felons the vote thus has a disparate impact on minorities and is impermissible.[139]

In a 2001 speech, Sotomayor rejected the notion advanced by Justices Ruth Bader Ginsburg and Sandra Day O'Connor that, in deciding cases, a wise old man and wise old woman would reach the same conclusion: "I would hope that a wise Latina woman with the richness of her experiences would more often than not reach a better conclusion than a white male who hasn't lived that life."[140]

The American Bar Association found that Sotomayor's dictum—that "gender and national origins may and will make a difference in our judging"—turns out to be true.[141] A study of twenty-two years of decisions from six federal circuits found that in racial harassment cases, plaintiffs lost 54 percent of the time when the judge was an African

American, but 79 percent of the time when the judge was white. Another study of 556 federal appellate court cases involving charges of sexual harassment and sex discrimination found that plaintiffs were twice as likely to emerge victorious if a female judge was on the panel.[142]

Decades ago, it was said that blacks in the Deep South could not get justice from an all-white jury. In the film version of *To Kill a Mockingbird*, in which Gregory Peck stars as Atticus Finch, defending a black man falsely accused of the attempted rape of a white woman, the issue is dramatized. Considering the O. J. Simpson murder trial, prosecutors now concede it is much more difficult to convict even patently guilty black felons if they are tried before largely black juries. Race-based justice may be America's future.

TRIBALISM IN THE FIFTIETH STATE

In Hawaii, the last state to join the American Union, tribalism is rising. A bill sponsored by Senator Daniel Akaka would create a racially exclusive native government independent of the state government and free from state taxes. This Hawaiian native government would be ceded a share of the 38 percent of land under public ownership. Some 400,000 Americans of Hawaiian ancestry would be eligible to vote, and a nine-member commission staffed by experts in genealogy would decide who they were. Gail Heriot, a member of the U.S. Commission on Civil Rights, asked Congress a pertinent question: "If ethnic Hawaiians can be accorded tribal status, why not Chicanos in the Southwest? Or Cajuns in Louisiana?"[143]

In 2010, the Akaka bill, backed by Obama, passed the House 245–164. "We have a moral obligation, unfulfilled since the overthrow of Queen Liliuokalani, that we are closer to meeting today," said Akaka. Should the bill become law, "The native governing entity will need to enter into negotiations with the State of Hawaii and the United States."[144]

As Irish independence led to demands for Scottish independence, a native government in Hawaii, restricted to persons of Hawaiian blood, would be a major step toward the creation of other ethnic enclaves inside the United States along the lines of the Indian nations.

In mid-2010, another nation within the American nation, the Iroquois Confederacy, refused to allow its lacrosse team to travel on U.S. passports to England for the Lacrosse World Championship. The invitation to participate as Iroquois was a rare example, they agreed, of international recognition of Iroquois sovereignty. But to require them to travel on U.S. passports was an attack on their real identity.[145]

Secretary of State Hillary Clinton interceded to let them leave using Iroquois passports. But the British refused to let them enter without U.S. passports. The team stayed home, but made its point. We are Iroquois first, American second.

ANGRY WHITE MEN

"[A]little rebellion now and then is a good thing, & as necessary in the political world as storms in the physical," wrote Jefferson of Shays's rebellion.

A rebellion is under way in America: a radicalization of the working and middle class, such as occurred in the Truman-McCarthy era, during the George Wallace campaigns, and in the anti-amnesty firestorm that killed the Bush-Kennedy-McCain push for citizenship for illegal aliens. What all these movements had in common was populist rage against a reigning establishment. But what explains the failure of the establishment to understand its countrymen?

When the urban riots of the 1960s exploded from Harlem in 1964 to Watts in 1965, to Detroit and Newark in 1967, to Washington, D.C., and scores of cities in 1968, liberals declared this to be a natural reaction to poverty, despair, and "white racism," as did the Kerner Commission appointed by LBJ. When campus radicals burned ROTC buildings, opposition to the war in Vietnam explained why the "finest young generation we have ever produced" was behaving so.

But when Tea Party dissidents came out to town-hall meetings to denounce Obamacare, the reaction was hysterical. To Harry Reid, they were "evil-mongers." To Nancy Pelosi their conduct was "un-American."

Robert Gibbs compared them to the "Brooks Brothers riot" of the Florida recount.[146] Some commentators saw racism at the root of the protests. In "Town Hall Mob," Paul Krugman wrote that "cynical political operators are.... appealing to the racial fears of working-class whites."[147] Cynthia Tucker calculated that 45 to 65 percent of the vocal opposition to Obama was driven by racial animus toward a black president.[148]

This hyperbole revealed how out of touch the left had become. For, six months later, a *Wall Street Journal/NBC News* poll found the Tea Party movement was more positively regarded—41 percent held a favorable view to 24 percent who held a negative view—than either political party.[149]

What explains the alienation of a vast slice of working-class America?

In "Decline of the American Male" in *USA Today*, David Zinczenko writes: "Of the 5.2 million people who've lost their jobs since last summer, four out of five were men. Some experts predict that this year, for the first time, more American women will have more jobs than men."[150]

Edwin Rubenstein, a former editor at *Forbes*, looking back to the beginning of the Bush II presidency, wrote that for every 100 Hispanics employed in January 2001, there were 124 holding jobs in July 2010. But for every 100 non-Hispanics employed in January 2001, only 97.8 were still working in 2010.[151]

Between January 2001 and July 2009, Hispanic employment surged by 3,627,000 positions. Non-Hispanic positions fell by 1,362,000.[152] For the white working class, the Bush decade did not begin well nor did it end well, which may explain why Obama did better among these voters than did Kerry or Gore.

Why the alienation in Middle America?

In their lifetimes, they have seen their Christian faith purged from schools their taxes paid for and mocked in movies and on TV. They have seen their factories shuttered and jobs outsourced. They have seen trillions of tax dollars go for Great Society programs, but have seen no Great Society, only crime, rising illegitimacy, and rising dropout rates.

They watch on cable as illegal aliens walk into their country and are re-warded with free health care and education for their kids, take jobs away from U.S. workers, and carry Mexican flags while marching in American cities to demand U.S. citizenship.

They see Wall Street banks bailed out and read that the bankers used the billions not to lend but to trade, and that the bonuses are back. They see their government shoveling billions out to Fortune 500 companies and banks to rescue the country from a financial crisis created by that same government, and by those same companies and banks. They sense that they are losing their country. And they are right.

5

DEMOGRAPHIC WINTER

Russia is disappearing. So is Japan. Europe is next to go.[1]
—JOHN FEFFER, 2010
Epoch Times

*Within a hundred years. . . . God will come down to earth with his big
ring of keys, and will say to humanity: "Gentlemen, it is closing time."*[2]
—PIERRE EUGÈNE MARCELLIN BERTHELOT (1827–1907),
French statesman

D emography is destiny.
Auguste Comte, the philosopher and mathematician known
as the father of sociology, is said to have coined the cliché. Yet
there is truth in it. Europeans crossing the Atlantic in the sixteenth, seventeenth, and eighteenth centuries sealed the fate of Native Americans.
That a defeated Germany's population was surging while that of France
was stagnant was a justifiable cause of grave apprehension in a Quay
d'Orsay that had pushed the Allies into imposing the vindictive peace of
Versailles, that dishonored, dismembered, and divided the defeated
Germany of November 1918.

Yet demography is not always destiny, for all human capital is not created equal. In making history it has often been the quality of a people
that mattered most. Consider what a handful of Greeks in fifth-century
Athens created, what three hundred Spartans at Thermopylae prevented, what a Galilean carpenter's son and a dozen disciples gave the

world. Consider what a few score men in Philadelphia in 1776 and 1787 achieved. By 1815, an island of eight million off the coast of Europe had seen off Napoleon, gained mastery of the world's oceans, and created an empire that would encompass a fourth of mankind. Consider what a dozen Bolshevik gunmen began when they stormed the Winter Palace and ran off a panicked ruling council.

But demography has taken on even greater importance in our time. Why?

First, because democracy is the religion of the West. In the American creed, political legitimacy comes solely from the consent of the governed, each of whom has the same single vote. Democracy is a force multiplier of demography. Numbers eventually equal power.

Second, with the surge of ethnonationalism worldwide, and of identity politics in America, demography will increasingly dictate the division and distribution of society's wealth and rewards. A third and related reason is egalitarianism, the ideology that holds that all ethnic groups are equal and where inequality exists institutional racism is the probable cause.

As the West worships at the altar of democracy, is deeply egalitarian, and has thrown open its doors to a Third World in which ethnonationalism is embedded, it is the West whose destiny will ultimately be determined by demography. What is that destiny? Consider the latest statistics from the Population Division of the United Nations Department of Economic and Social Affairs:

Between now and 2050,
- One in every six East Europeans, 50 million people, will vanish.
- Germany, Russia, Belarus, Poland, and Ukraine will lose 53 million people.
- Where, at liberation in 1990 Lithuania, Latvia, and Estonia had 8 million people, 2.3 million of them will have disappeared by 2050.

- Between liberation in 1990 and 2050, the former captive nations of Romania and Bulgaria will have lost between them 10 million people.
- Europeans and North Americans who accounted for 28 percent of world population in 1950 will have fallen to 12 percent in 2050 and be among the oldest people on earth with a median age close to 50.

Not one nation of Europe or North America, save Iceland, has a birth rate sufficient to replace its population. All have been below zero population growth (2.1 children per woman) for decades. Who inherits the Western estate? Between now and 2050, Africa's population will double to 2 billion, and Latin America and Asia will add another 1.25 billion people. By 2050, the populations of Afghanistan, Burundi, the Democratic Republic of the Congo, Guinea-Bissau, Liberia, and Uganda will have tripled since Y2K, with Niger's population quintupling from 11 million to 58 million.[3]

In a 2010 essay in *Foreign Affairs,* "The Population Bomb: The Four Megatrends That Will Change the World," Jack Goldstone documents how Western peoples, whose empires ruled mankind on the eve of the Great War, are aging, dying, and sinking toward insignificance:

> In 1913, Europe had more people than China, and the proportion of the world's population living in Europe and the former European colonies of North America had risen to over 33 percent....
>
> By 2003, the combined populations of Europe, the United States, and Canada accounted for just 17 percent of the global population. In 2050, this figure is expected to be just 12 percent—far less than it was in 1700.[4]

Our own and our parents' generations have witnessed an epochal event: the fall of Christendom. From the close of the Edwardian era, with the death of Edward VII in 1910, in a single century, it all happened. The great European powers fought two great wars. All lost their empires. All saw their armies and navies melt away. All lost their Christian faith. All saw their birth rates plummet. All have seen their populations begin to age and shrink. All are undergoing invasions from formerly subject peoples coming to the mother country to dispossess their grandchildren. All of their welfare states face retrenchment even as they face tribal decline and death.

> Reflecting on the fate of Rome, Charles Darwin's grandson bemoaned a pattern he saw through history: "Must civilization always lead to the limitation of families and consequent decay and then replacement from barbaric sources, which in turn will go through the same experience?"[5]

So wrote Phillip Longman, author of *The Empty Cradle*. And who will replace the unborn children of the West? We are witness to the unfolding of a brazen prophecy of Algerian president Houari Boumedienne before the United Nations in 1974.

> One day millions of men will leave the Southern Hemisphere of this planet to burst into the northern one. But not as friends. Because they will burst in to conquer, and they will conquer by populating it with their children. Victory will come to us from the wombs of our women.[6]

The conquest of Europe by peoples of color from the old colonies is well advanced. The numbers of those lined up waiting to come, and of those lined up behind them, stagger the mind.

By midcentury, the ten most populous nations will be, in order: India, China, the United States, Indonesia, Pakistan, Nigeria, Brazil, Bangladesh, the Democratic Republic of the Congo, and Ethiopia.[7] Five are in Asia, three in sub-Saharan Africa, and one in Latin America. The United States will be the only First World nation on the list. But, by 2050, America will be more of a Third World than a Western nation, as 54 percent of the 435 million people in the United States, according to the UN's 2006 *Population Prospects,* will trace their roots to Asia, Africa, and Latin America.

Incontrovertible realities emerge from the thousand pages of text and numbers in that UN report.

Peoples of European descent are not only in a relative but a real decline. They are aging, dying, disappearing. This is the existential crisis of the West. And among the peoples of color who will replace them, the poorest in the least developed nations are reproducing fastest. For the most productive peoples in Asia, too, like the Japanese and South Koreans, are also beginning to age and die.

In 2007, the Organization for Economic Cooperation and Development, which includes the major economic powers, voiced alarm at the sinking birth rates in the most advanced nations.

> Birth rates have declined sharply in most OECD countries, to just 1.6 children per woman—well below the average of 2.1 children per woman needed just to maintain current population levels.
>
> The most direct consequence of low birth rates is a "vicious circle" of decreasing population: fewer children today imply fewer women of childbearing age twenty years from now, so the cumulative momentum of current low birth rates will be difficult to reverse.
>
> The effect on society is significant. There will be fewer young adults to care for elderly family members, pensions and healthcare will take up an increasing share of public spending, the workforce will be older and less adaptable, and domestic savings may shrink.[8]

"Today, close to half of all children in most OECD countries grow up without siblings."[9] The OECD said birthrates had fallen in Japan and some Eastern and Southern European countries to 1.3 children per woman. This is not two-thirds of what is needed to replace an existing population. The brief concludes ominously: "In purely biological terms, it may still be possible to return to previous levels [of births] but the pace of such a recovery would be unprecedented in human history."[10]

The OECD is saying the death of Europe appears irreversible and imminent.

Already, in Portugal, Ireland, Greece, and Spain deficits and national debt far in excess of EU limits threaten to sink the European monetary union. These deficits are traceable to fewer and fewer young workers available to carry the load of pensions and health care for retiring and retired seniors. The riots that tore through Greece, France, and the UK in 2010 are rooted in the demographic crisis of the West and are harbingers of what is to come.

AGING TIGERS, SETTING SUN

Not only do the nations of Europe and North America have birth rates that portend extinction of the native born, two of the most dynamic nations of Asia are on the path to national suicide. Japan, its population peaking at 128 million in 2010, will lose 25 million people by 2050.[11] A fifth of her population will disappear and one in six Japanese will be over 80. Japan's median age will rise from 45 to 55. And these projections assume a rise in the fertility of Japanese women that is nowhere in sight.

In March 2010 came more grim news. *Marketwatch* reported the birth rate in Tokyo had fallen to 1.09 children per woman and if "current trends continued, Japan's population will fall to 95 million by 2050, from about 127 million now," a loss of 32 million people. At this rate, a fourth of the nation will vanish in four decades.[12] "With as much as 40 percent of its population over 65 years of age," wrote Joel Kotkin, of *Forbes*, "no matter how innovative the workforce, *Dai Nippon* will simply be too *old* to compete."[13]

Noting that births in Japan in 2008 were 40 percent below what they were in 1948, Nicholas Eberstadt writes, in *Foreign Affairs*, that "fertility, migration and mortality trends are propelling Japan into . . . a degree of aging thus far contemplated only in science fiction."[14]

In December 2010, Agence France-Press, citing the National Institute of Population and Social Security Research, reported: "On current trends, Japan's population of 127 million will by 2055 shrivel to 90 million."[15] Recognizing the gravity of the demographic crisis, the Democratic Party of Japan, which was swept into power in 2009, planned $3,000 allowances per child and assistance with child care for families with grade-school children. The need seems desperate. In a 2010 *Washington Post* story on the decline in Japanese students attending U.S. universities, Blaine Harden wrote, "The number of children [in Japan] under the age of 15 has fallen for 28 consecutive years. The size of the nation's high school graduating class has shrunk by 35 percent in two decades."[16]

In 2010, China overtook Japan as the world's second largest economy, a ranking Japan had held since surpassing Germany forty years ago. The *New York Times* concludes:

> China's rise could accelerate Japan's economic decline as it captures Japanese export markets, and as Japan's crushing national debt increases and its aging population grows less and less productive—producing a downward spiral.
>
> "It's beyond my imagination how far Japan will fall in the world economy in 10, 20 years," said Hideo Kumano, economist at the Dai-Ichi Life Research Institute in Tokyo.[17]

Japan's fertility level has been below replacement levels since the 1970s. By 2050, it will have been below zero population growth for eighty years. If the birthrate does not rise, Japan's population at century's end will be 20 percent of what it is today.

The aging of Japan, the oldest nation on earth, seems reflected in its economic performance. In the 1960s, Japan's economy grew by 10 percent a year; in the 1970s by 5 percent a year; in the 1980s by 4 percent, still a healthy growth rate. But in the 1990s, the "lost decade," Japan's

GDP grew by 1.8 percent a year.[18] In the twenty-first century, Japan has failed to maintain even this anemic growth rate and, due to the vast public works spending in the 1990s, now faces a national debt 200 percent of her GDP.

In 1988, eight of the ten largest companies in the world in capitalization were Japanese, led by Nippon Telegraph & Telephone. Today, Japan does not have a single company in the top twenty, and it has only six in the top 100. "China has also surpassed Japan in having the biggest trade surplus and foreign currency reserves," writes Tabuchi, "as well as the highest steel production. And next year China could overtake Japan as the largest automobile producer."[19] China already has.

South Korea's population is projected to reach 49.5 million in 2025 but will recede to 44 million by 2050, a loss of 10 percent in twenty-five years.[20] Few nations suffer losses like that in wars. In the Civil War, North and South lost 620,000, 2 percent of the population.

In 2050, the median age of South Koreans will have risen from thirty-eight today to fifty-four and a third of all South Koreans will be over sixty-five, an immense burden of retirees for the working population to carry.[21] "Korea may lose out in the global economic competition due to a lack of manpower," Health Minister Jeon Jae-hee told the *Korea Times*. "It is actually the most urgent and important issue the country is facing."[22]

Technologically, Japan is among the world's most advanced nations. South Korea is the largest and strongest of the Asian tigers. It is impossible to believe either can maintain its dynamism when, together, they will lose thirty million people and add a decade to their median age. By 2050, 40 percent of all South Koreans and Japanese will be over sixty years of age.[23]

Both nations appear prepared to accept their fate, a dying population and declining nation, rather than adopt the American solution: replacement of her departing native born with millions of immigrants.

Another tiger, Singapore, is advancing toward the same end with a birth rate only 60 percent of what is needed to replace the population. As we approach midcentury, Singapore's median age will rise from forty today to fifty-four, almost 40 percent of the population will be over sixty, and there will be twice as many deaths each year as births by 2040. So worried is Singapore over its birth dearth it is offering mothers a "birth bonus" of $3,000 for the first and second child and $4,000 for the third and fourth, plus paid maternity leave.[24]

Free Asia, an economic miracle of the twentieth century, seems content to enjoy the good life and then pass away. At the end of 2010, AFP reported that the birth rate in Singapore had fallen to 1.2 children per women, while in South Korea it had fallen to 1.1, and on Taiwan to 1.03.[25]

VANISHING VOLK

For no country has demography had a greater bearing on destiny than Germany.

Indeed, behind the two wars that tore Europe apart lay a British fear that Germany, after crushing France in 1870, had grown too populous and powerful. Balance-of-power politics dictated Britain's moving closer to colonial rivals Russia and France. Prime Minister Benjamin Disraeli recognized the earth-shaking importance of the Franco-Prussian War and of Bismarck's having united the German states and peoples under a Prussian king:

> The war represents the German revolution, a greater political event than the French revolution of the last century.... There is not a diplomatic tradition, which has not been swept away. You have a new world.... The balance of power has been entirely destroyed.[26]

For ten years, 1914–1918 and 1939–1945, Britons and Germans fought. By 1945, Germany was finished as a military power and Britain was finished as a world power. Now the Germans have begun to disappear. "Since 1972, Germany has not seen a single year where the number of newborns exceeded the number of deaths," writes Reiner Klingholz, of Berlin's Institute for Population and Development.[27]

The creeping population-shrinking process was only masked by high immigration that could camouflage the natural losses—at least until 2003. Since then, the overall population of Germany has declined; the Federal Statistics Office expects that the nation will have around eight million fewer inhabitants by mid-century—that is the equivalent of losing the population of Berlin, Hamburg, Munich, Cologne and Frankfurt combined.[28]

What Klingholz is saying bears repeating: Germans have been dying out for forty years and this has been covered up by counting Turks, East Europeans, and Arabs as Germans. Now, not even immigrants from the Muslim lands, Eastern Europe, and the Third World can mask the reality.

Astonishing. Not long after World War II, West Germany boasted the world's second largest economy. Now a united Germany is on schedule to become a retirement center, nursing home, and cemetery for the Germanic peoples, whose origins date back to before the birth of Christ.

Today, 20 percent of Germany's population is older than 65, and 5 percent are older than 80. In 2050, the 65-plus age group will make up 32 percent and the 80-plus group 14 percent.... By mid-century one out of seven Germans will be older than 80. The figures are similar in Spain and Italy.[29]

In Austria, where the fertility rate is down to 1.4 births per woman, eighty-five-year-old Carl Djerassi, who contributed a key discovery that made the birth control pill possible, calls Europe's demographic decline a "horror scenario," a "catastrophe." There is "no connection at all between sexuality and reproduction."[30] Donald Rumsfeld was on to something when he called it "old Europe."

Of Southern Europe, where the fertility rate among the Catholic native-born has fallen to two-thirds of what is required to keep those nations alive, Carl Haub of the Population Reference Bureau says:

[Y]ou can't go on forever with a total fertility rate of 1.2 [children per woman]. If you compare the size of the 0–4 and 29–34 age groups in Spain and Italy right now, you see the younger is almost half the size of the older. You can't keep going with a completely upside-down age distribution, with the pyramid standing on its point. You can't have a country where everybody lives in a nursing home.[31]

As Longman writes, "This isn't just a numbers game."

As the darkest recent chapters of European history suggest, the point of transition from growth to demographic decline can be an unsettling and dangerous one. Fascist ideology in Europe was deeply informed by Oswald Spengler's *The Decline of the West,* Lothrop Stoddard's *The Rising Tide of Color Against White World Supremacy,* and the writings of other eugenicists obsessed with the demographic decline of "Aryans."[32]

Today, a new generation of Europeans that feels besieged by Muslim immigration has begun to shift allegiance from working class and conservative parties to anti-Islamic and anti-immigration parties that are flourishing now in virtually every country. In some they already share power and the mainstream parties have begun to submit to their demands

"THERE'LL ALWAYS BE AN ENGLAND"

The United Kingdom appears to be the great exception to the shrinking of European populations. In its 2006 Population Projections, the UN predicted that the UK would, by 2050, add the 8.5 million people that Germany would lose. The 2008 revision pushed Britain's population projection at midcentury to 72.4 million, an increase of 10 million people in forty years.[33]

Yet one must look more closely at these numbers. Fertility in Britain has been below replacement level since the early 1970s. Even the revised 2008 figures say British fertility will remain 15 percent below zero population growth through 2050. Then, there are those reports of native-born Britons in the scores and even hundreds of thousands emigrating annually.

How can a nation add 10 million people when its women are not having enough babies to replace the existing population and its native born are departing? The answer is immigration. The Caribbean, African, Arab, and Asian population of Britain is keeping the birthrate up and new immigrants are assuring that the population grows by at least 8.5 million and perhaps 12 million as Germany's declines. Britain is growing and changing its complexion.

"A Fifth of Europe Will Be Muslim by 2050," ran an August 2009 headline in the *Telegraph*.[34] In a related article cited by Cal Thomas, "Muslim Europe: The Demographic Time Bomb Transforming Our Continent," the *Telegraph* wrote that "Britain and the rest of the European Union are ignoring a time bomb: a recent rush into the EU by migrants, including millions of Muslims, will change the continent beyond recognition over the next two decades, and almost no policy makers are talking about it."[35]

Oxford demographer David Coleman adds that Britain's nonwhite population is on course "to grow from 9 percent at the last census in 2001, to 29 percent by 2051."[36] That means 21 million of the 72 million British subjects in 2050 will trace their ancestry to Africa, the Middle East, South Asia, or the Caribbean, a demographic transformation of a country that has never assimilated a large number of immigrants. In late 2010, Coleman updated his projections. Britons—English, Welsh, Irish, and Scots—will be a minority by 2066 and immigrants will "transform" Britain. "The transition to a 'majority-minority' population, whenever it happens, would represent an enormous change to national identity—cultural, political, economic and religious."[37] That date, 2066, is the millenial year of the Norman Conquest.

Who are the newcomers to the old continent?

In *Reflections on the Revolution in Europe: Immigration, Islam and the West*, Chris Caldwell writes that conspicuous among the more than 15 million Muslims in Western Europe are "militants, freeloaders and opportunists."[38] Fouad Ajami describes them:

> The militants took the liberties of Europe as a sign of moral and political abdication. They included "activists" now dreaming of imposing the Shariah on Denmark and Britain. There were also warriors of the faith, in storefront mosques in Amsterdam and London, openly sympathizing with the enemies of the West. And there were second-generation immigrants who owed no allegiance to the societies of Europe.[39]

In a stunning revelation in 2009, Andrew Neather, speechwriter and adviser to Tony Blair and Home Secretary Jack Straw, revealed that Blair's Labor government had thrown open Britain's doors to mass immigration to socially engineer a "truly multicultural" country and "rub the Right's nose in diversity."[40] The government did not reveal what it was about, said Neather, as that might have driven Labor's "core working-class vote" to the British National Party of Nick Griffin.

"[T]he truth is out and it's dynamite," said Sir Andrew Green, the chairman of the think tank Migrationwatch. "Many have long suspected that mass immigration under Labor was not just a cock up but a conspiracy. They were right."[41] Under a clandestine Labor policy to alter the racial balance and change the face of Britain, three million immigrants, 5 percent of Britain's entire population, came in from the Third World, said Green.

Is it not treason to bring in foreigners, deceitfully, to swamp a people and dispossess them of their culture and country? What is the difference between what Labor stands accused of doing and what Stalin did in the Baltic republics in the 1940s—and what China is doing today in Tibet?

According to the *London Times*, from 2004 to 2008 the Muslim population surged by 500,000 to 2,422,000, and was growing at ten times the rate of the native-born population due to higher birthrates, immigration, and conversions. And more and more of these Muslims are asserting their Islamic identity as they see their brothers fighting the West in Iraq, Afghanistan, and Pakistan. Hindus in Britain tripled to 1.5 million in the first seven years of the century. The "Black British" from the Caribbean and sub-Sahara have risen to 1.45 million.[42] Although Hindus and Muslims and the black British are spread throughout the realm, they are heavily concentrated in what has come to be called Londonistan.

Some of the estimated one million Poles who migrated to Britain after Warsaw entered the EU have left for home where the wages were rising, as Britain entered the financial crisis and David Cameron's era of austerity.[43]

THE LOST TRIBES OF ISRAEL

"In Rama was there a voice heard, lamentation and weeping, and great mourning, Rachel weeping for her children, and would not be comforted, for they are no more," wrote the evangelist Matthew.

As their nation enters its sixty-fourth year, Israelis can look back with pride. Israel is a democracy with the highest standard of living in the Middle East. Her high-tech industries are in the first rank. From a nation of fewer than a million in 1948, her population has grown to 7 million. In seven wars—the 1948 War of Independence, the Sinai invasion of 1956, the Six-Day War of 1967, the Yom Kippur War of 1973, the Lebanon wars of 1982 and 2006, and the Gaza War—Israel has prevailed.

Israel has revived Hebrew, created a currency, immersed her children in the history, ancient and modern, of the Jewish people, and established a national homeland for Jews, millions of whom have come to settle. The nation is home to the largest concentration of Jews anywhere on earth.

Yet, Israeli realists must look forward with foreboding. For Israel became home to the largest Jewish population only because the number of American Jews plummeted in the 1990s from 5.5 to 5.2 million. Six percent of the U.S. Jewish population, 300,000 Jews, vanished in a decade. By 2050, the U.S. Jewish population will shrink another 50 percent to 2.5 million.[44] American Jews appear to be an endangered species.

Why is this happening? It is a result of the collective decision of Jews themselves. From Betty Friedan to Gloria Steinem in the 1970s to Ruth Bader Ginsburg today, Jewish women have led the battle for abortion rights. The community followed. A survey in 2000 by the Center for Jewish Community Studies in Baltimore found 88 percent of the Jewish public agreeing that "Abortion should be generally available to those who want it."[45]

As Jews were 2 to 3 percent of the U.S. population from *Roe v. Wade* to 2010, how many of the fifty million abortions since 1973 were performed on Jewish girls or women? How many Jewish children were never conceived because of birth control?

In Philip Roth's *The Counterlife,* a militant Israeli character says, "what Hitler couldn't achieve at Auschwitz, American Jews are doing to themselves in the bedroom."[46]

Stephen Steinlight, former director of National Affairs at the American Jewish Committee, sees in U.S. population numbers existential peril for Israel.

> Far more potentially perilous, does it matter to Jews—and for American support for Israel when the Jewish State arguably faces existential peril—that Islam is the fastest growing religion in the United States? That undoubtedly at some point in the next 20 years Muslims will outnumber Jews, and that Muslims with an "Islamic agenda" are growing active politically through a widespread network of national organizations? That this is occurring at a time when the religion of Islam is being supplanted in many of the Islamic immigrant sending countries

by the totalitarian ideology of Islamism of which vehement anti-Semitism and anti-Zionism form central tenets?[47]

"Will our status suffer," Steinlight asks, "when the Judeo-Christian cultural construct yields, first, to a Judeo-Christian-Muslim one, and then to an even more expansive sense of national religious identity?"[48] To listen to President Obama is to understand that post-Christian America has already arrived at that "more expansive sense of national religious identity."

ISRAEL'S EXISTENTIAL CRISIS

If demography is destiny, Israel's future appears grim. Her population of 7.5 million is 80 percent Jewish. But the Arab minority is growing faster, except for the ultra-Orthodox Jewish, known in Hebrew as "haredim," for whom eight children to a family is not unusual. Indeed, according to the Taub Center for Social Policy Studies in Israel, if present trends continue, by 2040, 78 percent of all primary school children in Israel will be either ultra-Orthodox or Arab.[49]

A point of an earlier chapter, that the more religious the community the larger the families and the more secular and agnostic a people the fewer the children, is underscored by Eric Kaufmann in *Shall the Religious Inherit the Earth?* According to Kaufmann, "Ultra-Orthodox Jews, whether in Israel, Europe or North America, have a two or threefold fertility advantage over their liberal-Jewish counterparts. Their eventual achievement of majority status within worldwide Jewry in the twenty-first century seems certain."[50]

An Israeli blogger writes that in Israel nearly 30 percent of all children one to four years old are Arab. And many Israelis, adds John Mearsheimer, now choose to live outside the country.

There are somewhere between 700,000 and 1 million Israeli Jews living outside the country, many of whom are unlikely to return. Since 2007, emigration has been outpacing immigration in Israel. According to scholars John Mueller and Ian Lustick, "a recent survey indicates that only 69 percent of Jewish Israelis say they want to stay in the country, and a 2007 poll finds that one-quarter of Israelis are considering leaving, including almost half of all young people."[51]

Housing minister Ariel Atias warns of a migration of the growing Arab population into Jewish sectors of Israel:

> I see [it] as a national duty to prevent the spread of a population that, to say the least, does not love the state of Israel.... If we go on like we have until now, we will lose the Galilee. Populations that should not mix are spreading there. I don't think it is appropriate [for them] to live together.[52]

"The mayor of Acre visited me yesterday for three hours and asked me how his town could be saved," Atias said, "He told me that Arabs are living in Jewish buildings and running them out." Atias urged that land be sold to Jews and Arabs separately, "to create segregation...between Jews and Arabs but also between other sectors, such as ultra-Orthodox and secular Jews."[53]

Not any Iranian weapon of mass destruction but demography is the existential crisis of the Jewish nation. According to UN figures, Israel's population will exceed 10 million by 2050. But the Arab share will be almost 30 percent. Palestinians in the West Bank, East Jerusalem, and Gaza, 4.4 million today, will then number more than 10 million. Jordan's population, 60 percent of which is Palestinian, will also double to 10 million.

By midcentury, then, Palestinians west of the Jordan River will outnumber Jews two to one. Add Palestinians in Jordan, it is three to one. And that does not count Palestinians in Egypt, Lebanon, Saudi Arabia, Syria, and the Gulf states, whose numbers will also double by 2050. Palestinians today have one of the highest fertility rates on earth, 5 children per woman, though an Israeli source says that in Israel it has fallen to 3.9 and, without the Bedouins of the Negev, 3.2 children per woman.[54] Only Orthodox Jews in Israel, of whom there are some 800,000, exceed that.

If Israel is to remain a Jewish state, a Palestinian state seems a national imperative. Yitzhak Rabin came to recognize this, but was assassinated. Ehud Barak came to recognize this and sought to bring it about. In his last days in office, Ehud Olmert warned, "if the two-state solution collapses," Israel will "face a South African-style struggle."[55]

Three months before he launched the Gaza war, Olmert told two journalists that peace would require a return of the Golan Heights to Syria, the surrender of almost the entire West Bank, and the return of East Jerusalem to the Palestinians.

> In the end, we will have to withdraw from the lion's share of the territories, and for the territories we leave in our hands, we will have to give compensation in the form of territories within the State of Israel at a ratio that is more or less 1:1.... Whoever wants to hold on to all of [Jerusalem] will have to bring 270,000 Arabs inside the fences of sovereign Israel. It won't work.[56]

Absent a Palestinian state, Israel has three options. First, annex the West Bank, the one-state solution. This would bring 2.4 million Palestinians into Israel, giving her a population 40 percent Arab. With their birth rate, the Palestinians would soon outnumber the Jews and vote to abolish the Jewish state—the end of the Zionist dream. Second is the Kahane solution. The late Rabbi Meir Kahane, assassinated in New York, urged the expulsion of all Palestinians from Judea and Samaria. But such ethnic cleansing would mean war with the Arabs, the isolation of Israel, and the alienation of the United States. The third option is no annexation, no Palestinian state, no expulsions—but permanent Israeli control of the West Bank and Gaza. This would entail making Gaza a penal colony of 1.5 million with no way out by land, sea, or air, save by leave of the Israeli Defense Force. On the West Bank, it would mean confinement of a burgeoning population of millions in enclaves wedged between the Israeli wall and the Jordan River, dotted by checkpoints and bisected by roads set aside for the exclusive use of Israelis. Travel in and out of the West Bank would be by sufferance of the IDF.

In January 2010, Defense Minister Barak implied that Prime Minister Netanyahu was leading Israel toward such a future, and that the Jewish people could not live with it.

> The lack of defined boundaries within Israel, and not an Iranian bomb, is the greatest threat to our future.... It must be understood that if between the Jordan and the [Mediterranean] sea there is only one political entity, called Israel, it will by necessity either not be Jewish or not democratic and we will turn into an apartheid state.[57]

Olmert echoed Barak: "As soon as that happens, the state of Israel is finished."[58]

THE NEIGHBORS

This is not the only demographic crisis Israel faces. According to UN population projections, by 2050, Syria's population of 22 million will increase to 37 million. Saudi Arabia's 26 million will increase to 44 million. Egypt will grow by 46 million to 130 million. The Islamic Republic of Iran, with a population of 75 million today, is expected to grow to 97 million by midcentury. And from Hamas in the south to Hezbollah in the north to the Muslim Brotherhood in the west, the Islamic faith of Israel's neighbors grows in militancy. If the threat within comes from a surging Palestinian population, the external threat comes from Israel's neighbors. To assess the magnitude of the problem, compare the population of Israel and the nations with which she went to war in 1967—to their projected populations in 2050.

Populations

Nation	1967 (Millions)	2050 (Millions)
Israel	2.7	10.5
Jordan	1.3	10.1
Syria	5.6	37.0
Saudi Arabia	5.0	44.0
Egypt	33.0	130.0

To this correlation of forces, add again this fact: Palestinians west of the Jordan today almost equal in number the Jewish population of Israel.

The Israeli right, led by Netanyahu's Likud Party and the Israel Our Home Party of Avigdor Lieberman, says it will never permit a Palestinian capital in Jerusalem, never negotiate with Hamas, and never accept a Palestinian state led by Hamas. Nor will it agree to a Palestinian state that does not give up the right of return, recognize Israel as a Jewish state forever, and accept severe limitations on its sovereignty. Harvard law professor Alan Dershowitz adds that any acceptance of a right of return for Palestinian Arabs to the lands from which their fathers and grandfathers were driven or fled, "would achieve demographically what the Arab nations have been unable to achieve militarily—destruction of the Jewish state." Israelis, says Dershowitz, need to "protect Israel against demographic annihilation."[59]

This means no Palestinian state. For no Arab leader could recognize a Palestine that gave up the right of return and agreed to cede all of Jerusalem to Israel forever, and survive. Behind Israel's stand lies an assumption not self-evidently true: time is on Israel's side. If demography is destiny, it transparently is not, for the Islamic world is exploding with new life.

Consider. In 1950, Goldstone writes, the populations of Bangladesh, Egypt, Indonesia, Nigeria, Pakistan, and Turkey added up to 242 million. Last year, these six most populous Muslim nations had a combined population of 885 million. The six are expected to add 475 million people by 2050 for a total of 1.36 billion, almost all of whom will be Muslim and poor. "Worldwide," writes Goldstone, "of the 48 fastest growing countries today—those with annual population growth of 2 percent or more—28 are majority Muslim or have Muslim minorities of 33 percent or more."[60]

OLD MOTHER RUSSIA

With the collapse of the empire and breakup of the Soviet Union, Russia seems to have lost the will to live. In an historic development, Russia's population has fallen from 148 million in 1991 to 140 million today and is projected to plunge to 116 million by 2050, a loss of 32 million Russians in six decades.[61] If these projections hold, six decades of freedom will have resulted in the disappearance of more Russians than seventy years of Bolshevism, from the October Revolution through the civil war of 1919–1920, to the starvation of the Kulaks, the Great Terror of the 1930s, the gulag, and all the dead of the Great Patriotic War with Nazi Germany from 1941 to 1945.

Of all the numbers in UN world population projections, the figures on Russia are the most depressing. Her fertility rate is two-thirds of what is needed to replace her people. Every year, for every thousand Russians, there are 11 births and 15 deaths. In 2007, the UN projected that Russia's population shrinkage would average 750,000 annually for the next forty years. And no end is in sight.

The revised figures of 2008 offered a more optimistic assessment. The fertility rate of Russian women will rise to three-fourths of what is needed to maintain zero population growth. However, the OECD, as of 2009, projects a Russian population under 108 million in 2050.[62] Martin Walker graphically describes what is happening to the late superpower and largest country on earth:

> In Russia, the effects of declining fertility are amplified by a
> phenomenon so extreme that it has given rise to an ominous

new term—hypermortality. As a result of the rampant spread of maladies such as HIV/AIDS and alcoholism and the deterioration of the Russian health care system, says a 2008 report by the UN Development Program, "mortality in Russia is 3–5 times higher for men and twice as high for women" than in other countries at a comparable stage of development. The report...predicts that within little more than a decade the working-age population will be shrinking by up to one million people annually. Russia is suffering a demographic decline on a scale that is normally associated with the effects of a major war.[63]

In "Drunken Nation: Russia's Depopulation Bomb," Nicholas Eberstadt, of the American Enterprise Institute, writes:

A specter is haunting Russia today. It is not the specter of Communism—that ghost has been chained in the attic of the past—but rather of depopulation—a relentless, unremitting, and perhaps unstoppable depopulation....as Russians practice what amounts to an ethnic self-cleansing.[64]

Marxist theory famously envisioned the "withering away" of the state. But, writes Eberstadt, "Russia has seen a pervasive and profound change in childbearing patterns and living arrangements—what might be described as a 'withering away' of the family itself."[65]

The death rate in Russia, especially among men, is now at levels found only in less-developed countries of the Third World. "History," writes Eberstadt, "offers no examples of a society that has demonstrated sustained material advance in the face of long-term population decline."[66]

One effect of Russia's vanishing population will be a constrained foreign policy. As former ambassador Richard Fairbanks wrote in the aftermath of the Russia-Georgia clash of 2008:

Russia's incursion into Georgia understandably evokes Cold War–era fears of a resurgent post-Soviet imperialism. But such concerns overlook a fundamental constraint. Russia is fast running out of young men.

Between 2010 and 2025, Russia's pool of potential military recruits, aged 20–29, will decline by 44 percent, according to the United Nations. This forecast is not subject to meaningful revision; it has been "written in stone" by births that have already occurred.[67]

Defense consultant William Hawkins echoes Fairbanks. Citing the National Intelligence Council's *Global Trends 2025,* Hawkins writes, "The loss of the Near Abroad and demographic declines within Russia itself have reduced its population base. By 2017, the NIC notes, 'Russia is likely to have only 650,000 18-year-old males from which to maintain an army that today relies on 750,000 recruits.'"[68]

Like the Aral Sea, the fourth largest lake in the world in 1960, which has lost 60 percent of its acreage and 80 percent of its volume, Russia's evaporating pool of young men will constrain Moscow's military. And there will be deficiencies across the Russian economy as the number of workers entering the labor force declines year after year. Ex-CIA director Michael Hayden believes Russia will have to import workers from the Caucasus, Central Asia, and China, exacerbating ethnic and religious tensions in a country with a history of xenophobia.[69]

Russia confronts yet another crisis in the rapid growth in her Muslim population, especially in Chechnya, Dagestan, and Ingushetia in the North Caucasus, where secessionist sentiment is strong. Grozny, capital of Chechnya, was leveled in the second Chechen war when Vladimir Putin restored the rebellious province at a heavy cost in blood.

Since 1989, Russia's Muslim population has risen 40 percent to 25 million, as Muslims, with high birth rates, pour in from the former Soviet republics. By 2020, Muslims are expected to be one-fifth of the nation. Arab news network Al Jazeera is projecting that, by 2040, half the people living in Russia will be followers of the Prophet. Adds *Foreign Policy,* "Throw into the mix anger about the ongoing Muslim insurgency in Chechnya and smoldering resentment about the demise of the Soviet Union, and you have a potent recipe for an ugly nationalist movement—or something worse."[70]

Mother Russia is dying and the geostrategic consequences will be earth-shaking. By 2050, Russia may still control twice the landmass of China, but with less than a tenth of China's population. In the Far East, six million Russians are outnumbered two hundred to one by Chinese.[71] These aging Russians sit on Earth's last great storehouse of oil, gas, timber, gold, coal, furs, and natural resources, which a huge and hungry China needs. In "Rivalries of the Bear and Dragon," the *Financial Times* writes that Russia is "paranoid about the thinly populated eastern third of its landmass."[72] And understandably so. Arnon Gutfeld of Tel Aviv University "predicts that by 2050 Russia will have insufficient human resources to control the territory it occupies."[73] Russia faces, says Putin, "the serious threat of turning into a decaying nation."[74]

Although Moscow is aligned with Beijing in the Shanghai Cooperation Committee, created to push the United States out of Central Asia, America is no threat to Mother Russia. Americans prefer to buy what the Chinese may one day be prepared to take.

With the populations aging and dying in Eastern and Southern Europe, there has been no shortage of ideas for dealing with the existential crisis of the West. Yet some environmentalists are imploring Europe not to interfere, not to grant incentives for families to have more than two children. "Women bearing children in an industrialized world...have an enormous impact on global warming," writes John Feffer, of *Foreign Policy in Focus.* "American women having babies generate seven times the carbon output of Chinese women having babies."[75] Feffer believes Western nations should not seek to raise birth rates but should open their doors to the people the Third World produces in abundance, who have tiny carbon footprints. In what is surely an understatement, Feffer argues, "It won't be easy to persuade Russians to welcome large numbers

of Chinese into Siberia or Italy to embrace more Nigerians."[76] His solution—a world migration summit.

> President Obama, the son of an immigrant, should spearhead
> the initiative. By pushing for a migration summit he can dem-
> onstrate that the United States is finally ready to play well
> with others. Such a Statue of Liberty play would be a fitting
> way for the president to spend the political capital of the No-
> bel Prize and secure his legacy as a global leader.[77]

It would also be a fitting way to expedite Obama's early return to Illinois.

SECOND THOUGHTS IN SHANGHAI

In December 2009, the *Washington Post* reported on a population crisis in
a country where few would expect it—the world's most populous nation, China, with 1.3 billion people.

"More than 30 years after China's one-child policy was introduced,
creating two generations of notoriously chubby, spoiled only children
affectionately nicknamed 'little emperors,'" wrote Ariana Eunjung Cha
from Shanghai, "a population crisis is looming in the country."[78]

> The average birthrate has plummeted to 1.8 children per cou-
> ple as compared with six when the policy went into effect,
> according to the UN Population Division, while the number
> of residents 60 and older is predicted to explode from 16.7
> percent of the population in 2020 to 31.1 percent by 2050.[79]

Using UN projections of a Chinese population of 1.4 billion by 2050,
this translates into 440 million people in China over age sixty, an immense burden of retired, elderly, and aging for the labor force to carry
and the country to care for. Shanghai is already approaching that point,

with more than 20 percent of its population over sixty, while the birth-rate is below one child per couple, one of the lowest anywhere on earth. Due to Beijing's one-couple, one-child policy, which has led to tens of millions of aborted baby girls, 12 to 15 percent of young Chinese men will be unable to find wives. As single males are responsible for most of society's violence, the presence of tens of millions of young single Chinese men portends a time of trouble in the Middle Kingdom. Peter Hitchens toured China to assess the impact of the draconian policy he calls "gendercide" for its systematic extermination of baby girls.

> By the year 2020, there will be 30 million more men than women of marriageable age in the giant empire....Nothing like this has ever happened to any civilization before.... [S]peculation is now seething about what might happen: a war to cull the surplus males, a rise in crime, a huge expansion in the prostitution that is already a major industry in every Chinese city, a rise in homosexuality.[80]

China is fortunate its one-couple, one-child policy, written into its constitution in 1978, was never an inescapable mandate. For it would have produced, in two generations, a nation with one grand-child in the labor force for every four grandparents. Already, writes Longman, China is "rapidly evolving into what demographers call a '4-2-1' society, in which one child becomes responsible for supporting two parents and four grandparents."[81]

Eberstadt points to another consequence of this birth dearth. China's "key manpower pool" of young workers aged fifteen to twenty-nine is expected to fall by 100 million, or about 30 percent, by 2030.[82]

Yet, psychologically, it may not be easy to wean Chinese couples off the one-child policy. The *Post* quoted a woman from China's human resources administration, herself an only child. "We were at the center of our families and used to everyone taking care of us. We are not used to taking care of and really do not want to take care of others."[83]

Across the Taiwan strait, the fertility rate has sunk to one child per woman and the government is offering a \$31,250 prize for the Taiwanese citizen who comes up with the best slogan to make people want babies.[84]

WHY THE WEST IS DYING

The reason the West is dying is simple: children are no longer so desirable. The child-centered society has been succeeded by the self-centered society. The purpose of life is the pursuit of pleasure, not the sacrifices required in the raising of children.

Freed from the moral constraints of Christianity, European and American young wish to enjoy the benefits of matrimony without the burdens. Society and science have accommodated them with contraceptives, the pill, the patch, sterilizations and abortion on request. And the social sanctions against sexual indulgence and the single life have largely disappeared.

Children are also less desirable because they are more expensive. In the first half of the twentieth century, one in five or one in ten children went to college. Young men left home in their late teens, married, and created their own families. Girls married young. Today, if parents wish to provide their children access to the good life, they must subsidize sixteen and often nineteen years of education for each child, the cost of which has soared into the hundreds of thousands of dollars, far beyond the means of most of the middle class.

Women are putting off having children to enter a labor market where their talents are rewarded and their social and economic independence can be won. Why get married and have babies and be tied down for years and fall behind? If one wishes to know the experience of motherhood, it can be had with a single child.

For those educated women who want the good life, a law degree or a doctorate is the way, not a husband and two kids. Many families can no longer get by on one salary. But when the wife goes to work, she often never goes home again. What was glamorous yesterday, the big two-parent family, is no longer so. The Huxstables of *The Cosby Show* and *The Brady Bunch* long ago gave way to *Sex and the City*.

For two generations, the West has known the sweet life. Now the bill comes due. With a shrinking pool of young workers due to the birth control practiced by and abortions submitted to by baby boomers and the follow-on generation, Europe no longer has the tax revenue to sustain the welfare states to assure the sweet life. A time of austerity is at hand. And from the riots across France to the anarchist attack on Tory Party headquarters in London to the garbage left piled and stinking on the streets of Marseille and Naples in the fall of 2010, Europe is not going gentle into that good night. But go she shall.

Yet some see the bright side. There is a growing school of thought that the fewer children one has, the better a global citizen one is, especially in America, where the per capita carbon footprint on Mother Earth is so high. Says Andrew Revkin of the *New York Times*, "Probably the single most concrete and substantive thing an American, young American, could do to lower our carbon footprint is not turning off the lights or driving a Prius, it's having fewer kids."[85]

The logic of Revkin's argument is irrefutable. By having one child, which means a more rapid death and disappearance of Western man, Western man thereby serves mankind. Greater love than this hath no man.

6

EQUALITY OR FREEDOM?

Equality of condition is incompatible with civilization.[1]
—JAMES FENIMORE COOPER

Utopias of equality are biologically doomed.[2]
—WILL AND ARIEL DURANT, 1968

Inequality . . . is rooted in the biological nature of man.[3]
—MURRAY ROTHBARD, 1973

We hold these truths to be self-evident, that all men are created equal," wrote Jefferson, in one of the most quoted sentences in the English language. On the Gettysburg battlefield in 1863, Lincoln hearkened back to Jefferson's words: "Four score and seven years ago our fathers brought forth on this continent, a new nation, conceived in Liberty, and dedicated to the proposition that all men are created equal." In our civil religion this is sacred text.

Barack Obama invoked the creed in his inaugural: "The time has come . . . to carry forward that precious gift, that noble idea, passed on from generation to generation: the God-given promise that all are equal, all are free, and all deserve a chance to pursue their full measure of happiness."[4]

Americans are taught that, unlike blood-and-soil nations, ours is a "propositional nation," an "ideological nation," built upon ideas.[5] What makes us exceptional, what gives purpose to our national existence is that America has been dedicated from birth to the advancement of equality and democracy for ourselves and all mankind. From 1776 on, said Lincoln, we have been "dedicated to the proposition that all men are created equal."

So our children are taught. To question the belief that America is and has always been about equality, democracy, and diversity is to mark one-self down as almost un-American. Yet this rendition of American history is a myth as great as that of the *Aeneid*, where the surviving hero of the sack of Troy sails the Mediterranean in exile to become founding father of Rome.

Today's egalitarian drive to make us all equal is no fulfillment of the vision of the Founding Fathers. Indeed, it is the thesis of this chapter that America is embarked on an ideological crusade to achieve a utopian goal, that we will inevitably fail, and that, in the process, we shall ruin our country.

WHAT THE FATHERS BELIEVED

The Founding Fathers did not believe in democracy. They did not believe in diversity. They did not believe in equality. From what Jefferson wrote and the fathers signed it is clear that the only equality to which they subscribed, as an ideal and an aspiration, was an equality of God-given rights. "We hold these truths to be self-evident, that all men are created equal, that they are endowed by their Creator with certain un-alienable rights, that among these are life, liberty and the pursuit of happiness."

Governments, wrote Jefferson, are formed to secure these rights, and when they fail to do so, they render themselves illegitimate, and the people have a right to rise up, overthrow those governments, and institute a new government based upon the consent of the people.

> [T]o secure these rights, Governments are instituted among Men, deriving their just powers from the consent of the governed,—That whenever any Form of Government becomes

destructive of these ends, it is the Right of the People to alter or to abolish it, and to institute new Government.

This is the idea that has inspired mankind.

To extract "all men are created equal" from the context in which it was written and assert it as an endorsement of an egalitarian society is to distort what Jefferson wrote and what the men of Philadelphia believed. Lest we forget, this was a declaration of *independence*! And in its closing words the Founding Fathers tell the world what they and the war are truly all about:

> We, therefore, the Representatives of the united States of America, in General Congress Assembled . . . do, in the Name, and by Authority of the good People of these Colonies, solemnly publish and declare, That these United Colonies are, and of Right ought to be Free and Independent States; that they are Absolved from all Allegiance to the British Crown, and that all political connection between them and the State of Great Britain, is and ought to be totally dissolved.

What made these men heroes was not Jefferson's phrase about an equality of rights but his blazing indictment of the king as a tyrant on the order of Ivan the Terrible and his assertion that Americans no longer owed him allegiance. The men of '76 put their lives, fortunes, and sacred honor on the line to overthrow British rule. Many would pay with their fortunes and lives for this act of treason.

From birth, America was the Party of Liberty. *Egalité*, on the other hand, was what the French Revolution claimed to be about. No American war was fought for egalitarian ends, postwar propaganda notwithstanding.

The War of 1812 was waged against the mother of parliaments in de facto alliance with the greatest despot of the age, Napoleon Bonaparte. It was about vindicating the rights of our citizens and seizing Canada. The Texas war of 1835–1836 was fought for independence from an autocratic and Catholic Mexico. How could it have been about equality when the Lone Star Republic that emerged from that war became the second slave nation in North America?

No one would suggest the Indian wars were about equality. They were about conquest and subjugation. As we shall see from Lincoln's own words, the Civil War was about restoring the Union. The Spanish-American War was fought to avenge the sinking of the *Maine* and drive the Spanish out of Cuba. It ended with our annexation of Puerto Rico, Hawaii, Guam, and the Philippines. In the Philippines we conducted the most unjust war in American history to deny Filipinos, who had trusted us, their right to be free and independent.

World War I was not fought "to make the world safe for democracy" but to crush the kaiser's Germany. We did not declare war until German U-boats began to sink our merchant ships carrying war materiel to Britain, and America, herself by then an empire, fought as an "associated power" beside five empires: the British, French, Russian, Japanese, and Italian. At war's end, the German and Ottoman empires and their millions of subjects were divided up among the victorious imperial powers—with Woodrow Wilson's blessing.

As for World War II, how could we have been fighting for democracy when we did not go to war until Japan attacked us and Hitler declared war on us? Our ally who did most of the fighting and dying was the Soviet Union of Stalin, Hitler's partner in starting the war and a monstrous tyrant whose victims before the war began outnumbered Hitler's one thousand to one. Were Hamburg, Dresden, Hiroshima, and Nagasaki about bringing democracy to Germany or Japan, or annihilating the Third Reich and the Empire of Japan?

WAS AMERICA ABOUT EQUALITY?

The Constitution and Bill of Rights are the foundational documents of the republic and the organic documents of American union. And the word "equality" does not appear in either. Nor does the word "democracy."

Can these be the ends for which the United States was established if they are not even mentioned in the nation's founding documents?

To determine if Jefferson believed in equality, let us set his words alongside the views he expressed and the life he led. Could this young Virginian truly believe all men are created equal when he presided over a plantation of slaves whom, with the exception of the Hemings family, he did not even free on his death half a century later?

In the bill of indictment against George III, Jefferson wrote: "He has excited domestic insurrections amongst us, and has endeavored to bring on the inhabitants of our frontiers, the merciless Indian Savages whose known rule of warfare, is an undistinguished destruction of all ages, sexes and conditions."

Did Jefferson believe that Native Americans, these "merciless Indian Savages," were equal to his countrymen, or should be made equal? Not until the Indian Citizenship Act of 1924 were Native Americans made full citizens. Not until this writer was in college did Indians in all states get the right to vote.

In that same indictment of George III, Jefferson describes the soldiers the king has sent across the ocean to put down the rebellion: "He is at this time transporting large Armies of foreign Mercenaries to compleat the works of death, desolation, and tyranny, already begun with circumstances of Cruelty & perfidy scarcely paralleled in the most barbarous ages, and totally unworthy the Head of a civilized nation." Clearly, Jefferson believed that English soldiers were superior to "foreign Mercenaries" and the King of England, as "Head of a civilized nation," ought not to behave like some barbarian ruler of ages past.

Among the evils the king visited upon his people was capturing colonists and impressing them into military service to fight fellow Americans and "become the executioners of their friends and Brethren."

"Brethren" appears repeatedly in Jefferson's declaration. For one of the great offenses of the king was that he was doing all this not to foreigners or "merciless Indian Savages" but to people of a common blood. Again and again, Jefferson invoked the ties of kinship and blood. "Nor have We been wanting in attention to our Brittish brethren." We have "conjured them by the ties of our common kindred," but they "have been deaf to the voice...of consanguinity." Hence, Jefferson writes, we must sever our bonds. No longer are the British brethren. "We must...hold them, as we hold the rest of mankind, Enemies in War, in Peace Friends."

Jefferson was saying that that the coming separation from England would not be simply a political separation. It would be the sundering of a nation, the dissolution of a people who belong together, as they are "brethren." In author Kevin Phillips's phrase, the Revolution was a "Cousins' War."[6]

In *Notes on the State of Virginia*, often cited as an illustration of his opposition to slavery, Jefferson wrote of the men and women who worked his plantation:

> Comparing them by their faculties of memory, reason and imagination, it appears to me, that in memory they are equal to the whites; in reason much inferior; as I think one could scarcely be found capable of tracing and comprehending the investigations of Euclid; and that in imagination they are dull, tasteless, and anomalous.[7]

Can one read a brutal passage like this and still maintain that Thomas Jefferson believed as literal truth that "all men are created equal"?

In 1813, Jefferson wrote John Adams, once his rival, now his friend:

> I agree with you that there is a natural aristocracy among men. The grounds of this are virtue and talents.... The natural aristocracy I consider as the most precious gift of nature for the instruction, the trusts, and government of society. And indeed it would have been inconsistent in creation to have formed man for the social state, and not to have provided virtue and wisdom enough to manage the concerns of the society. May we not even say that that form of government is the

best which provides the most effectually for a pure selection
of these natural *aristoi* into the offices of government?[8]

Jefferson is saying that he agrees with Adams that nature did not make all
men equal. Nature made us unequal. And we should be thankful for that
"precious gift" of a "natural aristocracy" of virtue and talent that "creation" has provided for us. For the *aristoi,* the best, have been conferred
upon us by nature to lead and instruct us. Not only are some individuals
superior, there are superior peoples. "The yeomanry of the United States
are not the canaille of Paris," Jefferson wrote to Lafayette in 1815.[9]

Jefferson and the other Founding Fathers saw themselves as belonging to an aristocratic elite in whose custody the republic was best entrusted. Jefferson never recanted these views. In his autobiography,
written forty-five years after the Declaration of Independence, Jefferson
was still writing of "the aristocracy of virtue and talent which nature has
wisely provided for the direction of the interests of society."[10]

On Jefferson and equality, Bertrand Russell observed: "In America
everybody is of the opinion that he has no social superiors, since all men
are equal, but he does not admit that he has no social inferiors, for, from
the time of Jefferson onward, the doctrine that all men are equal applies
only upwards, not downwards."[11]

THE SILENCE OF MR. MADISON

Remarkably, the Constitution not only does not mandate equality, it
does not mention equality. Writes Yale professor Willmoore Kendall, a
mentor of William F. Buckley Jr.:

> The Framers ... did not so much as mention the topic of equal-
> ity in the new instrument of government—not even in the
> Preamble, where, remember, they pause to list the purposes
> (a more perfect union, the blessings of liberty, justice, etc.) for
> which We the people ordain and establish the Constitution,

and, where, if nowhere else, one might expect them to recall that first proposition of the Declaration, under which and for which, remember, they had just fought a great war.[12]

In the Constitution James Madison largely drafted in Philadelphia in 1787, there is no reference whatsoever to the most famous words of the Declaration of Independence that his Virginia neighbor had written in Philadelphia in 1776. Nor is equality mentioned anywhere in *The Federalist Papers* of which Madison was principal author. Nor is equality mentioned in the Bill of Rights, the ten amendments to the Constitution Madison introduced in the first Congress, although the Virginia Declaration of Rights, in which Madison surely had a hand, "begins with at least a courtly bow to equality." Writes Kendall, "Publius . . . has a way, if I may put it so, of clamming up whenever (as does sometimes happen) the topic of equality heaves into sight."[13]

Publius was the pen name shared by Madison, Hamilton, and John Jay in *The Federalist Papers*. How can America have been dedicated from birth to the equality of all men when her birth certificate, the Constitution, does not mention equality, five of her first seven presidents, Madison included, were slave-holders, and the Supreme Court, seven decades after the Constitution was ratified, declared that slaves could never be citizens?

"WE CAN NOT . . . MAKE THEM EQUALS"

What of Lincoln? Did the author of the Emancipation Proclamation believe in the equality of all men?

The Lincoln Americans know, the father figure with the wise and wonderful wit who came out of Illinois to free the slaves, who would have marched with Martin Luther King—this Lincoln would be unrecognizable to his contemporaries. While as early as 1854 Lincoln condemned slavery as a "monstrous injustice" and bravely took the anti-slavery side in his debates with Stephen Douglas, here is the Republican Senate candidate on the stump, in Charleston, Illinois, on September 18, 1858, after having been baited by the "Little Giant" on where he stood on social and political equality:

> I will say then that I am not, nor ever have been in favor of bringing about in any way the social and political equality of the white and black races,—that I am not nor ever have been in favor of making voters or jurors of negroes, nor of qualifying them to hold office, nor to intermarry with white people; and I will say in addition to this that there is a physical difference between the white and black races which I believe will forever forbid the two races from living together on terms of social and political equality. And inasmuch as they cannot so live, while they do remain together there must be the position of superior and inferior, and I as much as any other man am in favor of having the superior position assigned to the white race.[14]

For a candidate to make such a white-supremacist statement today would mean the end of his career. Four years earlier, at Peoria on October 16, 1854, Lincoln confessed his ambivalence as to what should be done with the freedmen, were slavery to be abolished:

> If all earthly power were given me, I should not know what to do, as to the existing institution. My first impulse would be to free all the slaves, and send them to Liberia,—to their own native land.... [But] Free them, and make them politically and socially, our equals? My own feelings will not admit of this; and if mine would, we well know that those of the great mass of white people will not.... A universal feeling, whether well or ill-founded, can not be safely disregarded. We can not, then, make them equals.[15]

Lincoln is saying that a belief in white supremacy is a "universal feeling" of the "great mass of white people" in America. And he shares it. He

believed in freedom for all, but not equality for all, other than that black
and white share a common humanity and have an equal right to be free.
After his assertion "We can not...make them equals," Lincoln continued:

> I have never said anything to the contrary, but I hold that,
> notwithstanding all this, there is no reason in the world why
> the negro is not entitled to all the rights enumerated in the
> Declaration of Independence—the right to life, liberty and
> the pursuit of happiness. I hold that he is as much entitled to
> these as the white man. I agree with Judge Douglas, he is not
> my equal in many respects,—certainly not in color, perhaps
> not in moral or intellectual achievements. But in the right to
> eat the bread, without leave of anybody else, which his own
> hand earns, he is my equal, and the equal of Judge Douglas,
> and the equal of every living man.[16]

Eloquent, and, in its time, heroic.

At the time of the Dred Scott decision in 1857, which he deplored,
Lincoln explained his views as to what the Founding Fathers meant with
those famous words in Philadelphia:

> I think the authors of that notable instrument intended to in-
> clude all men, but they did not intend to declare all men equal
> in all respects. They did not mean to say all were equal in
> color, size, intellect, moral developments, or social capacity.
> They defined with tolerable distinctness, in what respects
> they did consider all men created equal—equal in "certain
> inalienable rights, among which are life, liberty, and the pur-
> suit of happiness." This they said, and this They meant.[17]

What Lincoln is saying is this: Negroes have the same God-given rights
to life, liberty, and the pursuit of happiness as white men and the declaration of 1776 is a promissory note they shall one day enjoy those same

rights. But while all men are equal in God-given rights, they are not equal in God-given talents.

A man must be measured against his time. "[J]udge not that ye be not judged!" said Lincoln in his Second Inaugural. His position on slavery, that it was evil and he would have no part in it, was that of a principled politician of courage. His views on equality were the views of his countrymen.

But if Lincoln did not go to war to make men equal, did he go to war to "make men free"? No. Lincoln went to war to restore the Union after the flag was fired on at Fort Sumter. In his first inaugural address, on March 4, 1861, he offered the seven seceded states the assistance of the federal government in running down fugitive slaves and endorsed an amendment to the Constitution to make slavery permanent in all 15 states where it existed. As he wrote Horace Greeley on August 22, 1862, "My paramount object in this struggle *is* to save the Union and is *not* either to save or destroy slavery. If I could save the Union without freeing *any* slave I would do it...."[18]

Nevertheless, on January 1, 1863, in his Emancipation Proclamation, Lincoln declared free slaves in rebel-held territory, and supported a constitutional amendment to free all slaves. And in his second inaugural, a month before his death in April 1865, Lincoln declared,

> Fondly do we hope—fervently do we pray—that this mighty scourge of war may speedily pass away. Yet, if God wills that it continue until all the wealth piled up by the bond-man's two hundred and fifty years of unrequited toil shall be sunk, and until every drop of blood drawn with the lash, shall be paid by another drawn with the sword, as was said three thousand years ago, so still it must be said, "the judgments of the Lord, are true and righteous altogether."

Lincoln's second inaugural could have been written by John Brown. Lincoln is saying that we Americans are being punished by God for having enslaved these people for two and half centuries and having failed to live up to the meaning of our creed. He is declaring the six hundred thousand American dead already piled up as God's righteous retribution upon us as a people.

Yet the Second Inaugural is not about the equality of all men. It is about the equal right of all to be free, about an end to slavery. Not for ninety years after the Declaration of Independence did the idea of equality—missing from the Constitution, the Bill of Rights, *The Federalist Papers,* and from national policy—appear. And then it was in the Fourteenth Amendment and was restricted to the "equal protection of the laws."

> No State shall make or enforce any law which shall abridge the privileges or immunities of citizens of the United States; nor shall any State deprive any person of life, liberty, or property, without due process of law; nor deny to any person within its jurisdiction the equal protection of the laws.

EQUALITY—THEN AND NOW

The Fourteenth Amendment did not mandate or mention social, political, or economic equality. The Congress that approved it in 1866 had established and segregated the Washington, D.C., public schools.[19] Twenty-four of the thirty-seven existing states at the time the Fourteenth Amendment was proposed segregated their schools.[20] In the 1875 Civil Rights Act, the issue of segregation in D.C. and the states did not even come up.[21] In *Plessy v. Ferguson* (1896), segregation was upheld by the Supreme Court as consistent with the Fourteenth Amendment.

In Washington, D.C., the public schools were segregated until *Brown v. Board of Education* (1954), which overturned *Plessy*. But Brown was not based on the Constitution. It was based on sociology. The headline on James Reston's story in the *New York Times* on May 13, 1954, read: "A Sociological Decision: Court Founded Its Segregation Ruling on Hearts and Minds Rather than Laws."[22]

Not until the 1960s did courts begin to use the Fourteenth Amendment to impose a concept of equality that the authors of the Declaration of Independence, the Constitution, the Bill of Rights, *The Federalist Papers,* and the Gettysburg Address never believed in. Before the 1960s, equality meant every citizen enjoyed the same constitutional rights and the equal protection of existing laws. Nothing in the Constitution or federal law mandated social, racial, or gender equality. While the nation by the 1960s supported federal action to end segregation where it still existed, it was understood that inequalities of incomes and rewards were the inevitable concomitant of a competitive and free society.

1963: "LET FREEDOM RING"

In August 1963 at the Lincoln Memorial in the centennial year of the Emancipation Proclamation, Martin Luther King rose to deliver one of the memorable addresses of American history. His theme, however, was not equality. He mentioned it but twice, first together with freedom and next when he quoted Jefferson: "I have a dream that one day this nation will rise up and live out the true meaning of its creed, 'We hold these truths to be self-evident, that all men are created equal.'" The goal of the famous March on Washington was "Jobs and Freedom" and the theme of King's speech was declared in his opening line: "I am happy to join with you today in what will go down in history as the greatest demonstration for freedom in the history of our nation."[23] Freedom is mentioned a dozen times by King and repeated another ten times in his closing refrain, "Let freedom ring."

What freedoms did King demand? Freedom from the "manacles of segregation and the chains of discrimination" and freedom from "a lonely island of poverty in the midst of a vast ocean of material prosperity."[24]

1965: "FREEDOM IS NOT ENOUGH"

In the Senate debate over the Civil Rights Act of 1964, Hubert Humphrey assured the nation that the law being enacted "does not require an

employer to achieve any kind of racial balance in his work force by giving any kind of preferential treatment to any individual or group."[25]

Not until 1965 did the goal of the civil rights movement shift from an
end to segregation to social and economic equality. The great leap forward came at Howard University in the 1965 commencement address,
when the freedom King had spoken of was superseded and replaced by
"equality as a fact and equality as a result."[26]

President Lyndon Johnson began that address by describing freedom
as but the first stage of "the revolution": "Freedom is the right to share,
share fully and equally, in American society—to vote, to hold a job, to
enter a public place, to go to school. It is the right to be treated in every
part of our national life as a person equal in dignity and promise to all
others."[27]

While the "beginning is freedom," said Johnson, "freedom is not
enough.... it is not enough just to open the gates of opportunity. All our
citizens must have the ability to walk through those gates."[28]

> This is the next and the more profound stage of the battle for
> civil rights. We seek not just freedom but opportunity. We
> seek not ... just equality as a right and a theory but equality as
> a fact and equality as a result....
>
> [E]qual opportunity is essential, but not enough, not enough.
> Men and women of all races are born with the same range of
> abilities. But ability is not just the product of birth. Ability is
> stretched or stunted by the family that you live with, and the
> neighborhood you live in—by the school you go to and the
> poverty or the richness of your surroundings. It is the product
> of a hundred unseen forces playing upon the little infant, the
> child, and finally the man.[29]

Law professor William Quirk wrote of Johnson's shift of national goals—
from no discrimination based on race to full equality of results based on
race: "The people never agreed to that. Every poll ever taken shows that

80 percent of the people do not agree with that. Nothing in the Constitution said that. None of the statutes the Congress has passed said anything like that."[30] Johnson had committed the nation to a concept of equality American novelist James Fenimore Cooper called an impossibility in civilized society:

> Equality in a social sense may be divided into that of condition and that of right. Equality of condition is incompatible with civilization and is found only to exist in those communities that are but slightly removed from the savage state. In practice, it can only mean a common misery.[31]

Johnson's equality of result would soon be expanded to include men and women and Anglos and Hispanics. In *Regents of the University of California v. Bakke* (1978), the Supreme Court declared that racial discrimination against whites to advance equality in America was now constitutional and moral. Said Justice Harry Blackmun: "In order to get beyond racism, we must first take account of race. There is no other way. And in order to treat some persons equally, we must treat them differently. We cannot—we dare not—let the Equal Protection Clause perpetuate racial supremacy."[32]

Blackmun was saying that if free and fair competition in our society repeatedly yields unequal results and rewards because one group has been crippled by history, the state must step in to assure an equality of prizes. Yet this concept of equality had no basis in the Constitution, the Fourteenth Amendment as written and intended, or in the civil rights laws of the 1960s to which Congress and the country assented. This idea of equality is rooted in an egalitarian ideology that is the antithesis of what the Founding Fathers and every president before Lyndon Johnson believed—if Johnson believed what he was saying.

Those who would change society begin by changing the meaning of words. At Howard University, LBJ changed the meaning of equality from the attainable—an end to segregation and a legislated equality of rights for African Americans—to the impossible: a socialist utopia. For where outside of socialist ideology is it dogma that "Men and women of all races are born with the same range of abilities." It is more true to say that no two men or women were ever born equal. Talents are unequally distributed not only within ethnic groups but within families. To impose an equality of rewards for unequal accomplishments is to nullify one of the goals of our Constitution—"to establish justice." It is to replace justice with injustice.

The only way to achieve equality when a free market, free associations, and free competition fail to deliver it is to use state power to forcibly bring about parities of income, influence, rewards, and riches. This is socialism.

At Howard, LBJ declared that the promise of America's Revolution was insufficient for his revolution. Noting the disproportionate levels of poverty and income in America, he declared:

> These differences are not [the result of] racial differences. They are solely and simply the consequences of ancient brutality, past injustice, and present prejudice.... For the Negro they are a constant reminder of prejudice. For the white they are a constant reminder of guilt. But they must be faced and they must be dealt with and they must be overcome, if we are ever to reach the time when the only difference between Negroes and whites is the color of their skin.[33]

Did Lyndon Johnson truly believe that all racial inequalities are due "solely and simply" to racism, that if the prejudice of white America is "overcome," then "equality as a fact and equality as a result" will magically appear, and "the only difference between Negroes and whites" will be "the color of their skin"?

Where is the empirical evidence for this assertion? There is none. This is pure egalitarian ideology. As Murray Rothbard wrote, "Since egalitarians start with the *a priori* axiom that all people and hence all groups of people, are...equal, it then follows for them that any and all group differences in status, prestige, or authority in society *must* be the result of unjust 'oppression' and irrational 'discrimination.'"[34]

The proof of LBJ's "a priori axiom" is nonexistent. Indeed, LBJ's speech contradicts itself. He says that unemployment for blacks and whites was the same in 1930, but black unemployment is now twice that of whites. He says that black teenage unemployment was less than that of whites in 1948, but has since tripled to 23 percent. He says that income disparity widened during the 1950s. In short, in the decades when segregation was dying out, blacks were falling further behind. How can improving white attitudes toward black Americans be the cause of worsening conditions in black America?

Aristotle said, "Democracy...arises out of the notion that those who are equal in any respect are equal in all respects." The Founding Fathers and Lincoln disbelieved in this "notion" of equality. LBJ embraced it. And ever since, we have been trying to create an egalitarian society based on that false notion. We will not succeed. The republic will die before we do.

"INEQUALITY IS NATURAL"

Historians Will and Ariel Durant, authors of an eleven-volume series of monumental books written over four decades, *The Story of Civilization*, arrived at the opposite conclusion.

In *The Lessons of History*, the Durants conclude: "Nature...has not read very carefully the American Declaration of Independence or the French Revolutionary Declaration of the Rights of Man."[35]

> [W]e are all born unfree and unequal: subject to our physical and psychological heredity, and to the customs and traditions of our group; diversely endowed in health and strength, in mental capacity and qualities of character. Nature loves differences as the necessary material of selection and evolution;

identical twins differ in a hundred ways, and no two peas are alike.[36]

Inequality "is not only natural and inborn, it grows with the complexity of civilization."[37] In refutation of everything LBJ said at Howard, the Durants declare:

> Nature smiles at the union of freedom and equality in our utopias. For freedom and equality are sworn and everlasting enemies, and when one prevails the other dies. Leave men free, and their natural inequalities will multiply almost geometrically, as in England and America in the nineteenth century under *laissez-faire.* To check the growth of inequality, liberty must be sacrificed, as in Russia after 1917.[38]

Again, "To check the growth of inequality, liberty must be sacrificed."

That is the point of this chapter. Where equality is enthroned, freedom is extinguished. The rise of the egalitarian society means the death of the free society. "Liberty by its very nature . . . is inegalitarian," writes Jude Dougherty, dean emeritus of the School of Philosophy at Catholic University: "Men differ in strength, intelligence, ambition, courage, perseverance and all else that makes for success. There is no method to make men both free and equal."[39]

When we consider the revolutions dedicated to equality—the French Revolution of Marat and Robespierre, the Russian Revolution of Lenin and Trotsky, the Chinese Revolution of Mao, the Cuban Revolution of Castro and Che Guevara—are the Durants not right? Is Dougherty not right?

The contention that men and women are equal is found in feminist ideology not human nature. Men are bigger, stronger, more aggressive. That is why men commit crimes and are imprisoned at a rate of ten to one over women.[40] That is why men fight wars, lead armies, and build empires. Men's intelligence levels range higher and lower than those of women. Men reach heights of achievement in mathematics, science, and philosophy few women attain. Men also reach greater depths of depravity. In sports, where Americans demand the best, men and women compete separately.

The first article of France's Declaration of Human Rights echoes Jefferson and Rousseau: "Men are born and remain free and equal in rights. Social distinctions may be founded only upon the general good." But are infants born free? And who decides what is the "general good"? As for equality of rights, yes, but children are not all born equal in the ability to learn. Half are below average. Two months into first grade, children know they are not equal. Some are bright, others slow. Some are athletic, others are not. Some can sing, others cannot. Some girls are pretty, others plain. "So far is it from being true that men are naturally equal that no two people can be half an hour together but one acquires an evident superiority over the other," said Samuel Johnson.[41]

In the Old and New Testament are all people equal? Jews were the Chosen People to whom God promised the messiah. The Son of God, his mother, and the twelve apostles were Jews. Among his disciples, Christ preferred John, elevated Peter to be the rock upon which he would build his church, and condemned Judas. In the parable of the talents, the servants are unequally endowed and each is expected to produce consistent with his talents. If Christ taught that some are more gifted than others, the egalitarianism espoused at Howard is in conflict with our Christian faith. Paul affirmed it in his letter to the Romans: "We have gifts differing according to the grace that has been given us."

THE DODO

Observing the contortions ideologues go through to ensure equality of result, one is reminded of the "Caucus-race" in *Alice's Adventures in Wonderland*. Everyone "began running when they liked, and left off when they liked," and "when they had been running half an hour or so ... the Dodo suddenly called out 'The race is over!' and they all crowded round it, panting, and asking, 'But who has won?'"

"At last the Dodo said, '*everybody* has won, and all must have prizes.'"[42]

The ideologue begins with an idea—all are equal and should have equal shares of the good things in life—then proceeds to try to force society to conform to this ideal. "The ideologue," wrote Russell Kirk, "thinks of politics as a revolutionary instrument for transforming society and even transforming human nature. In the march toward Utopia, the ideologue is merciless."[43]

To the ideologue, adds Professor Gillis Harp, of Grove City College, "Facts don't matter and character assassination is permissible."[44] The rampant use today in public discourse of terms of anathema and abuse such as "racist," "sexist," and "homophobe" testifies to how intolerant the egalitarian is toward those who disbelieve in the core doctrine of his faith.

"Utopias of equality are biologically doomed," said the Durants.[45] "You may drive out Nature with a pitchfork," said the Roman poet Horace, "yet she will always hasten back." Whether it be in sports, the arts, music, education, or politics, free and fair competition allows a natural aristocracy to assert and distinguish itself. Freedom produces a hierarchy based on intelligence, talent, and perseverance. The African American leader W. E. B. Du Bois wrote, in a 1903 essay, that the highest priority of his people should be to elevate and educate that natural aristocracy, "The Talented Tenth" of black America.

> The Negro race, like all races, is going to be saved by its exceptional men. The problem of education, then, among Negroes must first of all deal with the Talented Tenth; it is the problem of developing the Best of this race that they may guide the Mass away from the contamination and death of the Worst, in their own and other races.[46]

A nation dedicated to the proposition that all are equal and entitled to equal rewards must end up constantly discriminating against its talented tenth, for that is the only way a free society can guarantee social and economic equality. And consider the costs incurred, the injustices done, the freedoms curtailed—all in the name of equality.

- Hundreds of thousands of children have been ordered bused out of their neighborhoods to inferior and often dangerous schools, igniting racial conflict, causing white flight, abandonment of urban schools, and the ruin of public education—a crown jewel of American civilization.
- The right of businesses to hire and promote based on ability and performance has been subjected for decades to policing by tens of thousands of government agents. If a labor force does not reflect gender equality or the racial composition of the community, the company may be prosecuted.
- Governments impose de facto race and gender quotas that add hugely to the cost of doing business. Scores of billions have been siphoned off from companies in class action law suits brought for alleged discrimination in one of the more lucrative rackets in American history.
- The top 1 percent of wage and salary earners now carries 40 percent of the entire income tax load while the bottom 50 percent carry none of it. Was it not the Communist Manifesto that called for a "heavy progressive or graduated income tax"?
- In a nation once renowned for its freedom of speech, censorship is spreading with speech codes on campuses and hate crimes laws that punish speech offensive to the egalitarian dogma that all races, all ethnic groups, and all sexual orientations are to be equally respected.
- To assure equality of all religions, Christianity, our cradle faith, has been purged from the nation's public schools and public square and treated as just another religion.
- Universities are now required by Title IX to equalize expenditures on men's and women's sports, leading to the

elimination of men's sports teams and the creation of women's teams for which there is little or no demand.

- Almost all men's colleges have been forced to admit women.
- VMI and the Citadel were forced to admit female cadets although the schools, the alumni, and the mothers, wives, and sisters of VMI and Citadel cadets and graduates protested this judicially mandated end to their 150-year-old tradition.
- Men have been discriminated against so relentlessly that women with jobs now outnumber them, and men sustained 70 to 80 percent of all job losses in the Great Recession.[47]
- Southern states must still appeal to Justice Department bureaucrats for permission to make minor changes in election laws.
- Dunbar High, perhaps the finest elite black high school in America, which produced generals and senators and sent a higher share of its graduates to college than any Washington, D.C., institution, was converted in the name of equality into a neighborhood school and became one of the most troubled schools in the city.
- In *Baker v. Carr* (1962), the Supreme Court forbade all states from modeling their legislatures on Congress and mandated that all states be apportioned on population alone. Purpose: impose one-man, one-vote democracy, which our fathers rejected when they gave Delaware and Rhode Island the same number of senators as Massachusetts and Virginia.
- In the name of equality, the Supreme Court has declared the practice of homosexuality to be a constitutional right.
- Vaughn Walker, a gay federal judge in San Francisco, has ruled that same-sex marriage is guaranteed by the Fourteenth Amendment. Can anyone believe this absurd notion of equality was intended by or written into the Constitution by the Congress that produced the 14th Amendment?

- Although gay marriage has been rejected in thirty-one states in referenda, judges continue to declare that such unions be treated as marriages. An idea of equality rejected democratically by voters is being imposed dictatorially.
- In December 2010, a repudiated liberal Congress imposed its San Francisco values on the armed forces by ordering homosexuals admitted to all branches of the service. Indoctrination of recruits, soldiers, and officers into an acceptance of the gay life style will transfer authority over the military, the most respected institution in America, to agents of a deeply resented and widely detested managerial state.
- To bring black and Hispanic home ownership to parity with that of whites, George W. Bush pushed banks into making millions of sub-prime mortgages, defaults on which may yet bring down our free-enterprise system. Egalitarianism may prove to be the murder weapon of American capitalism.
- In the name of equality for all the world's peoples, the Immigration Act of 1965 threw open the nation's doors converting America into what Theodore Roosevelt called a "polyglot boarding house" for the world.

When one considers the scores of thousands of bureaucrats in federal, state, and local government, at colleges and in corporations, all working to insure proportional representation of races, ethnic groups, and genders, we begin to see how equality and freedom are at war and why America is a failing nation.

The pursuit of race, gender, ethnic, and economic equality is utopian. Imagine that a regime committed to absolute equality confiscated all the property and wealth of the nation and redistributed it in equal portions. How long would it be before the more able and aggressive citizens would repossess that wealth? Confiscation and redistribution would have to begin anew.

"An egalitarian society," wrote Rothbard, "can only hope to achieve its goals by totalitarian methods of coercion; and, even here, we all believe and hope the human spirit of individual man will rise up and thwart any such attempts to achieve an ant-heap world."[48]

No two men were more unlike than Rothbard and George Kennan. Here they agreed. "I am anything but an egalitarian," Kennan told Eric Sevareid. "I am very much opposed to egalitarian tendencies of all sorts."[49] Biographer Leo Congdon says that Kennan "viewed the passion for equality as the product of envy and resentment."[50]

Yet even professed conservatives have succumbed to the siren's call of egalitarianism. When Californians voted in Proposition 8 to restrict marriage to a man and a woman, former solicitor general Ted Olson said the voters had violated the equal protection clause of the Constitution. "The Constitution of Thomas Jefferson, James Madison and Abraham Lincoln does not permit" denying homosexuals the right to marry.[51]

Is Olson aware that the Constitution of Jefferson, Madison, and Lincoln did not contain the words "equal" or "equality" or have an equal protection clause? All three presidents were dead before the Fourteenth Amendment was added. Is Olson aware that Jefferson equated homosexuality with rape and believed homosexuals should be castrated and lesbians punished by "cutting thro' the cartilage of her nose a hole of one half inch diameter at the least"?[52]

This is no endorsement of Jefferson's proposal, but it is further proof that the egalitarian extremism of the late twentieth and the early twenty-first centuries is rooted not in the history of this republic but in the ideology of modern man.

EQUALIZING TEST SCORES

Nowhere has the egalitarian impulse proven more costly or failed more dismally than in the drive to close the racial gap in test scores. And it is not as though we were not warned.

In 1966, a year after LBJ enacted his Elementary and Secondary Education Act, moving the federal government massively into the state and local province of public education, came the famous Coleman Report of 1966. In a review of the performance of two-thirds of a million children, writes Charles Murray, the Harvard- and MIT-trained social scientist:

> To everyone's shock, the Coleman Report...found that the quality of schools explains almost nothing about differences in academic achievement. Measures such as the credentials of the teachers, the curriculum, the extensiveness and newness of physical facilities, money spent per student—none of the things that people assumed were important in explaining educational achievement were important in fact. Family background was far and away the most important factor in determining student achievement.[53]

Nature and nurture, heredity and home environment, brains and motivation, the study found, these are the primary determinants of pupil performance.

In 1971, the *Atlantic Monthly* ran a cover article by Harvard's Richard Herrnstein. His thesis was that even if we are able to equalize the home and school environment of all children, natural academic ability will enable some children to outperform others. No matter how much money is invested in reducing class size and enhancing teacher training, an "hereditary meritocracy" will arise in a public school system where expenditures are equal.[54]

Coleman and Herrnstein were teaching predestination in education. They were implying that the national effort just launched to raise the test scores of minority children to parity with the scores of white children was an experiment noble in purpose but doomed to fail. But pessimism about the ability of government to succeed in its ambitions was not in vogue when government was being hailed as architect and builder of the Great Society.

America plunged forward. U.S. and state governments and local school districts began the most massive investment in education in all of history.

Expenditures per pupil doubled and tripled. Head Start, a preschool program for low-income children established in 1965, was lavishly funded. Perhaps $200 billion was poured into Title I of the Elementary and Secondary Education Act, which provided additional funds to schools based on their population of low-income students.

What were the results? Writes Murray, "no evaluation from Title I from the 1970s onward has found credible evidence of a significant positive impact on student achievement.... A 2001 study by the Department of Education revealed that the gap widened rather than diminished."

George W. Bush attacked the disparity between majority and minority school achievement anew with his No Child Left Behind law. The Department of Education budget doubled again. What was accomplished? Judging by test scores, writes Murray, "NCLB has done nothing to raise reading skills despite the enormous effort that has been expended."

> The notion that we know how to make more than modest improvements in [children's] math and reading performance has no factual basis ... even the best schools under the best conditions cannot overcome the limits of achievement set by the limits on academic ability.[55]

Heather Mac Donald, of the Manhattan Institute, provides corroborating evidence. "On the 2006 SAT, the average score in the critical-reading section was 434 for blacks, 527 for whites, and 510 for Asians; in the math section 429 for blacks, 536 for whites, and 587 for Asians."[56]

In a 2005 ranking of fifty states and Washington, D.C., by how much each spent per pupil, New York ranked first, D.C. third.[57] The fruits of this investment of tax dollars: in some D.C. high schools, half of all minority students drop out. Of those who graduate, half are reading and doing math at seventh-, eighth-, or ninth-grade levels. Near the top of the nation in tax dollars spent per pupil, Washington, D.C., is at the bottom in academic achievement.

In 2007, the U.S. graduation rate for high school students fell for the second straight year to 69 percent.[58] Forty-six percent of blacks, 44 percent of Hispanics, and 49 percent of Native American students failed to earn a diploma in four years. Back in 1969, 77 percent of high school students earned their diplomas in four years. America is not treading water. America is sinking.

In 2009 came a report from New York that made D.C. schools look like MIT. Some two hundred students in their first math class at City University of New York were tested on basic skills. Two-thirds of these college freshmen could not convert a decimal into a fraction. Ninety percent could not do simple algebra.[59]

Hailing his schools chancellor Joel Klein, Mayor Michael Bloomberg boasted in 2009, "We are closing the shameful achievement gap faster than ever." When the 2010 state test scores came in, however, the achievement gap was back. "Among the students in the city's third through eighth grades," wrote the *Times,* "33 percent of black students and 34 percent of Hispanic students are now proficient [in English], compared with 64 percent among whites and Asians." School officials now acknowledge "a test score bubble."[60]

When Klein stepped down, the *Daily News* summed up his record: "Test scores went up steadily until last year, when they plunged to abysmal levels when exams got tougher."[61] As Klein was resigning, the Council of the Great City Schools issued a report containing what it described as "jaw-dropping data." The *New York Times* story began:

> An achievement gap separating black from white students has long been documented—a social divide extremely vexing to policy makers and the target of one blast of school reform after another.
>
> But a new report focusing on black males suggests that the picture is even bleaker than generally known.[62]

Using the highly respected National Assessment for Educational Progress tests, the council found that poor white boys eligible for free meals at school performed as well in math and reading as black boys from middle class and affluent neighborhoods. Said Ronald Ferguson, director of the Achievement Gap Initiative at Harvard:

> There's accumulating evidence that there are racial differences in what kids experience before the first day of kindergarten.... They have to do with a lot of sociological and historical forces. In order to address those, we have to be able to have conversations that people are unwilling to have.[63]

The council report naturally urged Congress to "appropriate more money for schools."[64] Yet there are people willing to have those "conversations." One is Robert Weissberg, professor of political science emeritus at the University of Illinois and author of *Bad Students, Not Bad Schools*, who agrees with Charles Murray that "the 'democratization' of schooling—a diploma for nearly everyone—that brings those into the classroom who can barely master the material and, critically, to insist that these youngsters can be proficient is romantic foolishness."[65] The beginning of real school reform is not to babysit indolent or unruly students but to get them out of the schools.

> If one single genuine "magic bullet" cure for America's education decline exists, it would be to eliminate the bottom quarter of those past 8th grade. Unfortunately, the "democratization" of education seems to be irresistible as educational reformers increasingly call for enrolling semiliterates in college as if a degree itself certifies proficiency.[66]

Weissberg believes we should push students to the limits of their ability, then push them again, and, when they have ceased to learn, push them out the door and accept the reality that all are not equal in their aptitude for and attitude about academic learning. This used to be called common sense.

THE GLOBAL GAP IN TEST SCORES

"That speaks about who is going to be leading tomorrow," said Angel Gurria, secretary-general of the Paris-based Organization for Economic Cooperation and Development (OECD), which, every three years, holds its Program for International Student Assessment tests of the reading, math, and science skills of fifteen year olds worldwide.[67] Gurria was referring to the results of the 2009 Program for International Student Assessment tests. Sixty-five nations competed. Chinese students swept the board. The schools of Shanghai finished first in math, reading, and science. Hong Kong was third in math and science. Singapore, a city-state dominated by overseas Chinese, was second in math and fourth in science.

And the United States? America ranked seventeenth in reading, twenty-third in science, thirty-first in math. "This is an absolute wake-up call for America," said Education Secretary Arne Duncan. "We have to face the brutal truth. We have to get much more serious about investment in education."[68]

Yet a closer look at the PISA scores reveals some unacknowledged truths. While Northeast Asians are turning in the top scores, followed by Europeans, Canadians, Australians, and New Zealanders, looking down the list of the top thirty nations, one finds not a single Latin American nation, not a single African nation, not a single Muslim nation, not a single South Asian or Southeast Asian nation (save Singapore), not a single nation of the former Soviet Union except Latvia and Estonia. Among the OECD's thirty-four members, the most developed nations on earth, Mexico, the principal feeder nation for U.S. schools, came in dead last in reading.

Steve Sailer got the full list of sixty-five nations, broke down the U.S. reading scores by ethnicity, and measured American students against the continents and the countries from which their families originated. What he found was startling. Asian American students outperformed all Asian students except those from Shanghai. White Americans outperformed the students from all thirty-seven predominantly white nations except Finland. U.S. Hispanics outperformed the students of all eight Latin American countries that participated. African American kids outperformed the only black country to participate, Trinidad and Tobago, by 25 points.[69]

America's schools are not all abject failures. They are successfully educating immigrants and their descendants to outperform the kinfolk their parents or ancestors left behind when they came to America. What America's schools are failing at, despite the trillions poured into schools since the 1965 Primary and Secondary Education Act, is closing the racial divide. We do not know how to close test-score gaps in reading, science, and math between Anglo and Asian students on one hand and black and Hispanic students on the other. And, judging from the PISA tests, neither does the world.

The gap between the test scores of East Asian and European nations and Latin American and African nations mirrors the gap between Asian and Anglo students in the United States and black and Hispanic students in the United States.

As the Heritage Foundation reported after analyzing the PISA reading test results, "If white American students were counted as a separate group, their PISA reading scores would rank them third in the world. Hispanics and black Americans, however, would score 31st and 33rd respectively."[70]

"America's educational woes reflect our demographic mix of students," writes Weissberg:

> Today's schools are filled with millions of youngsters, many of whom are Hispanic immigrants struggling with English plus millions of others of mediocre intellectual ability disdaining academic achievement.... To be grossly politically incorrect most of America's educational woes vanish if these indifferent, troublesome students left when they had absorbed as much as they were going to learn and were replaced by

learning-hungry students from Korea, Japan, India, Russia, Africa, and the Caribbean.[71]

Education reformer Michelle Rhee asserts that, "It is abundantly clear from the research that the most important school factor in determining a child's success is the quality of the teacher in the front of the classroom."[72]

But is this really "abundantly clear"? With the Coleman Report and Charles Murray, Weissberg dissents, arguing that 80 percent of a child's success depends on the cognitive ability and disposition he or she brings to class, not on textbooks or "the teacher in front of the classroom." If brains and a desire to learn are absent, no amount of spending on schools, teacher salaries, educational consultants, or new texts will matter.

Even if we could equalize the home environment, and the school environment, for all children, we would still not get equal test scores. As *Discover* magazine science blogger Razib Khan writes, "When you remove the environmental variance, the cognitive variance remains."[73]

BURNING HERETICS

A refusal to accept what human experience teaches is the mark of the ideologue. At a January 2005 academic conclave, Harvard President Larry Summers was asked why there were so few women receiving tenure in mathematics and the hard sciences. Summers volunteered that it might be due to unequal abilities of men and women. "In the special case of science and engineering, there are issues of intrinsic aptitude, and particularly of the variability of aptitude," said Summers, wading out into treacherous waters. These may cause "the different availability of aptitude at the high end."[74]

"I felt I was going to be sick," said MIT biology professor Nancy Hopkins. "My heart was pounding and my breath was shallow.... I just couldn't breathe because this kind of bias makes me physically ill." Had she not fled the room, said Hopkins, "I would've either blacked out or thrown up."[75]

A year later, Summers was subjected to a "lack-of-confidence" and censure vote by the Faculty of Arts and Sciences—and was gone. Egalitarianism is an ideology not terribly tolerant of dissent.

A year after Summers's departure, Dr. James Watson, winner, with Dr. Francis Crick, of the 1962 Nobel Prize for their discovery of the double-helix structure of DNA, volunteered to the *Sunday Times* that he was "inherently gloomy about the prospect of Africa," as "all our social policies are based on the fact that their intelligence is the same as ours—whereas all the testing says not really."[76]

Watson's 2007 autobiography, *Avoid Boring People: Lessons from a Life in Science*, was then found to contain this heresy:

> There is no firm reason to anticipate that the intellectual capacities of peoples geographically separated in their evolution should prove to have evolved identically. Our wanting to reserve equal powers of reason as some universal heritage of humanity will not be enough to make it so.[77]

Watson's address to London's Science Museum was immediately canceled, as was his book tour. And he was compelled to resign as the director of Cold Spring Harbor Laboratory, where he had served for forty years.

"I disapprove of what you say but I will defend to the death your right to say it," said Voltaire to Rousseau. "Error of opinion may be tolerated where truth is free to combat it," said Jefferson. What does it say about twenty-first-century liberalism, and what does it say about twenty-first-century America, that one of her greatest scientists can be flogged, fired, and forced to recant beliefs he has formed from a lifetime of study and experience?

In *Human Accomplishment: The Pursuit of Excellence in the Arts and Sciences, 800 B.C. to 1950,* Murray looked at four thousand significant figures and the world's greatest achievements in science, art, music, philosophy, and mathematics. He concluded that 97 percent of the most significant figures and 97 percent of the greatest achievements in astronomy, biology, earth sciences, physics, mathematics, medicine, and technology came from Europe or North America. An astonishing record for one civilization. Women were credited with 0 percent of the achievements in philosophy, 1.7 percent in the sciences, 2.3 percent of the greatest Western art, 4.4 percent of great Western literature, and two-tenths of 1 percent of great Western music.[76]

It is a time for truth. As most kids do not have the athletic ability to play high school sports, or the musical ability to play in the band, or the verbal ability to excel in debate, not every child has the academic ability to do high school work. No two children are created equal, not even identical twins. The family is the incubator of inequality and God its author. Given equal opportunities, the gifted will rise and the less talented, athletically, artistically, academically, will trail. Yet for forty years, writes Charles Murray, "American leaders have been unwilling to discuss the underlying differences in academic ability that children bring to the classroom."[79]

In "The Inequality Taboo," an essay in the September 2005 issue of *Commentary,* Murray writes that the mistaken assumption behind affirmative action is that if all socially imposed impediments to equality were removed, true equality would exist.

> Affirmative action ... assumes there are no innate differences between any of the groups it seeks to help and everyone else. The assumption of no innate differences among groups suffuses American social policy. That assumption is wrong.
>
> When the outcomes that these policies are supposed to produce fail to occur, with one group falling short, the fault for the discrepancy has been assigned to society. It continues to be assumed that better programs, better regulations, or the right court decisions can make the differences go away. That assumption is also wrong.[80]

Watching America's exertions to achieve an unattainable equality—through affirmative action, quotas, set asides, progressive taxes, and a mammoth welfare state—brings to mind Nathaniel Hawthorne's "The Birth-Mark." In that short story, the scientist Aylmer, passionately in love with his beautiful young wife, Georgiana, becomes obsessed with a small red birthmark on her cheek in the shape of a hand. Coming to hate the birthmark, Aylmer conducts a dangerous surgery to remove it—to make his wife perfect. He removes the imperfection, and his wife dies. Our pursuit of the perfect, an ideal nation where at last all are equal, is killing the country.

EQUALITY AS POLITICAL WEAPON

In revolutions where equality is the enthroned idol—in the French, Russian, Chinese, and Cuban revolutions—the dispossession of the old regime was often a merciless affair. Political and propertied classes, priests and poets, were sent to the guillotine, the Lubianka, the gallows, the firing squad, or the labor camp. And as the old order went off to jails, exile, and graves, the revolutionary elite, uglier and more brutal than those they displaced, moved into the palaces, mansions, and dachas.

George Orwell's *Animal Farm* got it right. The revolution rises on the slogan, "All animals are equal." But once power is attained, the pigs move up into the farmhouse and the slogan is amended to read, "All animals are equal, but some animals are more equal than others." The revolution to establish equality for all invariably ends up establishing the dictatorship of the few.

"Every revolution must have its myth," writes Duncan Williams, British professor of literature, "and the most persistent of these, and the one which, contrary to all human experience, has gained the most 'romantic' adherence over the past century and a half is the belief in the 'equality of man.'" From her life's work as an anthropologist, Margaret Mead concluded that this belief in equality is rooted in myths and dreams: "The assumption that men were created equal, with an equal ability to make an effort and win an earthly reward, although denied every day by experience, is maintained every day by our folk-lore and our day dreams." "In the realm of sport this belief seems curiously absent," writes Williams. "No man in his senses would dare to presume that he has, on the grounds of equality, an inalienable right to represent his country in the Olympic games, any more than a boy would imagine he can automatically claim a place in his school football team."[81] Sports are too important to Americans to indulge such myths as the equality of all men.

Over the past half-century, we have plunged trillions of dollars into public education, a large share of which has gone toward efforts to close racial gaps. But we have never come close to achieving equality in test scores. We have created a mammoth welfare state, but the percentage below the poverty line stopped dropping four decades ago. We have exempted half the nation from income taxes and laid three-fourths of the burden on the talented tenth. But we have never created equality of wealth and never will as long as we are a free people. Indeed, the more we become an economy based on knowledge, not manual labor, the wider the inequalities become. To create the egalitarian society that exists only in the minds of ideologues we are killing the wonderful country we inherited from the Greatest Generation.

For decades, we have maintained standing armies of bureaucrats whose pay and benefits far exceed those of the taxpayers who subsidize and sustain them. Eventually one realizes that this transfer of wealth and power from one class to another is really what the "equality" game is all about:

> The doctrine of equality is unimportant, because no one save perhaps Pol Pot and Ben Wattenberg really believes in it, and no one, least of all those who profess it most loudly, is seriously motivated by it.... The real meaning of the doctrine of equality is that it serves as a political weapon.[82]

So wrote author and essayist Sam Francis. A century and a half earlier, Tocqueville had seen through egalitarianism—to the drive for power that lay behind it.

> [T]he sole condition which is required in order to succeed in centralizing the supreme power in a democratic community, is to love equality, or to get men to believe you love it. Thus the science of despotism, which was once so complex, is simplified, and reduced ... to a single principle.[83]

Bertrand de Jouvenel, who lived through the Nazi occupation, echoed Tocqueville: "It is in the pursuit of Utopia that the aggrandizers of state power find their most effective ally. Only an immensely powerful apparatus can do all that the preachers of panacea government promise."[84]

Long before him, the Italian philosopher Vilfredo Pareto wrote that equality "is related to the direct interests of individuals who are bent on escaping certain inequalities not in their favor, and setting up new inequalities that will be in their favor, this latter being their chief concern."[85]

Cui bono?—Who benefits?—is ever the relevant question. When a new class advances preaching the gospel of equality, who gets the power?

7

THE DIVERSITY CULT

*Never in recorded history has diversity been
anything but a problem.*[1]
—ANN COULTER, 2009

Diversity's beauty is in the eye of the beholder.[2]
—PETER SKERRY
"Beyond Sushiology: Does Diversity Work?"

I firmly believe the strength of our Army comes from our diversity.[3]
—GENERAL GEORGE W. CASEY,
Army Chief of Staff

O n July 4, 1776, the Continental Congress moved that on the
Great Seal of the United States there be emblazoned the motto
E pluribus unum. The men of Philadelphia understood that only
their unity gave them the strength to defy the mighty British Empire.

On the eve of war Patrick Henry had declared, in the Virginia House
of Burgesses, "The distinctions between Virginians, Pennsylvanians, New
Yorkers, and New Englanders are no more. I am not a Virginian, but an
American." If Americans were to win their freedom, national identity
must supersede all others. "We must all hang together," said Franklin, "or
most assuredly we shall all hang separately."

Yet it is now fashionable to assert that America's greatness comes
from her diversity. A corollary is that the more diverse America becomes, the better and stronger country she becomes, and America will
not realize her true destiny until she evolves into—in the title of Ben

Wattenberg's 1991 book—*The First Universal Nation,* embracing all the races, tribes, creeds, cultures, and colors of planet Earth.

"The non-Europeanization of America is heartening news of an almost transcendental quality," Wattenberg trilled.[4] Yet one wonders: what kind of man looks with transcendental joy to a day when the people among whom he was raised have become a minority in a nation where the majority rules? This is normally a disorder of the left.

"The full-blown modern style of ethnomasochism," writes John Derbyshire, the *National Review* columnist, "is, like many other psychosocial pathologies, a product of Anglo-American progressivism. It was already showing up in its finished form among pre-boomers such as Susan Sontag (b. 1933) and Ann Dunham (b. 1942)."[5]

> We read about Ann in her son's autobiography... refusing to accompany her Indonesian husband to dinner parties with visiting American businessmen. These were her own people, Ann's husband would remind her; at which, the son tells us, "my mother's voice would rise to almost a shout. They are not my people."[6]

Ann Dunham's son is Barack Obama.

Americans who seek stricter immigration control have been charged with many social sins: racism, xenophobia, nativism. Yet none has sought to expel any fellow American based on color or creed. We have only sought to preserve the country we grew up in. Do not people everywhere do that, without being reviled? What motivates people who insist that America's doors be held open wide until the European majority has disappeared?

What is their grudge against the old America that eats at their heart?

In 1976, presidential candidate Jimmy Carter defended ethnic enclaves formed by free association and pledged not to use federal power to reengineer them.

I am not going to use the Federal Government's authority
deliberately to circumvent the natural inclination of people to
live in ethnically homogeneous neighborhoods.... I think it is
good to maintain the homogeneity of neighborhoods if they've
been established that way.[7]

To define these communities Carter used the phrase "ethnic purity": "I
have nothing against a community that's made up of people who are
Polish or Czechoslovakian or French-Canadian, or black, who are trying
to maintain the ethnic purity of their neighborhoods. This is a natural
inclination on the part of people."[8]

What Carter said of neighborhoods is what Americans who oppose
mass immigration say about their country: "This is a natural inclination
on the part of people." It is those who are so repelled by the ethnic character of the old America that they wish to see it expunged whose motivations need to be explored and explained.

When the 1992 Los Angeles riot erupted in the spring of that year,
and Koreans and whites were attacked in the worst urban violence since
the New York draft riot of 1863, Vice President Dan Quayle was in
Japan. When his host inquired if perhaps the United States was not suffering from too much diversity, Quayle responded, "I begged to differ
with my host. I explained that our diversity is our strength."[9]

One imagines the Japanese were unpersuaded. So fearful is Japan of
the diversity Dan Quayle celebrates, the Japanese refuse to open the
country to immigration, even with a birthrate that is more accurately
described as a death rate. Has Japan suffered from a lack of diversity?
Though reduced to rubble in 1945, and only the size of Montana with
fewer resources, Japan still boasts an economy one-third that of the
United States and is in some ways our superior in manufacturing and
technology.

DIVERSITY AS IDEOLOGY

All of us appreciate a diversity of restaurants and food—French, Chinese, Japanese, Italian, Mexican, Serb, Thai, and Greek, for example. This adds spice to life. A diversity of views in politics makes for more interesting debate and better decisions. Thus freedom of speech and the press are protected. Academic freedom is sheltered in colleges and universities for the same reason. We learn from hearing what we did not know and from those with whom we may not agree.

There is also a beneficial diversity of function in society. In building a home, one needs an architect, carpenters, electricians, plumbers, masons, roofers, and a foreman. In a symphony orchestra, there is a diversity of talents and instruments: strings, woodwinds, brass and percussion— violins, cellos, clarinets, trumpets, French horns, trombones, tubas, harps, all synchronized by one conductor. On an NFL team, quarterbacks have different talents than running backs. Tight ends are bigger and stronger, but slower than wide receivers. Linebackers and safeties have complementary but different duties. Place kickers and punters are specialists. The diversity with which this chapter deals is an ideological concept. As Peter Wood, executive director of the National Association of Scholars and author of *Diversity: The Invention of a Concept*, writes, *diversity* (which he italicizes) refers to a "contemporary set of beliefs...distinct from its older meanings."[10]

> *Diversity* bids us to think of America not as a single garment but as divided up into separate groups—on the basis of race, ethnicity, or sex, for starters—some of which have historically enjoyed privileges that have been denied the others.
>
> *Diversity*....is above all a political doctrine asserting that some social categories deserve compensatory privileges in light of the prejudicial ways in which members of these categories have been treated in the past and the disadvantages they continue to face.[11]

The ideology of *diversity* instructs us that, as women and people of color were discriminated against in our past, justice dictates that they receive preferential treatment in hiring, promotions, admissions, and contracts until the equality of sexes and races is achieved.

Beyond being simple justice, we are told, *diversity* is morally and socially beneficial, leading America to a better place than any nation has ever been. The exhilaration that marks the *diversity* enthusiast is akin to that of journalist Lincoln Steffens when he came home from Lenin's Russia exclaiming, "I have been over into the future—and it works!" Again, Wood writes:

> The ideal of *diversity* is that once individuals of diverse backgrounds are brought together, a transformation will take place in people's attitudes—primarily within the members of the formerly exclusive group, who will discover the richness of the newcomers' cultural background.[12]

Wood is saying that, under this ideology, as *diversity* takes hold of America, white men, whose fathers ran the country to the exclusion of women, African Americans, and Native Americans, will come to appreciate and embrace what their fathers never knew—the beauty and beneficence of *diversity*. America is striding toward a brave new world that will make her the envy and model for all mankind. Here is Wood describing the "ideal of *diversity*."

> *Diversity* will breed tolerance and respect, and because it increases the pool of skills, will enhance the effectiveness of work groups and contribute to economic prosperity. In the more extended flights of the diversiphile's imagination, *diversity* creates good will and social betterment in every direction. The African-American manager, the gay white secretary, and the Latino consultant learn from each other's distinctive cultural experience and become better workers, better citizens, better persons.[13]

In *We Are Doomed: Reclaiming Conservative Pessimism,* Derbyshire capital-
izes diversity when using it in Wood's context, and advances his own
"Diversity Theorem":

> Different populations, of different races, customs, religions
> and preferences, can be mixed together *in any number or pro-
> portions at all,* with harmonious result. Not only will the result
> be harmonious, it will be *beneficial* to all the people thus mixed.
> They will be better and happier than if they had been left to
> stagnate in dull homogeneity.
>
> A corollary to this Diversity Theorem states that if the ex-
> periment were to be carried out on a nation...then the nation
> would be made stronger and better by an increase in Diversity,
> so long as the system was controlled by properly approved and
> trained Diversity managers. It would be more peaceful, more
> prosperous, better educated, more cultivated, better able to
> defend itself against its enemies. Diversity is our strength![14]

Diversity, as Woods and Derbyshire describe it, is utopian, in that it en-
visions a nation that has never before existed. Yet, this utopian vision has
America's elite enraptured. "America's diversity is our greatest strength,"
said Bill Clinton.[15] "Diversity is one of America's greatest strengths,"
echoed George W. Bush.[16] Google the exact quote, "Diversity is our
greatest strength," and you get around twenty thousand results.

To former NATO commander Wesley Clark, a candidate for his
party's presidential nomination in 2004, "Democrats have always believed that our diversity is our greatest strength whether in our schools,
our workplaces, our government or our courts."[17] Well, not exactly, as the
general, who grew up in Arkansas, knows well. For it was his Democratic
Party that maintained segregation for a century after slavery, and his
Democratic governor Orval Faubus who, in 1957, could not tolerate the
presence of a single black student at Little Rock High School. As Wood
writes:

Once upon a time Americans encountered the world's diversity with awe, anger, prejudice, disgust, erotic excitement, pity, delight—and curiosity. Then we recast ourselves as champions of tolerant diversity, became fearful of inconvenient facts, and lost interest.[18]

Indeed, the old concept of America, as melting-pot nation, was about melding immigrant Irish, Italians, Germans, Jews, Poles, Greeks, Czechs, and Slovaks into Americans. The melting pot was about the abolition of diversity and the Americanization of immigrants, which is why our multiculturalists reject it as an instrument of cultural genocide.

THE FOUNDERS' FEARS

"In our diversity is our strength" is now an article of faith of our ruling class. To ridicule the notion as risible, unrooted in history, and an affront to common sense is to identify oneself as a reactionary or racist.

When did diversity and multiculturalism become national treasures? For this was surely not so in colonial times.

The first decision of the Jamestown settlers was to build a fort to protect themselves from the Indians they held responsible for exterminating the colony known as Roanoke. An Indian raid in 1622, resulting in the massacre of a third of all the Jamestown colonists, appeared to vindicate their judgment that "red men" were mortal enemies who must be driven out of the lands they claimed in the name of England.

The colonists were WASP supremacists. Without moral qualms, they drove the Indians over the mountains and established a society of white and Christian men and women along with African slaves. Catholics were unwelcome. Priests were put back on the boats that brought them. Virginia had been named for the "Virgin Queen" Elizabeth, who was determined to complete the work of her father, Henry VIII, who sought to end religious diversity in England by eradicating Catholicism.

America was largely settled by colonists from the British Isles. Nearly two centuries after Jamestown and Plymouth Rock, when Washington took his oath as president, the thirteen states were 99 percent Protestant. In 1790, U.S. citizenship was opened up for "free white persons" of "moral character." No others need apply.

To the English, Scots-Irish, Welsh, and Dutch, however, there had been added Germans whose presence in Pennsylvania alarmed that icon of the Enlightenment, Benjamin Franklin.

> Those who come hither are generally of the most ignorant Stupid Sort of their own Nation…and as few of the English understand the German Language, and so cannot address them either from the Press or Pulpit, 'tis almost impossible to remove any prejudices they once entertain.… Not being used to Liberty, they know not how to make a modest use of it.…
>
> Why should Pennsylvania, founded by the English, become a Colony of Aliens, who will shortly be so numerous as to Germanize us instead of our Anglifying them, and will never adopt our Language or Customs, any more than they can acquire our Complexion.[19]

With the end of the French and Indian War, German immigration receded, easing the concerns of Dr. Franklin. Yet General Washington shared his fears. In peril at Valley Forge, he did not mean to entrust the cause to immigrants: "Let none but Americans stand guard tonight."

In Federalist No. 2, John Jay looked out and saw a nation of common blood, faith, language, history, customs, culture, and principles:

> Providence has been pleased to give this one connected country to one united people—a people descended from the same ancestors, speaking the same language, professing the same religion, attached to the same principles of government, very similar in their manners and customs, and who, by their joint counsels, arms, and efforts, fighting side by side throughout a

long and bloody war, have nobly established general liberty and independence.[20]

Jay is describing the nation of Washington, Adams, Hamilton, and Jefferson, and he is saying it is our *sameness* that makes it possible for us to endure and succeed as a great nation. Jay goes on to issue this warning:

> This country and this people seem to have been made for each other, and it appears as if it was the design of Providence, that an inheritance so proper and convenient for a band of brethren, united to each other by the strongest ties, should never be split into a number of unsocial, jealous, and alien sovereignties.[21]

Here Jay expresses the fear that this country, so fitting for a "band of bretheren, united to each other by the strongest ties," could be lost, should the nation "split into a number of unsocial, jealous and alien sovereignties."

Today we embrace what our fathers feared.

Celebrants of diversity point to the Irish immigration of the 1840s and the great wave of immigration from Southern and Eastern Europe from 1890 to 1920. America, they argue, despite nativist fears, successfully integrated these diverse peoples into one nation. They ignore the crucial elements that made America work.

All these people were Europeans. All were white. Almost all were Christian. After each wave of immigration, there were long periods of little or no immigration that gave America time to assimilate the newcomers. And before they were fully assimilated, their children and grandchildren passed through deeply patriotic public and parochial schools where they were immersed in the language, literature, history, and traditions of this unique people. Today, however, those schools have been converted into madrassas of modernity where it is forbidden to invoke the faith of our fathers and American history is often taught as a series of crimes against peoples of color.

Until 1965, U.S. immigration laws were written with one goal: to pre-serve the European character of the country. During the debate on the Immigration Law of 1965, Edward Kennedy, chairman of the subcommittee conducting the hearings, was passionate in his reassurances that the new law would not break with tradition or alter the nation's ethnic character.

> [O]ur cities will not be flooded with a million immigrants an-nually. Under the proposed bill, the present level of immigra-tion remains substantially the same.... Secondly, the ethnic mix of this country will not be upset.... Contrary to the charges in some quarters, [this bill] S. 500 will not inundate America with immigrants from any other country or area, or the most populated and deprived nations of Africa and Asia.[22]

Only haters would tell such lies, Kennedy stormed: "The charges I have mentioned are highly emotional, irrational, and with little foundation in fact. They are out of line with the obligations of responsible citizenship. They breed hate of our heritage."[23]

Kennedy was assuring a nation that, in a 1965 Harris poll, said that, by two to one, it did not want any increase at all in immigration.

What has happened since 1965, the diminution and displacement of the European majority, was done against the will of the majority of Americans. For decades, Americans have told pollsters they want immi-gration restricted and illegal aliens sent home. But what Americans want no longer seems to matter.

"A FUTURE RICH WITH PROMISE"

Hua Hsu, author of "The End of White America?" awaits eagerly the day when white Americans are a minority. "For some, the disappearance of this centrifugal core heralds a future rich with promise," he writes, and quotes President Bill Clinton's "now-famous address to students at

Portland State University," where he declared, "In a little more than 50 years, there will be no majority race in the United States." Professor Hsu continues,

> Not everyone was so enthused. Clinton's remarks caught the attention of another anxious Buchanan—Pat Buchanan, the conservative thinker. Revisiting the president's speech in his 2001 book, *The Death of the West,* Buchanan wrote: "Mr. Clinton assured us that it will be a better America when we are all minorities and realize true 'diversity.' Well, those students [at Portland State] are going to find out, for they will spend their golden years in a Third World America."
>
> Today, the arrival of what Buchanan derided as "Third World America" is all but inevitable.[24]

What Clinton and Hsu see as inevitable is so only if the American people permit it to happen. Still, one wonders, why does the ascendancy and eventual rule of America by people of color mean a better America? Where is the multiracial, multiethnic country that is a better place than the country we grew up in? Everywhere we look, racially and ethnically diverse nations are tearing themselves apart.

Historians will look back in stupefaction at twentieth- and twenty-first-century Americans who believed the magnificent republic they inherited would be enriched by bringing in scores of millions from the failed states of the Third World.

Where has diversity not been a cause of division?

Is a diversity of languages a strength? Ask the Canadians and Belgians whose countries are forever on the cusp of breaking up over language differences.

"Language is only the most obvious problem introduced by diversity," writes Brookings Institution Senior Fellow Peter Skerry in "Beyond Sushiology: Does Diversity Work?" He uses "sushiology" to describe the syndrome that afflicts those who see "the extraordinary variety and quality of ethnic cuisine now available in the United States as evidence of the unalloyed benefits from our racial and ethnic diversity."[25]

In Genesis, the pride-intoxicated people of Earth decide to build a great tower to reach up to heaven—in a challenge to Yahweh.

> And the Lord said, Behold, the people is one, and they have all one language; and this they begin to do: and now nothing will be restrained from them, which they have imagined to do....
>
> [L]et us go down, and there confound their language, that they may not understand one another's speech.
>
> So the Lord scattered them abroad from thence upon the face of all the earth....
>
> Therefore is the name of it called Babel; because the Lord did there confound the language of all the earth: and from thence did the Lord scatter them abroad upon the face of all the earth.

Did the God of the Pentateuch strengthen the people he had created when he destroyed the unity of their language and scattered them to the four corners of the earth? To hear men endlessly recite this mindless mantra, "Our diversity is our strength," when tribal, ethnic, and religious diversity is tearing nations to pieces, is to recall Orwell: Only an intellectual could make a statement like that. No ordinary man could be such a fool.

THE FLIGHT FROM DIVERSITY

Do today's Americans truly cherish diversity? Why, then, when free to associate, do so many Americans separate and segregate themselves?

In his essay "Equality," Harvard professor Orlando Patterson writes that though they "have been almost wholly accepted into the public sphere of American life,"

[B]lack Americans remain remarkably excluded from most regions of the nation's private sphere. They are more segregated now than ever, have astonishingly few intimate friendships with non-blacks, and are the most endogamous group in the nation.... This apartness...has worsened even as blacks' public integration has progressed apace.[26]

In his "nation-of-cowards" address, introducing Black History Month at the Department of Justice, Attorney General Eric Holder lamented the persistence of self-segregation, half a century after the triumph of the civil rights movement:

[O]utside the workplace the situation is even more bleak in that there is almost no significant interaction between us. On Saturdays and Sundays America in the year 2009 does not, in some ways, differ significantly from the country that existed some fifty years ago. This is truly sad. Given all that we as a nation went through during the civil rights struggle it is hard for me to accept that the result of those efforts was to create an America that is more prosperous, more positively race conscious and yet is voluntarily socially segregated.[27]

Holder echoes Obama's 2008 speech on Rev. Jeremiah Wright in which he invoked the "old truism that the most segregated hour in American life occurs on Sunday morning."

Several months later, Patterson, writing in the *New York Times,* echoed Holder:

In private life blacks are almost as isolated from whites today as they were under Jim Crow.... The crucial questions that the country now faces are these: How can white citizens, who publicly embrace black citizens as athletic heroes, matinee idols, pop-music kings, talk-show queens, senators, governors

and now president, continue to shun them in their neighborhoods, schools and private lives?[28]

Patterson poses a follow-up question: "In their insistent celebration of
racial identity, how complicit are black Americans in their own social
isolation?"[29]

What Holder and Patterson are saying is that, left to themselves,
black and white separate and segregate. The evidence bears them out.
In 2010 the *New York Times* reported on the failed effort to persuade
African Americans to come and bring their children to our national
parks:

> [V]isitors to the nation's 393 national parks—there were 285.5
> million of them in 2009—are overwhelmingly non-Hispanic
> white, with blacks the least likely group to visit. That reality
> has not changed since the 1960s, when it was first identified as
> an issue. The Park Service now says the problem is linked to
> the parks' very survival.... no group avoids national parks as
> much as African-Americans.[30]

If Americans of color have no interest in the national heritage of our
national parks, a shrinking white majority will be unable to sustain
them.

No longer mandated by courts, busing for integration is being abandoned and segregation is returning to the public schools. Parents who
cannot afford private schools move away from neighborhoods when Hispanics and African Americans move in.

"It's getting to the point of almost absolute segregation in the worst of
the segregated cities—within one or two percentage points of what the
Old South used to be like," says Gary Orfield, of the Civil Rights Project.
"The biggest metro areas are the epicenters of segregation. It's getting
worse for both blacks and Latinos, and nothing is being done about it." In
the Charlotte-Mecklenburg School District of North Carolina, site of a

famous integration decision in the Nixon era, "About half of its elementary schools have 10 percent or fewer white students, or 10 percent or fewer African American students." Two-thirds of Latino and black children in major cities attend schools that are less than 10 percent white.[31]

Why? First, white students are declining as a share of public school enrollment. Second, white parents seek neighborhoods for their children to grow up in that are like the ones they themselves grew up in.

"Segregation means people are being deliberately assigned to schools based on skin color," says Roger Clegg of the Center for Equal Opportunity, "If it simply reflects neighborhoods, then it's not segregation."[32]

A LOST SENSE OF NATIONHOOD

In *The Big Sort: Why the Clustering of Like-Minded America Is Tearing Us Apart,* journalist Bill Bishop and sociologist Robert Cushing report that Americans are self-segregating not only by income and race but by social values and political beliefs. In one of their more arresting findings, they report that 27 percent of all the counties in the United States in 1976 were "landslide counties." They went by 20 points or more for Carter or Ford. By 2004, however, 48 percent of all counties went by 20 points or more to Kerry or Bush.[33]

"People prefer to be with people like themselves," writes *Washington Post* columnist Robert Samuelson.

> For all the celebration of "diversity," it's sameness that dominates. Most people favor friendship with those who have similar backgrounds, interests and values. It makes for more shared experiences, easier conversations, and more comfortable silences. Despite many exceptions, the urge is nearly universal. It's human nature.[34]

Samuelson's observation tracks that of a more famous American who discovered something about his fellow man on a pilgrimage to Mecca.

I tucked it in my mind that when I returned home I would tell Americans this observation: that where true brotherhood existed among all colors, where no one felt segregated, where there was no "superiority" complex, no "inferiority" complex—then, voluntarily, naturally, people of the same kind felt drawn together by that which they had in common.[35]

Mr. Samuelson, meet Malcolm X.

Reviewing *The Big Sort* in the *New York Times,* Scott Stossel wrote:

The three-network era of mass media, which helped create a national hearth of shared references and values, is long gone, displaced by a new media landscape that has splintered us into thousands of insular tribes.... Conservatives watch Fox; liberals watch MSNBC. Blogs and RSS feeds now make it easy to produce and inhabit a cultural universe tailored to fit your social values, your musical preferences, your view on every single political issue. We're bowling alone—or at least only with people who resemble us, and agree with us.[36]

Again, Bishop and Cushing:

We have built a country where everyone can choose the neighbors (and church and news shows) most compatible with his or her lifestyle and beliefs. And we are living with the consequences of this segregation by way of life: pockets of like-minded citizens that have become so ideologically inbred that we don't know, can't understand, and can barely conceive of "those people" who live just a few miles away.[37]

Our retreat into enclaves of race and identity is far advanced. States cannot secede as they did in 1861, but people can—to places where they hope to rediscover the sense of community they recall in an America forever gone.

In *Whitopia*, Rich Benjamin describes what white Americans are re-treating to:

> Whitopia is whiter than the nation, its respective region and
> its state. It has posted at least 6 percent population growth
> since 2000. The majority of that growth (often upward of 90
> percent) is from white migrants. And a whitopia has a *je ne sais
> quoi*—an ineffable social charisma, a pleasant look and feel.[38]

Among the new whitopias are St. George, Utah; Coeur d'Alene, Idaho; Bend, Oregon; Prescott, Arizona; and Greeley, Colorado. These mi-grants to whitopia have seceded from the new America to the old nation they grew up in.

Americans, writes Bishop, "lost their sense of a nation by accident in the sweeping economic and cultural shifts that took place after the mid-1960s. And by instinct they have sought out modern-day recreations of the 19th-century 'island-communities' in where and how they live."[39]

Bishop's point bears repeating. Since the middle of the last century we Americans have been losing our sense of nationhood, our sense that we are one nation and one people. Out of one, we have become many.

Nor are Americans out of step with the world. In a 2007 Pew poll of 45,000 people in 47 countries, "people from nations rich and poor worry about losing their traditional culture. In 46 of 47 countries, majorities say their traditional way of life is getting lost.... 73 percent of Ameri-cans fretted about the trend." Three in four U.S. respondents wanted new restrictions on immigration.[40]

Do Americans believe our diversity is our strength? Do they love the "beautiful mosaic" America is becoming? In December 2009, the *Na-tional Journal* reported on a USA Network poll by Peter Hart which found that "just 25% ... believe America's diversity is an indisputable advantage for the country [while] fifty-five percent believe discord among Americans of different stripes has worsened in the last ten years." More than half the nation says America remains excessively divided on ethnic lines while only one in twenty says race relations are no longer a problem.[41]

Among the unmentionables that explain racial separation is crime. An analysis of "single offender victimization" figures from the FBI for 2007 finds blacks committed 433,934 violent crimes against whites, eight times as many as the 55,685 that whites committed against blacks. Interracial rape is almost exclusively black-on-white, with 14,000 assaults on white women by African American males in 2007. Not one case of white sexual assault on a black female was found in the FBI study.[42] Are not such crimes of both interracial violence and sexual degradation hate crimes?

Newspapers rarely or never report such statistics. But in making decisions about where to live, shop, and socialize, people act on this reality. In retort to Eric Holder's nation-of-cowards speech, Heather Mac Donald wrote that before "Holder and his attorneys" start blaming racism for racial separation, he might glance at those crime statistics:

> For instance, the homicide rate for black men between the ages of 18 and 24 is well over ten times that of whites.... In New York City ... 83 percent of all gun assailants were black during the first six months of 2008, according to victims and witnesses, though blacks make up only 24 percent of the city's population. Add Hispanic perps and you account for 98 percent. That explains why someone might feel a sense of trepidation when approached by a group of black youths. That's not racism, it's the reality of crime.[43]

If Mac Donald's statistics are accurate, 49 of every 50 muggings and murders in New York are the work of minorities. That might explain why black folks have trouble getting a cab. Every New York cabby must know the odds, should he pick up a man of color at night. They are forty-nine to one that if he is assaulted or never makes it home his assailant will be a man of color.

In "Is Racial Profiling Racist?" *Washington Times* columnist Walter Williams, himself black, explains the practice and defends the profilers.

> If racial profiling is racism, then the cab drivers of Washington, D. C., they themselves mainly black and Hispanic, are all for it. A District taxicab commissioner, Sandra Seegars, who is black, issued a safety-advice statement urging D.C's 6,800 cabbies to refuse to pick up "dangerous-looking" passengers. She described "dangerous looking" as a young black guy...with shirttail hanging down longer than his coat, baggy pants, unlaced tennis shoes.[44]

Seegars also urged cabbies to stay out of poor black neighborhoods.

After a cabbie in New York City was shot four times by a robber wearing a hooded sweatshirt, identified by police as Hispanic, Fernando Mateo, president of the New York State Federation of Taxi Drivers, advised his drivers to profile blacks and Hispanics for their own protection. Said Mateo, "the God's honest truth is that 99 percent of the people that are robbing, stealing, killing these drivers are blacks and Hispanics."[45]

Mateo is himself black and Hispanic.

When charges of race discrimination were lodged against Papa John's pizza delivery service in St. Louis, Williams writes, more than three-fourths of the drivers were black. They refused to deliver in the neighborhoods where they lived—out of fear of muggings or worse.

Even Jesse Jackson seems to understand that racial profiling is not necessarily racist. Said the reverend: "There is nothing more painful to me at this stage in my life than to walk down the street and hear footsteps and start thinking about robbery—then turn around and see somebody white and feel relieved."[46] When Jackson attended a "Rebuild America" rally in Detroit on Labor Day in 2010, the Cadillac Escalade chauffeuring him around was stolen and stripped. Detroit Mayor Dave

Bing's official vehicle, a GMC Yukon Denali, also went missing and was found sitting on bricks, wheels and rims gone.[47]

SELF SEGREGATION

In its editorials the *New York Times* may deplore "Resegregation Now,"[48] yet what is taking place reflects the decisions of free people about where they wish to live and with whom they wish to socialize. And if ours is to remain a free society, neither Big Brother nor the social engineers should interfere with that freedom of association.

In 2009, under a banner headline, "Black Sorority Protests 'Old South' Days," the *Montgomery Advertiser* ran a story supporting Orlando Patterson's thesis about black complicity in "their own social isolation."[49]

> Tuscaloosa—Members of a black sorority at the University of Alabama had gathered for an anniversary celebration when the street in front of their house filled with white men, some wearing Confederate uniforms and carrying rebel flags.
>
> It was Kappa Alpha Order's annual parade celebrating the antebellum South, and it prompted members of the black sorority to ask university officials to stop the event in the name of racial sensitivity.[50]

What was surprising was not white students wearing Confederate uniforms and carrying the Rebel battle flag. Reenactments of Civil War battles and gatherings of Sons of Confederate Veterans are common occurrences in the South. Moreover, Kappa Alpha Order was founded in 1865 at Washington and Lee while Robert E. Lee was the college president.

What was noteworthy was the phrase "black sorority." Half a century after Governor George Wallace stood in the schoolhouse door to block integration, many of the brightest black women at the University of

Alabama still voluntarily segregate themselves in sororities. Indeed, Alpha Kappa Alpha, the sorority offended by the Rebel marchers, had just celebrated the centennial of its birth at Howard University in 1908 and invited Michelle Obama to join. AKA is one of the "Divine Nine" black sororities and fraternities that date back a century. That they endure, fifty-seven years after the *Brown* decision, testifies to the truth of what Holder had asserted: Americans remain committed to desegregated schools and sports teams, but when it comes to socializing, they prefer their own. Our political elites preach a gospel of diversity, but the people do not practice the faith in their private lives.

Still, while the self-segregated black sororities and fraternities endure, the Kappa Alpha Order, because of the incident in Tuscaloosa, has banned the wearing of Confederate uniforms at Old South week celebrations.[51]

IS DIVERSITY A STRENGTH?

Are Americans a stronger people because tens of millions of immigrants and their children speak a language other than English in their homes and our fastest growing radio and TV stations broadcast in Spanish? Do we diminish ourselves by demanding that new citizens read English and immigrant children be immersed in English in public schools?

What other nation truly believes that its diversity is its greatest strength? Great Britain is a far more diverse nation than it was in the Days of Hope and Glory of Victoria and Churchill. Is she a stronger and better nation now that London is Londonistan, now that mullahs defend Muslim bombers, now that there are race riots every year? If diversity is truly a strength, why do Scots and Welsh seek to follow the Irish into secession and independence?

Has the ethnic diversity of the Balkans been a source of strength? Is Germany stronger for the diversity the Turks brought? Is France stronger for the five to eight million alienated Muslims in the banlieues of Paris?

Do the Israelis seek to build a multiethnic society, or do they wish to preserve a land where Jews alone are welcome to come and settle? Do they welcome the return of the Palestinians who once inhabited the land? Has the religious and ethnic diversity of Lebanon—Christian and Muslim, Sunni and Shia, Arab and Druze—been a blessing? Or does its diversity portend the breakup of Lebanon?

If diversity is a strength, how have such monochromatic nations as South Korea and Japan been so successful? Does Beijing believe "diversity is our strength" as it moves millions of Han Chinese into Tibet and Xinjiang to swamp Tibetan Buddhists and Uighur Muslims?

If diversity is a blessing, why does Mexico treat Guatemalans crossing into Mexico so harshly? Are the Mexicans fools for failing to appreciate the beauty and benefits of diversity? Or are we the fools for inviting the world into our own country?

Has the ethnic diversity of Africa—Kikuyu, Luo, and Masai in Kenya; Mashona and Matabele in Zimbabwe; Zulu, Xhosa, Bantu in South Africa; Hutu and Tutsi in Rwanda and Burundi; Yoruba and Ibo in Nigeria—proven a blessing for those countries? Or has diversity been the primary cause of the massacre of millions? Would not these peoples have all been happier, had their national boundaries been drawn up along tribal lines?

"At the end of their careful review of 40 years of research on diversity (including racial and ethnic) in organizations," writes Skerry, "psychologists Katherine Williams and Charles O'Reilly conclude: 'the preponderance of empirical evidence is that diversity is likely to impede group functioning.'"[52]

Which raises some questions.

Where is the empirical evidence behind General Casey's assertion that "the strength of our Army comes from our diversity"? Is the diverse army of today really superior to Lee's Army of Northern Virginia that resisted the Union's mighty Army of the Potomac for four years? Is it superior to the U.S. Army that went ashore at Normandy? How so? Where is the evidence that an army enhances its strength when its enlisted ranks and officer corps become a mosaic of white, black, Asian, Hispanic, male, female, straight, and gay soldiers?

No one would say a surgical team or hockey team or debating team was superior because it included people of all races and ethnic groups. We would judge each team by its performance. What General Casey seems to be saying is that the strength of the U.S. Army stems from the fact that we now have a smaller share of white male soldiers. Does anyone really believe that?

In an amicus brief supporting the University of Michigan's right to discriminate against white applicants to increase racial diversity, General Motors and dozens of Fortune 500 companies declared, "There can be little doubt that racial and ethnic diversity in the senior leadership of the corporate world is crucial to our Nation's economic prospects."

After GM went belly-up, perhaps it is unfair to bring up the episode. But how does GM, de facto, become a better company if the number of white male executives who made it the greatest company on earth is reduced? And if "diversity in the senior leadership of the corporate world is crucial to our Nation's economic prospects," how did we become the greatest manufacturing and economic power in history before the coming of the Age of Diversity?

Today, there are countless thousands of bureaucrats—government, corporate, academic, media—beavering away to insure diversity in the bureaucracy, the corporate suite, the workplace, the student body, and the newsroom, who deal annually with hundreds of thousands of complaints regarding ethnic, race, and gender bias. The cost of enforcement and compliance runs into the scores of billions of dollars. Eight years ago, *Forbes* put the cost of diversity training at $10 billion.[53] Enormous sums have been transferred from companies to diversity lawyers and aggrieved workers in class-action suits. In December 2010, Congress voted to send 75,000 black farmers and ex-farmers an average of $50,000 each to compensate them for alleged racial discrimination, two decades ago, by the Department of Agriculture.[54]

In May 2011, the Department of Agriculture voluntarily offered $1.3

billion to Mexican American and women farmers as compensation for the discrimination they suffered in the previous thirty years, plus $160 million in loan forgiveness. Lawyers for the Mexican Americans farmers protested. The $50,000-per-farmer settlements offered were below those of African Americans, some of whom were getting up to $250,000. Moreover, Mexican-American farmers had to produce the applications they made for USDA loans that were denied, a standard that black farmers did not have to meet.[55]

Frederick Pfaeffle, the department's deputy assistant secretary for civil rights, met with farmers in Florida to expedite the settlements. However, as the Associated Press reported, "No farmers in Florida had come forward with discrimination allegations."[56] The search for victims continues.

"Every large company or institution must have a vice president for diversity—if not, as is increasingly the case, a chief diversity officer," writes John Derbyshire. "The CDO at Washington State University has an annual budget of $3 million and a full-time staff of 25."[57]

All this bureaucracy makes us less free. Does it make us a stronger and better country? No, answers Thomas A. Kochan, one of our more respected human resource scholars. After a five-year study of diversity's impact on business, he concluded, "The diversity industry is built on sand. The business case rhetoric for diversity is simply naive and overdone."[58]

Diversity training itself may even damage corporate efficiency, writes Hans Bader in Openmarket.org, for it often "triggers workplace conflict and lawsuits, by compelling employees to talk about contentious racial or sexual issues, with resulting acrimony, and remarks that are misinterpreted or perceived as racially or sexually biased."[59] Anyone who has been in a debate on a racially charged issue like the false allegations of the rape of a black woman by members of the Duke lacrosse team knows how fast the room temperature can rise.

Even President Obama cannot satisfy the diversiphiles. His press office, though integrated, failed to pass muster with CNN's Roland Martin:

I got an e-mail Tuesday listing all of the various press folks and contact information, and hardly any African-Americans or Hispanics were listed. Granted, the deputy press secretary is African-American and the director of broadcast media is Hispanic. That's not sufficient.... Just because there's a black president doesn't mean that issues like diversity should be cast aside.[60]

One wonders what Roland Martin is complaining about, for whatever the conditions in Barack Obama's press office, affirmative action has been flourishing in the federal government—even under George W. Bush.

Though just 10 percent of the U.S. civilian labor force, African Americans comprise 18 percent of all federal workers, 25 percent of the employees at Treasury and Veterans Affairs, 31 percent of State Department employees, 37 percent of Department of Education employees, and 38 percent of HUD employees. They comprise 42 percent of the employees at the EEOC and the Pension Benefit Guaranty Corporation, 55 percent of employees at the Government Printing Office, and 82 percent of the employees at the Court Services and Offender Supervision Agency.[61]

The federal Office of Personnel Management has hiring "targets" for women, Hispanics, African Americans, and Asian Americans—but none for white males.

When the Obama administration proposed shutting down Fannie Mae and Freddie Mac, the mortgage giants whose losses of $150 billion have had to be borne by taxpayers, the *Washington Post* warned, in a story headlined "Winding Down Fannie and Freddie Could Put Minority Careers at Risk," that 44 percent of Fannie's employees and 50 percent of Freddie's were people of color.[62]

And if diversity is so beneficial, why do so many famous diversiphiles pay premium prices to live in communities far from the loveliness of which they sing? Writing to Senator Moynihan, James Q. Wilson saw desegregation as both complementary to and compatible with the freedom of people to separate and socialize with their own.

Erecting walls that separate "us" from "them" is a necessary correlate to morality since it defines the scope within which sympathy, fairness, and duty operate. The chief wall is the family/clan/village, but during certain historical periods, ethnicity defines the wall. The great achievement of Western culture since the Enlightenment is to make many of us peer over the wall and grant some respect to people outside it; the great failure of Western culture is to deny that walls are inevitable or important.[63]

In short, good fences make good neighbors.

COURT SEATS AS SET-ASIDES

For decades, the Supreme Court has been the target of demands for greater diversity and a broader representation of women and minorities. President Obama's nomination of Sonia Sotomayor was hailed as a great step forward.

Nixon and Ford were the last presidents to maintain WASP hegemony on the Court. Nixon sent up six nominees, Ford one. All seven were White Anglo-Saxon Protestants: Warren Burger, Clement Haynsworth, Harrold Carswell, Harry Blackmun, Lewis Powell, William Rehnquist, and John Paul Stevens.

Even before Nixon, however, Democrats were into the "new" ethnic politics. Most of the older ethnics—Germans, Irish, Italians, Poles, Slovaks, Greeks—were out. Since 1940, no Democratic president has named an Irish Catholic to the Court. No Democratic president has ever named an Italian or Polish Catholic. The party of the Daleys, Rizzos, and Rostenkowskis is dead. Not since JFK named Byron R. White half a century ago has any Democratic president named a white Christian man or woman to the Court, though white Christians remain the vast majority of all Americans.

Seven names have been sent up since 1962 by Democratic presidents:

Arthur Goldberg, Abe Fortas, Thurgood Marshall, Ruth Bader Ginsburg, Stephen Breyer, Sonia Sotomayor, and Elena Kagan—one African
American, one Puerto Rican, and five Jews. This is the Democratic Party's idea of diversity on the Court. It might also be labeled: no white
Christians need apply.

Under President Reagan, Republicans got into the diversity game,
though their approach seemed more inclusive. Reagan's first choice was
Sandra Day O'Connor, the first woman nominated. His second choice
was Antonin Scalia, the first Italian American. His third was Robert
Bork, a white Protestant. When Bork was rejected by the Senate, Reagan
chose Douglas Ginsburg, a Jewish colleague of Bork's on the U.S. Appellate Court for the District of Columbia. When Ginsburg's name was
pulled because of a marijuana incident in college, Reagan went with an
Irish-Catholic from his home state of California, Anthony Kennedy.

George H. W. Bush nominated David Souter, a white Protestant, and
the African American Clarence Thomas. In replacing Rehnquist and
O'Connor with John Roberts and Sam Alito, George W. Bush replaced
two white Protestants with two white Catholics, one of whom is only the
second Italian American nominated. Thus the Court today consists of
six Catholics and three Jews, but not a single Protestant for the first time
in U.S. history, although Protestants make up one-half of our entire
population. The historic character of this change was noted by the Associate Dean of Notre Dame Law School, Richard Garnett:

> When the Supreme Court first met in 1790, there were only
> about 30,000 Catholics and 2,500 Jews in the United States.
> The Court's first Catholic did not join the bench for almost 50
> years, with Roger Taney's selection in 1836. It would be 80
> more years until the confirmation of the first Jewish justice,
> Louis Brandeis.[64]

The day confirmation hearings began for Elena Kagan, Harvard law
professor Noah Feldman, in a *New York Times* op-ed, "The Triumphant

Decline of the WASP," rhapsodized over our first WASP-free Supreme Court. "It is a cause for celebration that no one much cares about the nominee's religion," wrote Feldman, congratulating the WASPs on their dethronement.[65]

> Unlike almost any other dominant ethnic, racial or religious group in world history, white Protestants have ceded their socioeconomic power by hewing voluntarily to the values of merit and inclusion, values now shared broadly by Americans of different backgrounds. The decline of the Protestant elite is actually its greatest triumph.[66]

Religion may not be an issue to Professor Feldman, but it is to others. For the most underrepresented group on the Supreme Court is evangelical Christians. More numerous than Catholics and Jews combined, who hold all nine seats, Evangelicals have not held a single seat in modern times. George W. Bush tried to remedy this with his nomination of Harriet Miers, but failed.

While Republicans demand strict constructionists and Democrats demand justices who will retain *Roe v. Wade*, tribal politics is now the norm for both parties in making nominations to the Court and other positions of power. And, for the first time, fewer than half of the nine cabinet-level officers and fewer than half of the top White House aides are white males. Minorities and women are coming to dominate the federal government as they do the Democratic Party.

This "reflects both the changing face of the nation," said ex-White House communications director Anita Dunn, "as well as this president's very strong belief that different backgrounds do make for stronger decision-making." Princeton University's presidential scholar Fred Greenstein said that the diversity of Obama's power elite "suggests a true changing of the guard."[67] Indeed, throughout the federal government, civilian and military, the guard is changing.

DUMBING DOWN THE NAVY

"Naval Academy Professor Challenges Rising Diversity," ran the head-line.[68] The positive character of the opening paragraphs caused one to wonder: Had some faculty sorehead protested because more minority youngsters were coming to Annapolis?

> Of the 1,230 plebes who took the oath of office at the Naval Academy in Annapolis this week, 435 were members of minority groups. It is the most racially diverse class in the nation's 164-year history.
>
> Academy leaders say it's a top priority to build a student body that reflects the racial makeup of the Navy and the nation.[69]

Eventually the *Washington Post* got around to the charge by Bruce Fleming, an English professor at Annapolis for twenty-two years, that a double standard had been used to create a class that was 35 percent minority. According to Fleming, who once sat on the board of admissions, white applicants to the Academy had to have all As and Bs and scores of 600 or higher on both the English and math parts of their Scholastic Aptitude Test to qualify for a "slate" of ten applicants, from which one is drawn. But if you checked a box indicating you are an African American, Hispanic, Native American, or Asian:

> SAT scores to the mid 500s with quite a few Cs in classes... typically produces a vote of qualified...with direct admission to Annapolis. They're in and given a pro forma nomination to make it legit....Minority applicants with scores and grades down to the 300s, and Cs and Ds also come, though after a remedial year at our taxpayer-supported remedial school, the Naval Academy Preparatory School.[70]

If this is true, the Naval Academy is running a two-tiered admissions system of the kind that kept Jennifer Gratz out of the University of Michigan and was declared unconstitutional by the Supreme Court. If true, the Academy is racially discriminating against hundreds of white students every year, who studied their whole lives for the honor of an appointment to the U.S. Naval Academy. If true, what Annapolis is doing is worse, because it was premeditated and programmed, than what the New Haven city government did in denying Frank Ricci and other white firefighters the promotions they earned in competitive exams. At least New Haven could say it acted out of fear of being sued.

Yet, the Chief of Naval Operations and Academy superintendent appear proud of what they are doing. Fleming quotes CNO Admiral Gary Roughead as saying, "diversity is the number one priority" at the Naval Academy.[71] Roughead's predecessor, Chairman of the Joint Chiefs Admiral Mike Mullins, has described diversity as a "strategic imperative." The Academy website calls diversity "our highest personnel priority."[72] Superintendent Vice Admiral Jerry Fowler has been quoted as saying he wants graduating classes that "looked like" the fleet, where 42 percent of enlisted personnel are nonwhite.[73]

A recent incident involving the elite color guard at Annapolis testifies to the absurd lengths to which our politically correct Naval Academy will go to remain in sync with the temper of the times.

> Leaders of the U.S. Naval Academy tinkered with the composition of the color guard that appeared at a World Series game last month [November 2009] so the group would not be exclusively white and male.... The net result was that one of the six who marched on Yankee Stadium's field, Midshipman 2nd Class Hannah Allaire, was selected because her presence would make the service academy look more diverse before a national audience.[74]

What would Nimitz, Spruance, and "Bull" Halsey think of this?

Academy graduates and retired officers were outraged at the removal of a midshipman from color guard honors because of his race and gender. Yet, in *Military Officer,* Roughead described today's Navy officer corps, NCOs, and civilian leadership as too male and too white: "If you look at the Navy today, it looks like America, but if we look at just the officers, I see a bunch of white guys. The same is true for our senior enlisted and senior civilians. The nation will be more diverse in 2040 and I believe the Navy must look like its nation."[75] Is it also the admiral's goal to have the navy consist of 50 percent women and 27 percent folks over 60, with a significant fraction of gays and lesbians? Because that is what the admiral will have to shoot for if he wants the navy to "look like its nation." Or do we want the finest navy we can put to sea without regard to race, color, creed, or political correctness?

How do Roughead's diversity midshipmen do at Annapolis?

They are overrepresented, says Fleming, in "pre-college lower track courses, mandatory tutoring programs and less-challenging majors. Many struggle to master basic concepts."[76] Though unqualified for college work, they will soon be operating the most complex weapons systems in the history of naval warfare: carriers, Aegis cruisers, and nuclear submarines. What would Admiral Hyman ("Why Not the Best?") Rickover, the tough-minded genius who built our nuclear navy, think of Roughead's affirmative-action fleet?

"[W]e're dumbing down the Naval Academy," says Fleming, and "we're dumbing down the officer corps." Supporting his contention, 22 percent of incoming plebes in 2009 had SAT scores in math below 600, as compared to 12 percent in 2008.[77] This is also an issue of justice. If hundreds of Hispanic and black youth were rejected by the Naval Academy, year in and year out, though they had superior grades and SAT scores, Roughead and Fowler would be explaining to a congressional committee why they ought not to be relieved of their posts for blatant race discrimination.

In July 2010, the *Washington Times* unearthed an e-mail from a "Diversity Accountability" admiral to flag officers, directing them to prepare a list to "identify our key performers by name," as CNO Roughead "is interested in who are the diverse officers with high potential and what is the plan for their career progression. He may ask what is being done within to ensure they are considered for key follow on billets within the Navy." The message added, "The list must be held very closely."

Of course it must, for it amounts, as the *Times* wrote, to "blatant invidious discrimination.... If you are a white male, it might be time to set sail and seek opportunities elsewhere."[78]

Were this being done to promote white officers over black officers, those responsible would be instantly cashiered. The secrecy with which the navy is doing this testifies to the shamefulness of it all. Yet the navy only seems to be following Ivy League tradition.

BIAS, BIGOTRY, AND IVY

A dozen years ago, the *Wall Street Journal* carried an essay by a Jewish Harvard graduate, Ron Unz, about racial and religious underrepresentation at our elite colleges. According to Unz, at Harvard, Hispanic, and black enrollment had reached 7 percent and 8 percent, slightly less than their respective 10 and 12 percent of the population. And this had been a cause of protests by black and Hispanic students demanding proportional representation.

Unz also found, however, that nearly 20 percent of the student body was Asian, and 25 to 33 percent was Jewish. Asians were then 3 percent of the U.S. population and Jewish Americans 2.5 percent. When Unz, himself Jewish, factored in foreign students, athletes, children of alumni and faculty, what emerged was a student body where white Christians, then 70 percent of the U.S. population, were down to 25 percent of Harvard's enrollment.[79]

The composition of the student bodies at Yale, Princeton, Columbia, Berkeley, and Stanford was much the same, wrote Unz. And as Hispanics, Asians, blacks, and Jewish Americans vote heavily Democratic, the

picture that emerged was of an Ivy League elite salving its social conscience by cheating white Christians out of first-class tickets into society's top tier, and giving them instead to Harvard's preferred minorities.

Nor is this a minor matter, for the Ivy League preselects America's
leaders. Michelle and Barack Obama are where they are because, in getting into Princeton, Columbia, and Harvard Law, and onto law review,
they benefited from affirmative action, as did Sonia Sotomayor at
Princeton and Yale Law School.

Barack Obama himself conceded the point in 1990, when, as president of *Harvard Law Review,* he wrote in defense of its affirmative action
policy:

> As someone who has undoubtedly benefited from affirmative
> action programs during my academic career, and as someone
> who may have benefited from the Law Review's affirmative ac-
> tion policy when I was selected to join the Review last year, I
> have not personally felt stigmatized.[80]

These Ivy League schools "act as a natural springboard to elite careers in law, medicine, finance and technology," wrote Unz, and "many
of these commanding heights of American society seem to exhibit a
similar skew in demographic composition."[81] Exactly. If a Philadelphia
bricklayers union or Alabama police department set aside as many slots
for their own kids as Ivy League schools do for the children of faculty
and alumni and their favored minorities, they would have the Justice
Department breathing down their necks. But what is forbidden in fly-
over country is permissible, even praiseworthy, at Harvard and Yale.

Where does this leave Middle America?

From the Naval Academy to the Ivy League, the white working and
middle class is being made to pay disproportionately for America's past
sins. If the admissions policies of all the elite colleges and graduate
schools are structured so that half the students are Asian, Jewish, and
the progeny of previous graduates, and another fourth come in through

affirmative action, while white Christians are always underrepresented, there is no doubt as to who will be running the country and who will be riding in the back of the bus.

When Unz's analysis appeared, A. Kenneth Ciongoli, president of the National Italian American Foundation, wrote:

> Euro-Catholics, the American middle class, have paid the price ... of affirmative action, while the establishment perpetrators have hypocritically protected themselves.... Italian Americans, 8 percent of America's population, are 3 percent of Ivy League student bodies and less than 1 percent of the faculties.[82]

Italian Americans were more underrepresented at Harvard than were Hispanics or African Americans.

Growing up Catholic, one knew the Ivy League was inhospitable terrain. Few Ivy League recruiters showed up at Catholic high schools to offer scholarships to deserving boys. In 2009 a study by Princeton University sociologists Thomas Espenshade and Alexandria Radford confirmed that a deep bias against white conservative Christians pervades America's elite colleges.

The Espenshade-Radford study "draws from ... the National Study of College Experience ... gathered from eight highly competitive private colleges and universities (entering freshman SAT scores: 1360)," writes Princeton's Russell K. Nieli, who summarized the findings. When admissions officers at elite colleges talk of diversity, Nieli writes, what they mean is that the African American contingent on campus should be 5 to 7 percent and Hispanics about equal. And to achieve these goals, the discrimination practiced against white and Asian kids is astounding. As Nieli puts it, "To have the same chance of gaining admission as a black student with a SAT score of 1100, an Hispanic student otherwise equally matched in background characteristics would have to have 1230, a white student a 1410, and an Asian student a 1550."[83]

Was this what the civil rights movement was about, requiring boys and girls whose parents came from Taiwan, Korea, or Vietnam to get a perfect SAT score of 1600 to be given equal consideration with a Nigerian or a Haitian kid who gets 1150? What are the historic and moral arguments for discriminating against students whose parents came from Poland in favor of those whose parents came from Puerto Rico?

Another form of bigotry prevalent among our academic elite is a throwback to the WASP ascendancy. While Ivy League recruiters prefer working-class to affluent black kids with the same test scores, with white kids the opposite is true. White kids from poor families, who score as well as those from wealthy families, not only get no break, they appear to be the least desirable of all students.

While applicants are given points for their extracurricular activities, especially leadership roles and honors, if you played a leading role in Future Farmers of America, 4-H Clubs, or junior ROTC, leave it off your resume or you may be blackballed. "Excelling in these activities is 'associated with 60 or 65 percent lower odds on admissions,'" Nieli writes, adding: "Poor Whites Need Not Apply" seems to be the unwritten rule for admissions officers at America's top colleges.[84]

At our most celebrated universities, diversity is a code word for their own private prejudices. For these schools have zero interest in a diversity that would embrace:

> born-again Christians from the Bible belt, students from Appalachia and other rural and small-town areas, people who have served in the U.S. military, those who have grown up on farms or ranches, Mormons, Pentecostals, Jehovah's Witnesses, lower-middle-class Catholics, working class "white ethnics," social and political conservatives, wheelchair users, married students, married students with children, or older students first starting into college after raising children.[85]

As Nieli writes, "Students in these categories are often very rare at the most competitive colleges, especially the Ivy League." Furthermore,

"Lower-class whites prove to be all-around losers. At elite schools, they are rarely accepted. Lower-class Asians, Hispanics and blacks are seven-to-ten times more likely to get in with the same scores."[86]

That blatant bigotry against white Christians is rampant in 2010 at institutions that prattle about how progressive they are is disgusting. That Republicans who purport to speak for a Middle America whose families bear the brunt of this bigotry remain silent is shameful. In an essay, "Diversity and the Myth of White Privilege," Senator James Webb wrote of the hardships of the Southern and Appalachian peoples whence his Scots-Irish ancestors came and called for an end to discrimination against them:

> Nondiscrimination laws should be applied equally among all citizens, including those who happen to be white.... Our government should be in the business of enabling opportunities for all, not in picking winners. It can do so by ensuring that artificial distinctions such as race do not determine outcomes.[87]

Our most competitive public and private colleges and universities benefit from tax dollars through grants and student loans. The future flow of these funds should be made contingent on Harvard, Yale, and all the rest ending practices that went out at Little Rock Central High in 1957.

Harvard's penitence for its past sins against minorities of color, however, is all-pervasive. Having discovered a decade ago that of the 750 oil portraits hanging in libraries, dining commons, and undergraduate residences, all but two were of white men or women, Harvard has been frantically hanging portraits of blacks, Asians, Hispanics, and other people of color all over campus to produce the effect of a rainbow coalition of academic icons.[88]

Yet, again, what is the social impact of ever-greater racial, ethnic, religious, and cultural diversity on our nation? Has it made us a more united, cooperative, and caring people?

DEPLETED SOCIAL CAPITAL

"Americans of all ages, all conditions, and all dispositions constantly form associations," Tocqueville marveled:

> They have not only commercial and manufacturing associations…but associations of a thousand other kinds.…Wherever at the head of some new undertaking you see the government in France, or a man of rank in England, in the United States you will be sure to find an association.[89]

What explains this American trait—to associate and cooperate for a common goal? Tocqueville thought it was because we had no aristocracy, no hereditary community of privileged and powerful men who were expected to unite people dependent upon them. An aristocracy was lacking in America, said Tocqueville, due to "equality of conditions."

> Amongst democratic nations, all the citizens are independent and feeble; they can hardly do anything by themselves, and none of them can oblige his fellow-men to lend him their assistance. They all, therefore, become powerless if they do not learn to voluntarily help each other.[90]

This tendency to come together for common goals is an essential element of what Robert Putnam, author of *Bowling Alone,* calls "social capital." According to the Heritage Foundation's Jason Richwine, who took Putnam's classes at Harvard, Putnam defined social capital as "social networks and the associated norms of reciprocity and trustworthiness."[91]

"Social capital turns out to be an exceptionally valuable commodity," writes Richwine. "Building complex networks of friends and associates, trusting others to keep their word, and maintaining social norms

and expectations all grease the wheels of business by enabling cooperation."[92]

When social capital in a community is high, adds Richwine,

> People...tend to have more friends, care more about their
> community, and participate in civic causes. Where social capi-
> tal is greater, Putnam says, "children grow up healthier, safer
> and better educated; people live longer, happier lives; and de-
> mocracy and the economy work better."[93]

When social capital evaporates, we enter Hobbes's world, where it is every man for himself and let the devil take the hindmost.

In *Bowling Alone*, Putnam perceived a lowering of the reservoir of social capital since the 1950s—a growing separation of Americans from
one another, a withdrawal into the self, alienation, and rising levels of
distrust. Social capital was drying up, Putnam concluded, and undertook a massive study to learn why. "E Pluribus Unum: Diversity and
Community in the 21st Century" is the title of Putnam's five-year study.
His conclusions make hash of the cliché "Our diversity is our strength."

After thirty thousand interviews, Putnam concluded that ethnic and
racial diversity devastates communities. In diverse communities, people
not only do not trust strangers, they do not trust their own kind. They
withdraw into themselves, they support community activity less, they
vote less. "People living in ethnically diverse settings," said Putnam, "appear to 'hunker down,' that is, to pull in like a turtle."[94]

In October 2006, the *Financial Times* reported on Putnam's findings of
the social devastation that diversity has wrought.

> A bleak picture of the corrosive effects of ethnic diversity has
> been revealed in research by Harvard University's Robert
> Putnam, one of the world's most influential political scientists.
> His research shows that the more diverse a community is, the

less likely its inhabitants are to trust anyone—from their
next-door neighbour to the mayor.[95]

"Prof Putnam," said the *FT,* "found trust was lowest in Los Angeles, 'the
most diverse human habitation in human history.' "[96] In diverse cities
and towns people tend to:

> withdraw even from close friends, to expect the worst from
> their community and its leaders, to volunteer less, give less to
> charity and work on community projects less often, to regis-
> ter to vote less, to agitate for social reform more but have less
> faith they can actually make a difference, and to huddle un-
> happily in front of the television.[97]

"Putnam adds a crushing footnote," writes columnist John Leo. His findings "may underestimate the real effects of diversity on social withdrawal."[98]

Confirming Putnam, in 2011, *Travel and Leisure* revealed in its annual
readers' survey that New York had been replaced as the "rudest city" in
America by what was once the sunny, laid-back capital of Southern California, Los Angeles. And though L.A. is the second largest city in America, every NFL team that ever moved there has eventually moved out
for lack of public support. The L.A. Rams moved to Anaheim and then
St. Louis. The L.A. Chargers moved to San Diego. The L.A. Raiders
came from Oakland, and then moved back.

DIVERSITY'S DOWNSIDE

And Putnam is not alone. After Obama's speech on race in Philadelphia
in 2008, the *New York Times*'s Eduardo Porter reviewed a series of studies
by economists and academics confirming Putnam's findings and added a
conclusion of his own: "Racial and ethnic diversity undermine support
for public investment in social welfare."[99]

Harvard economists Alberto Alesina and Edward Glaeser traced the gap in social spending between Europe and America—Europe's is far higher—"to the United States' more varied racial and ethnic mix."[100] In Europe, people believe that money spent on government programs will go to people like themselves. Americans suspect it will not.

Why, then, do Americans give more than Europeans to charity? In philanthropy one can be more certain the money will go to those one wishes to help. Harvard economist Erzo F. P. Luttmer found that support for welfare increases when recipients belong to the same racial group as taxpayers.

A study of charity by Notre Dame economist Daniel Hungerman "found that all-white congregations became less charitably active as the share of black residents in the local community grows." A study by Alesina, Reza Baqir of the IMF, and William Easterly of New York University found that municipal spending—on roads, sewage, education, and trash clearance—is smaller in racially diverse cities. A 2003 study by Julian Betts and Robert Fairlie of the University of California "found that for every four immigrants who arrived in public high schools, one native student switched to a private school."[101]

The elites love diversity in the abstract. In reality, it seems no one does. Putnam's findings are echoed by criminologists Jerome Skolnick and David Bailey: "Police-community reciprocity can be achieved only when there is a genuine bonding of interests between the police and the served citizenry.... That may turn out to be progressively difficult to accomplish in demographically complex urban areas, with their increasingly ethnic diversity."[102] Have not such episodes as the accusation of "racist cops" in the L.A. trial that acquitted O. J. Simpson, to the charges of "racial profiling" against New Jersey state troopers, to the uproar over the police shooting of Amadou Diallo in the Gotham of Rudy Giuliani, underscored this point?

"By making racially diverse societies out of previously homogeneous ones," writes political scientist Gary Freeman, "migration has complicated political and social cleavages."[103] Freeman is saying that the country of the Eisenhower-Kennedy era has been balkanized politically and socially by a mass immigration no one ever voted for. Arthur Schlesinger underscored the point in *The Disuniting of America:* "The hostility of one tribe for another is among the most instinctive human reactions.... Mass migrations have produced mass antagonisms since the beginning of time."[104]

Putnam's conclusion is ominous: a diversity of races and ethnic groups in a society risks disintegration of that society. Yet America is on track to add 130 million people in four decades, mostly Third World immigrants and their children. Every U.S. city will resemble Los Angeles today. And Putnam found Los Angeles to be the textbook case of a multiracial, multiethnic, multilingual stew in which the levels of suspicion and distrust were higher than he had ever measured anywhere before. Adds Richwine:

> Looking at his list of the most trusting places, Putnam found whole states such as New Hampshire and Montana, rural areas in West Virginia and East Tennessee, and cities such as Bismarck, North Dakota, and Fremont, Michigan. Among the least trusting places were the cities of Los Angeles, San Francisco, and Houston. The most trusting places tended to be homogeneous white, while the least trusting places were highly diverse.[105]

Although Putnam's finding that ethnic diversity causes community tensions and social disintegration has been known for years, U.S. leaders seem oblivious to the risks they are taking with our national unity.

"Consider how surprising this is," Richwine writes, noting that diversity has become a declared national goal:

> Achieving diversity, especially ethnic diversity, is an explicit goal of all major corporations, universities and government agencies. The U.S. Supreme Court has declared that diversity is a "compelling state interest" that overrides legal prohibitions on race-based school admissions. Top politicians routinely utter the phrase "Our diversity is our strength" in speeches.[106]

Remarkable. Our elites, who vacation at beaches and ski resorts and send their children to schools that are predominantly white, celebrate a racial diversity that fifty years of white flight, common sense, and social science tell us may make an end of our country. Such is the power of ideology to blind men to the evidence of their own eyes. Whom the gods would destroy they first make mad.

A QUESTION OF POWER

Some contend that naïveté and utopianism cannot explain the relentless drive to abolish America's majority, that malevolence and a will to power are at work. Conservative scholar Paul Gottfried writes:

> Multiculturalists speak incessantly about tolerance, but not everyone is to be assigned the same expressive and cultural rights. Those who are awarded victim status by virtue of a group affiliation have preferential rights to self-identity, whereas those identified with repression, such as Southern whites in America, are accorded no right to a sense of pride in a shared past.[107]

To the late columnist Sam Francis, like egalitarianism, multicultur-alism was "a deliberate device by which the power-hungry can subvert a culture, whose moral codes deny them power, and build an alternative culture, whose different moral codes yield power for themselves." Our cultural elite allies itself with those out to overthrow the old Christian order—ethnic militants, feminists, atheists—anticipating they will ride the revolution to power. They are succeeding. Our traditional Christian culture has been driven from the temple of our civilization. "By enforc-ing 'diversity' as both an ideal and an actual practice through affirmative action, forced integration, mass immigration, and multiculturalism," wrote Francis, "the dominant culture undermines ... the traditional cul-ture and renders its continued functioning impossible." He concludes:

> [T]he weakening of families, the erosion of communities, the inversion of sexual morality, and all the other chants of the litany of decline.... are symptoms of the decadence of traditional culture...but they are also signs of the triumph of the dominant culture, which regards them at worst as insignificant irritants or at best as indications of impending liberation from traditional restraints, and the defeat of its adversary, traditional culture.[108]

Francis quotes Nietzsche: "The values of the weak prevail because the strong have taken them over as devices of leadership," adding, "What Nietzsche grasped and what most modern conservatives, who dislike Nietzsche almost as much as Karl Marx and Hillary Clinton, don't grasp is that what looks like decline, decadence and decay to conservatives appears to the champions of such trends as progress and the birth of a new civilization."[109] In short, this is no accident, comrade.

A decade ago, in *Coloring the News: How Political Correctness Has Corrupted American Journalism,* columnist William McGowan concluded that "diversity is the new religion."[110] Reviewing McGowan's latest book, historian H. A. Scott Trask wrote that he had understated the case. Diversity, wrote Trask, is a "state religion, the new faith of the clerical class and a means of social control of the plutocracy."[111] To disparage diversity is punishable heresy.

DIVERSITY'S DEADLY SIDE

Nidal Malik Hasan was two men. One was the proud army major who wore battle fatigues to mosque; the other, the proud Arab American who wore Muslim garb in civilian life. What brought Hasan's two identities into conflict was his conviction that Iraq and Afghanistan were immoral wars and his shock that he was to be deployed to serve in the Afghan war against fellow Muslims, a sin against Allah. Hasan was torn.

Which was his higher loyalty? Which, in Michael Vlahos's phrase, was his "fighting identity"?

Hasan told friends he was "a Muslim first and an American second." On November 5, 2009, when he told his neighbor, "I am going to do good work for God" and gave her his Koran, the call of jihad had prevailed over his oath of loyalty as an army officer.[112]

Reportedly shouting "Allahu Akbar!" as he fired, Hasan killed thirteen and wounded twenty-nine U.S. soldiers at Fort Hood, Texas. [113] An Internet posting over the name "Nidal Hasan" had equated suicide bombers with Medal of Honor winners who fall on grenades to save fellow soldiers.

Although this was an act of wartime treason and terrorism, Hasan saw himself as a hero-martyr who had put God and faith above his allegiance to a nation waging immoral wars against Muslim peoples.

Such conflicts of loyalties are not uncommon in war.

President Woodrow Wilson feared that if he took America into the European war on the side of Britain, Irish Americans would rise in protest and German Americans march on Washington. FDR was so fearful that the blood ties of resident Japanese would trump any loyalty to the United States, he ordered 110,000 transferred out of California to detention camps.

Among American Muslims, Hasan is atypical, but not alone. Other Muslims have been apprehended plotting terror attacks. In Arkansas in 2008, a Muslim shot two soldiers at a recruitment center. In Kuwait, before the invasion of Iraq, a Muslim sergeant threw a grenade and fired into the tent of his commanding officer, killing two and wounding fourteen.

Why didn't the army discharge Hasan, whose extreme views were known? "Army specialists were warned about the radicalization of Major Nidal Malik Hasan years before [the massacre]," says the *Boston Globe,* "but did not act in part because they valued the rare diversity of having a Muslim psychiatrist, military investigators wrote in previously undisclosed reports." The reports concluded that "because the Army had attracted only one other Muslim psychiatrist in addition to Hasan since 2001, 'it is possible some were afraid' of losing such diversity 'and thus were willing to overlook Hasan's deficiencies as an officer.'"[114]

Our diversity cult may have been responsible for the worst massacre on a U.S. military base in memory.

"It may be hard to comprehend the twisted logic that led to this tragedy," said President Obama.[115] But why? To John Derbyshire, the rationale was clear.

> [I do not] find Hasan's logic twisted or hard to comprehend. His loyalty was to Islam; he believed America to be making war on Islam; therefore his loyalty commanded him to kill Americans. Seems perfectly logical to me—a darn sight more logical than the Army continuing to promote him long after they knew what was in his head.[116]

Major Hasan's massacre should rivet our attention on the issue of dual loyalties in the hearts of men in a country wedded to the idea that the greater our religious, racial, and ethnic diversity, the more moral a people we become.

What Hasan saw as a higher loyalty to Islam moved him to murder fellow soldiers. What Alger Hiss saw as a higher loyalty to his political faith, Communism, moved him to transfer America's secrets to Soviet agents in Stalin's time. What Jonathan Pollard saw as his sacred identity as a Jew moved him to betray his oath, loot America's vital secrets, and transfer them to an Israeli agent.

Homegrown Americans have been responsible for the massacres of fellow Americans from Oklahoma City to Columbine to Tucson, where six were killed and thirteen wounded, including Congresswoman Gabrielle Giffords. But unassimilated immigrants have also been responsible for mass murder.

The 1993 Long Island railroad massacre where six died and nineteen were wounded was the work of Jamaican Colin Ferguson, who hated whites. The Virginia Tech slaughter where thirty-two died and twenty-five were wounded was carried out by a Korean student. The massacre at the Binghamton immigration center in 2009, where thirteen people were shot to death, was the work of Jiverly Wong, a Chinese man from Vietnam. Asked by a fellow worker if he liked the New York Yankees, Wong replied, "No. I don't like that team. I don't like America. America sucks."[117]

No longer are we one nation and one people. Tens of millions have arrived, and more are coming, whose loyalties remain to the countries they left behind and the faiths they carry in their hearts. And if, in our "Long War" against "Islamofascism," we are perceived as trampling upon their true nations, faiths, or kinfolk, they will see us, as Hasan came to see us, as the enemy of their sacred identity, the enemy of what they hold most dear.

Years ago, the concept of America as melting pot was rejected by an Establishment that now rhapsodizes about the most multiracial, multiethnic, multicultural country on earth. Yet, such societies contain within the seeds of their own destruction, the ever-present peril of disintegration.

Writes Vlahos:

[M]ultiethnic and multireligious societies have big identity problems. The bigger and more complex they are ... the more these cultures are vulnerable to the tug and pull of identities between culture and subculture. This can be a creative and enriching tension. Yet so often it also creates contradictions within and competition over who owns the sacred identity— big identity.[118]

Major Hasan faced just such contradictions and competition. Forced to choose, he chose his sacred identity. Today, those same contradictions, that same competition of identities grows stronger, as the nation grows ever more diverse—racially, ethnically, religiously, culturally, ideologically, and politically.

Why, then, are we surprised by ethnic espionage, the cursing of our country in U.S. mosques, news that Somali immigrants are going home to fight our Somali allies, Pakistani American boys departing to train in al-Qaeda camps, and illegal immigrants marching under Mexican flags?

Eisenhower's America was a nation of 160 million with a European-Christian core and culture all its own. We were a people then. And when, in 2050, we have become a stew of 435 million, of every creed, culture, and color, from every country on earth, what will hold us together?

Pressed by ABC's George Stephanopoulos as to the motivation of Major Hasan in killing and wounding forty-two fellow soldiers, Army Chief of Staff General Bernard Casey declined to speculate, but volunteered his deeper concern:

"This terrible event would be an even greater tragedy if our diversity becomes a casualty."[119]

8

THE TRIUMPH OF TRIBALISM

Wars between nations have given way to wars within nations.[1]
—BARACK OBAMA, 2009
Nobel Prize Address

Ethnic ... rivalry is as old as sin, and as inextinguishable.[2]
—SIR CHRISTOPHER MEYER, 2008
British Diplomat

*Ethnic and racial conflict, it seems evident, will now replace the conflict
of ideologies as the explosive issue of our times.*[3]
—ARTHUR SCHLESINGER, 1991

*[N]ationalism is not resurgent; it never died. Neither did racism.
They are the most powerful movements in the world today.*[4]
—ISAIAH BERLIN, 1991

A 2008 cover article in *Foreign Affairs* by Jerry Z. Muller, "Us and Them: The Enduring Power of Ethnic Nationalism," argues that the relentless tug of tribal ties of blood and kinship will imperil the unity and survival of all of the multiethnic nations in the twenty-first century.

Americans generally belittle the role of ethnic nationalism in politics. But ... it corresponds to some enduring propensities of the human spirit, it is galvanized by modernization, and in one form or another, it will drive global politics for genera-tions to come. Once ethnic nationalism has captured the imagination of groups in a multiethnic society, ethnic disaggregation or partition is often the least bad answer.[5]

Muller maintains that the drive of ethnic groups to separate and create nation-states in which their own unique culture, language, and faith are predominant and their own kind rule is among the most powerful drives of man. Remorseless and often irresistible, ethnonationalism caused the world wars and tore apart the Soviet Union and Yugoslavia, he argues. And the wisest policy for the United States may be to get out of its way.

The West, Muller contends, has misread and mistaught itself its own history. A familiar and influential narrative of twentieth-century European history argues that nationalism twice led to war, in 1914 and then again in 1939. Thereafter, the story goes, Europeans concluded that nationalism was a danger and abandoned it. In the postwar era, Western Europeans enmeshed themselves in a web of transnational institutions, culminating in the European Union.[6]

This is not how it happened, writes Muller:

> The creation of ethnonational states across Europe, a consequence of two world wars and ethnic cleansing, was a precondition of stability, unity and peace. With no ethnic rivals inside their national homes, European peoples had what they had fought for, and were now prepared to live in peace with their neighbors.
>
> As a result of this massive process of ethnic unmixing, the ethnonationalist ideal was largely realized: for the most part, each nation in Europe had its own state, and each state was made up almost exclusively of a single ethnic nationality. During the Cold War, the few exceptions to this rule included Czechoslovakia, the Soviet Union, and Yugoslavia. But these countries' subsequent fate only demonstrated the ongoing vitality of ethnonationalism.[7]

Czechoslovakia, the Soviet Union, and Yugoslavia were dictatorships, held together by monolithic Communist parties. Had they not been police states, all would have disintegrated long before they did.

Muller holds that what happened in Europe in the twentieth century, the breakup of empires and nations into their ethnic components, is happening in Africa, the Middle East, and Asia. The will to secede and establish one's own national home, like the will of a son to leave his father's house and start his own family, is more powerful than any ideology, be it communism, socialism, fascism—or democracy.

> [E]thnonationalism has played a more profound role in modern history than is commonly understood, and the processes that led to the dominance of the ethnonational state and the separation of ethnic groups in Europe are likely to reoccur elsewhere. In areas where that separation has not yet occurred, politics is apt to remain ugly.[8]

The ethnic violence rampant in Asia, the Middle East, and Africa is a reenactment of what Europe went through, a sorting out of tribes.

Muller's contention that ethnonationalism is embedded in human nature and ethnic homogeneity may be a precondition of liberal democracy and peace echoes Robert Putnam. And if these men are right, the more multiethnic and multiracial we make America, the closer we advance to the *bellum omnium contra omnes,* the war of all against all. In *Pandaemonium,* published in 1993, Senator Moynihan noted the remarkable blindness of foreign policy scholars to the power of ethnonationalism in our time:

> There are today just eight states on earth which both existed in 1914 and have not had their form of government changed by violence since then. These are the United Kingdom, four present or former members of the Commonwealth, the United States, Sweden and Switzerland. Of the remaining 170 or so

contemporary states, some are too recently created to have known much recent turmoil, but for the greater number that have gone, by far the most frequent factor involved has been ethnic conflict.[9]

"Yet it is possible," Moynihan marveled, "to have studied international relations through the whole of the twentieth century and hardly to have noticed this."[10] Since *Pandaemonium* appeared, the United Kingdom, the United States, Sweden, and Switzerland have been torn by racial or religious divisions. And a look back to the last century confirms Muller's thesis.

THE BALKAN WARS

The twentieth century opened during the longest European war since Napoleon. It was fought in Africa, where the Dutch-speaking Boer republics of the Transvaal and the Orange Free State were fighting to maintain their identity and independence. Not until Lord Kitchener set up his concentration camps for Boer women and children, to deprive Louis Botha's guerrillas of the support of their people, did the Boers yield in 1902.

Three years later, Norway, which had been detached from Denmark and ceded to Sweden when the Danes chose the wrong side in Napoleon's wars, broke free. The Norwegians were prepared to fight for independence, as were some Swedes to deny it to them. But statesmanship prevailed and the Norwegians departed to establish their own ethnonational home.

What happened in the Balkans, however, was anything but peaceful.

In the 1820s, the Greeks had broken free of the Ottoman Turks in a war of liberation to establish a nation of, by, and for Greeks alone. Of that struggle, Lord Byron, who perished in it, wrote:

The mountains look on Marathon—
And Marathon looks on the sea;

And musing there an hour alone,
I dream'd that Greece might still be free;
For standing on the Persians' grave,
I could not deem myself a slave.[11]

By the twentieth century, Serbia, too, had her independence.

But the Balkans, which Bismarck dismissed as "not worth the bones of a single Pomeranian grenadier," were a boiling cauldron of ethnic discontent and conflict between The Habsburg, Romanov, and Ottoman empires. They were the "powder-keg" of Europe. Indeed, Bismarck had warned that when the Great War came, it would likely come "out of some damn fool thing in the Balkans."

In 1908, with Emperor Franz Josef in the sixtieth year of his reign, Austria annexed Bosnia-Hercegovina in violation of the 1878 Treaty of Berlin. With Russia reeling from her defeat by Japan and the revolution of 1905, Czar Nicholas II did nothing. For Vienna had the backing of the mightiest power in Europe, the Second Reich of Kaiser Wilhelm II.

By 1912, however, under Russian auspices, a Balkan League had been formed that included Bulgaria, Serbia, Greece, and Montenegro. Its goal: tear Macedonia away from an Ottoman Empire preoccupied by a war with Italy over what is today Libya.

On October 8, Montenegro declared war and was joined, ten days later, by her allies. With the league marshaling 750,000 soldiers, the Turks were routed on every front. The Bulgarians crushed them in Thrace and drove to the outskirts of Constantinople. Serbs and Montenegrins seized Skopje, the capital of Macedonia. Greeks occupied Thessalonika. Albania, Macedonia, and Thrace, the three European provinces of the Ottoman Empire, had been lost. On December 3, the Turks agreed to an armistice.

On January 13, 1913, however, after "The Young Turks" effected a coup in Constantinople, war resumed. Again, the Balkan League triumphed. On May 30, 1913, at the London Conference, Albania was declared independent at the insistence of the Great Powers, but Macedonia was divided among the victorious Balkan allies.

The First Balkan War was an ethnonational war of race, tribe, and religion. Christian Slavs had united to expel Muslim Turks from a peninsula whose peoples detested them for their centuries of harsh rule.

In mid-1913, the Second Balkan War erupted over Macedonia. The Bulgarians felt cheated of their fair share and laid claim to Salonika. Greece and Serbia, forced to yield their shares of Albania at the London Conference, formed an alliance. The Second Balkan War lasted from June 16 to July 18.

The Bulgarians were routed, as Romanians and Turks joined Greece and Serbia to strip Sofia of all her gains in the First Balkan War. Bulgaria lost Southern Dobruja to Romania, Eastern Thrace to the Turks. Greece and Serbia divided Macedonia, creating an ethnonational quarrel that endures and bedevils NATO. Athens refuses to recognize Macedonia, except as FYROM, the Former Yugoslav Republic of Macedonia. To Greeks the name and land of Philip of Macedon and his son Alexander the Great belong exclusively to Greece.

SARAJEVO, 1914

After her victories in the First and Second Balkan Wars, Serbia was aflame with nationalism, determined to bring all Serbs into a national home, including those living under Austrian rule in Bosnia-Hercegovina. This was impossible—without a war with the Habsburg Empire. On June 28, 1914 in Sarajevo, the Bosnian capital, Serb nationalist Gavrilo Princip, dispatched from Belgrade by elements in the security services, shot and killed the Archduke Francis Ferdinand, heir to the Austrian throne, and his wife. That act of ethnonational terror eliminated a reformer who had meant to redress the grievances of his Slav subjects when he took the throne of Franz Josef, now in the sixty-sixth year of his reign. Ferdinand had intended to grant the Slavs autonomy and equality with Austrians and Hungarians. His assassination succeeded beyond the wildest dreams of the secret Black Hand society plotters in Belgrade.

Austria issued an ultimatum to Serbia. When her ten demands were not met in full, Vienna declared war and shelled Belgrade from across the Danube. Czar Nicholas mobilized his armies in support of Russia's little Slav brothers. The Kaiser ordered mobilization to counter the Russians. When Russia's ally, France, refused to declare neutrality, Germany declared war. And when the German army crossed into Belgium, the British cabinet reversed itself to back war for Belgium and France.

None were more stunned than the Marxists who had predicted that the working-class sons of Europe would never take up arms to kill one another for their rulers. The proletariat, they believed, would stand as one against a capitalists' war. Many Marxists never recovered the faith they lost when the party in which they had invested their greatest hopes, the German Social Democrats, voted to a man for the kaiser's war credits. The call of socialist solidarity was drowned out by the call of tribe and blood. In London, Paris, St. Petersburg, and Berlin, boys and men were cheered wildly as they marched off to kill their Christian neighbors.

The Italian Socialist Party leadership denounced its sister parties in Germany and Europe, which had backed the war, and, in a 12–1 vote, passed a resolution declaring, "We will be faithful to our flag; and on this flag is written: Proletarians of all the world unite!" The sole dissenter was Benito Mussolini.[12]

After four years, nine million soldiers had perished and four empires had fallen. Ethnonationalism had plunged the continent and the world into the worst war in history.

PARIS, 1919

When Lenin came to power in 1917, he began to publish the secret treaties in the Romanov archives, revealing how, at war's end, the Allies—Britain, France, Russia, Italy, Romania, and Japan—had planned to carve up the world. The Great War seemed suddenly to be naught but an amoral imperial struggle for land and loot.

To counter this depiction of why millions of young men had been sent to early graves, President Wilson, whose nation had entered the war in April 1917 "to make the world safe for democracy," issued his Fourteen Points. Here, Wilson told the world, is what we Americans are fighting for. At the heart of his vision was the idea of self-determination. On February 1, 1918, Wilson laid down his preconditions for a just and lasting peace:

> There shall be no annexations.... People are not to be handed about from one sovereignty to another by an international conference.... "Self-determination" is not a mere phrase.... Every territorial settlement involved in this war must be made in the interest and for the benefit of the population concerned, and not as part of any mere adjustment or compromise of claims amongst rival States.[13]

Before the peace conference opened, however, U.S. Secretary of State Robert Lansing had confided to his diary his alarm at the explosive potential of Wilson's words:

> The more I think about the president's declaration as to the right of "self-determination," the more convinced I am of the dangers of putting such ideas in the minds of certain races....
> The phrase [self-determination] is simply loaded with dynamite. It will raise hopes which can never be realized. It will, I fear, cost thousands of lives....What a calamity that the phrase was ever uttered! What misery it will cause![14]

What came out of the Paris peace conference, that "riot in a parrot house," in British diplomat Harold Nicholson's phrase, justified Lansing's fears and spat upon Wilson's hopes. Wilson's fears had been realized. The Hohenzollern, Habsburg, and Ottoman empires were demolished, but the nations birthed through the treaties of Versailles, St. Germain, Trianon, Neuilly, and Sèvres were insults to Wilson's ideals.

After accepting an armistice based on Wilson's Fourteen Points, Germany lost Northern Schleswig to Denmark through plebiscite, and Eupen and Malmedy to Belgium for the damage done during the German occupation. Alsace and Lorraine went to France, as this was No. 8 of Wilson's points. The Saar was torn from Germany, along with its people, who were to be granted a vote in fifteen years on whether they wished to return. A long slice of Germany, from Silesia to the sea, cutting her in two and separating East Prussia from Berlin, was ceded to Poland. Danzig, an East Prussian town and Hanseatic League port, was put under Warsaw's control to give Poland an outlet to the sea. Memel would be seized by Lithuania.

Versailles stripped Germany of one-tenth of her people and an eighth of her territory. By 1920, Germans chafed under the rule of Danes, Belgians, French, Italians, Czechs, Poles, and, soon, Lithuanians. The Allies had produced a peace to end all peace. Germany had proven herself the most powerful nation in Europe, having defeated Russia, Romania, and Italy, and fought Britain and France to a draw for four years, with not one foreign soldier on German soil. When Germany got back on her feet, she would come looking for those she had lost.

Ethnonationalism, the demand that lost German lands and peoples be restored, became an almost universally supported plank in the platform of the new National Socialist Party.

After Germany mounted the scaffold came the turn of the Habsburg Empire. Under the treaties of St. Germain and Trianon, that ancient empire was dissolved. Northern provinces went to Poland. Czechoslovakia, which had emerged in 1918 under Thomas Masaryk, a great favorite at Paris, was granted custody of 3.5 million ethnic Germans, 2.5 million Slovaks, 800,000 Hungarians, 500,000 Ruthenians, and 150,000 Poles. All resented being forced to live in a nation dominated by 7 million Czechs.

Whether to force 3 million Germans under a Czech rule most of them despised was fiercely debated at Paris. The U.S. delegation's Archibald Coolidge called it a grave mistake. South Africa's Jan Smuts warned that the Czech lust for Hungarian and German land could bring disastrous results: "With some millions of Germans already included in Bohemia in the north, the further inclusion of some 400,000 or 500,000 Magyars in the south would be a very serious matter for the young state, besides the grave violation of the principles of nationality involved."[15] The "millions of Germans" in Bohemia to whom Smuts referred lived in a place the world would come to know as the Sudetenland.

The Allies did not heed Smuts. They listened to Eduard Benes, the Czech foreign minister who promised to model Czechoslovakia on the Swiss federation, where minorities would enjoy equal standing and large measures of autonomy. On the eve of Munich, Lloyd George would accuse Benes of having lied to the Allies at Paris.

South Tyrol, with 250,000 Tyroleans, Austrian for six centuries, was ceded to Italy as war booty for switching sides and joining the Allies in 1915. Vienna, seat of one of the great empires of Christendom, became the capital of a tiny landlocked country of fewer than 7 million.

Hungary was reduced from an imperial domain of 125,000 square miles to a nation of 36,000. Nearly half the Magyar population had been transferred to foreign rule. Transylvania and its 2 million Hungarians was given to Romania for joining the Allies. Slovakia, which a largely Catholic Hungary had ruled for centuries, was given to the Czechs, along with its 800,000 Hungarians. Other Hungarian lands went to the Kingdom of Serbs, Croats, and Slovenes. When Romania invaded to overthrow the Hungarian Soviet Republic of Bela Kun, which had seized power and instituted a Red Terror, Admiral Miklós Horthy led a National Army into Budapest and promised to restore all lost Magyar lands and peoples. His determination would propel the admiral into partnership with Hitler.

What made Versailles a calamity was not only the injustice of forcing millions of Hungarians and Germans under alien rule, nor the hypocrisy of the Allies, who had professed their devotion to self-determination, but what Smuts had called "the grave violation of the principles of nationality." The Allies had signed birth certificates for nations that were as multiethnic and multilingual as the demolished Habsburg Empire, but wholly lacked that empire's lineage and legitimacy.

The new Kingdom of Serbs, Croats, and Slovenes contained Bosnian Muslims, Albanians, Macedonians, Montenegrins, Hungarians, and Bulgarians. Poland ruled millions of Germans, Ukrainians, White Russians, Jews, and Lithuanians. Romania contained millions of Hungarians and Bulgarians. These minorities ruled by Belgrade, Prague, Warsaw, and Bucharest had been consigned to those capitals against their will and in violation of Wilson's promise that self-determination would be the basis of the peace. Believing they had been betrayed and subjugated, they seethed with a resentment that would explode in a second European war in which the butcher's bill would dwarf that of the Great War.

"THE NATURAL MAP OF THE WORLD"

In his 1920 *Outline of History*, H. G. Wells bewailed the folly of herding ethnic groups into artificial states: "There is a natural and necessary political map of the world which transcends these things," Wells wrote.

> There is a best way possible of dividing any part of the world into administrative areas and a best possible kind of government for every area, having regard to the speech and race of its inhabitants, and it is our common concern to secure these divisions and establish those forms of government quite irrespective of diplomacies and flags, "claims" and melodramatic "loyalties," and the existing political map of the world.[16]

Democracy notwithstanding, wrote Wells, "The natural political map of the world insists upon itself. It heaves and frets beneath the artificial political map like some misfitted giant."[17] Wells understood that not parchment, but language, literature, blood, soil, history, and faith make a nation; that a nation is an organic living thing, not some fabricated construct. As for the multicultural, multilingual, multiethnic nations crafted in Paris by presidents and prime ministers, they were artificial nations, ever at risk of falling apart.

> It is extraordinarily inconvenient to administer together the affairs of peoples speaking different languages and so reading different literatures and having different general ideas, especially if those differences are exacerbated by religious disputes. Only some strong mutual interests, such as the common defensive needs of the Swiss mountaineers, can justify a close linking of peoples of different languages and faiths.[18]

Now that the natural nations of Europe had seen millions of their kinsmen consigned to the rule of alien ethnicities whom they detested, Wells sensed what was coming.

THE IRISH REBELLION

When Disraeli observed, "All is race. There is no other truth," he meant what Churchill meant when he spoke of "this island race," a unique people, separate from all others, united by borders, language, culture, history, and blood.[19] Disraeli saw the Irish, though part of Britain, as a breed apart: "This wild, reckless, indolent, uncertain and superstitious race have no sympathy with the English character. Their ideal of human felicity is an alternation of clannish broils and coarse idolatry [i.e., Catholicism]. Their history describes an unbroken circle of bigotry and blood."[20] The Duke of Wellington was of similar mind. Reminded that he had been born in Dublin, the Iron Duke retorted, "Being born in a stable does not make one a horse."[21] A contemporary of Wellington and Disraeli, Thomas Carlyle regarded the Irish as "human swinery."[22]

The Irish saw themselves as a people apart, even when they fought alongside Englishmen and Scots. In "An Irish Airman Foresees His Death," Yeats spoke for his people:

I know that I shall meet my fate
Somewhere among the clouds above;
Those that I fight I do not hate,
Those that I guard I do not love;
My country is Kiltartan Cross,
My countrymen Kiltartan's poor,
No likely end could bring them loss
Or leave them happier than before.[23]

England's cause was not Ireland's cause. England's enemies were not Ireland's enemies. No sooner had the Great War ended than the Troubles began. Fresh in memory was the Easter Rising of 1916, when 2000 rebels, in that year of the Somme Offensive, seized the General Post Office in Dublin to stoke a rebellion. While a botched affair that initially earned its leaders ridicule and contempt, the British immediately villainized themselves—by arresting thousands more than had participated in the rising and sending fifteen of the leaders before firing squads, creating a fatal breach between British and Irish. Wrote Yeats, in "Easter 1916":

I write it out in a verse—
MacDonagh and MacBride
And Connolly and Pearse
Now and in time to be,
Wherever green is worn,
Are changed, changed utterly:
A terrible beauty is born.[24]

Changed they were, from blunderers who had committed an act of wartime treason into martyrs of Irish independence. In 1918, needing fresh troops after the losses halting Ludendorff's offensive, Lloyd George decided to conscript the Irish. That was the end of the Irish Parliamentary

Party of John Redmond, who had lost a son in the war. Sinn Féin now spoke for Ireland.

In 1919, a guerrilla war began with the killing of constables and Irish collaborators of the British government. London sent in veterans of the Western Front, the Black and Tans. From 1919 to 1921, hundreds died on each side until rebel commander Michael Collins went to London to negotiate peace with Churchill. An Irish Free State was created, but six northern counties of Ulster remained with the United Kingdom. The treaty Collins brought home ignited a civil war that ended only with his assassination.

Few better examples exist of the power of ethnonationalism. Here were British subjects, citizens of a free nation who enjoyed all the rights of Englishmen, who were represented in Parliament, who belonged to the greatest empire since Rome at the apogee of her power and glory and in the hour of her greatest triumph. Yet they wished to be free of her, and were willing to fight and die to have Ireland, an impoverished land of a few million, take her place alongside the nations of the world. What caused the Irish to prefer separation to union?

Ethnonationalism. Though they had lived alongside the English for centuries, the Irish saw themselves as the English saw them: as separate. They were Celts, not Anglo-Saxons, Church of Rome, not Church of England. Gaelic was their language, not English. The history on which they brooded was not the history of England or the empire but a centuries-long catalog of crimes against the Irish—from Drogheda and Wexford to the Penal Laws and the Potato Famine to the executions of the Easter Rising. Long after their war for independence had been won, hatred of England was a defining feature of diaspora Irish, a part of their DNA.

When, in 1939, Britain declared war against Hitler's Germany, Canada, South Africa, New Zealand, and Australia declared war in solidarity with the Mother Country. Ireland proclaimed a neutrality that she maintained through Dunkirk, the Battle of Britain, and America's entry—indeed, to the end of the war.

England's war was not Ireland's war.

THE YOUNG TURKS

Unlike the secession of Norway from Sweden in 1905, many new ethnostates of the twentieth century were birthed in blood.

In the first decade of the century the Ottoman Empire, the "Sick Man of Europe," in the cruel depiction attributed to Czar Nicholas I, had begun to die, and Western powers and former subject nations had begun to bite off provinces. In 1908, "Young Turks" first executed a coup in Salonika. From 1911 to 1918, Enver Bey, the future Enver Pasha, ran a virtual military dictatorship. His goal was to "Turkify" the empire by forcing subjects to use the Turkish language, accept national education, and have their sons serve in a national army. As there were millions of Christian Slavs, Greeks, and Armenians (as well as Muslim Arabs and Kurds) in the empire that stretched from the Maghreb to Mesopotamia, Turkification was resisted. In 1914, Turkey cast its lot with the Central Powers and won a legendary victory at Gallipoli after repelling a British-French fleet in the Dardanelles. That Allied naval disaster cost First Lord Winston Churchill his post. In that same year, 1915, the Turks, enraged at Armenians fighting alongside an invading Russian army, perpetrated a series of massacres and expulsions of their Armenian subjects that may have cost as many as 1.5 million lives. Armenians and others regard what the Turks did as genocide.

In 1918 the Turks went down to defeat, and the Treaty of Sèvres, imposed in Paris in 1920, marked the end of the empire. Under the secret Sykes-Picot agreement, Palestine, Transjordan, and Mesopotamia went to the British, and Syria and Lebanon to France. Arabs were denied the independence promised by Lawrence of Arabia. Three of the victorious Allies, France, Italy, and Britain, occupied parts of Turkey, while Greeks controlled western Anatolia almost to Ankara. Offered a mandate over Constantinople, in which Wilson was interested, the Americans wisely declined. The United States had never declared war on Turkey.

Came now the hour of Ataturk.

His army first forced out the French and Italians, then drove the Greeks out of Anatolia, slaughtering thousands in Smyrna, then confronted the British at Chanak. The British stood down and sailed away. By the 1923 Treaty of Lausanne, ethnic cleansing was legitimized. Some 1.4 million Greeks were forced to leave Turkey and 400,000 Turks were forced out of lands that now belonged to Greece.

The caliph was put on the Orient Express. Mehmet VI, the last sultan of the Ottoman Empire, left Constantinople on a British warship. Under the hero of Gallipoli, the Republic of Turkey was born as a secular nation, its institutions modeled on the West. Save for the Kurds, whose ethnonational drive for a home of their own would bedevil her to this day, Turkey was a land of, by, and for Turks alone. Out of the carcass of the Ottoman Empire had come the first modern ethnonational state in the Middle East.

The tribal conflict between Greek and Turk endures on the island of Cyprus. The Turks invaded in 1974 to prevent annexation by Greece and a Turkish Republic of Northern Cyprus remains a headache for NATO.

"EIN VOLK"

That Hitler was the personification of the German race was dogma in his party. And it was the treaties of Versailles and St. Germain that forced millions of Germans under alien rule that provided Hitler with the program he rode to power. To understand the rage in the German soul Hitler stoked, one must understand the history of the Great War, from the German point of view. By spring 1918, Germany was victorious on three fronts. Romania had been routed in 1916. The royal family had fled. The Italians had been broken at Caporetto in 1917. The Russians had thrown down their rifles, the czar had abdicated, and the Bolsheviks had signed away Russia's European empire at Brest-Litovsk by March 1918. By spring, Ludendorff was back on the Marne. Had it not been for the Americans pouring into Allied lines at the rate of 250,000 soldiers a month, Germany might have won an armistice that would have left her undefeated on the Western Front and triumphant in the east.

The dramatic reversal of 1918—the shock of defeat for the Germans—was tremendous. Then, after they had accepted an armistice on Wilson's Fourteen Points, laid down their arms, and delivered the High Seas Fleet to Scapa Flow, the Allies proceeded to divide and dismember Germany.

By declaring the kaiser a war criminal, tearing off German provinces, disarming them and leaving them naked to their enemies, making them wage slaves of the victorious powers, forcing Germany to accept sole moral responsibility for causing the war and the damage done, then starving them until their leaders signed the treaty, the Allies stoked the ethnonationalism of Germans more than Bismarck had with his victory over Napoleon III. As all Germans from Prussia to Bavaria had fought and bled together and suffered together on the home front, so all believed that they had been lied to and betrayed by Wilson and the Allies and that the lands and people taken from them must be restored. In his pledge to bring all lost Germans home to the Reich, Hitler had the support of Germans everywhere.

"Nationalism is an infantile disease," said Einstein. "It is the measles of mankind."[25] But in Germany in 1933, it was a rather more serious malady, from which Dr. Einstein would flee to America.

In 1935, the Saar, severed at Paris but promised a plebiscite to decide whether to remain outside Germany, voted by 90 percent to return. Catholic and socialist, Saarlanders preferred a Nazi regime that crushed unions and persecuted the Church to life apart from their kinsmen. Such is the power of ethnonationalism.

When, in March 1936, German troops marched into the demilitarized Rhineland for the first time since 1918, there was wild rejoicing. Anschluss, the invasion and incorporation of Austria into the Reich, undertaken by Hitler to prevent a plebiscite on the permanent separation of his birth country, was celebrated in both nations. Many Austrians, who shared a culture with Germany, willingly exchanged nationhood and independence for a new life inside the new Reich.

The Czech crisis of 1938 that led to Munich and the Danzig crisis of 1939 that provoked Hitler's attack on Poland, came out of ethnonational demands.

Hitler, an Austrian who grew up in Linz near the Czech border when Czechs were ruled from Vienna, was determined to bring the Germans of Bohemia and Moravia out from under Prague and back under German rule, where the Sudetenlanders wished to be. At Munich, the British and French acceded to Hitler's demand.

Poles and Hungarians then seized the Czech lands where their kinfolk lived. Slovaks, too, struggled to break free of Czech rule and create a nation. Ethnonationalism tore Czechoslovakia apart. This caused a panicked British government to extend a war guarantee to Poland, then involved in a dispute with Berlin over return of 350,000 Danzigers to a Fatherland from which they, too, had been severed against their will at Paris. Poland's refusal to discuss Danzig provoked Hitler into invading the country on September 1, 1939.

Both world wars came out of ethnonational quarrels the great powers created or ignored. World War II is depicted as the Good War in which democracy triumphed over fascism. But the crises that caused the war were rooted in ethnic conflict, not ideology. German, Slovakian, Polish, Hungarian, and Ruthenian ethnonationalism tore Czechoslovakia to pieces in 1938 and 1939. German ethnonationalism in Danzig that Poland refused to address caused Hitler to destroy Poland, not the Polish form of government, to which Hitler had no objection.

THE GREAT TRIBAL WAR

Obsessed with race, Hitler wanted all Jews out of the Reich. But on ideology, he was pragmatic and flexible. While preferring nationalist allies like Franco's Spain, Mussolini's Italy, Horthy's Hungary, Tiso's Slovakia, and Pilsudski's Poland, he partnered with Stalin and the Bolsheviks to retrieve what belonged to Germany, and admired the British, democratic at home and imperialist abroad. Britain was to Hitler the ideal ally.

Churchill loved the empire as much as he loathed many of its subjects, especially Indians. Historian Andrew Roberts writes that his views were not only "more profoundly racist than most," they influenced his conduct as a statesman:

> Churchill's racial assumptions occupied a prime place both in his political philosophy and in his views on international relations. He was a convinced white—not to say Anglo-Saxon—supremacist and thought in terms of race to a degree that was remarkable even by the standards of his own time. He spoke of certain races with a virulent Anglo-Saxon triumphalism which was wholly lacking in other twentieth-century prime ministers, and in a way which even as early as the 1920s shocked some Cabinet colleagues.[26]

Stalin, born Joseph Vissarionovich Dzhugashvili in Gori, Georgia, put ideology on the shelf when Russia was invaded. He let Orthodox priests and bishops out of prison and called on Russia's sons to defend the Rodina from rape by Teutonic hordes who were the Mongols of modernity. The Great Patriotic War was a race war. German treatment of Jews and Untermenschen, Russian treatment of Magyar and German women, testify to tribal war. Here is a sampling from Stalin's propagandist, Ilya Ehrenburg, when Germans occupied great swaths of Russian soil in 1942. It was titled "Kill."

> Germans are not human beings. Henceforth the word German means to us the most terrible curse. From now on the word German will trigger your rifle. We shall not speak any more. We shall not get excited. We shall kill. If you have not killed at least one German a day, you have wasted that day....

If you leave a German alive, the German will hang a Russian and rape a Russian woman. If you kill one German, kill another—there is nothing more amusing for us than a heap of German corpses.... Kill the German—this is your old mother's prayer. Kill the German—this is what your children beseech you to do. Kill the German—this is the cry of your Russian earth. Do not waver. Do not let up. Kill.[27]

Japan's war in Asia was a race war. In Nanking, Japanese soldiers bayoneted Chinese babies for sport, their mothers and fathers for practice. Korean girls and women were conscripted as sex slaves for Japanese troops. America's war of revenge against Japan was a race war. Newsreels, movies, magazines, comic books, headlines treated "Japs" as a repulsive race whose extermination would benefit mankind. General Curtis LeMay boasted, of his B-29 saturation bombing of the Japanese capital, "We scorched and boiled and baked to death more people in Tokyo that night of March 9–10 than went up in vapour in Hiroshima and Nagasaki combined."[28]

Only well after the war was over was it rebranded a war to bring the blessings of democracy to Germany and Japan.

The war brought death to millions but produced a new Europe. After the ethnic cleansing of fifteen million Germans from Prussia, Brandenburg, Pomerania, Silesia, Moravia, Bohemia, and the Balkans, an exodus two hundred times as large as the Trail of Tears under Andrew Jackson, Europe from Eire to the Elbe consisted of almost all homogeneous states. The Germans were in Germany, the French in France, the Italians in Italy, the Irish in Ireland.

But among the subjects of Europe's surviving empires came now an explosion of ethnonationalism. The India of Gandhi gained independence in 1947. East and West Pakistan seceded. A religious and ethnic war costing millions of lives followed. In May 1948, the Jews declared independence. Arabs went to war to eradicate the "Zionist entity" while

Arab civilians in the war zone fled to UN camps where they would live for generations as a new nation, Palestine, was conceived in their hearts.

In 1946, Vietnamese who had chafed under colonial rule and suffered under Japanese occupation rose up to resist the return of the French. "We have a secret weapon," said Ho Chi Minh, "it is called Nationalism."[29]

Four decades later, when the Berlin Wall fell, ethnonationalism went about its work, tearing apart the Soviet Empire and then the Soviet Union—into fifteen nations. Czechoslovakia split in two as in March 1939. Yugoslavia, born at Paris in 1919, disappeared from the map as Slovenia, Croatia, Bosnia, Serbia, Montenegro, Macedonia, and Kosovo sprang to life. The secessions of Croatia and Bosnia were fiercely resisted. Thousands died. Kosovo, the cradle of Serbia, was torn loose only after seventy-eight days of U.S. bombing.

"Once the iron fists of the former Soviet Union and Tito's Yugoslavia had been removed," said Christopher Meyer, "nationalist and ethnic tensions broke surface with the murderous velocity of the long suppressed."[30]

Spain, Greece, Slovakia, Romania, and Cyprus all refuse to establish diplomatic relations with Kosovo. All fear providing an impetus to secession-minded minorities at home.

What the disintegration of the USSR and Yugoslavia into twenty-two nations reveals is this: absent an authoritarian regime or dominant ethnocultural core, all multiracial, multiethnic, and multilingual nations are ever at risk of disintegration. A corollary: as autocracies give way to democracy, new nations will break out of the old, and the more divided and discordant the world will become. A UN that began with 52 member nations now has 193 and counting. Balkanization, that often bloody breakdown and breakup of nations along racial, tribal, religious, and cultural fault lines, may be the defining force of our time.

THE LAST EUROPEAN EMPIRE

What happened to the Soviet Union—that so few foresaw?

Marxism-Leninism, the ideology imposed on the Russian Empire in 1917 that set out to conquer the world, died in the soul of Soviet man. By the later years of the Cold War, few still believed in its tenets or the inevitability of its triumph. The church militant, the party of Lenin and Stalin, built on the now-moribund faith, had come to be seen less as a spear point of revolution to create paradise on earth than as a monolith to preserve the power and privileges of a corrupt *nomenklatura*.

With the collapse of the Soviet Empire and the end of the Cold War, the Soviet state lost its reason for being. And as the party lost the loyalty of the people, the instruments of state security, the Red Army and KGB, were left to hold the USSR together. They no longer had the will. Ethnonationalism outlasted Marxist ideology—and proceeded to tear apart the prison-house of nations. To his eternal credit, Mikhail Gorbachev let it happen. The old nations, Lithuania, Latvia, and Estonia, broke free first. Then came Belarus, Ukraine, Moldova. Armenia, Georgia, and Azerbaijan in the Caucasus followed. In Central Asia, five nations were born: Kazakhstan, Turkmenistan, Uzbekistan, Tajikistan, and Kyrgyzstan.

Yet this was but the end of the beginning. Minorities inside the new nations now wanted their place in the sun and the Caucasus would take on the aspect of the early twentieth-century Balkans.

Transnistria fought its way free of Moldova. Nagorno-Karabakh, an Armenian enclave inside Azerbaijan, declared independence, producing war between Armenia and Azerbaijan. Chechnya sought to break free of Russia. Moscow would fight two wars to hold on, in which half a million perished and Grozny, the Chechen capital, would be reduced to Berlin 1945. South Ossetia and Abkhazia broke from Georgia. In 2008, a Georgian invasion of South Ossetia was swiftly routed by Russia, which has now recognized the breakaway provinces as independent states.

In 2009, Dagestan's interior minister was assassinated. Ingush President Yunus-Bek Yevkurov was almost killed by a suicide bomber who swerved into his motorcade with a Toyota Camry loaded with explosives.[31] Maksharip Aushev, an opposition leader in Ingushetia, was murdered by assassins who sprayed his vehicle with automatic gunfire.[32]

By 2010, attacks and assassinations were occurring almost daily in Ingushetia, Dagestan, and Chechnya and President Medvedev declared the North Caucasus Russia's greatest domestic crisis. In March 2010, forty people were killed in twin suicide blasts in the Moscow subway, with one bomb exploding at Lubianka station. The bombers were women reportedly trained and dispatched by Caucasus Emirate, a militant Islamic group that demands secession of the North Caucasus and creation of a caliphate.[33] At summer's end, a suicide car bomber hit the main entrance of a mall in North Ossetia's capital, killing 16 and wounding 133.[34] "Russia's Muslim North Caucasus," writes Leon Aron, director of Russian studies at AEI,

> is today barely governable, mired in poverty and unemployment, and swept up in relentless fundamentalist Islamic terrorism. Nary a day passes, especially in Dagestan and Ingushetia, without an official—a police officer, judge, prosecutor, local functionary—being killed by terrorist attacks.[35]

In January 2011, a suicide bomber walked into the international arrivals hall of Moscow's Domodedovo International Airport and detonated his explosives, killing 36 and injuring 180. Rebel leader Doku Umarov, in a video, claimed that he ordered the attack as a blow in a "total war" against Russia for an independent Islamist nation in the Caucasus and called on Muslims in the Volga regions of Tartarstan and Bashkortostan to join the insurgency.[36] Vladimir Putin pledged, "Revenge is inevitable."[37] Wrote Elena Milashina, of *Novaya Gazeta,* "The entire North Caucasus region is on fire, and suicide bombers pay a leading role on this gruesome stage."[38]

Putin is not a man easily intimidated, as the last Chechen war demonstrated. Still, it is hard to see how Russia, its population shrinking by half a million to a million people a year, can hold on to a region where the disposition to kill and the willingness to die is so deeply rooted. Almost two hundred years ago, Pushkin wrote, "Cossack! Do not sleep.... In the gloomy dark, the Chechen roams beyond the river."[39]

Charles King, author of *Extreme Politics: Nationalism, Violence and the End of Eastern Europe,* writes that failure to cope with ethnic terror in the Caucasus could lead to a rightist uprising in Russia.

> If the Kremlin cannot contain the cycle of attacks and counterattacks, then Russian nationalist groups—many of which spew chauvinistic rhetoric demonizing Russia's non-Christian minorities—could gain traction in Russian politics. Such groups have already been involved in mob attacks and killings of Muslim migrants from the Caucasus and Central Asia. The possibility of street violence is very real and potentially destabilizing.[40]

Adds King, "Muslims make up as much as 15 percent of Russia's population, with more than two million living in Moscow alone."

And the mixture is explosive. In December 2010, the killing of a 28-year-old Russian fan of the Spartak soccer team in a midnight brawl with young men from the Caucasus led to a huge demonstration outside Red Square. "Russia for the Russians!" they chanted, "Moscow for the Muscovites!" Many gave the Nazi salute. When the crowd dispersed, mobs assaulted police and the Moscow subway witnessed "a wave of beatings and stabbings of people from the Caucasus or Central Asia."[41]

In the southern city of Rostov, where a Russian student was killed by an Ingush classmate, another demonstration was held. There the chants were "Rostov is a Russian town" and "All for one and one for all."

Archpriest Vsevolod Chaplin, of the Russian Orthodox Church, said if authorities did not act, "massive ethnic clashes may break out."[42] President Medvedev decried the "pogroms," warning, "Ethnic violence threatens the stability of the state."[43] Wrote the *Financial Times:*

Russia's ultra-right has for two decades been little more than a curiosity: fodder for hand-wringing academics writing about "Weimar Russia." But in the wake of the biggest ethnic riots Russia has seen since the Soviet Union's fall, this formerly marginal if violent movement has arisen as a fearsome new political power.[44]

In Kyrgyzstan in 2010, the April overthrow of President Kurmanbek Bakiyev ignited violence that took hundreds of lives and imperiled the U.S. lease on Manas air base outside Bishkek, a vital link to Afghanistan. In June, thousands were killed and wounded in massacres of Uzbeks in the southern cities of Osh and Jalal-Abad. Hundreds of thousands fled into Uzbekistan. An ethnic war that tears Kyrgyzstan apart remains a distinct possibility.[45] Time is not on the side of the multinational nation.

TRIBALISM RETURNS TO EUROPE

Lately, the West has witnessed a revival of something it thought it had outgrown: ethnonationalism in Old Europe where it now manifests itself in secessionism. Three hundred years after the Act of Union, Scots seek what their Celt cousins won under Michael Collins: separation and independence. Many English would be happy to see them go.[46]

Separatism is alive in the Basque country, Catalonia, and Flanders. Turks and Greeks segregate on Cyprus. The Northern League seeks secession from Rome, Naples, and Sicily. Corsica has sought independence from France. The Srpska Republic may break from Bosnia to join its Serb brethren. Serbs in northern Kosovo are unlikely to remain in an Albanian Muslim nation. What is causing this?

An end to the Days of Hope and Glory has made the subjects of Elizabeth II less proud of being British than of being Scottish, Welsh, English, or Scots-Irish. With the EU evolving into a super-state no one loves, and with nations surrendering their sovereignty to Brussels, people are transferring their love and loyalty back to the homelands whence their people came. And a new factor is fueling secession in Europe's financial crisis: a sense that one's own are being exploited by neighbors who do not work as hard. In the small town of Arenys de Mar in October 2009, 96 percent of those who came out for a referendum voted for Catalonia's secession. "It's brutal," said the mayor. The rest of Spain is "bleeding us.... Now it's not about language and literature.... For the first time in history, the independence movement is coming via the people's purses."[47]

In July 2010, a million Catalans gathered in the streets of Barcelona "to demand greater regional autonomy and to protest a recent court ruling forbidding the prosperous region from calling itself a nation."[48]

Europe's debt crisis has breathed new life into the secessionist Northern League of Umberto Bossi, who sees autonomy first, then independence for Padania, the five regions of Italy centered on Piedmont, Lombardy, Veneto, and Trentino-Alto Adige (the old South Tyrol).

Mr. Bossi's central claim is that natives of Padania, an ambiguous area around the Po River that includes the cities of Milan, Turin, and Venice, descend from the northern Celtic tribes. The Celts, Mr. Bossi regularly reminds his fans, were a hard-working people unlike the Romans, warriors whose productivity was based on slave workers. His supporters often show up at rallies with Celtic-inspired swords and horned helmets.[49]

Bossi sees himself as a latter-day "Braveheart."

The greatest cause of alienation from Europe's governments is the mass immigration that stirs the ethnic consciousness of the native-born who are turning to populist parties. "Radical anti-immigration parties are gaining ground across the continent," the *Financial Times* warned in 2010, alerting politicians that "ignoring the warnings sent by the rising far-right would be far more dangerous" than addressing their concerns.[50]

> The latest evidence came in last week's Italian regional elections, where the xenophobic Northern League won 13 percent of the vote. In France, the far-right National Front has also

made a comeback in recent regional elections—polling well over 20 percent of the vote in parts of the country. The British National Party may do well in next month's general elections. And anti-immigrant themes will also play a big role in the June election in the Netherlands.[51]

Alarmed at the threat to their ethnic identity, the anti-immigration parties are striding toward respectability and power. Austrian nationalists scored a triumph in 2008 when the Freedom Party and Alliance for Austria's Future together won 29 percent of the vote. In 2010, two weeks after doubling its vote in Styria, the Freedom Party under Heinz-Christian Strache, its leader since Jörg Haider's death, won 26 percent of the vote in Vienna's municipal elections, almost doubling its strength there. Strache is talked of as a future chancellor of Austria. Who is he, and what does he stand for?

> His Freedom Party is anti-EU and anti-foreigner. During their [2008] campaign, senior party members complained that immigration had brought an end to the good old days when Austrians ate Wiener schnitzel and sausages instead of "kebabs, falafel and couscous, or whatever that stuff is called." At rallies, Mr Strache pledged to set up a government ministry with the sole task of deporting unwanted foreigners.[52]

The National Front of Jean-Marie Le Pen humiliated Paris in 2009, winning more than half the vote in a suburb of Marseilles. The Swiss People's Party of Christoph Blocher, largest in Bern, was behind the referendum to change the constitution to outlaw new minarets and wearing of burkas. Fifty-eight percent of the Swiss voted with Blocher. "More than half the voters in the five biggest European economies believe women should be banned from wearing the burka."[53] When the center-right Fidesz Party ousted the socialists in 2010 in Hungary, the shocker to the *FT* was that the Jobbik Party of "right-wing extremists," which "sits squarely in Europe's most repulsive arch-nationalist tradition and which blames Jews and Roma for the hardships of other Hungarians," pulled 17 percent and entered parliament for the first time.[54]

In a *Washington Post* essay on a dying EU, Charles Kupchan, of the Council on Foreign Relations, wrote,

> Elsewhere [in Europe], rightwing populism is on the upswing—a product, primarily, of a backlash against immigrants. This hard-edged nationalism aims not only at minorities, but also at the loss of autonomy that accompanies political union.... Hungary's Jobbik Party, which borders on xenophobic, won 47 seats in elections this year—up from none in 2006.[55]

Three weeks after Kupchan wrote, the anti-immigration Sweden Democrats captured 6 percent of the vote and entered parliament for the first time with 20 seats, joining right-wing folk parties in Norway and Denmark. In April, 2011, the True Finns, nationalist, Euroskeptic, and anti-immigration, stunned Europe by capturing 19 percent of the vote and raising their representation in the 200-seat parliament from 5 to 39.

Nick Griffin, of the British National Party, who wants to "take back Britain" by providing incentives to nonwhite immigrants to go back home, appeared on the BBC's late-night *Question Time.* As John Burns of the *New York Times* wrote, the show normally attracts "a modest pre-bedtime audience."[56] Griffin drew 8.2 million viewers, on a par with World Cup games, as demonstrators excoriated the BBC for giving him a forum.

Censorship is grounded in fear. And the European establishment has begun to betray its fear of the ethnonational parties. Vlaams Blok, the most popular party in Flanders in 2004, was banned by the courts for portraying some immigrants as "criminals who take bread from the mouths of Flemish workers."[57] Vlaams Blok disappeared, and Vlaams Belang was born.

Griffin was prosecuted for inciting racial hatred for calling Islam a "wicked and vicious faith."[58] The Austrian Freedom Party's Susanne

Winter was given a three-month suspended sentence and a 24,000 euro fine "for incitement to hatred and degradation of religious doctrines." Observing that one of the Prophet's wives was only nine, Winter called Muhammad a pedophile and warned that Europe faces a "Muslim immigration tsunami."[59]

Geert Wilders, a rising figure in Dutch politics and a member of the European Parliament, was charged with hate speech for equating Islam and Nazism.[60] In June 2010, his Freedom Party became the third strongest, surpassing the ruling Christian Democrats, who lost half their parliamentary strength. "More security, less crime, less immigration, less Islam—that is what the Netherlands has chosen," said Wilders.[61] A prominent Australian Muslim cleric, Feiz Muhammad, called for the beheading of Wilders, "this Satan, this devil."[62]

That same June 2010, the disastrous performance of Les Bleus, the French soccer team in the World Cup that failed to win a single match, ignited a raucous, racially tinged debate that "focused on lack of patriotism, shared values and national honor on a team with many members who are black or brown and descended from immigrants." President Sarkozy, who called Les Bleus' performance on and off the field a "disaster," was echoed by his education minister, Luc Chatel, who denounced its Senegal-born leader. "A captain of the French team who does not sing 'the Marseillaise' shocks me.... When one wears the jersey, one should be proud to wear the colors."[63]

The 1998 French team that won the World Cup had been praised for its multiracial character—black, white, and Arab—and seen as a symbol of a new diverse France. But the 2010 team, thirteen of whose twenty-two players were men of color, was denounced by French leaders and legislators as "scum," "little troublemakers," "guys with chickpeas in their heads instead of a brain," and "a gang of hooligans." The Algerian-born minister for the banlieues criticized Sarkozy for emphasizing "national identity" and warned that the "tendency to ethnicize" the attacks on Les Bleus was "building a highway for the National Front" of Le Pen.[64]

That same summer of 2010 saw North African youth go on a rampage in Grenoble, causing President Sarkozy to declare that France was "seeing the consequences of 50 years of insufficiently controlled immigration, which have ended up in the failure of integration." Sarkozy proposed a law to strip North Africans of citizenship if they attack police officers. Critics saw the French president as "pandering to racists and xenophobes" to win back support he was bleeding to Le Pen's National Front. Said former socialist prime minister Michel Rocard of the new Sarkozy hard line, "We haven't seen this sort of thing since the Nazis."[65] Such charges did not deter Sarkozy, his eye on 2012, from deporting 18,000 Roma Gypsies, despite their EU citizenship and their right to travel the continent.

When EU Justice commissioner Viviane Reding compared the Sarkozy expulsion of Gypsies to Vichy's expulsions of Jews, Sarkozy exploded: "The comparison with the second world war and what happened in our country—it is an insult. It is a wound. It is a humiliation. It is an outrage."[66] He vowed to continue breaking up the illegal camps and deporting the Roma.

Yet, by spring 2011, in a poll of voter sentiment in the presidential election of 2012, Sarkozy was running behind Marine Le Pen, who had taken over the National Front from her father in January.[67]

Italy, with 800,000 Romanians, most of them new arrivals since 2007 and many of them Gypsies, is following France's lead. Milan is dismantling its authorized Triboniano camp as a den of thieves, said the *Washington Post*, and "bulldozing hundreds of small impromptu camps inhabited by newer arrivals and issuing mass eviction notices to Roma families." "Our final goal is to have zero Gypsy camps in Milan," said vice mayor Riccardo de Corato, "These are dark-skinned people, not Europeans like you and me.... They prostitute their wives and children."[68]

Germany, too, in the summer of 2010, played host to an ethnic row. In *Germany Does Away with Itself,* Thilo Sarrazin claimed his nation was being "dumbed down" by Turks and Kurds with higher birthrates but lower intelligence than Germans and Jews. "Hereditary factors" play a role in the disparity, wrote Sarrazin.[69] His book sold 300,000 copies in seven weeks. By early 2011, it had sold 1.2 million. Polls found 31 percent of Germans agreed that Germans are "becoming dumber," while 62 percent called Sarrazin's comments justified. Merkel denounced him, but half of Germany opposed the move to oust Sarrazin from the Social Democratic Party.

A few years ago, Sarrazin's book would not have been published. Now, concedes a *New York Times* headline, "Long Dormant After Wartime, German Pride Begins to Blink and Stir."[70]

> In ways large and small, Germany is flexing its muscles and reasserting a long-repressed national pride.... There are fears of emerging (or resurgent) chauvinism, seen recently in broadsides against Muslims by Thilo Sarrazin, who is stepping down from the board of the German Central Bank, after publishing a divisive best seller saying that Muslim immigrants are draining the social-welfare state and reproducing faster than ethnic Germans.[71]

A month after the Sarrazin affair, Merkel told young CDU members in Potsdam that Germany's attempt to build a multicultural society where Turks, Arabs, and Germans live side by side had "utterly failed." Thirty percent of Germans said in a survey that their country was now "overrun by foreigners," while an equal number believe the foreigners had come for the social benefits.[72] Within a few months of Merkel's repudiation of multiculturalism, David Cameron had seen the light, declaring "state multiculturalism" a failure.[73] He was instantly parroted by Sarkozy.

After New Year's Day, 2011, Greek Interior Minister Christian Papoutsis announced the building of a 128-mile wall on the Turkish border after more than 100,000 people had crossed over in 2010. Greece has become the main entry point into the EU for Asian and African migrants. "The Greek public has reached its limits in taking in illegal immigrants.... Greece can't take it anymore," said Papoutsis.[74]

Ethnonationalism within nations manifests itself in tribalism. Belgium, created by the Great Powers in 1831, is likely the next nation in Europe to split—into a Dutch-speaking Flanders tied to Holland by language and culture and a French-speaking Wallonia.

Flanders is conservative, capitalist, wealthy. Wallonia is poor, socialist, statist. Flanders's 60 percent of the population generates 70 percent of GDP and 80 percent of the exports. The Flemish grow weary of seeing their taxes—the top rate is 50 percent—going to sustain Wallonia where unemployment is three times as high. Flanders also seethes over a government decision to bring in French-speaking North Africans to give Walloons control of Brussels. The capital, though in Flanders, now has a French-speaking majority. By one poll, 43 percent of Flemish wish to secede.

"The enmity is everywhere," writes the *New York Times* of this last binational and bilingual country in Western Europe, save Switzerland.[75] Belgium, writes Muller, is "close to breaking up."[76] Bismarck was right, after all: "Whoever speaks of 'Europe' is wrong. It is a geographical expression."[77]

The disintegration of the nations of Old Europe will likely be a nonviolent affair. Aging countries of an old and dying continent are not going to fight to prevent people from going their separate ways. But nonviolence is not likely to be the way the Asian and African nations come apart.

SECESSIONISTS IN THE MIDDLE KINGDOM

So grave was the crisis that Hu Jintao canceled his meeting with President Obama, broke off from the G8, and flew home. Hundreds had been killed and over a thousand injured, mostly Han Chinese, in ethnic street battles with Uighurs in Xinjiang, the huge oil-rich western province that extends deep into Central Asia. The Uighurs are a Turkic-speaking Muslim people who seek to create a new nation: East Turkestan. The surge of Chinese troops into Xinjiang bespoke Beijing's fear that what happened to the Soviet Union could happen here. Unlike Mikhail Gorbachev and Boris Yeltsin, the Chinese, as they have demonstrated in Tiananmen Square and Tibet, will not blanch at bloodletting to crush secession.

China's anti-Uighur policy, writes Carl Gershman, president of the National Endowment for Democracy, "encourages Han Chinese settlement and employment in the western Xinjiang region while jobless Uighurs, especially young women, are recruited to work in factories in eastern China. The focus on women is not accidental." Said exiled Uighur leader Rebiya Kadeer, "We believe it is part of the authorities' effort to threaten our continuity as a people," as the Chinese "are taking these women out of their communities at the time they would be getting married and starting families."[78]

Beijing has sought to ensure permanent possession of Inner Mongolia, Manchuria, Xinjiang, and Tibet by swamping the indigenous populations with Chinese settlers. This was Stalin's way in the Baltic states: flood them with Russians and drown their culture, language, and identity. In July 2010, a front-page story in the *New York Times,* datelined Lhasa, Tibet, began:

> They come by the new high-altitude trains, four a day, cruising 1,200 miles past snow-capped mountains. And they come by military truck convoy, lumbering across the roof of the world.
>
> Han Chinese workers, investors, merchants, teachers and soldiers are pouring into remote Tibet. After the violence that ravaged this region in 2008, China's aim is to make Tibet wealthier—and more Chinese.[79]

Beijing's need to emphasize ethnic solidarity has been made more acute by the death of Maoism. Under the Great Helmsman, China had proclaimed herself vanguard of the world Communist revolution—the land of the true believers. Unlike the Soviet Union of Khrushchev and Brezhnev that had lost the faith, China had an ideological identity. Today, China has no ideology to hold the nation together. On the sixtieth anniversary of the revolution, Professor Zhang Ming of Renmin University in Beijing told the *New York Times*, "There is no ideology in China anymore."

> The government has no ideology. The people have no ideology. The reason the government is in power is because they can say, "I can make your lives better every day. I can give you stability. And I have the power." As long as they can make people's lives better, it's O.K. But what happens on the day when they no longer can?[80]

Excellent question.

What the Chinese do have is five thousand years of history and pride in their rise from European and Japanese subjugation in the nineteenth and twentieth centuries to world power in the twenty-first. Most critically, though there is no one language, 90 percent of her people are Han Chinese—but 100 million are not.

What holds China together if a time of troubles begins?

On the sixtieth anniversary of Mao's triumph, Michael Wines wrote that in China, "Patriotism is a staple of the education system, and citizens are exhorted to equate the state and the homeland.... [but] none of the Chinese narrative bears on the communists and their government."[81]

> [T]he official ideology of socialism and the revolutionary struggle against capitalist roaders, though still taught in universities and factory halls, is treated as dull propaganda by all except a dwindling number of true believers.
>
> Historians and sociologists say that socialist ideology once was a bedrock of Chinese patriotism and support of the government. Paradoxically, it was killed by the reform and the opening of China that began thirty years ago and brought the economic miracle of today.[82]

China's Communist rulers face an inevitable crisis of legitimacy.

By abandoning Maoism and revolution, the party built a mighty nation, but destroyed the rationale for its monopoly of power. As long as China succeeds, the Communists can say: our party is indispensable. But what does the party fall back on should China begin to fail? How do they answer if the people say, "China is failing. It is time for you to move on and for us to find new leaders with new ideas, and try a new road"? What is the justification for a Communist Party retaining absolute power if that party no longer delivers the capitalist goods the Chinese people have come to expect?

Patriotism is said to be the last refuge of the scoundrel. Patriotism and the race card may be the last refuge of the Chinese Communists. This could mean trouble for the Taiwanese and the ethnic neighbors with whom Beijing has border and territorial quarrels: Russia, Japan, India, and the other claimants to the Paracel and Spratly Islands in the South China Sea.

Yet, the contrast between a serious China and an insouciant America on this issue of national identity is startling. Beijing floods its borderlands with Chinese and smothers religious and ethnic diversity to keep China whole and one. America, declaring, "Our diversity is our strength!" invites in the world to swamp her native-born. China sees ethnonationalism among its unhappy minorities as an existential threat. The U.S. elite regard ethnicity as the obsession of the underclass.

THE GLOBAL BALKANS

Ethnonationalism is on the boil across what Zbigniew Brzezinski calls the global Balkans. And India, the other emergent great power in Asia, is even more vulnerable than China, as she is more diverse. In Kashmir, India's Muslim-majority state, a separatist movement is entrenched and the summer of 2010 saw some of the worst violence in years. Since independence in 1947, India has fought three wars with Pakistan, with Kashmir always at issue. New Delhi is also erecting a 2,500-mile fence around Bangladesh to keep arms smugglers and Muslim extremists out.[83] Though a Hindu nation, India is also the world's third largest Muslim nation with an estimated 150 million believers. In recent decades a rising Muslim militancy has called into being a Hindu party, the BJP, which is now India's second largest.

But India's troubles only begin in Kashmir. The Tamils in the south still seethe over their kinsmen's failure to carve a nation out of Sri Lanka, apart from the Sinhalese. Tens of thousands died in that island's civil war that ended in May 2009. Delhi intervened in 1987 in what came to be called India's Vietnam.

Nagaland, one of India's smallest states, the size of Connecticut and Rhode Island, borders Burma and, with a Christian population, has hosted an independence movement since 1947. Perhaps the most powerful forces that threaten India's stability and unity are the Maoist Naxalites who have battled New Delhi since 1967 and boast ten to twenty thousand fighters. In a recent ambush, 76 Indian soldiers were massacred. In May 2010, a high-speed train was derailed when Maoists cut out a foot of track. Eighty-one civilians were killed, more than 200 wounded. Naxalites are our "first enemy," says Home Secretary G. K. Pillai.[84] Prime Minister Manmohan Singh told police chiefs in Delhi the violence is increasing in the Naxalite war that has already taken 6,000 lives and the Maoists are winning the struggle to carve out a Communist state: "I have consistently held that in many ways, left-wing extremism poses perhaps the gravest internal security threat our country faces."[85]

Other secessionists are battling to break apart India's twenty-eight states. The strongest is the drive to separate Talangana from Andhra Pradesh. Hunger strikes by Talangana leaders and suicides by students have brought the cause to the attention of the world and put it on the docket of the Congress Party.

Given the tension between Muslim and Hindu, the language and cultural differences, the disparities of wealth between middle and upper classes and the dirt-poor hundreds of millions, India is a prime candidate for ethnonational insurrections throughout the twenty-first century.

In Burma, the junta has deployed thousands of troops to the north to put down Kokang, Wa, and Kachin rebels. The Kokang, many of whom are ethnic Chinese, have fled in the tens of thousands to China's Yunnan.[86] In the east, the Karen have conducted the world's longest-running insurgency, since Burma became a nation in 1948. With the release of Nobel laureate and pro-democracy heroine Aung San Suu Kyi from house arrest, a question arises: Would a democratic Burma suppress the rebels to hold Burma together as the junta has done?

Ethnic minorities make up 40 percent of the population and the tribes have resisted domination since Britain gave Burma its independence. "Social conflict based on ethnicity has been at the heart of Burma's political failure for decades," says Andrew Heyn, the British ambassador in Rangoon.[87]

In Thailand, Malays have attacked Buddhist monks and temples and officials of the government. Their goal: an Islamic Malay nation wedged between Thailand and Malaysia. "Terrorist attacks in the villages of southern Thailand have reached an all-time high, as schools become breeding grounds for young fighters," reports the *Washington Times*. "Thailand Muslims reject anything modern and forms of entertainment, including televisions, except to watch soccer matches," said a counselor at the Thai embassy.[88]

On December 31, 2009, after a court ruling in Malaysia granted Christians the right to use the name Allah when speaking of God, seven churches were firebombed. As religion correlates with race in Malaysia—the constitution equates Muslim and Malay—critics charged the regime with exploiting a religious clash to incite race resentment. The Chinese and Indian minorities are Buddhist, Hindu, and Christian.[89]

Jacqueline Ann Surin, editor of a Malaysian news site, told the *New York Times*, "Malaysia is peculiar in that we have race-based politics and over the past decade or so we have seen an escalation of the notion that

Malay Malaysians are superior. . . . So it's a logical progression that if the Malay is considered superior by the state to all others in Malaysia, then Islam will also be deemed superior to other religions."[90]

In Mindanao, a Moro separatist movement has been fighting on and off for the half millennium since the Spanish conquered the Philippines and Catholicism became the national faith. Their religion and their resistance have created a new people. "We don't believe we are Filipinos," says Kim Bagundang, of the Linguasan Youth Association. "That's the essential problem." The Moros seek to have the Muslim lands of Mindanao declared an "ancestral domain" where they will rule and their Islamic faith and culture will be dominant.[91]

In Central Mindanao in late 2009, a convoy of 57 journalists and lawyers and the wife and relatives of a local vice mayor was intercepted by 100 armed men.[92] The women were raped, the entire party murdered, with many mutilated in what is called the Maguindanao massacre. The atrocity was "unequaled in recent history," said an adviser to President Arroyo. "The Muslim insurgency has killed about 120,000 people since the 1970s," the *Washington Post* reported, an astonishingly high figure.[93] On accepting his Nobel peace prize, Barack Obama recognized the new reality that many statesmen yet fail to see:

> [The] old architecture is buckling under the weight of new threats. . . . wars between nations have increasingly given way to wars within nations. The resurgence of ethnic or sectarian conflicts, the growth of secessionist movements, insurgencies and failed states . . . have increasingly trapped civilians in unending chaos.[94]

"It is useless to say that nationalism and ethnic tribalism have no place in the international relations of the 21st century," says the British diplomat Sir Christopher Meyer. "If anything the spread of Western-style democracy has amplified their appeal and resonance."[95]

"OUR GREATEST ENEMY IS ETHNIC NATIONALISM"

In the fall of 2009, Jundallah (God's Brigade) of Sistan-Baluchistan carried out a spectacular act of terror, killing forty Iranians including a brigadier general of the Revolutionary Guard. Tehran accused the United States of fomenting ethnic separatism to break up the country or bring about regime change. A million Baluch live in Iran where Arabs, Azeris, Kurds, and other minorities constitute half the population, with Persians the other half.

There are five million Baluch in Pakistan where the oil- and gas-rich province of Baluchistan is 40 percent of the national territory. Baluchi grievances against the army and regime are mounting. "Baluch nationalism is more broad-based, is a more serious phenomenon than at any time in the past," says Selig Harrison, of the Center for International Policy, an authority on the Baluch, who seek to carve a new nation out of Pakistan and Iran.[96]

Iraq is Sunni, Shia, and Christian; Arab, Kurd, and Turkomen. No one rules out a return to sectarian or civil war when the Americans depart, or an Arab-Kurd clash over Kirkuk. Kurds in Turkey's south and east number, by some counts, 20 to 25 million. This Kurdish enclave looks over the border to Iraqi Kurdistan with its population of five million as model and magnet. In July 2010, the president of Iraq's Kurdish region, Massoud Barzani, told an Egyptian television station, "The Kurdish nation ... should have its own state like the Turkish, Persian and Arab nations. We are not claiming we are stronger than them, but we have nothing less than those nations."[97] Were one to wager on new nations being born, Kurdistan, Baluchistan, Palestine, and Pashtunistan would be among the favorites.

The Pashtun, from whom many of the Taliban came, are the largest Afghan tribe, occupying the nation's south and east, while the Hazara are in the central mountains. Tajiks and Uzbeks made up most of the Northern Alliance the Americans conscripted to take down the Taliban. There may be 35 to 40 million Pashtun, a population larger than that of many European nations. Most live in Pakistan, where they give sanctuary to their Afghan cousins. That Tajiks are coming to dominate the army is certain to deepen Pashtun resistance to the American-backed regime of President Hamid Karzai.

"Ethnic chauvinism, which has long bedeviled this fiercely tribal country and fueled a destructive civil war in the 1990s, is erupting again," wrote *Washington Post* foreign correspondent Pamela Constable from Kabul on Christmas Eve 2010.[98]

In the 2010 elections, the Hazara, a repressed Shia minority, converted themselves into a tribal party and won every seat in the province of Ghazni. The majority Pashtun, divided in their loyalties between Karzai and the Taliban, threatened with reprisals if they voted, stayed home. The Hazara came out and won 50 of 249 seats in the lower house of parliament. But they are understandably nervous over their success. "This is a multiethnic country, and all groups need to be represented," said Dr. Amin Ahmadi, dean of two small Hazara Shiite colleges in Kabul. "Our greatest enemy is ethnic nationalism."[99]

THE ENDURING TRIBALISM OF AFRICA

Nigeria's civil war, where a million perished, was an ethnonational war of secession by the Ibo. When, after years of civil war, Rhodesia became Zimbabwe, the Mashona of Robert Mugabe proceeded to massacre 7,000 Matabele of rival Joshua Nkomo's tribe to teach him a lesson. In Rwanda, Hutu massacred Tutsi. After the 2008 elections in Kenya, the Kikuyu of Mau Mau chief and founding father Jomo Kenyatta were ethnically cleansed by the Luo.

"More than 2,000 people have been killed this year in ethnically driven battles" in southern Sudan, reported the *New York Times* in 2009. The massacres were the work of Nuer warriors against Dinka villagers in Jonglei state.[100] The Muslim north may have been stirring up tribal war to divide the Christian and animist south before the 2011 election to determine whether the south would secede. Between north and south, the conflict is religious and racial. Within the south it is tribal.

In January 2011, the south voted 99–1 to secede and create the Republic of South Sudan, a decision described by one Cairo press observer as a "dangerous precedent in an Arab world looking increasingly fractured along sectarian and ethnic lines." Salama Ahmed Salama, of al-Shorouk, dissented: "The lesson we must all learn is that secession... can be the road to safety when union becomes a heavy and unbearable burden on people."[101]

Across the Red Sea, war-torn Yemen, with Sanhan, Mareb, and Jahm among the dominant tribes, is in danger of splitting apart. In the oil-rich but poor and populous south, which includes the old British colony of Aden that became a Marxist state before uniting with the north in 1990, a secessionist movement is building. A north-south civil war was fought in 1994. The forces pulling Yemen apart are religious—the Houthi rebels in the north are Shia—and tribal. Says Gregory Johnson, of Princeton:

> Secession is a major problem for Yemen...the government's inability to put down the rebellion in the north has certainly emboldened calls for secession in the south. If the Yemeni state falls apart, I do not believe it will separate into two pieces along the pre-unification lines prior to 1990. It will be much messier and much more chaotic than a simple bifurcation would suggest.[102]

A fractured Yemen that shares a border with Saudi Arabia would be perilous for Riyadh and create new opportunities for al-Qaeda, which already has a presence there and across the Red Sea in Somalia.

In Lebanon, the divisions are ideological, religious, and ethnic: Falange and Hezbollah, Muslim and Christian, Sunni and Shia, Arab and Druze. According to scholar Donald L. Horowitz:

> Connections among Biafra, Bangladesh, and Burundi, Beirut, Brussels, and Belfast were at first hesitantly made—isn't one "tribal," another "linguistic," another "religious"?—but that is true no longer. Ethnicity has fought and bled and burned its way into public and scholarly consciousness.[103]

The point is crucial. As Catholicism was integral to Irish identity in the 1919–1921 rising and to Polish identity in resistance to Communism, religion has become a feature of sacred identity.

Two days after the fall of Egypt's Hosni Mubarak, Colonel Muammar Khadafi in Libya, suddenly threatened himself, sought to redirect Arab rage against the West by melding religious and racial identity. On the birthday of the Prophet, he issued a call to Muslim countries to join forces, saying the world was divided into white, denoting America, Europe, and Israel, and green, for the Muslim world.

"The white colour has decided to get rid of the green colour," said Khadafi. "These [Muslim] countries should be united against the white colour because all of these white countries are the enemies of Islam."[104]

When a rebellion erupted to depose him, and America intervened to prevent what Obama said was an imminent massacre in Benghazi, Khadafi instantly played the tribal card, declaring "colonialist crusaders," i.e., white Christians, are coming again to conquer our Arab and Muslim land.

Under Prime Minister Recep Tayyip Erdogan and his Justice and Development Party, Turkey is shedding a secular identity formalized by the founding father of modern Turkey, Mustafa Kemal Ataturk, in 1923, and reassuming its religious identity as an Islamic nation that belongs with the Islamic world as much or more than it does with the West. Their Islamic identity has also made of Hamas in Gaza and Hezbollah in Lebanon far more formidable foes of Israel than Yasser Arafat's secular PLO ever was.

Israel is a nation where constant conflict rages between democratist ideology, Zionist ethnonationalism, and religious fundamentalism. Netanyahu and Likud insist that, as a precondition for a Palestinian state,

the Palestinians must recognize Israel as a "Jewish state" whose character must forever remain Jewish. This will not be easy to sustain, as the
Palestinian Central Bureau of Statistics has identified 2014 as the year
when Arabs west of the Jordan—in Israel, Jerusalem, Gaza, and the West
Bank—at 6.1 million, equal and begin to outnumber the Jewish population.[105]

The goal of Foreign Minister Avigdor Lieberman and his nationalist
party, Yisrael Beiteinu, is "ethnic cleansing," writes the *American Prospect*:
"[A]s the creepy name (which translates into 'Our Home Is Israel') suggests, Yisrael Beiteinu believes the million-plus Arab citizens of Israel
must be expelled."[106] Lieberman's politics are described by the former
editor of the *New Republic*, Peter Beinart:

> In his youth, he briefly joined Meir Kahane's now banned
> Kach Party, which . . . advocated the expulsion of Arabs from
> Israeli soil. Now Lieberman's position might be called "pre-
> expulsion." He wants to revoke the citizenship of Israeli Arabs
> who won't swear a loyalty oath to the Jewish state. . . . He said
> Arab Knesset members who met with representatives of Hamas
> should be executed. He wants to jail Arabs who publicly mourn
> on Israeli Independence Day, and he hopes to permanently
> deny citizenship to Arabs from other countries who marry
> Arab citizens of Israel.[107]

What is Avigdor Lieberman but an ethnonationalist?

Israel's demand that she be formally recognized as a "Jewish state,"
even by her own non-Jewish citizens, represents a claim that Israel is an
ethnonational state of, by, and for Jews. Former Israeli ambassador to the
United States David Ivry, who claims he persuaded an aide to Secretary
of State Colin Powell to insert the phrase "Jewish state" for the first time
in a major U.S. address on the Middle East, defines its ethnonational
meaning precisely and coldly: "The Palestinians should have no right of
return; only Jewish refugees can ever come back."[108]

THE INDIGENOUS PEOPLES' REVOLT

Evo Morales was elected president in 2005 determined to redistribute Bolivian wealth to his own Aymara tribe and the "indigenous peoples" he claims were robbed by white men who came after Columbus. With Hugo Chávez, Morales is goading the Indians to take back what was allegedly stolen from them. And he has met with no small success.

"Vote Reflects Racial Divide," ran the banner over a story datelined Santa Cruz that began, "The Bolivian vote to approve a new constitution backed by Leftist President Evo Morales reflected racial divisions between the nation's Indian majority and those with European ancestry."

While the predominantly white and mestizo provinces voted against Morales's constitution, it won huge majorities among the Indian tribes of the western highlands. For the new constitution is about group rights. By Article 190, Bolivia's thirty-six Indian areas are authorized to "exercise their jurisdictional functions through their own principles, values, cultures, norms and procedures." Tribal law is to become provincial law and, one day, national law. Pizarro's triumph over the Incas is to be overturned. Governor Mario Cossío of Tarija province, which voted no, says the new constitution will create a "totalitarian regime" run by an "ethnically based bureaucracy."[109] Opponents, reports the *Economist,* say the "community justice" provisions of the constitution "will politicize justice ... and legitimize mob justice in the form of lynchings and stonings, which have become more common over the past two years."[110]

Morales replies: "Original Bolivians who have been here for a thousand years are many but poor. Recently arrived Bolivians are few but rich."[111]

Josh Partlow, of the *Washington Post,* writes that the dividing line in Bolivia "transcends economics and has laid bare cultural and geographic differences as well. People from the Andean highlands, with its indigenous majority, often accuse those of Spanish descent in the lowlands [of Santa Cruz] of having a racist agenda."[112]

"Everything looks bad to the people who used to be in power,"
said Felipe Montevilla, 55, a man of the Aymara ethnic group
who attended a Morales rally in the town of Viacha, on the
high plateau above the national capital, La Paz. "For 500 years,
they never had to tip their hat to an indigenous man. This
problem is primarily racist," Montevilla said.[113]

Morales is using principles and procedures invented by white men—
universal franchise and majority rule—to dispossess white men. He is
using democratic means for tribal ends, imposing Indian law where Indians are the majority. The nineteenth-century French rightist Louis
Veuillot explained how anti-democrats would dispossess the democrats: "When I am the weaker I ask you for my freedom because that is
your principle; but when I am the stronger I take away your freedom
because that is my principle."[114]

Upon what ground do democratists stand to tell Morales he cannot
use democracy to dispossess the European minority and empower his
own race? What does the future hold for the West when people of European descent become a minority in nations they created, and people of
color decide to vote themselves proportionate or larger shares of the
national wealth?

In 2009, Morales was reelected in a landslide. Nor is Bolivia alone
among nations where ethnicity and democracy are coming together to
overturn the verdicts of free markets.

"WORLD ON FIRE"

Our situation may be about to become even more grim.

How much more is told in *World on Fire: How Exporting Free Market
Democracy Breeds Ethnic Hatred and Global Instability.* Amy Chua's book is
about those "ethnic minorities who ... tend under market conditions to
dominate economically, often to a startling extent, the 'indigenous' majorities around them."[115]

Examples are the overseas Chinese, the Indians of East Africa, whites in south Africa, and Europeans in the Andean countries. Chua, whose aunt was a Chinese national whose throat was cut by a Filipino chauffeur resentful of her wealth, argues that while free markets often concentrate a nation's wealth among ethnic minorities, democracy gives power to impoverished ethnic majorities. This has proven a combustible and lethal cocktail.

> In these circumstances, the pursuit of free-market democracy becomes an engine of potentially catastrophic ethnonationalism, pitting a frustrated "indigenous" majority, easily aroused by opportunistic vote-seeking politicians, against a resented wealthy ethnic minority. This confrontation is playing out in country after country, from Indonesia to Sierra Leone, from Zimbabwe to Venezuela, from Russia to the Middle East.[116]

In 1965, as recounted in the Mel Gibson film *The Year of Living Dangerously,* Indonesian mobs massacred hundreds of thousands of Chinese, the market-dominant minority. Chua describes what happened in 1998, when Suharto, Sukarno's successor, who had protected the 3 percent of Chinese who controlled much of the nation's wealth, was in turn ousted:

> Indonesians were euphoric. After the words "free and fair elections" hit the U.S. headlines, Americans were euphoric. Democratic elections, it was thought, would finally bring to Indonesia the kind of peace and legitimacy perfect for sustaining free markets....
>
> That's not what happened in Indonesia. The fall of Suharto's autocracy was accompanied by an eruption of ferocious anti-Chinese violence in which delirious, mass-supported

Muslim mobs burned, looted and killed anything Chinese, ultimately leaving two thousand people dead.[117]

Across the Malacca Strait a similar script was played out.

In May 1969, riots in Malaysia brought death to hundreds of Chinese, the rape of their women, suspension of parliament and erection of a system of race preferences. As Malays, *bumiputra*, sons of the soil, were 62 percent of the population but had only 2 percent of the wealth, the government "adopted sweeping ethnic quotas on corporate equity ownership, university admissions, government licensing, and commercial employment.... It also initiated large scale purchases of corporate assets on behalf of the Malay majority."[118]

Chinese companies were forced to set aside 30 percent of equity for Malays, but given no choice as to who their new partners would be. Firms seeking to list on the stock exchange were required to have 30 percent *bumiputra* ownership. Not until 2009 did Malaysia's ruling coalition, facing recession, rising Chinese and Indian protests, and competition for foreign investment, relent and roll back the 30 percent rule.[119]

Third World nationalizations in the postcolonial era, writes Chua, by and large did not seek to abolish private property but to transfer it from the market-dominant minority to the largest and most powerful tribe or ethnic group:

> In Uganda...the politically dominant groups of the north have repeatedly subjected the economically powerful Baganda of the south to bloody purges. In Nigeria in 1966, tens of thousands of Ibo were slaughtered indiscriminately by furious mobs. In Ethiopia, the relatively prosperous Eritreans were recently expelled en masse.... [I]n Rwanda, the genocidal massacre of the Tutsi minority is inextricably connected with their historic economic dominance.[120]

In 1972, Idi Amin gave the 75,000 Indians who ran small businesses ninety days to get out of Uganda. Their property was confiscated and turned over to Africans.

At "liberation" in 1979, the whites of Zimbabwe controlled most of the wealth. In three decades they have been picked clean. In a 2010 essay on "The White Tribes," Joshua Hammer writes, "But nowhere was white flight more dramatic than in Zimbabwe, where the white population dropped from a peak of around 296,000 in 1975 (five percent of the population) to 120,000 in 1999 to just 30,000 today."[121]

Mugabe has now gone after the last four thousand white-owned farms that account for almost all of Zimbabwe's exports—to hand them to loyalists. Zimbabwe is now a basket case, its starving people fleeing to a South Africa that has started down the same path.

On April 3, 2010, Eugène Terre'Blanche, a white nationalist and last-ditch defender of apartheid, was hacked to death by two black employees on his farm. The murder came, wrote the *Financial Times*, as "Julius Malema, the demagogic leader of the ruling African National Congress's powerful youth wing, has been touring the country calling for nationalization of private businesses and singing the Apartheid-era song containing the lyrics 'Kill the Boer.'"[122] Since the end of apartheid, agricultural unions claim three thousand white farmers have been killed.[123] Half the white population has left the country.

Though a South African court declared "Kill the Boer" hate speech, Malema continued to sing it and traveled to Zimbabwe to hail Mugabe for his violent seizures of white-owned farms. The *FT* urged President Jacob Zuma to steal the thunder of his ANC youth leader with a more rapid redistribution of white-owned land to black South Africans. Since the end of apartheid, fifteen million acres of farmland have been transferred to black owners.[124]

South Africa's regime, writes Robert Guest of the *Economist*, wants "about 25% of most industries to be in black hands by 2010. The new black capitalists are supposed to pay a 'market' price for their acquisitions, but they don't have the money, so they don't."

Instead, the focus is on redistribution. And not the conventional sort, from rich to poor, but from white to black, which is not the same. South Africa has embarked on probably the most extreme affirmative action program anywhere. Private companies above a certain size are obliged to try to make their workforces "demographically representative" (75 percent black, 50 percent female, etc.) from factory floor to boardroom.[125]

Under the Employment Equity Act and Black Economic Empowerment Act, companies are required to discriminate in hiring against white males in favor of white women, persons of color, people with disabilities, and those from rural areas. The government employment act establishes a quota of 80% of all new jobs for blacks.[126]

A racial-ethnic spoils system may be the future in the Third World, leading, as in Africa, to dispossession and departure of whites and Indians whose ancestors were brought there by the British to help run the empire, and were abandoned when the British departed. In Australia, an open-borders policy that has brought millions in from Asia, writes ethologist Frank Salter, has begun to threaten social cohesion and national unity:

> Ethnic stratification is taking place.... Anglo Australians... are presently being displaced disproportionately in the professions and in senior managerial positions by Asian immigrants and their children. The situation is dramatic at selective schools which are the high road to university and the professions. Ethnocentrism is not a White disorder and evidence is emerging that immigrant communities harbour invidious attitudes towards Anglo Australians, disparaging their culture and the legitimacy of their central place in national identity.[127]

Nor are Americans strangers to race violence over who has what. Korean grocers are a visible presence in black communities and the

Korean aptitude for entrepreneurship is legendary. A 2002 census report found 95,000 black-owned businesses in America to 57,000 Korean-owned businesses, though blacks outnumber Korean Americans twenty-five to one.[128] Thus, a Korean American is fifteen times as likely to own a business with employees as an African American. Of all Asian ethnic groups, Koreans have the highest rate of business ownership. Nor has this gone unnoticed. In his 1991 rap song, Ice Cube reminded Korean shopkeepers who was boss in the 'hood.

> *So pay respect to the black fist*
> *or we'll burn your store, right down to a crisp....*
> *Cause you can't turn the ghetto—into Black Korea.*[129]

The following April, in the worst race violence in twentieth-century America, mobs poured out of South Central to attack Koreatown.

Three years later, after protests at Jewish-owned Freddy's Fashion Mart in Harlem featuring chants of "Burn down the Jew store," a berserk African American burst in and shot four employees, then set fire to the store, killing seven in all.

How deep does the resentment run?

In 2006, Andrew Young, former UN ambassador and former Atlanta mayor, was asked if he thought it right that Walmart, whose spokesman he was, was killing mom-and-pop stores in the African American community. An agitated Young fired back.

> Well, I think they should; they ran the "mom-and-pop" stores out of my neighborhood.... But you see those are the people who have been overcharging us—selling us stale bread and bad meat and wilted vegetables. And they sold out and moved to Florida. I think they've ripped off our communities enough. First it was Jews, then it was Koreans, now it's Arabs; very few black people own these stores.[130]

The Korean presence in the black community seems ever on the mind, especially the Korean monopoly of the "black hair" market.

"Whether you're in the suburbs of Houston or on MLK Boulevard in Anytown, USA," writes R. Asmerom, in the *Atlanta Post*, "that image of the few Koreans in the neighborhoods only existing behind the cash register of liquor, beauty supply and other retail shops is still perplexing." Asmerom reported that in September 2010, "[T]here are over 9,000 Korean-owned beauty supply stores serving a billion dollar market for Black hair." The Korean "concentration in these businesses promoted a shroud of secrecy and protectiveness" that "fueled part of the tension between Korean business owners and the urban African-American community which famously erupted during the 1992 Los Angeles riots."[131]

Asians and whites are America's market-dominant majority. In half a century, they will become the minority. Already, they are shrinking minorities in major cities. By Chua's thesis, racial and ethnic majorities will use electoral power to elevate politicians to expropriate the wealth of the minority as is happening with ever-heavier taxes on the upper middle class and wealthy, Asian and white, in California.

The Obama Democrats, who campaigned for abolishing "tax cuts for the rich," individuals earning $200,000 and families earning $250,000, may be a harbinger of what is to come with the rise of Third World America.

"WHITE PEOPLE WITH BLUE EYES"

Chua exposes a fatal flaw of democracy in multiethnic nations.

Free markets concentrate wealth in the hands of a market-capable ethnic minority. Democracy empowers the ethnic majority. When the latter begin to demand a larger share of the wealth, demagogues arise to meet those demands. Hugo Chávez, Evo Morales, Ollanta Humala, Daniel Ortega all profess to speak for the indigenous Indians they claim were robbed by the Portuguese, Spanish, and other Europeans who came after Columbus.

In the United States, MEChA, the "Movimiento Estudiantil Chicano de Aztlán," or "Chicano Student Movement of Aztlán," which is present on hundreds of campuses and in the barrios of the Southwest, is a replica of these indigenous peoples' movements in Latin America. In *World on Fire,* Chua writes of how Hugo Chavez vaulted to power in one of the wealthiest nations of South America.

> Chavez swept to his landslide victory on a wave of explicit ethnically based populism. Demanding "a social revolution," Chavez aroused to impassioned political consciousness Venezuela's brown-skinned pardos, who make up 80 percent of the population, who are largely destitute, and, who, like "The Indian from Barinas"—as Chavez refers to himself—have "thick mouths" and "Chinese-looking eyes." "He is one of us," wept cheering, growth-stunted washerwomen, maids, and peasants. "We've never had another president like that before."[132]

Two hundred years after Spanish America broke free of Madrid, a deep division between the Spanish and white and the Indian and African, on the lines of race, class, and income, endures. In Colombia that division is on display every November in rival beauty contests.

At the Naval Museum in Cartagena in 2010, writes the *New York Times,* "light-skinned daughters of prominent families" competed for the title of Miss Colombia and "sashayed about flashing perfect smiles and impossibly high cheekbones."[133]

A few miles away in a slum called Boston, another beauty contest was being held to crown Miss Independence, queen of the slums. As Colombia has the largest black population of any Spanish-speaking nation, the new Miss Independence was the dark-skinned daughter of a maid who earned six dollars a day cleaning houses of the Cartagena rich. Only once in the seventy-six-year history of the Miss Colombia pageant has an Afro-Colombian candidate won.[134]

Clashes along these same dividing lines—race, class, income—may decide the future of all of Latin America, and not only Latin America.

During the financial crisis, President Lula da Silva, speaking at a press conference with Gordon Brown, stoked the racial resentment of black and brown against the market-dominant minority of the Global Economy:

> This crisis was caused by the irrational behavior of white people with blue eyes, who before the crisis appeared to know everything and now demonstrate that they know nothing....I do not know any black or indigenous bankers so I can only say [it is wrong] that this part of mankind which is victimized more than any other should pay for the crisis.[135]

When riots broke out in Jamaica in May 2010, Orlando Patterson wrote, echoing Chua, "The violence tearing apart Jamaica, a democratic state, raises serious questions...[about] the link between violence and democracy itself."[136]

> In diverse democracies, the temptation of leaders to exploit ethnic identity for political ends is an all too frequent source of major conflict, sometimes culminating in oppression of minorities and even genocide. We saw this happen in Rwanda in 1994 and the former Yugoslav states in the 1990s. Dennis Austin, who has studied political strife in India and Sri Lanka, has concluded that in such societies, "democracy is itself a spur to violence," adding "depth to the sense of division."[137]

In the spring 2010 violence in Kyrgyzstan that toppled the president and triggered the ethnic cleansing and killing of Uzbeks, Kyrgyz set out to pillage a Chinese-owned mall. "Armed with iron bars and clubs," reported the *Washington Post*, "the mob stormed into the Guoying center in the middle of the night, looting, smashing and then burning the best-known emblem of China's economic presence here in the capital."[138]

Ethnonationalism and populism seem everywhere on the rise, with animosity toward "overseas Chinese" spreading across the Third World where they have settled and succeeded. "It is getting very difficult to be Chinese here," said the leader of a trade group in Bishkek.[139] Race resentment and ethnic envy have produced many horrors of our world, but only a fool will deny their power or try to define them out of existence. They are real and we must live with them.

What Amy Chua implies in *World on Fire* bears repeating.

America's crusade for global democracy may, if successful, ensure endless ethnic warfare. For free markets enrich the economically able, the winners in society—Chinese, Indians, Ibo, Tutsis, whites—while democracy empowers the ethnic majority, the losers. Rulers, dependent on the majority, like Mugabe on his Shona, will then use the law or vigilante justice to reward the people on whom they depend for power, by stripping the minority of its wealth and condoning the humiliation of and violence against that minority. Again and again and again it has happened.

Consider Chua's law on a global scale. The market dominant minority for five hundred years has been Europeans, now down to a sixth of the world's population and fated to be a tenth or less in 2060. The world's majority will be African, Arab, Latin, Asian. Yet, these billions of people have only a fraction of the world's wealth. Is it not inevitable that there will arise an irresistible worldwide clamor that the few who have so much transfer more of what they have to those who have so little?

Why would Western nations further empower, though transnational institutions, a world majority that believes we are rich because they are poor? Chávez is the hero type of Frantz Fanon's *Wretched of the Earth*. As Chua writes, "Like Bolivia's Amerindian rebel leader Mallku and Ecuador's Villavicencio, Chavez generated mass support by attacking Venezuela's 'rotten' white elites."[140] Is Hugo Chavez a harbinger of what is to come?

An alarmed Russian ambassador to NATO, Dmitry Rogozin, thinks so, and has implored the white nations to unite or fall one by one:

> There is an enormous distance between Europe and the Third World. There is a new civilization emerging in the Third World that thinks that the white, northern hemisphere has always oppressed it and must therefore fall at its feet now. This is very serious. If the northern civilization wants to protect itself, it must be united: America, the European Union, and Russia. If they are not together they will be defeated one by one.[141]

CURSE OR BLESSING

Is ethnonationalism a genetic disease of mankind that all good men should quarantine wherever it breaks out? Or is this drive of awakened peoples to create nations of their own where their own kind come first a force of nature that must be accommodated if we are ever to know peace? To many who lived through the twentieth century, the poisonous fruit of ethnonationalism, the horrors it produced from Nanking to Auschwitz to Rwanda, answer the question with finality: ethnonationalism is a beast that must be chained. Yet ethnonationalism liberated the captive nations and brought down the "evil empire." And with the rise of Solidarity and its crushing by General Wojciech Jaruzelski on Moscow's orders, America's cry was "Let Poland be Poland!" Ethnonationalism gave birth to scores of African and Asian nations that came out of the old European empires. Many are prosperous and peaceful.

America was herself a product of ethnonationalism, the awakening consciousness of the colonists that while we were the children of Europeans we were also a new people, unique, separate, and identifiable: Americans.

Ethnonationalism was behind the pogroms of Europe but created the nation of Israel. Ethnonationalism led to the exodus of six hundred thousand Arabs from their homes in Palestine, the Nakba, or catastrophe, of 1948, but it also birthed in the refugee camps and two intifadas a new people. Palestinians will, God willing, soon have a nation of their own.

If ethnonationalism has been behind terrible crimes, have not great crimes been committed in the name of religion? Do we therefore decry all religions? "Nations are the wealth of humanity, its generalized personalities. The very least of them wears its own special colors, and bears within itself a special facet of divine intention," said Solzhenitsyn.[142]

We may deny the existence of ethnonationalism, detest it, condemn it. But this creator and destroyer of empires and nations is a force infinitely more powerful than globalism, for it engages the heart. Men will die for it.

Religion, race, culture, and tribe are the four horsemen of the coming apocalypse. But let us give the last word to Professor Jerry Muller: "Americans . . . find ethnonationalism discomfiting both intellectually and morally. Social scientists go to great lengths to demonstrate that it is a product not of nature but of culture. . . . But none of this will make ethnonationalism go away."[143]

9

"THE WHITE PARTY"

The face of America is changing. It's not Joe the Plumber.[1]
—SOLEDAD O'BRIEN, NOV. 4, 2008
CNN Anchor

The Republican Party is becoming the monochromatic party.[2]
—GLORIA BORGER, NOV. 4, 2008
CNN Commentator

*If you look at folks of color . . . they're more successful in the Democratic Party
than they are in the white, excuse me, in the Republican Party.*[3]
—HOWARD DEAN, AUGUST 2008
Democratic Party Chairman

Agaffe, said Michael Kinsley, is when a politician blurts out an impermissible truth, then hastily recants lest he cripple his career.

In the quotation above, Howard Dean committed a gaffe. He told an inconvenient truth. For the Republican Party may be fairly described as the white party, though this was not always true. Before the New Deal, the Democrats were the white party, as they had almost zero black support, having been the party of secession and segregation while Republicans were the party of Lincoln and emancipation. In the Depression year of 1932, a majority of black Americans voted for Hoover and against FDR.

Franklin Roosevelt swiftly ended that tradition in the North, where his New Deal drew support from black voters, even as his Dixiecrat allies continued to deny African Americans the right to vote in the eleven states of the old Confederacy.

How did presidential nominees like Al Smith and FDR of New York and Adlai Stevenson of Illinois sustain the alliance of northern liberals and Southern segregationists? By balancing progressive candidates with Southern or border-state segregationists on every national ticket between 1928 and 1960, except 1940. Those vice presidential nominees were Joe Robinson, of Arkansas, in 1928; John Nance Garner, of Texas, in 1932 and 1936; Harry Truman, of Missouri, who had flirted with the Klan, in 1944; Alben Barkley, of Kentucky, in 1948; John Sparkman, of Alabama, in 1952, who would sign the Southern Manifesto denouncing the *Brown* decision; and Estes Kefauver, of Tennessee, in 1956.

Before offering the vice presidency to Henry Wallace in 1940 as a replacement for "Cactus Jack" Garner, FDR sounded out Senator James Byrnes of South Carolina. "Jimmy" Byrnes, a protégé of "Pitchfork" Ben Tillman, was a white supremacist. "This is a white man's country and will always remain a white man's country," he once declared.[4]

Byrnes, regarded as a Southern moderate, had led the Senate battle against the anti-lynching law and helped filibuster it to death in 1938. Offered the vice presidency in 1940, he turned it down, fearing his record on race would hurt FDR in the North. Had Byrnes accepted the vice presidency, he would almost surely have become president when FDR died in 1945, giving America a white supremacist to lead her into a postcolonial era.[5] On his accession to the presidency, Truman, who also admired Byrnes, named him secretary of state.

Democratic presidents also rewarded their segregationist allies with Supreme Court seats. Wilson named the anti-Semite James C. McReynolds to the Court in 1914. The 1924 official photograph of the Court was never taken, as McReynolds refused to sit beside Jewish Justice Louis Brandeis.[6]

FDR named former Klansman Hugo Black of Alabama to the Court in 1937. As a lawyer, Black had won an acquittal for a Methodist pastor and Klansman who admitted to murdering the Catholic priest who presided at his daughter's wedding to a Puerto Rican.[7] Black's law partner was a Cyclops of the Birmingham Klavern. His senate campaign manager was the Grand Dragon of the Alabama Klan. After election to the Senate, Black, who had marched and spoken in robes, hood, and mask, accepted a lifetime membership in the Klan. As Black tells it, FDR was fully aware of his Klan associations.[8]

When McReynolds stepped down in 1941, FDR replaced him with Byrnes. Despite NAACP protests, Byrnes was confirmed by a Democratic Senate, eight minutes after his nomination was submitted. This is the buried past of the Democratic Party of which Bruce Bartlett has written.

For almost a century, since Roger Taney, there had been a tradition of one Catholic Justice on the court. When Justice Frank Murphy died in 1949, Truman terminated that tradition. Eisenhower restored it with William Brennan.

In the two presidential campaigns of Wilson and the four of FDR, Democrats swept every Confederate state all six times. The Democratic candidate in 1924, John W. Davis, carried every Confederate state and, with the exception of Oklahoma, only Confederate states. Truman took seven Southern states to Strom Thurmond's four. Dewey got none. In 1952 and 1956 most of the electoral votes Adlai Stevenson got came from the most segregated states of the South. Only when Nixon swept the South in his forty-nine-state landslide of 1972 did a "Southern Strategy" become the mark of the beast.

Among the two dozen senators to sign the 1956 Southern Manifesto, which urged resistance to the *Brown* decision, were such grandees as John Sparkman, Walter George, Richard Russell, John Stennis, Sam Ervin, Strom Thurmond, Harry Byrd, John McClellan, Russell Long, Jim Eastland, J. William Fulbright, and George Smathers, a carousing buddy of JFK. All were Democrats. House Democrats who signed the manifesto and would play major roles in national politics included Wilbur Mills, Carl Vinson, Hale Boggs, and Mendel Rivers. In all, ninety-nine Democrats signed the Dixie Manifesto, but only two Republicans.

With the Civil Rights Act of 1964 and the nomination of conservative Barry Goldwater, black allegiance to the party of Lincoln ended. Although a majority of votes against the bill were cast by Southern Democrats, Goldwater voted with them. He had been a member of the National Association for the Advancement of Colored People (NAACP), had contributed to its campaign to desegregate Phoenix schools, and had desegregated his own department store and the Arizona Air National Guard when he was chief of staff. But Goldwater was a constitutionalist who believed desegregating public accommodations was a state, not a federal, responsibility.

Nevertheless, perceived as hostile to black aspirations, Goldwater lost the African American vote to Lyndon Johnson by sixteen to one, and Republicans have never since found the favor with African Americans that they had in national elections for the century after Lincoln.

Half a century ago, however, the black vote was not as significant as today. Blacks could not vote in any numbers in the South. Democrats ruled Dixie as a fiefdom and used a variety of ruses to prevent African Americans from going to the polls. Northern blacks did not register or vote to the same extent as whites. And when they did, they gave the party of Lincoln one vote for every two they delivered to the party of FDR. Eisenhower got 39 percent of the black vote in 1956. Running against John F. Kennedy, Richard Nixon won 32 percent. Goldwater's share of the African American vote was only 6 percent.[9]

With the Voting Rights Act of 1965, the mass registration of African Americans began. And with the Immigration Act of 1965, which led to tens of millions coming from the Third World, the ethnic and racial composition of the American electorate was changed forever.

THE GOP'S EXISTENTIAL CRISIS

America is a different country from the one many of us grew up in. In thirty years, Americans of European descent, whose forebears founded the republic and restricted citizenship to "free white persons" of "high moral character," will be a minority. Hispanics will outnumber blacks two to one. America will have become a nation unrecognizable to our parents. Consider how dramatic the change has been.

In 1960, whites comprised 89 percent of a population of 160 million. They now comprise 64 percent of a population of 310 million. In 2041, they will represent less than 50 percent of a population of 438 million and a much smaller share of the young. No nation has undergone so radical a transformation in so short a time. And these numbers portend an existential crisis for the GOP.

Three political events have contributed to the crisis. The first was the ratification, in March 1961, of the Twenty-third Amendment, granting Washingtonians the right to vote and the District of Columbia the same three votes in the Electoral College as Alaska, Montana, Wyoming, North and South Dakota, Delaware, and Vermont. The District of Columbia is not a state, has no senators, and is one-twentieth of the size of Rhode Island. By population (600,000), D.C. is outranked by twenty-six other U.S. cities. By land area, D.C.'s sixty-eight square miles is exceeded by that of 150 other U.S. cities.

With this amendment the Democratic Congress elected in 1958 added three electoral votes to their party's total in every future presidential contest, for D.C. has never voted Republican. Also, in treating D.C. like a state, Congress opened the door to the possibility of statehood and electoral votes for Puerto Rico, Guam, the Virgin Islands, and American Samoa. The drive to make Puerto Rico the fifty-first state, which would add six new members to the House and two U.S. senators and would make America a bilingual nation, is steadily advancing, with Republican support.

Washington, D.C., votes for the Democrats in every election, municipal or national, as Washington depends on government for survival. And as more Americans come to depend on government for their health, education, and incomes, more and more will vote for that same Party of Government.

The second event was the Immigration Act of 1965, which brought in scores of millions from the Third World to break a Republican lock on the presidency that Nixon and Reagan had given the party for a quarter century. Third was the decision of a Democratic Congress and President Nixon to impose the eighteen-year-old vote on the states.

In extending the 1965 Voting Rights Act, Congress in 1970 added a rider declaring that eighteen-year-olds had the right to vote in federal elections. This was blatantly unconstitutional, as it had required one constitutional amendment, the fifteenth, to guarantee former slaves the right to vote, and another, the nineteenth, to guarantee women the right to vote.

As a special assistant, this writer urged President Nixon to veto the bill. For presidents take an oath to defend the Constitution, and Nixon himself believed the eighteen-year-old vote could not be accomplished by statute. As Nixon wrote:

> As passed, the bill contained a "rider" which I believe to be unconstitutional: a provision lowering the voting age to 18 in Federal, State and local elections. Although I strongly favor the 18-year-old vote, I believe—along with most of the Nation's leading constitutional scholars—that Congress has no power to enact it by simple statute, but rather it requires a constitutional amendment.[10]

Nixon should have vetoed the bill. Instead, declaring that he had "misgivings," he signed it and directed Attorney General John Mitchell to seek an expedited review. The Supreme Court ruled swiftly. The rider was unconstitutional. But by now state legislators and governors, assuming the eighteen-year-old vote was inevitable with Nixon backing it, rushed to support a constitutional amendment so as not to offend the young people likely to vote in 1972. Thus was the Twenty-sixth Amendment approved by the requisite thirty-eight states in July 1971, adding millions of eighteen-, nineteen-, and twenty-year-olds to the electorate forever.

To understand the existential crisis of the GOP, brought on by these reforms, let us look back to the voting results of the 2008 presidential election.

A CORONER'S REPORT ON
THE MCCAIN CAMPAIGN

To study the exit polls from the McCain-Obama race is to see stark and clear what a coroner might declare to be the cause of death of the Grand Old Party.

An April 2009 analysis of Census Bureau data by the Pew Research Center reveals that white voters made up 76 percent of the electorate in 2008. (In 1960, they had comprised 94 percent.)[11] African Americans comprised 12 percent of all voters in 2008; Hispanics, 7.4 percent; and Asians, 2.5 percent.

According to the exit polls from November, McCain got 55 percent of the white vote, 31 percent of the Hispanic vote, and 4 percent of the black vote, the same share of the black vote David Duke got when he ran for governor of Louisiana.

But if black America has become a bloc vote in presidential years, white America is a house divided. In Alabama, Mississippi, and Louisiana, McCain won 85 percent of the white vote. In Washington, D.C., McCain lost 85 percent of the white vote. In August 2008, 8 percent of white voters said race was the most important factor in the upcoming election, and 13 percent cited race as one of several important factors. More than one-third of the whites who said the race of the candidate was important said they were voting for Obama.[12] Obama almost surely got millions of white votes *because* he is African American.

As for the black vote in 2008, the *New Yorker* writes:

Judging from exit polls, black voters made up about 1.1 percent of the McCain electorate, which is lower than the historical average, but not by much. (In 1984, when President

Reagan was reelected in a landslide, black voters accounted for only about 1.5 per cent of his total.) American politics has been segregated for decades; the election of a black President only made that segregation more obvious.[13]

By religious affiliation, Protestants accounted for 54 percent of the electorate; Catholics, 27 percent; and Jews, 2 percent. McCain won 54 percent of the Protestant vote, 45 percent of the Catholic vote, and 21 percent of the Jewish vote. Using basic arithmetic, one finds that 64 percent of McCain's voters were Protestant and 27 percent Catholic. Thus, 91 percent of McCain voters were Christian, and 91 percent were white. White Christians are the Republican base.

Black Americans made up 1 percent of McCain's vote, Jews less than 1 percent. Although few senators have been more pro-Israel than McCain, who wanted to put Senator Joe Lieberman, a Jewish independent Democrat, on his ticket, he lost the Jewish vote by a staggering 57 points. Norman Podhoretz explains:

> [F]or most American Jews.... liberalism has become more than a political outlook. It has for all practical purposes superseded Judaism and become a religion in its own right. And to the dogmas and commandments of this religion they give the kind of steadfast devotion their forefathers gave to the religion of the Hebrew Bible. For many, moving to the right is invested with much the same horror their forefathers felt about conversion to Christianity.[14]

Republican courtship of the Jewish vote has failed. And given its shrinking share of the national vote, this seems barren terrain, though the Obama collisions with Netanyahu and his Likud party suggest the GOP should not write off the Jewish vote (critical in Florida) in 2012. But so long as Obama is the voice and face of his party, the African American vote, six to seven times as large as the Jewish vote, is gone. This is not an argument for writing off any voters. But it does tell Republicans where the fish are not biting.

Consider younger voters. McCain lost voters aged eighteen to twenty-nine by a margin of 66 to 32 percent. George W. Bush also lost this age group twice, but by smaller margins. Yet, for the third straight presidential election, the GOP lost young voters. What makes this worrisome for the party is that lifetime voting habits are formed in a voter's first few elections.

Nor can one ignore the ethnic and religious factors among the young. As Chuck Todd and Sheldon Gawiser write, in *How Barack Obama Won:*

> Young voters are more diverse racially and ethnically than older voters and are growing more so over time. Just 62% of voters under 30 are white, while 18% are black and 14% Hispanic. Four years ago, this age group was 68% white; in 2000, nearly three-quarters, 74%, were white. They are also more secular in their religious orientation and fewer report regular attendance at worship services, and secular voters tend to vote Democratic.[15]

One thus returns to the criticality of the white vote to the GOP, and the approaching and perhaps terminal crisis caused by its support for an open-borders immigration policy that is shrinking the party's base into America's newest minority. As Thomas Edsall writes, in the *Huffington Post,*

> The trend is striking. In 1976, 89 percent of the electorate was white. That number fell ... to 88 percent in 1980, 86 percent in 1984, 85 percent in 1988, 83 percent in 1996, 81 percent in 2000, 77 percent in 2004, and 74 percent last year. The only exception was 1992, when the presence of independent candidate Ross Perot drove the white percentage of the electorate up to 87 percent.[16]

Republican analyst Bill Greener wrote, after the 2008 election:

> In 1976, 90 percent of the votes cast in the presidential election came from non-Hispanic whites. In 2008, John McCain won this vote by a 56–43 margin. Had John McCain run in 1976 instead of 2008, not only would he have won, he would have won the popular vote before a single non-white vote was cast.[17]

Greener drives the point home:

> So, despite all the chatter about the impact of Sarah Palin, despite the unpopularity of President Bush, despite the difficulty of the same party winning a third consecutive national election, despite the charisma of Barack Obama (and the love shown to him by the mainstream media), despite the financial meltdown of September, despite any other factor anyone can cite, if John McCain had been the candidate at a time when non-Hispanic whites were the overwhelming majority of the voters, he would be president now.[18]

The message bears repeating. White Americans, who provide nine out of ten Republican votes every presidential year, have fallen to less than two-thirds of the U.S. population and three-fourths of the electorate. Meanwhile, the number of people of color is growing, both as a share of the population and as a share of the electorate. And in presidential elections, people of color vote Democratic—in landslides. Asians vote 60 percent Democratic, Hispanics 60–70 percent, and African Americans 90–95 percent.

Despite the Republican sweep in 2010, the "number of House districts where minorities constitute at least 30 percent of the population has roughly doubled, from one-fourth in the 1990s to one-half now."[19] This means more and more congressional districts are moving to where they will be safely Democratic, even in Republican-wave elections like 2010.

Through its support of mass immigration, its paralysis in preventing twelve to twenty million illegal aliens from entering and staying in this country, and its failure to address the "anchor-baby" issue, the Republican Party has birthed a new electorate that will send the party the way of the Whigs. After Bush's defeat of John Kerry, Michael Moore consoled liberals:

> ...88% of Bush's support came from white voters. In 50 years, America will no longer have a white majority. Hey, 50 years isn't such a long time! If you're ten years old and reading this, your golden years will be truly golden and you will be well cared for in your old age.[20]

"The demographic that Palin attracts is in decline," writes Frank Rich. "That demographic is white and non-urban."[21]

While he relishes the decline of the Sarah Palin demographic, Rich is not wrong. Political scientist Alan Abramowitz projects that minorities will make up 34 percent of the electorate in 2020.[22] Whites will comprise 66 percent. A GOP presidential candidate could then win the same 60 percent of the white vote the GOP won in 2010 and still be 10 points away from a tie in the popular vote.

INDIAN SUMMER OF THE GOP?

On November 2, 2010, the Republican Party swept to its greatest off-year triumph since before World War II, picking up 5 governorships, 6 Senate seats, 63 House seats, and 680 state legislators. As of January 2009, few predicted such a comeback, though some of us said that Obama, like Hoover, would be blamed for the tough times ahead, even though a major recession had been baked into the cake, before he arrived. Many analysts were writing the GOP's obituary. James Carville's

2009 book was titled *40 More Years: How the Democrats Will Rule the Next Generation.*

The issues that caused the defection from the Democrats are not in dispute. They include the 9.5 percent unemployment for fourteen months before the election; the failure of the $787 billion stimulus to stop the hemorrhaging of jobs; fear of deficits of 10 percent of GDP and a national debt surging to a hundred percent of GDP; the public's rejection of Obamacare; the belief that the federal government is seizing too much power; the sinking popularity of the president; Nancy Pelosi; Harry Reid; and the rise of the Tea Party—not necessarily in that order.

But the real story of the 2010 election is about who stayed home and who came out to vote. The Republican Party rolled to the most stunning off-year election victory in living memory because white America came out to vote and minorities and the young stayed home.

According to a *New York Times* postelection analysis, the white vote rose from 75 percent of the electorate in the McCain-Obama race of 2008 to 78 percent in 2010, and the Republican share rose from 55 percent in 2008 to 62 percent. In the South, the Republican share of the white vote rose to 73 percent, inundating Blue Dog veterans like John Spratt of South Carolina and Gene Taylor of Mississippi.[23]

In the Deep South, where segregation endured the longest, segregation has returned, this time to politics. "Of the nine Democratic representatives that remain from states of the Deep South, only one, John Barrow of Georgia, is white. Of the 28 Republicans, only one, the newly elected Tim Scott of South Carolina, is black."[24]

Says Dave "Mudcat" Saunders, a strategist to Southern Democrats, "Right now in most of Dixie it is culturally unacceptable to be a Democrat. It's a damn shame, but that's the way it is."[25]

In "White Flight," his analysis of the 2010 congressional election, Ron Brownstein of *National Journal* put the Republican share of the white vote at 60 percent and the Democratic share at 37 percent, but he notes that the alienation of white America from Obama and his policies is even more pronounced:

Exactly 75 percent of minority voters said they approved [of Obama's performance]; only 22 percent said they disapproved. Among white voters, just 35 percent approved of the president's performance, while 65 percent disapproved; a head-turning 49 percent of whites said they *strongly* disapproved. (Those whites voted Republican last fall by a ratio of 18-to-1.)[26]

Republicans again lost the youth vote, 18–29, by a margin of 56–42 percent, but this was a far better showing than John McCain's, who lost them by more than two to one. Republicans won all other age groups, including seniors by 20 points. However, Democrats carried 73 percent of nonwhites, including Asians, Hispanics, and African Americans.[27]

Catholics and Protestants were 89 percent of the electorate and the GOP won 55 percent of the Catholics and 61 percent of the Protestants. Once again, the Republican vote was over 90 percent Christian and over 90 percent white.

The crisis of the GOP can be stated simply: due to immigration and higher birthrates among people of color, America is becoming less white and less Christian—and, therefore, inevitably, less Republican.

The Democratic base is growing, and the Republican base is dying.

THE DEMOCRATIC BASE

In the early aftermath of Obama's victory, Brownstein saw GOP hopes of recapturing the White House fading like the Cheshire Cat in *Alice's Adventures in Wonderland*. And his case was rooted in recent political history:

In the five presidential elections beginning with Clinton's victory in 1992, and ending with Obama's in 2008, eighteen states and the District of Columbia, with 248 electoral votes, voted Democratic all five times. In not one of the eighteen states or D.C. did McCain come within 10 points of Obama. In New York, Illinois and California, McCain did not come within 20 points.[28]

The eighteen states include all of New England except New Hampshire; New York and New Jersey; the mid-Atlantic states of Pennsylvania, Delaware, and Maryland; four major midwestern states—Michigan, Illinois, Wisconsin, and Minnesota; the three Pacific coast states of California, Oregon, and Washington; and Hawaii. Moreover, Iowa, New Hampshire, and New Mexico have gone Democratic in four of the last five presidential contests.

Even after 2010, there are only two Republican congressmen in all of New England, both from New Hampshire.

In Massachusetts one sees a Republican party on the way to extinction. Every statewide elected official except Senator Scott Brown is a Democrat, as are all the congressmen. There are four Republicans among 40 state senators and 30 Republicans in the 160-member state assembly. Not since the 1950s has the GOP controlled either house. "Uniquely among the 50 states," writes analyst Jon Keller, in *The Bluest State,* "Massachusetts over the past few decades has been a Democrats' Burger King: They always have it their way."[29]

Consider the nation's most populous state, with one-fifth of the electoral votes needed to win the presidency. California went for Nixon in all five elections in which he was on the national ticket, and for Reagan all four times he ran. Now, not only has California gone Democratic in five straight presidential elections, McCain's share of the state vote fell below Goldwater's. In 2010, Meg Whitman and Carly Fiorina, despite well-funded campaigns, lost by 10 points or more to Jerry Brown and Barbara Boxer. Brown, who won the governorship, and Boxer, who won the Senate seat, had been around for decades. While Democrats were shedding sixty-three U.S. House seats, in California they did not lose a single one and added to their strength in Sacramento, where Democrats control both houses of the legislature. California has added ten million people since 1988, but Republican registration is below what it was in 1988. The GOP does not hold one statewide office. As the *L.A. Times* wrote, in an autopsy of the Republican defeat, "the party's white and coneservative voter base is giving way to the state's non-white and non-partisan population."[30]

Adds Michael Blood, of the Associated Press, "[T]he party of Richard Nixon and Ronald Reagan is slowly sinking in the West."[31]

High among the reasons the GOP has lost California is, again, immigration and the socioeconomic and ethnic character of the immigrants. Nearly 90 percent now come from the Third World and are mostly poor or working class. They rely on government for help with health care, housing, education, incomes. "If there is one group you could say that does not share the Republican small-government philosophy, it's Latinos," says Antonio Gonzalez, president of the Southwest Voter Registration Education Project. "We are Big-Government, government-safety-net, activist-government [voters]."[32]

Indeed, in "Demographic Change and the Future of the Parties," written for the Center for American Progress, Ruy Teixeira comes to a conclusion that will be impossible for the party of Reagan to accept:

> These data suggest that there is really only one way for the GOP to effectively compete for minority voters, and it's a way that Republicans have rejected so far. The party must, quite simply, become less conservative. They will have to jettison their bitter hostility to active government, spending on social services, and immigration reform and develop their own approach in these areas that minorities might find appealing.[33]

If a historian were to write *The Decline and Fall of the House of Reagan*, he could find no better place to study than Orange County, birthplace of Richard Nixon, home of John Wayne, Goldwater country, and a bastion of the John Birch Society. In this Alcázar of the old Right, Reagan thumped Carter three to one. Yet, Obama ran McCain close to a dead heat, for the Orange County of yesterday is gone. Republican registration has fallen to 43 percent. Forty-five percent of residents speak a language other than English in their homes. Writes Adam Nagourney, of the *New York Times:*

> Whites make up only 45 percent of the population; this county is teeming with Hispanics as well as Vietnamese, Korean, and Chinese families. Its percentage of foreign-born residents jumped to 30 percent in 2009 from 6 percent in 1970, and visits to some of its corners can seem like a trip to a foreign land.[34]

In 2010, Loretta Sanchez, who captured the Orange County seat of Bob Dornan in 1996 in a photo finish in which illegal aliens allegedly provided her margin of victory, raised the specter of Hispanics in peril of losing a seat to a rival ethnic group. Sanchez told Jorge Ramos on Univision's *Al Punto* program, "The Vietnamese [are] trying to take away this seat...from us and give it to this Van Tran, who's very anti-immigrant and very anti-Latino."[35]

The old ideological politics of Orange County has given way to a new tribal politics. The county was once a microcosm of and metaphor for Middle America. But immigration has changed its character forever. The new Hispanic poor and working class depend on government and vote for government. Vietnamese, Koreans, and Chinese no longer see the Republican Party as their natural home, as the Cold War anticommunism of the GOP has become irrelevant in the new century. A loss of manufacturing and outsourcing of jobs have changed Orange County from a middle-class bastion into a place where the disparities of wealth have visibly widened.

"[T]he political texture of this county, which is larger in population than Nevada or Iowa," writes Nagourney, "is changing, and many officials say it is only a matter of time before many Republican office-holders get swept out with the tide."[36] As Orange County goes, so goes California, and as California goes, so goes America.

Another cause of the approaching Republican crisis is the division of the nation into taxpayers and tax consumers. Since Reagan, tax cuts have dropped one-third of all wage earners off the tax rolls. When tax credits are factored in, 47 percent of U.S. workers pay no U.S. income tax. A study by the Congressional Joint Committee on Taxation found that, in 2009, fully 51 percent of all households owed no federal income tax. If one pays no federal income tax, yet reaps a bonanza of federal benefits, it makes sense to vote for the party of government and against a party that would cut the government. Two centuries ago, John C. Calhoun, who studied the failings and failures of democracies, precisely described our present condition:

> The necessary result, then, of the unequal fiscal action of the government is, to divide the community into two great classes; one consisting of those who, in reality, pay the taxes, and... bear exclusively the burthen of supporting the government; and the other, of those who are the recipients of their proceeds, through disbursements, and who are, in fact, supported by the government; or, in fewer words, to divide it into taxpayers and tax-consumers.[37]

Calhoun's division of the nation describes the America of today. Were the taxing power to be exploited, he warned, "for the purpose of aggrandizing and building up one portion of the community at the expense of the other.... it must give rise to two parties and to violent conflicts and struggles between them, to obtain the control of the government."[38]

Calhoun was forecasting the Tea Party revolution. We are today engaged in his "conflicts and struggles," a synonym for class warfare. For the vast majority of the 4.4 million on welfare, the 22 million on government payrolls, the 23 million receiving EITC checks, the 44 million on food stamps, the 50 million on Medicaid, the 70 million wage earners who pay no income tax, the Democratic Party is their party.

We are approaching the tipping point where there will be more tax consumers than there are taxpayers. Reports the *Wall Street Journal:*

Nearly half of all Americans now live in a household in which someone receives government benefits, more than at any time in history [while] the fraction of American households not paying federal income taxes has also grown—to an estimated 45% in 2010, from 39% five years ago.[39]

Thirteen percent of U.S. households do not even pay Social Security taxes.[40] Why should scores of millions of people who pay no taxes but partake of a cornucopia of benefits vote for a party committed to cutting benefits? H. L. Mencken's quip in the 1930s about the New Deal has become reality in the twenty-first century. America has indeed been divided "into those who work for a living and those who vote for a living."[41]

The Republican lock on the presidency, crafted by Nixon and patented by Reagan, has been picked. Will 2010 prove to be the Indian summer of the Republican Party before an endless winter sets in?

THE AUDACITY OF HOPE

Consider again the numbers cited above, which raise insistent questions that the Republicans of this generation refuse to address. In 2008, black and Jewish voters each gave McCain just one percent of his vote. Why then the GOP obsession with African American voters who went 24–1 for Obama, but are outnumbered by white voters 6–1? Why does the GOP spend so much time courting Jewish voters, who are outnumbered by Catholic voters 13–1 and by Protestant voters 25–1? And Jews are more deeply dyed-in-the-wool Democrats than are Catholics or Protestants. Even Ronald Reagan never came close to carrying the Jewish vote.

You go hunting where the ducks are, said Barry Goldwater. As whites remain three-fourths of the electorate and Christians four-fifths, this is where the GOP will find victory or defeat. If Republicans can raise their 2012 nominee's share of the Catholic vote from 45 to 52 percent—what Bush won against Kerry and the party won again in 2010—that seven-point gain would add more votes than would going from 20 percent of the Jewish vote to 100 percent.

Which of these two feats is easier for the party to accomplish?

Not only is the Catholic vote 13.5 times the Jewish vote, it is more receptive to the Republican stance on moral and social issues—for prayer in school and right-to-life on abortion, and against embryonic stem-cell research, euthanasia, same-sex marriage, and affirmative action.

Consider again the black vote. By one estimate, Nixon, running in 1972 against a South Dakota liberal who lacked Hubert Humphrey's heroic standing in black America, won 18 percent of the black vote. In 2010, McCain got 4 percent. For a half-century, 18 percent and 4 percent have been the high and low water marks for the GOP with black voters. In 2012, with Obama running, the GOP figure will likely remain close to that 4 percent.

But if the Republican candidate can raise the GOP share of the white vote from McCain's 55 percent to the 58 percent Bush got in 2004, that would have the same impact on GOP vote totals as raising the party's share of the African American vote from 4 percent to 21 percent.

And if the GOP can simply win again in 2012 the same 60–62 percent of the white vote the party won in 2010, a presidential victory is almost assured.

Demographer William H. Frey, of the Brookings Institution, emphasizes this crucial point:

> While the significance of minority votes for Obama is clearly key, it cannot be overlooked that reduced white support for a Republican candidate allowed minorities to tip the balance in many slow-growing "purple" states.
>
> The question I would ask is if a continuing stagnating economy could change that.[42]

What these numbers and Frey's point demonstrate is that McCain, who refused to focus on issues of concern to Christians, such as same-sex marriage and right to life, and issues of concern to the white working and middle class, such as affirmative action, illegal immigration, NAFTA, and the racist rants of Rev. Wright, forfeited his chance to be president. Only once during the election did McCain move into the lead. That was for the two weeks after he chose Sarah Palin, a charismatic Christian with immense appeal to Evangelicals and Nashville-NASCAR "real Americans."

Frank Rich, though socially and culturally repulsed by Palin and those for whom she speaks, recognized her appeal to the forgotten Americans.

> [Palin] stands for a genuine movement: a dwindling white nonurban America that is aflame with grievances and awash in self-pity as the country hurtles into the 21st century and leaves it behind.... The real wave she's riding is a loud, resonant surge of resentment and victimization.[43]

Rich is talking of those "bitter" folks, clinging to their Bibles, bigotries, and guns, Obama spoke of at that closed-door fund-raiser in San Francisco, where he explained why white Pennsylvanians were not rallying to him. The resentment to which Palin appeals, writes Rich, as he sketched his caricature of Middle America, "is in part about race":

> When Palin referred to Alaska as "a microcosm of America" during the 2008 campaign, it was in defiance of the statistical reality that her state's tiny black and Hispanic populations are unrepresentative of her nation. She stood for the "real America," she insisted, and the identity of the unreal America didn't have to be stated explicitly for audiences to catch her drift.[44]

There is some truth in what Rich writes. In the fortnight following Palin's selection, McCain vaulted from eight points down to four points up for the first time in the election year. Those "bitter" folks of Obama's derisive depiction, who gave Hillary her crushing victories in Pennsylvania, West Virginia, and Kentucky, had suddenly swung over to John McCain.

What the above points to is a strategy from which Republicans will recoil, a strategy to increase the GOP share of the white Christian vote and increase the turnout of that vote by specific appeals to social, cultural, and moral issues, and for equal justice for the emerging white minority. If the GOP is not the party of New Haven firefighter Frank Ricci and Cambridge cop James Crowley, it has no future. And although Howard Dean disparages the Republicans as the "white party," why should Republicans be ashamed to represent the progeny of the men who founded, built, and defended America since her birth as a nation?

In 2009, Virginia and New Jersey showed the way. In Virginia, the GOP candidate for governor, Bob McDonnell, got 9 percent of the black vote to McCain's 8 percent. No gain. But the white share of the electorate rose from 70 percent in 2008 to 78 percent in 2009, and McDonnell won 67 percent of that vote to McCain's 60. Thus did McDonnell turn McCain's 6-point defeat in the Old Dominion into a 17-point Republican landslide.

In New Jersey, Republican Chris Christie got 9 percent of the black vote to McCain's 8 percent. But Christie took 59 percent of the white vote to McCain's 50 percent, and won the governorship.

In January 2010, Scott Brown pulled off the upset of the century, capturing a Senate seat held for almost sixty years by John F. Kennedy and his brother Edward. How did Brown turn Obama's 26-point victory over McCain into a 6-point victory over Attorney General Martha Coakley? By sweeping the white vote as massively as had Obama.

In the 2008 election, 79 percent of Massachusetts voters were white. Obama carried them by 20 points. While there were no exit polls from the Brown-Coakley race, analysts believe the white vote was over 80 percent and Brown carried two-thirds of it. For the independents in the Bay State who went overwhelmingly for Brown are largely white folks who have left the Democratic Party, while blacks and Hispanics have stayed loyal. Brown won a huge majority of those independents.

Moreover, the clash between Sergeant Crowley and Professor Gates took place in Cambridge. And when Obama rushed to judgment to charge

Crowley with having "acted stupidly," his support sagged in white America but sank in the Bay State, where Governor Deval Patrick joined Obama in piling on the Cambridge cop.[45]

The McDonnell, Christie, and Brown campaigns have shown a light on the path to victory over Obama in 2012. The Republican road to re-capture of the White House lies in increasing white turnout and raising the party's share of that turnout—three-fourths of the entire electorate—from McCain's 55 percent closer to the two-thirds won by Nixon and Reagan.

In the final analysis, however, a serenely confident Bill Clinton was probably right. Asked by David Gregory on *Meet the Press* if the "vast right-wing conspiracy" Hillary had identified was "still there," Clinton replied, "Oh, you bet. Sure it is. It's not as strong as it was because America has changed demographically."[46]

WHAT PANDERING PRODUCED

At the 1988 convention that nominated him, Vice President George H. W. Bush promised a "kinder and gentler" administration, which caused conservatives to ask, "kinder and gentler than whom?" The campaign Bush was conducting, however, as he spoke that August night, was anything but kind and gentle.

Far behind after the Democratic convention in late July, Bush and campaign chief Lee Atwater turned a 17-point deficit on August 1 into an 8-point lead by Labor Day that Bush never lost. How did they effect a 25-point turnaround in five weeks? They eviscerated Michael Dukakis on social and cultural issues: specifically, Dukakis's veto of a bill that mandated recitation of the pledge of allegiance in schools, his opposition to the death penalty, his pride in being "a card-carrying member of the ACLU," and his weekend furloughs for convicts and killers like Willie Horton.

After the Houston convention of 1992, however, President Bush—Lee Atwater having passed away—recoiled from social and cultural issues and sought to win on foreign policy and the economy, where his approval rating was only 16 percent. The social issues could have derailed Clinton, which is why James Carville told the War Room to stay laser-focused: "It's the economy, stupid!" Bush and James Baker seemed to think social and cultural issues beneath the dignity of a president. So it was that George H. W. Bush ceased to be president.

Under Bush II, the GOP sought to broaden its base by pandering to liberal minorities at the expense of its base. In July 2005, Ken Mehlman, the chairman of the Republican National Committee, traveled to the NAACP convention in Milwaukee to apologize for a Southern Strategy that from 1968 to 1988 produced five GOP victories in six presidential elections and two forty-nine-state landslides. "Some Republicans gave up on winning the African American vote, looking the other way or trying to benefit politically from racial polarization," said Mehlman. "I am here today as the Republican chairman to tell you we were wrong."[47] White House Press Secretary Scott McClellan seconded Mehlman.

Yet Bush was even then boycotting the NAACP convention for the fifth year. And understandably so. For the NAACP had run ads in 2000 implying that Bush had been indifferent to the dragging death of James Byrd, a disabled black man in Waco, Texas. NAACP chairman Julian Bond had compared his cabinet choices to mullahs. President Bush, said Bond, had "selected nominees from the Taliban wing of American politics, appeased the wretched appetites of the extreme right wing and chose Cabinet officials whose devotion to the Confederacy is nearly canine in its uncritical affection."[48]

A month after Mehlman's apology, Katrina struck, and some in the black community charged that Bush had failed to act swiftly to rescue New Orleans because most of the victims were black. Bush had won 9 percent of the black vote in 2000 and 11 percent in 2004. He saw his approval among African Americans plunge to 2 percent.

Mehlman would lead the GOP into 2006, where the party would lose both houses of Congress. He resigned and went to work for Henry Kravis on Wall Street. How did his outreach effort succeed? In 2008, McCain would lose the African American vote 24–1. In 2010, Ken Mehlman came out of the closet and went to work in support of same-sex marriage.

"ILLIBERAL DEMOCRATS"

"I have a much broader base to build a winning coalition on," Hillary Clinton boasted to *USA Today* in May 2008, speaking of her stronger appeal to white voters. She cited an AP article, which, in her words,

> found how Sen. Obama's support among working, hard-working Americans, white Americans, is weakening again, and how whites in both states who had not completed college were supporting me.... These are the people you have to win if you're a Democrat in sufficient numbers to actually win the election. Everybody knows that.[49]

The Democratic Party can't win with just "eggheads and African-Americans," Paul Begala added helpfully.[50]

What Hillary and Begala were saying was politically incorrect but palpably true. She was describing "Reagan Democrats," white folks who would give her 10-point victories in Ohio and Pennsylvania and 41- and 35-point victories in West Virginia and Kentucky. Obama's success in bringing them home in November cost John McCain the election.

Who are these Democrats, half of whom had said in exit polls from North Carolina and Indiana that if Hillary lost the nomination they would stay home or vote for McCain? In his derisive way, Frank Rich described them:

> a constituency that feels disenfranchised—by the powerful and well-educated who gamed the housing bubble, by a news media it keeps being told is hateful, by the immigrants who have taken some of their jobs, by the African-American who has ended a white monopoly on the White House. Palin is

their born avatar. She puts a happy, sexy face on ugly emotions, and she can solidify her followers' hold on a G.O.P. that has no leaders with the guts or alternative vision to stand up to them or to her.[51]

They are working class and middle class, Protestant and Catholic, small-town and rural, often unionized, middle-aged and seniors, surviving on less than $50,000 a year. In the forty years from 1968 to 2008, two Democrats won the presidency. Both did so only after connecting with these folks.

In 1976, Carter ran as an Annapolis graduate, Navy submariner, nuclear engineer, born-again Baptist Sunday-school preacher, and peanut farmer from Plains, Georgia, who wished to preserve the "ethnic purity" of northern neighborhoods. In 1992, Bill Clinton ran as a death-penalty Democrat from Hope, Arkansas, who had the nerve to diss Sister Souljah right in front of Jesse Jackson.

The morning after the 2006 Democratic capture of both houses of Congress, Jacob Weisberg identified the new breed of Democrat that was now the decisive swing vote on Capitol Hill as "economic nationalists" and "illiberal Democrats":

> Most of those who reclaimed Republican seats ran hard against free trade, globalization, and any sort of moderate immigration policy. That these Democrats won makes it likely that others will take up their reactionary call. Some of the newcomers may even be foolish enough to try to govern on the basis of their misguided theory.[52]

After losing the Pennsylvania primary, Obama, to appeal to these people, reinvented himself as a proud patriot whose grandfather fought in Patton's army, who enjoyed a bottle of Bud like the next guy, a kid raised in poverty by a single mom who had turned his back on Wall Street to fight for steelworkers laid off when the mills closed in south Chicago.

McCain, a POW and war hero, was a natural for middle Pennsylvania and middle Ohio. But on the populist issues, the outsourcing of American jobs and the invasion of illegals from Mexico, he stood with the *Wall Street Journal,* the K Street lobbyists, and corporate America—for NAFTA and for amnesty.

Like Bush I in 1992, McCain recoiled from cultural and social issues. He denounced Tarheel Republicans for linking Obama to the Reverend Wright. He berated a conservative talk show host who mocked Barack's middle name. He went to Canada to swear allegiance to NAFTA. The mainstream media applauded, but, before Palin arrived, the Republican base was sullen and the Reagan Democrats were silent.

McCain's diffidence on right to life, affirmative action, and gay rights, his embrace of amnesty and NAFTA, explain the enthusiasm gap. On election day, twice as many voters were excited about the prospect of an Obama presidency as were about a McCain presidency.

McCain would learn his lesson. In 2010, when challenged by former congressman J. D. Hayworth in a GOP primary, McCain ceased to be the maverick beloved of the national press and did a passable imitation of Tom Tancredo. He ran a tough-talking television advertisement charging that illegal aliens were responsible for "home invasions [and] murders." The ad ended with McCain walking the border with a sheriff and demanding, "Complete the danged fence!"

COMEBACK ROAD

For conservatives, *How Barack Obama Won* reads like something out of Edgar Allan Poe's tales of the macabre. Yet, on closer reading, one can discern the Republican path to victory in 2012, even as the light shone upon that path in 2010.

First, the bad news.

Obama raised the black vote to 13 percent of the national vote, then carried it 95–4 percent. The Republican share of the Hispanic vote—9 percent of the electorate in exit polls, 7.4 percent in census figures—fell from Bush's 40 percent in 2004 to 32 percent for McCain. Young voters aged eighteen to twenty-nine went for Obama by a margin of 66–31 percent. Obama ran stronger among white voters with a college education than Kerry or Gore.

Put starkly, the voting groups that are expanding as a share of the electorate—Hispanics, Asians, African Americans, and whites with college degrees—were all trending ever more Democratic in 2008. The voters most loyal to the GOP—white folks without college degrees and religious conservatives—were shrinking as a share of the electorate.

Where were the signs of hope?

First, in 2008, 75 percent of voters thought the country was headed in the wrong direction. Obama won these voters 62–36 percent. But if the country is seen as headed in the wrong direction in 2012, as most Americans believe today, this will cast a cloud over Obama's candidacy. McCain's albatross in 2008 would become Obama's in 2012.

Second, only 27 percent of voters in 2008 approved of Bush's performance by election day. Only Truman, as a sitting president in an election year, had a lower rating, 22 percent in 1952. That year, Democrats lost the White House and both houses of Congress.

Todd's point is dramatic: "With the single exception of Missouri, which barely went for McCain, Obama won every state where Bush's approval rating was below 35% in the exit polls, and he lost every state where Bush's approval was above 35%."[53]

Obama rode Bush's coattails to victory. Had Bush been at 35 or 40 percent on election day, McCain might have won. In 2012, Obama will not have George Bush to kick around anymore.

Third, on election day, 93 percent rated the economy as not so good or poor. The GOP will not have to wear those concrete boots in 2012. Obama will, as he wore them in the 2010 wipeout.

Fourth, on candidates' qualities, the situation looks even rosier for Republicans. In 2008, no less than 34 percent of the electorate said the most important consideration in a candidate was that he be for "change." Not only was Obama the "change candidate," he patented the issue and carried this third of the nation looking for change by an astounding 89–9 percent. But in 2012, Obama will be the candidate of continuity, the incumbent. The candidate of change will be his Republican opponent.

Fifth, the second most critical consideration of voters in choosing a president was "values." Thirty percent of the electorate put values first. Among that 30 percent, McCain won 65–32.

Values issues are the GOP's ace in the hole.

What that two to one McCain advantage argues is that the neoconservatives instructing the GOP to dump values issues should themselves be dumped.

Traditional values are a powerful magnet for the most Democratic of minorities. African Americans gave McCain 5 percent of their votes in California, but gave Proposition 8, the proposal to outlaw gay marriage, 70 percent of their votes. "[N]o ethnic group anywhere," said the *Washington Post*, "rejected the sanctioning of same-sex unions as emphatically as the state's black voters."[54] California Hispanics gave McCain 23 percent of their votes, but gave 53 percent of their votes to Proposition 8. Why would the GOP throw away these cards?

McCain lost Colorado by 10 points. But the Colorado Civil Rights Initiative, which would have outlawed race and gender preferences, lost in a dead heat. In Michigan, California, Washington, and Nebraska, the ban on affirmative action has won a huge majority of whites and a larger share of black, Hispanic, and Asian voters than did John McCain. If the conservative side of these issues is more popular than the GOP, why would the GOP abandon them?

THE SOCIAL ISSUES

Those who urge Republicans to call a truce in the culture wars are uneasy with social issues and prefer to pound the table for lower taxes and less spending, common ground upon which all Republicans can stand.

But if Republicans are conservatives, what do they wish to conserve, if not the lives of unborn children and matrimony as ordained by God? The traditional family is the cinder block of a good society. When it crumbles, society crumbles. Can we not see the consequences of the collapse of traditional morality and marriage in a country where 41 percent of all children are born out of wedlock?

Where is the evidence that the social issues are losing issues?

- A CBS poll in April 2008 found that when asked, "Would you like to see religious and spiritual values have more influence in the schools than they do now, less influence, or about the same influence?" 49 percent called for more influence, and only 16 percent said less influence.[55]
- In a 2005 Pew poll, two-thirds of Americans felt liberals have "gone too far in trying to keep religion out of schools and government." By 75 to 21, blacks agreed. Independents, 2 to 1, endorsed the proposition that liberals have gone too far in de-Christianizing America.[56] Is this not ground to stand on to drive a wedge between liberals and black folks whose religious affiliation rate is higher than that of any ethnic group?
- Fully 64 percent of Americans believed that creationism should be taught alongside evolution. Only 26 percent disagreed. Thirty-eight percent went so far as to say that the theory of evolution should be tossed out of the classroom and only creationism taught to children.[57]
- A Pew Research Center poll in 2006 saw some attrition, but, by 58 to 35 percent, Americans still favored the teaching of both creationism and evolution.[58]

A majority of Americans gave public schools poor to failing grades in how they deal with the issues of evolution, religion, and homosexuality.[59]

What do these number shout out?

America remains a predominantly Christian country. Those three Iowa Supreme Court judges who ruled that the state constitution requires recognition of same-sex marriages were denied retention. They were fired by the people of Iowa. In Oklahoma, a proposition to prohibit use of Sharia law in state courts passed with 70 percent of the vote.

Social and moral conservatism has a greater appeal to the American people than does the Republican Party. Why would Republicans abandon a host of issues that are far more popular than they are?

HISPANICS AND IMMIGRATION

In early 2000, veteran GOP strategist Lance Tarrance addressed the Republican National Committee. "For the last three decades we've had a Southern strategy," said Tarrance. "The next goal is to move to a Hispanic strategy for the next three decades."[60]

With Hispanics expected to double their share of the population to close to 30 percent by mid-century, Tarrance would seem to have a point. And Bush and Rove pursued an Hispanic strategy. The focus of their effort was on amnesty for the 12 to 20 million illegals in the country, though there was no evidence this is Hispanics' highest priority. Amnesty, however, is a voting issue for tens of millions of Americans, the vast majority of whom oppose it.

After the Republican rout of 2006, Bush shifted this Hispanic strategy into high gear. To succeed Mehlman as party chairman he chose Senator Mel Martinez, who began his tenure with a press conference in Spanish and English. In 2007, McCain took the lead on Capitol Hill for the Bush-Kennedy bill providing a path to citizenship for illegals. This was to be his road to the Hispanic vote, and the White House.

However, an uproar ensued, magnified by cable TV, talk radio, the Web, and syndicated columns. And though it had the support of the political, corporate, and media establishments, the Bush-Kennedy-McCain immigration reform bill, amnesty by any other name, was stopped cold.

McCain had almost derailed his presidential campaign. In that same election cycle, Hillary Clinton had to withdraw her support of Governor Eliot Spitzer's plan to give driver's licenses to illegals and Spitzer had to abandon the idea when 70 percent of New Yorkers opposed it. By the primaries, every Republican candidate was sounding like Tom Tancredo.

What did the Bush-McCain leadership in pushing a path to citizenship for illegal aliens avail them or their party? McCain lost the Hispanic vote by a margin of 67 to 32 percent. By 2009, Rove was doing commentary on Fox News. And Martinez had resigned his chairmanship, quit the Senate, and was berating his party.

> [T]he very divisive rhetoric of the immigration debate set a very bad tone for our brand as Republicans....there were voices within our party, frankly, which if they continue with that kind of rhetoric, anti-Hispanic rhetoric, that so much of it was heard, we're going to be relegated to minority status.[61]

On the issue of immigration, what do the polls, political experience, and pubic referenda teach us? Consider the following:

- California's Proposition 187 in 1994, designed to prohibit social welfare for illegal aliens, was supported by 64 percent of whites, 57 percent of Asian Americans, 56 percent of African Americans, and 31 percent of Hispanics. Governor Pete Wilson, behind by 20, rode Prop 187 to a 10-point victory.
- In Arizona in 2004, Proposition 200, mandating a cutoff in social services to illegal aliens, won in a landslide, despite the opposition of McCain and the GOP congressional delegation. Fully 47 percent of Hispanics voted for Prop 200.
- According to a 2010 Rasmussen Poll, Americans by 87 to 9 percent believe English should be the official language of the United States.[62] According to a Zogby poll, 71 percent of

Hispanics agree.[63] In Missouri a proposition mandating that all state agencies use English passed by nearly 7 to 1.

- A Rasmussen poll found that 77 percent of all Americans oppose giving driver's licenses to illegals and 66 percent think it "very important" that the government secure the border and halt illegal immigration.[64]

- In 2011, three Rasmussen polls were conducted. Results: 61 percent favor having their state adopt a version of Arizona's law requiring police to ID any suspect they think may be here illegally; 61 percent oppose granting automatic citizenship to children born to illegal aliens; and 82 percent believe businesses should have to use the federal E-Verify system to determine the immigration status of new employees.

Washington views the immigration issue as finding a way to bring illegal aliens "out of the shadows." America sees the issue as securing the border and sending illegals back home.

As Obama prepared to take the oath, the Pew Hispanic Center reported that only 31 percent of Hispanics rated immigration as an "extremely important" issue for the new president to address, while 57 percent said the economy was extremely important.[65] Immigration was listed as the sixth most important issue by Hispanic voters.

Immigration is also an issue on which the GOP is more in tune with African Americans. Some 56 percent of black Californians voted for Prop 187. A 2006 Field Poll found 59 percent would punish employers who hire illegals; 66 percent supported building a wall on the border; and only one in four favored letting illegals have driver's licenses.[66]

"Amnesty for illegal workers is not just a slap in the face to black Americans," argues T. Willard Fair, president of the Urban League of Greater Miami. "It's an economic disaster. I see…the adverse impact that [illegal immigration] has on the political empowerment of African Americans, and the impact it has on the job market."[67]

Few Republicans better exemplify the power of the issue than Lou

Barletta, mayor of Hazleton, Pennsylvania, a state McCain lost by 10 points, though he invested more money and time there than in any other state.

After imposing a tough local ordinance on illegal immigrants in his hamlet of 23,000, which had been overrun, Barletta was so popular he won the GOP primary with 94 percent and the Democratic primary as a write-in, with 63 percent. In 2008, Barletta challenged eleven-term incumbent Paul Kanjorski in the Eleventh Congressional District, which Gore and Kerry won by wide margins and Kanjorski won with 73 percent in 2006. While Obama was carrying Pennsylvania by 10 points, Barletta came within 3 points of unseating Kanjorski, who revised his stance on immigration and came out sounding like a Minuteman to win. In November 2010, Lou Barletta routed Kanjorski to become the new congressman in the Eleventh C.D.

WINNING THE YOUNG

When Michael Steele was elected RNC chair to succeed Martinez, he said he would bring the traditional values party into untraditional precincts. "We want to convey that the modern-day GOP looks like the conservative party that stands on principles. But we want to apply them to urban-suburban hip-hop settings."[68]

To whom Steele was appealing here was uncertain, as two thirds of African Americans regard rappers as poor role models. But there are two issues, critical to the Republican base, with which the young of the nation agree with the GOP: immigration and affirmative action.

In 2010, Harvard University's Institute of Politics conducted its 17th Biennial Youth Survey on Politics and Public Service. On the proposition "Qualified Minorities should be given special preferences in colleges and hiring," 14 percent of young people agreed, and 57 percent disagreed. Asked if immigration had done more good than harm, 23 percent of the young said it had been beneficial, 34 percent said harmful.[69]

Should illegal immigrants get driver's licenses? Only 24 percent of the young agreed, while 58 percent disagreed. "Should illegal immigrants get financial aid at state universities?" Of the young responding, 29% said yes; 50 percent said no aid.[70]

Despite the cult of diversity in which they are immersed from day care center days to college dorm, American's young yet believe in equal justice for all and special privilege for none.

BALKANIZATION OF BARACK'S PARTY

The Democratic Party has been described as a gathering of warring tribes that have come together in the anticipation of common plunder. While the party has, since FDR, claimed the allegiance of more Americans than the GOP, it is an unstable coalition. In Steve Sailer's phrase, it is the party of the four races—blacks, whites, Asians, and Hispanics—led by an African American, as vulnerable to being pulled apart at its ethnic and ideological seams as was the New Deal coalition that was shredded by Richard Nixon.

Obama emerged from 2008 with 45 percent of the white vote, 64 percent of the Asian vote, 68 percent of the Hispanic vote, 95 percent of the African American vote. But by fall 2010, his support among whites had plunged to 37 percent, and white Americans had become the most energized of all anti-Obama voters.

Other fissures and fractures have become visible. The Florida Senate race between GOP Governor Charlie Crist and Tea Party favorite Marco Rubio, which "evolved into a battle…tearing apart Democrats," exposed one division. Democrats had nominated Kendrick Meek, the only black candidate with a chance of winning a Senate seat. Al Gore, Bill Clinton, and Obama all went to Florida to campaign for Meek. But Meek's ex-House colleague Robert Wexler, who represented Palm Beach County while Meek represented Broward, "all but ordered the state's many Jewish voters to back Crist."[71]

With Meek lacking the solid support of his own party, Bill Clinton eventually urged him to drop out in favor of Crist. Meek refused and ran third. The Senate Democratic caucus now contains twelve Jewish senators, but not one African American.

Tensions have also arisen over campaign contributions from wealthy Jewish Democrats that have helped to defeat members of the Black Caucus deemed hostile to Israel. In 2011, when Bill Clinton went to Chicago to campaign for Rahm Emanuel, who was running for mayor, the ex-president had the race card played against him, again, as he had had in the 2008 primaries. Former U.S. Senator Carol Moseley Braun, an African American running against Rahm, called Clinton's endorsement of Rahm a "betrayal" of blacks.

> President Bill Clinton does not live or vote in Chicago. He's an outsider parachuting in to support another outsider. For him to come on the day following Dr. Martin Luther King's birthday to insert himself in the middle of a mayoral race, when the majority of the population and mayoral candidates are African American and Latino, is a betrayal of the people who were most loyal to him.[72]

Translation: Cities where people of color are the majority should be run by people of color. Representative Danny Davis, another African American in the race, agreed emphatically.

> The African American community has enjoyed a long and fruitful relationship with the Clintons, however it appears as though some of that relationship may be fractured and perhaps even broken should former President Clinton come to town and participate overtly in efforts to thwart the legitimate political aspirations of Chicago's Black community.[73]

In short, the mayor of Chicago should be a black man or woman, not a white like Rahm Emanuel, and Clinton is thus depriving the black people of Chicago of what rightly belongs to them by virtue of their numbers.

Muslim Americans and Arab Americans, both now part of the Democratic coalition, are also growing in number and side with the Palestinians. But these are not the only fissures in the Obama coalition. There is a chasm between blacks and gays. Prop. 8, the California initiative to outlaw same-sex marriage, won 70 percent of African American voters. Black preachers implored their congregations to vote to ban as an "abomination" what gays, lesbians, and liberals regard as the civil rights cause of the new century. On social issues like abortion, Hispanics and blacks often vote against white liberals.

The forty million African Americans and fifty million Hispanics, living side by side in urban America, often clash over spoils and turf. In New Orleans, after the damage caused by Katrina, black resentment at Mexican workers coming to take jobs rebuilding the city spilled out into public acrimony. In California, black and Hispanic gangs are waging a civil war. Black-white prison violence has been eclipsed by black-Hispanic violence.

On referenda to cut off social services to illegal aliens and keep them from getting driver's licenses, blacks vote like Republicans. Having been displaced as America's largest minority, blacks see Hispanics as rivals for the benefits of affirmative action, which was first established to undo the consequences of slavery and segregation, from which few Hispanics ever suffered.

When it comes to race preferences in hiring, promotions, and college admissions, Asians are often classified with whites and are increasingly the victims of reverse discrimination. Their interest in ending affirmative action may one day drive Japanese, Chinese, Korean, and Indian Americans out of Jesse Jackson's Rainbow Coalition.

When black Mayor Adrian Fenty picked Korean American Michelle Rhee to shape up D.C.'s failing public schools, and Rhee fired scores of black teachers, the black wards east of the Anacostia River cut Fenty dead.

As the Party of Government, Democrats find common ground on growing the government and redistributing the wealth of the private sector to the public sector, from those who have to those who have not. When the pie is expanding, everyone can have a larger slice.

The crisis of the Democratic Party is that while it prospers by expanding government, we have entered an era when millions detest government, and America's fiscal crisis mandates that we cut government. In brief, as America enters this era of austerity, the compelling U.S. national interest in reducing the size of government will clash repeatedly with the vital interests of the Democratic Party.

The question now is not who gets what, but who gets cut. The tribes that make up the Democratic coalition could be at war with each other over who gets cut. Successful politics is about addition, not subtraction. But in the coming age of a Balkanized America, politics will also be about division.

THE NATIONAL QUESTION

On the national question, Americans are united.

There still exists in their hearts the will to remain one nation under God and one people united by history, heritage, and language, committed to the proposition that in America men and women are to be judged "not by the color of their skin but by the content of their character." Americans still believe that we are all equal in rights, not because of where we came from but because of who we are: Americans.

In all thirty-one states where referenda have been held, traditional marriage has been affirmed, and same-sex marriage has been rejected. In every state but one where Ward Connerly's "civil rights initiative" that outlaws race, ethnic, and gender preferences has been put on the ballot, it has won. In every state where making English our official language has been put to the voters, they have said yes. In almost every state, county, and municipality where restrictions on public benefits for illegal aliens have been put to the vote, they have been endorsed by wide majorities. The agenda of the Left—de-Christianizing America, multiculturalism, racial preferences, and unrestricted immigration—has been imposed from above and resisted by a people who do not understand the strength that is theirs if they will but unite and fight.

10

THE LONG RETREAT

He who defends everything defends nothing.[1]
—FREDERICK THE GREAT

The bubble of American triumphalism has burst.[2]
—ANDREW BACEVICH, 2009

[T]he idea of "the West" has been fading for a long time on both sides of the Atlantic.[3]
—ANNE APPLEBAUM, 2009
Washington Post

In 1954, the French Empire in Indochina fell with the surrender at Dien Bien Phu. In Algeria, another war of national liberation began against a French rule first imposed in 1830.

By 1958, the Algerian war had outraged world opinion in that anti-colonial era and brought down the Fourth Republic. Charles de Gaulle, the hero of World War II, was recalled. Gaullists believed the general would crush the rebellion and restore *Algérie française* forever. But de Gaulle came to see the war as unwinnable and organized a vote that the forces of independence won. The Évian accords, granting independence in 1962, followed.

The one million *pied noirs* whose families had lived in Algeria for generations saw de Gaulle as a second Pétain who had surrendered sacred soil, but the general would survive assassination attempts and rule for seven more years. Eventually, the French came to see de Gaulle's decision as the submission of a statesman to the inevitable.

The wars in Indochina and Algeria brought down the French Empire. And the wars in Iraq and Afghanistan have brought America to her own de Gaulle moment. But how did the world's last superpower come to this pass?

SIREN'S CALL TO EMPIRE

In 1991, with the disintegration of America's Cold War rival, the Soviet Empire, and his 100-hour triumph in Desert Storm, President George H. W. Bush went before the UN to declare that America intended to create a "New World Order." At that moment, we succumbed to the temptation of all great powers to what Garet Garrett called the "greater thought."

> It is our turn.
> Our turn to do what?
> Our turn to assume the responsibilities of moral leadership in the world.
> Our turn to maintain a balance of power against the forces of evil everywhere—in Europe and Asia and Africa, in the Atlantic and Pacific, by air and by sea. . . .
> Our turn to keep the peace of the world.
> Our turn to save civilization.
> Our turn to serve mankind.[4]

"But this is the language of empire," wrote Garrett:

> The Roman Empire never doubted that it was the defender of civilization. Its grand intentions were peace, law and order. The Spanish Empire added salvation. The British Empire added the noble myth of the white man's burden. We have added freedom and democracy. Yet, the more that may be added to it, the more it is the same language still. A language of power.[5]

Hubris was in the air in that hour.

In *The End of History* Francis Fukuyama wrote of the inevitable "triumph of the West" and the coming of a new world where liberal democracy would be the "final form of human government embraced by all." Charles Krauthammer spoke of a "unipolar moment" when America ought to "go all the way and stop at nothing short of universal dominion." William Kristol dismissed the "misguided warnings of imperial overstretch" and called for a *Weltpolitik* of "benevolent global hegemony."[6] Madeleine Albright instructed mankind on why America had a right to bomb into submission a small nation, Serbia, that had never injured us. "If we have to use force, it is because we are America. We are the indispensable nation. We stand tall and ... see further into the future."[7]

Thomas Friedman became the troubadour of globalization, "which on closer examination," said Andrew Bacevich, "turned out to be a euphemism for Americanization.":

> The ultimate goal, Friedman wrote in 1999, was "the spread of free-market capitalism to virtually every country in the world"—a process that would put "a Web site in every pot, a Pepsi on every lip, [and] Microsoft Windows in every computer." Yet none of this was going to occur without the backing of hard power. "The hidden hand of the market will never work without a hidden fist," Friedman declared. "And the hidden fist that keeps the world safe for Silicon Valley's technologies is called the United States Army, Air Force, Navy, and Marine Corps."[8]

Heeding the call after 9/11, George W. Bush launched his "global democratic revolution," and, in the one memorable line of his second inaugural, set as America's "ultimate" goal "ending tyranny in our world."

But now the songbirds of empire have all fallen silent.

THE COLD WAR CONSERVATIVES

"Historians will remember the past two decades not as a unipolar moment," wrote Bacevich, "but as an interval in which America succumbed to excessive self-regard. That moment is now ending with our economy in shambles and our country facing the prospect of permanent war."[9]

If world history is the world's court, as Hegel said, severe judgment is being passed upon this hubristic generation. Indeed, when one compares the reticence and restraint of our most successful Cold War presidents, Eisenhower and Reagan, to the reflexive interventionism of Bush I and Bush II, the contrasts are startling. Eisenhower ended the Korean War in six months and gave us seven and a half years of prosperity and peace, some of the best years of our lives. He refused to intervene to save the French army in Indochina. He refused to intervene to save the freedom fighters of the Hungarian revolution in 1956. He ordered Britain, France, and Israel to get their invasion armies out of Egypt. He inserted marines into Lebanon to prevent a coup after the Iraqi revolution of 1958, and withdrew them as soon as the crisis passed.

Eisenhower created defensive alliances in the Middle and Far East modeled on NATO and built an arsenal so awesome it enabled Kennedy to back Khrushchev down in the Cuban missile crisis. But after he had ended the war he inherited he never got into another, and he left office with a prophetic warning about the dangers to the republic of a "military industrial complex" with a vested interest in a long Cold War.

Reagan was another conservative of the old school, not looking for a fight. Believing, as Eisenhower did, in "Peace Through Strength," he began a steady buildup of strategic and conventional forces, countered Moscow's deployment of SS-20 missiles in Eastern Europe with Pershing and cruise missiles in Western Europe, and aided anti-Communist rebels on the periphery of the Soviet Empire—in Nicaragua, Angola, and Afghanistan. But Reagan never sought direct confrontation or conflict with the Soviet Union. When Solidarity was crushed on Moscow's orders in 1981, Reagan declined to escalate the crisis and restricted U.S. support to the moral and material.

Reagan deployed measured military force three times. He sent U.S. Marines into Lebanon, liberated Grenada after a Marxist coup, and struck Libya after Gaddafi's bombing of a Berlin discothèque frequented by U.S. soldiers. After the terrorist attack on the Beirut barracks killed 241 of those marines, Reagan removed them and regretted ever having sent them in. He would call it the worst mistake of his presidency. In his last days in office, Reagan negotiated an arms control treaty for the removal of all U.S. and Soviet intermediate-range missiles from Europe. He had steered America to a peaceful end to the Cold War. Having begun his presidency decrying the "evil empire," he ended it being patted on the back by smiling Russians in Red Square while walking side by side with Mikhail Gorbachev.

In the decades after Reagan left and before Bush II departed, hubris became the hallmark of American foreign policy. Bush I intervened in Panama, attacked Iraq, liberated Kuwait, planted U.S. forces in Saudi Arabia, and intervened in Somalia, leading to a massacre of Delta Force troopers in Mogadishu in a bloody engagement that came to be known as Black Hawk Down.

Clinton invaded Haiti, intervened in Bosnia, bombed Serbia for seventy-eight days, and sent U.S. troops to effect a secession of her cradle province of Kosovo.

George W. Bush invaded Afghanistan, declared Iran, Iraq, and North Korea an "axis of evil," warned the world that we would maintain military supremacy in every vital region of the globe, declared a Bush Doctrine of preventive war and used it to invade and occupy an Iraq that had never threatened or attacked us, and launched a global crusade for democracy that featured demonstrations to dump over governments and install pro-American regimes in Serbia, Ukraine, Georgia, Kyrgyzstan, and Lebanon, as Kermit Roosevelt and the CIA had done in Iran in 1953.

Clinton and Bush II pushed NATO right up to Russia's front porch, bringing six former Warsaw Pact nations—East Germany, Hungary, Poland, the Czech Republic, Bulgaria, and Romania—and three Baltic states that had been part of the Soviet Union into an alliance created to contain Russia. Only European resistance stopped Bush II from putting Ukraine and Georgia on a fast track to NATO membership, which would have meant that should there be a Moscow-Tbilisi clash, America would instantly be eyeball to eyeball with a nation possessing thousands of nuclear weapons.

Barack Obama doubled U.S. forces in Afghanistan, began drone strikes in Pakistan, and launched a war on Libya.

And what has all this compulsive interventionism availed us?

We are less secure, less respected, less confident, and less powerful than we were in 1991. And is the world a better place?

RECEDING TIDE

The American empire has begun the long retreat.

In Lebanon and Ukraine the "color-coded revolutions" have been reversed. The U.S. commitment to Afghanistan has topped out at 100,000 troops and they have begun coming home. Military withdrawal from Iraq is to be done by year's end. These two wars may prove the last hurrahs of neo-imperialism, unless the nation is stampeded into another "preventive war" on Iran.

Looking back, the long retreat of American empire began decades ago. U.S. forces left Southeast Asia in the early 1970s and U.S. bases on Taiwan were abandoned. In the 1990s, the United States was ordered to vacate Clark air base in the Philippines and the U.S. naval base at Subic Bay. The U.S. footprint in Japan is shrinking. U.S. forces in South Korea are at the lowest level in sixty years. The eastward march of NATO has halted and the door has been closed to Ukraine and Georgia. America is not going to fight Russia over Tbilisi's clam to South Ossetia or who has sovereignty in the Crimea. The ballistic missile defense Bush II began to erect in Poland and Czechoslovakia has been put on hold.

The long retreat comports with the national interest and the will of the people. In 2009, the Pew Research Center found that 49 percent of

Americans thought the nation should "mind its own business internationally and let other countries get along the best they can on their own."[10] Only 44 percent of respondents disagreed. This is a dramatic reversal from a decade ago when 30 percent thought America should mind its own business, and 65 percent disagreed. Not in forty years had a survey found anti-interventionist sentiment this strong. Americans are growing weary of playing Atlas, holding up the world.

For those who have argued since the fall of the Berlin Wall in 1989 for the shedding of Cold War alliances and war guarantees and a return to a traditional policy of nonintervention, if U.S. interests are not imperiled, this is welcome news. What is less welcome are the reasons for America's retreat.

A relative decline in strategic power is not necessarily a crisis. The U.S. share of world power declined from 1945 to 1960, due to the recovery of Europe and Japan. America's real power grew under Eisenhower. Her recent decline, however, has been both relative and real. Its causes:

First, wars in Iraq and Afghanistan that have cost us 6,000 dead, 40,000 wounded, and over $1 trillion. These wars destroyed our post-9/11 national unity, alienated the Islamic world, and enlarged the pool in which al-Qaeda fishes.

Second, our imperial arrogance caused nations to unite to resist our hegemony, and we deliberately antagonized nations like Russia that had wanted to associate with us. People treated like untrustworthy friends and potential enemies often end up becoming so.

Third, the financial meltdown brought on by the collapse of a housing bubble that government policy created, the easy money policy of the Federal Reserve, and the amorality and casino mind-set of Wall Street.

Fourth, the dismantling of America's industrial base and its export to China under a trade policy that puts the profits of transnational corporations ahead of the prosperity of the republic. Our economic independence is history. We rely on foreign factories to produce the necessities of our national life, and on foreign governments for the loans to pay for them.

Fifth, the failure of the U.S. government to secure our border with Mexico and stop a poor peoples' invasion that is bankrupting our states and will, left unchecked, end our existence as one nation and people.

Sixth, the rise of rival powers that exploit for nationalist ends the global economic system established by the United States.

Seventh, a blindness in our leaders to see that the interdependent world for which they and we were made to sacrifice so much, a world of old and new democracies tied together by trade, is a mirage. Nations put national interests first.

ASSETS AND LIABILITIES

In *U.S. Foreign Policy: Shield of the Republic*, published in 1943, the famed columnist Walter Lippmann looked back on the division in the nation over going to war, and our unpreparedness at Pearl Harbor. We Americans, he wrote, "had forgotten the compelling and, once seen, self-evident common principle of all genuine foreign policy."

> A foreign policy consists in bringing into balance, with a comfortable surplus of power in reserve, the nation's commitments and the nation's power. The constant preoccupation of the true statesman is to achieve and maintain this balance.[11]

When a nation lacks the power to honor its treaty obligations or defend its vital interests, its foreign policy is insolvent. Examples abound when U.S. foreign policy was bankrupt, in that we had undertaken obligations which we lacked the power to honor. Had it not been for the Royal Navy guaranteeing the Monroe Doctrine, whereby we instructed the great powers of Europe they were to cease seeking colonies in our hemisphere, that doctrine would have been an embarrassing joke.

During the Civil War, we could do little about the annexation of Mexico by France's Napoleon III in the most flagrant violation of the Monroe Doctrine before the Cuban missile crisis. But when the Confederacy fell and

Andrew Johnson sent General Sheridan to the border with 40,000 battle-hardened Union troops, and Secretary of State Seward sent a general to Paris to tell Napoleon to get out of Mexico or we would come in and throw him out, we had that "surplus of power" to enforce our will and uphold Monroe's doctrine.

By 1941, U.S. foreign policy had been bankrupt for two decades. For Wilson had agreed at the 1919 Paris peace conference to a Japanese mandate over the Marshall, Mariana, and Caroline Islands, which lay between Hawaii and the Philippine Islands. And Harding had signed a Washington Naval Agreement that scuttled the fleets needed to defend the Philippines, leaving Japan's navy dominant in the western Pacific. Wrote Lippmann, "We are today liquidating in sweat and blood and tears, and at our mortal peril, the fact that we made commitments, asserted rights, and proclaimed ideals while we left our frontiers unguarded, our armaments unprepared, and our alliances unformed and unsustained."[12]

It is a thesis of this book that U.S. foreign policy is again insolvent. For the commitments we have undertaken over six decades cannot be covered by our overstretched and declining military power. If several outstanding IOUs were called in at once, U.S. strategic bankruptcy would be apparent to the world.

On the asset side of the balance sheet, the United States still possesses thousands of nuclear weapons and the ability to deliver them anywhere on earth, more than enough to deter Russia and China, the only nations with the weapons to inflict mortal wounds on us. Nor is there any quarrel between us and either of those powers to justify nuclear confrontation.

The U.S. Navy, though not half of the six-hundred-ship armada Reagan built, remains larger than the combined fleets of the next thirteen largest naval powers. According to former Secretary of Defense Robert Gates, the U.S. Navy can carry twice as many planes as all the other navies of the world combined. The U.S. Air Force is unequaled. No nation has a bomber force to match America's B-52s, B-1s, and B-2s, or her thousands of fourth- and fifth-generation fighters. U.S. defense spending is four times that of Russia and China combined and 44 percent of world military spending.[13]

But when the number of Americans on active duty is factored in—one-half of 1 percent of the population—the picture changes. Although we have commitments to defend scores of nations in Europe, the Middle East, Asia, and Oceania, U.S. forces are but one-tenth the size of our active-duty forces at the end of World War II, and not half the size of the peacetime army of Eisenhower. And these forces are spread all over the world. We have 50,000 troops in Iraq, 100,000 in Afghanistan, 28,000 in Korea, 35,000 in Japan, 50,000 in Germany.

If the responsibilities of the U.S. military were restricted to defense of our homeland and hemisphere and the seas around us, we possess that surplus of power of which Lippmann spoke. What, then, is the problem?

It is the other side of the ledger: the liabilities, the commitments we have made.

Although we spend more on defense than the next ten military powers combined, we can no longer defend every ally to whom we have given a war guarantee in the six decades since NATO was born. Two relatively small wars by twentieth-century standards, in Afghanistan and Iraq, have stretched the army and Marine Corps to the limit.

AN INVENTORY OF EMPIRE

While we have more than enough power to secure the republic, we cannot sustain the empire. Pax Americana is coming to an end. The only question is whether the liquidation of the empire will be done voluntarily and rationally, or after some strategic debacle like Saigon 1975 or a financial and economic collapse like that of 1929. One way or another, the last Western empire is coming down.

The signs are everywhere. After a decade of war, the United States has failed to convert either Iraq or Afghanistan into a pro-Western bastion or democratic beacon. As U.S. forces depart Iraq, that Shia-dominated nation is tilting toward Iran and the rising political figure is the anti-American Moqtada al-Sadr. As U.S. troops prepare to depart Afghanistan, the Taliban are closer to a return to power than they have been since 2001.

Should North Korea invade the South we would not have a fraction of the troops to send that we did in 1950. Should Moscow decide on teaching Estonia a lesson, how would we honor our NATO commitment to treat an attack on Estonia as an attack on the United States? Russia's chastisement of Georgia, when Tbilisi tried to retrieve its lost province of South Ossetia, showed that NATO's writ does not run to the Caucasus. Ukraine, sensing the shift in the balance of power, has agreed to Russia's demand to keep her naval base at Sevastopol in the Crimea until 2042. As U.S. force levels in Asia and the Pacific are drawn down, China's real and relative power, augmented by annual double-digit increases in defense spending, grows.

Where the Chinese have hard currency reserves of $3 trillion, we borrow from Europe to defend Europe. We borrow from the Gulf States to defend the Gulf States. We borrow from Japan to defend Japan. Is it not a symptom of senility to be borrowing from the world so we can defend the world? How long before we borrow our country into bankruptcy, so our foreign policy elites can continue to play the empire game?

Every year, the U.S. Government goes tens of billions deeper in debt to finance foreign aid. Why? A January 2011 CNN poll found that 81 percent of Americans want foreign aid cut.[14] At the Copenhagen summit, Secretary Clinton pledged the United States would take the lead in raising $100 billion a year to help Third World nations cope with climate change. Where is our $20 billion annual share to come from? From borrowing? But the foreign bankers lending us the money to sustain the empire are awakening to the truth that an America running regular deficits of 10 percent of GDP will never pay them back in dollars of the same value as the ones they are lending us.

How can the United States draw down its forces to help put its house in order, while defending what is vital? The first place to look is at the global archipelago of U.S. military bases. According to author Laurence

Vance, "There are, according to the Department of Defense's 'Base Structure Report' for FY 2009, 716 U.S. military bases on foreign soil in thirty-eight countries."[15]

Yet, according to an expert on the subject, the late Chalmers Johnson:

> "The official figures omit espionage bases, those located in war zones, including Iraq and Afghanistan, and miscellaneous facilities in places considered too sensitive to discuss or which the Pentagon for its own reasons chooses to exclude—e.g., in Israel, Kosovo or Jordan." Johnson places the real number of foreign bases at 1,000.[16]

According to the Department of Defense's "Active Duty Military Personnel Strengths by Regional Area and by Country," U.S. troops are in 148 countries and 11 territories.

This worldwide archipelago of bases may have been justified when we confronted a Communist bloc spanning Eurasia from the Elbe to the East China Sea, armed with thousands of nuclear weapons and driven by imperial ambition and ideological animus against the United States. But the Cold War is history. It is absurd to contend that 1,000 overseas bases are vital to U.S. security. Indeed, it is our pervasive military presence abroad, our support of despotic regimes, and our endless interventions and wars that have made America, once the most admired of nations, among the world's most resented and detested.

Liquidation of this empire should have begun at the end of the Cold War. Now it is being forced upon us by a deficit-debt crisis that the cost of that empire helped to produce. We cannot continue to kick the can up the road, for we have come to the end of the road.

Britain's John Gray got it right:

> The irony of the post-Cold War period is that the fall of communism was followed by the rise of another utopian ideology.... The collapse of American power that is underway is the

predictable upshot. Like the Soviet collapse, it will have large geopolitical repercussions. An enfeebled economy cannot support America's over-extended military commitments for much longer. Retrenchment is inevitable and it is unlikely to be gradual or well planned.[17]

The "utopian ideology" of which Gray writes is the idea we drank deep of at the end of the Cold War: that America, now the last superpower, had a mission from Divine Providence to use our wealth and power to lead mankind to a promised land of freedom, peace, prosperity, and democracy, even if it required decades of sacrifices of American blood and treasure in a new heroic "Long War." Our inevitable disillusionment is now at hand.

So, what criteria should determine which alliances should be allowed to lapse, which bases should be closed, and which troops brought home? The yardstick should be whether the nations involved are truly vital to the national security of the United States.

OUT OF RUSSIA'S SPACE

From Churchill's speech at Fulton, Missouri, in 1946, declaring an "iron curtain" had fallen across Europe, to Reagan's stroll through Red Square in 1988, the United States was consumed by the Cold War. At times in that protracted conflict—the Berlin blockade of 1948, the Cuban missile crisis of 1962—confrontation threatened to erupt into a world war.

By the grace of God and wise statesmanship, we avoided those wars, unlike the great powers in the first half of that bloodiest of centuries. And when, two decades ago, the Soviet Union dismantled its empire, withdrew the Red Army from Europe, allowed the USSR to disintegrate into fifteen nations, and jettisoned Communist ideology, the *casus belli* of the Cold War disappeared. America's Cold War mind-set and military alliances should have disappeared as well. Unfortunately, they did not.

Reagan would have seized the opportunity to convert Russia into a strategic partner and ally. For here was a great nation, still twice as large as the United States, with whom we no longer had a quarrel and whose hand was extended in friendship. Instead, cynically and opportunistically, we seized on Russia's moment of weakness to bring six former allies and three former republics of the USSR, all of which had been set free by Moscow, into an alliance aimed against Moscow.

Why? If the crushing of the Hungarian Revolution and the suppression of Poland's Solidarity movement in 1981 were not enough to rupture our relations with Russia, when did those countries become so vital to our security that we should go to war over them? If George H. W. Bush barely protested Gorbachev's sending special forces into the Baltic republics in 1990, when did Lithuania, Latvia, and Estonia become matters over which we should fight Russia, as we are now committed to do by our NATO alliance?

This was hubris of a high order. We obligated ourselves to defend nine new allies who added nothing to U.S. security, while antagonizing the world's largest nation, which had sought our friendship. We added to our strategic liabilities, but added no strategic assets. We alienated a superpower to call Latvia an ally.

Why? The Russians had done as we wished—let the captive nations go, abandoned Communism, dissolved the empire, allowed fourteen ethnic minorities to establish new nations—and we treated them like Clemenceau treated the Weimar Republic. And we wonder why they resent us?

Anti-Americanism is rampant in Russia and is not going to disappear. But the United States can alleviate this hostility by ceasing to deceive ourselves about our commitments and interests in the Baltic, the Caucasus, Central Asia, and Russia itself. We are not going to fight Russia over South Ossetia or Abkhazia or Georgia. We are not going to war over the Baltic republics. Nor is there any vital interest of ours at risk if Ukraine and Russia move closer. These nations have historic, cultural, and ethnic ties that go back to before the United States existed, and both face a world where their numbers are dwindling while the populations of

Asian and Muslim neighbors are growing. A closer alignment of Ukraine and Russia seems natural and presents no threat to us.

As we have economic but not strategic interests in Russia's "near abroad," the United States should tell Moscow that, after we leave Afghanistan, we will close all U.S. military bases in her border states and Central Asia and restrict military sales to Georgia, Ukraine, and the Baltic republics to defensive weapons. And we would expect reciprocity in Russian military sales to Caribbean countries and Central America. If we want Russia as a friend, let us get out of Russia's space and get out of Russia's face.

This is not to declare indifference to the fate of the Baltic republics. It is to say simply that these are not nations over which we can risk war. The same holds for Ukraine and Georgia. Both were part of the Russian empire of the Romanovs. And as the August war of 2008 showed, where we stood by as Russia thrashed Georgia for killing its peacekeepers and invading South Ossetia, America is not going to fight the largest country on earth over some statelet in the Caucasus.

In coming decades, a Russia whose population is shrinking is almost certain to lose land and people in the Caucasus and the Far East, where its population is outnumbered 100 to 1 by Chinese. There is nothing we can do about this and the Russian reaction to its diminution and its ethnonational dismemberment is unlikely to be pleasant. As this is none of our business, let us get out of the way, now.

WHITHER NATO?

At the end of the Cold War, NATO was acclaimed as "the most successful alliance in history." But it faced a dilemma, as did the March of Dimes when Drs. Salk and Sabin found the cure for polio. What does an alliance created to defend Europe from the Red Army and the Warsaw Pact do when the Red Army has gone home and the Warsaw Pact has ceased to exist? How does one defend the Elbe River line when the Elbe no longer divides Germany and Europeans travel freely from the Atlantic to the Urals?

As Russia had gone home, some of us urged back then, America should come home, cede NATO and all the U.S. bases in Europe to the Europeans, and become again what UN ambassador Jeane Kirkpatrick called "a normal country in a normal time." Our foreign policy elites, however, could not accept that the play was closing after a forty-year run and America's starring role as defender of the West against a mighty and malevolent Soviet Empire was coming to an end.

"We are about to do to you the worst possible thing we can do," said Georgi Arbatov, of Moscow's USA Institute. "We are going to take your enemy away."[18] Writer John Updike echoed Arbatov: "Without the Cold War, what's the point of being an American?"[19] Senator Richard Lugar stated the obvious. With the Iron Curtain lifted, the Berlin Wall down, and Europe free from Lisbon to Latvia, NATO "has to go out of area, or go out of business."[20]

America was not going to let NATO go out of business. Too many rice bowls would be broken. Thus, going back on a commitment we had made to Gorbachev, we brought the Warsaw Pact and three former Soviet republics into NATO. If the Russians feel like victims of a bait-and-switch, can we blame them?

Today, the sixty-year-old alliance is facing what may be a terminal crisis. After 9/11, NATO went out of area to go nation building in Afghanistan. We are now late in the tenth year of that war. Some NATO allies have already left Afghanistan. Others are scheduled to. Others impose restrictions on use of their troops, such as no combat. U.S. troops, too, are supposed to end major combat by 2014, though, as General Stanley McChrystal conceded last year, the Taliban have fought us to a draw.[21]

Should NATO fail in Afghanistan, what is its future? Who does NATO then contain or deter? Who would NATO fight? With the Baltic republics in the alliance, NATO is committed to treat an attack on Estonia as an attack on England. Can anyone believe Germany or France or Italy would declare war on Russia over Estonia?

When, in the Arab Spring of 2011, rebels rose up to depose Colonel Khadafi, whose army was about to crush the last stronghold of resistance in the east, Benghazi, Britain and France prevailed upon Obama to conduct air and missile strikes to prevent a massacre. No such massacre had occurred in any city Khadafi had retaken, but Obama, with aides warning him that inaction could mean a new Rwanda, was stampeded into war.

Ten days of U.S.-led air strikes sent Khadafi's forces reeling. Then, Obama handed the mission over to NATO. But without U.S. air and naval power, NATO could do no more than maintain a stalemate in a civil war in a militarily enfeebled nation of six million people. Without the United States, the claim that NATO is a great power is fiction.

Moreover, Europeans are facing a debt crisis that is forcing new cuts in their already anemic military budgets. "[A]ll over Europe governments with big budgets, falling tax revenues and aging populations are experiencing rising deficits, with more bad news ahead," reports the *New York Times:*

> With low growth, low birthrates and longer life expectancies, Europe can no longer afford its comfortable lifestyle... without a period of austerity and significant changes. The countries are trying to reassure investors by cutting salaries, raising legal retirement ages, increasing work hours and reducing health benefits and pensions.[22]

The armed forces of Britain, France, Germany, and Italy, shadows of the million-man armies of their grandfathers, face even deeper cuts in personnel. By 2050, according to the European Commission, the number of Europeans over 65 will double. In 1950, there were 7 workers for every retired European. In 2050, the ratio will be 1.3 to one.[23] Europe is aging and dying. Why would Europeans conscript their dwindling number of sons to fight in far-off lands? Why not rely, as always, on the Americans, who seem to relish the role? Out of area or out of business, said Senator Lugar. Having gone out of area, and come home disillusioned, NATO Europe must soon come to see the wisdom of the alternative.

EXITING THE ISLAMIC WORLD

Since 1991, the United States has fought a Persian Gulf war to liberate Kuwait, invaded and occupied Iraq and Afghanistan, used Special Forces and Predator drones to strike enemies in Somalia, Yemen, and Pakistan, imposed crippling sanctions on Iran, backed Israel in its wars in Lebanon and Gaza, and led a NATO attack on Libya.

We fight them over there, it is said, so we will not have to fight them over here.

Yet no Afghan or Iraqi or Somali or Yemeni or member of Hezbollah or Hamas ever attacked us—over here. September 11 was largely the work of fifteen Saudis sent by a Saudi, Osama. And while we are able to smash armies and depose despots, we have proven incapable of building nations or winning the hearts of peoples whose lands we have occupied. After sinking the wealth of an empire into Iraq, we have a regime that asked Tehran to bless its coalition, and that owes its existence to Moqtada al-Sadr.

The cost of our war in Iraq has been high: 4,400 dead, 37,000 wounded, $700 billion sunk, 100,000 Iraqi women widowed, hundreds of thousands of children orphaned. Sunni have been cleansed from Baghdad. Christians have endured pogroms and martyrdoms. Four millions Iraqis have been uprooted from their homes. Two million have left the country. As was said of the Romans: *Ubi solitudinem faciunt pacem appellant.* Where they make a desert they call it peace.

Across the Islamic world, we have broadened and deepened the reservoir of hate in which Al Qaeda fishes. "From the Mediterranean to the Indus Valley," writes Geoffrey Wheatcroft, quoting diplomat Aaron David Miller, America is "not liked, not feared, and not respected."[24]

The "inconvenient truth about the Arab world today," writes Eugene Rogan, an historian of the Arabs, "is that, in any free election, those parties most hostile to the United States are likely to win."[25] Elections in Egypt, Lebanon, Palestine, and Iran in the Bush years bear him out.

In the Middle East, democratization means Islamization, as seen in the recent Turkish elections in which the masses voted to deliver the coup de grâce to Ataturk's secular state. Should the National Endowment for Democracy succeed in bringing free and fair elections to post-Mubarak Egypt, Jordan, and Saudi Arabia, allies of the United States could be swept away.

We came to Afghanistan as liberators, but are seen now as occupiers, imposing our ideas, values, and satraps. After eight years of war in Iraq and ten in Afghanistan, we are coming home with Iraq going its own way and Afghanistan tipping toward the Taliban.

Why did we not succeed? First, because we are poor imperialists who lack the patience and perseverance of the British. Second, because the age of imperialism is over. What all peoples demand today is self-determination, sovereignty, and freedom from foreign domination. Third, because it was always utopian to believe we could impose a system rooted in Western secular values on people steeped for ten centuries in Islam. The war to do so has only made us enemies where they did not exist.

We failed to understand what motivated our attackers. They did not come to kill us because they abhor our Constitution, or wish to impose Sharia on Oklahoma. They were over here because we are over there. They came to kill us in our country because we will not get out of their countries. Terrorism is the weapon of the weak who wish to be rid of foreign domination. From Plains Indians to Afghan mujahideen, from Menachem Begin's Irgun to the Algerian FLN, from the IRA of Martin McGuinness to the ANC of Nelson Mandela, it has ever been thus.

Terrorism is the price of empire.

Anti-Western terror comes out of countries where the West is seen as overlord. When the British left Palestine, the Stern Gang attacks stopped. When the French left Algeria, the Paris bombings ended. When the Russians pulled out of Afghanistan, the mujahideen did not follow. When the U.S. Navy stopped shelling and the marines left Beirut, the attacks on Americans in Lebanon ceased. Osama bin Laden ordered 9/11 because U.S. troops were stationed on sacred Saudi soil that is home to Mecca. We will never end terrorist attacks on this country, until we remove our soldiers from those countries.

If we have a vital interest in that part of the world, it is that no hostile power should be able to shut off the flow of oil, the lifeblood of the industrial West. But the countries of the Middle East also have a vital interest in seeing to it that the oil flows. Without oil exports and the revenue they produce, the Middle East would sink to the level of the sub-Sahara.

CHINA'S CHALLENGE

In a 2008 survey of two dozen countries by the Pew Global Attitudes Project, the nation that emerged first, measured by the satisfaction of its people, was China. No other nation came close. "Eighty-six percent of Chinese people surveyed said they were content with the country's direction, up from 48 percent in 2002.... And 82 percent of Chinese were satisfied with their national economy, up from 52 percent."[26]

Considering whence the Chinese had come, out from under the mad murderous rule of Mao, support for the course set by Deng Xiaoping is understandable. Yet, for decades, China has denied couples the right to have a second child and its people the right to choose their leaders. The regime persecutes Tibetans, Uighurs, and Christians. Marxist ideology has been set aside but has been replaced by an ethnic chauvinism reminiscent of Central Europe in the 1930s. Yet, 86 percent of all Chinese were content with their country's direction.

High among the reasons for the sense of satisfaction and pride is that China had been growing 10 to 12 percent a year for decades. Rising prosperity and burgeoning power, national unity and international respect, seem more important to the Chinese than freedom of speech, religion, assembly, or the press.

Contrast the contentment of the Chinese with the dissatisfaction of our own countrymen. In that Pew survey, only 23 percent of Americans said they approved of the nation's direction. Only one in five was satisfied with the economy. And that was before the October 2008 crash. While this was in the final days of the Bush presidency, negative views about the direction of the country had returned by the end of Obama's first year.

Democratic capitalism now has a rival: autocratic capitalism. In Asia, Africa, and Latin America, nations are looking to China as a model, as, in the 1930s, European and Latin nations looked to the Italy of Il Duce, where the trains ran on time, and the Germany of Hitler, with its stunning recovery from the depression. Yet, while China, having doubled its share of the world economy in two decades, is the rising power and America a declining power, the imperative remains—avoiding what happened between a fading Britain and a rising Germany in the twentieth century: ten years of war that bled and bankrupted both.

There are no issues between America and China that would seem to justify conflict. But, in the event of an economic reversal such as Japan suffered in the 1990s, Beijing could provoke a crisis to unite and divert a vast population that saw its prosperity disappear and hopes dashed. The most likely site for such a crisis is the Taiwan Strait.

While the United States is not going to war with China over an island every president since Nixon has conceded is a part of China, we could not sit passively by and watch as Taiwan, our former ally, was attacked, blockaded, or invaded. Beijing needs to understand that a price would be imposed. But, given the thickening ties between Taiwan and the Mainland, it is hard to see why China would risk alarming Asia and enraging America by provoking a crisis. Indeed, Asian apprehension over the rising power of China offers the best hope of containing Beijing.

Consider: China occupies thousands of square miles of Indian land in Jammu and Kashmir seized in the 1962 war. Her claims to the Paracel and Spratly Islands in the South China Sea clash with the territorial claims of half a dozen nations. Her claim to the Senkakus in the East China Sea puts her at odds with Japan. China has also warned U.S. warships, especially carriers, to stay out of the Taiwan strait and the Yellow Sea.

In the fall of 2010, Japan arrested the Chinese captain of a trawler that had rammed one of her patrol boats in the Senkaku chain. Threatening a cut-off of "rare-earth" materials only China produces in abundance, Beijing forced Tokyo to release the captain, then demanded an apology and compensation.

South Korea is angered by China's support of the regime in the North that in 2010 torpedoed and sank one of its warships, killing four dozen sailors, and shelled a South Korean island, killing four.

Russia has to fear a China from whom the czars took a vast tract of land in the nineteenth century. Gazing north at the world's last great storehouse of natural resources, Beijing is surely contemplating one day doing to Russia what czarist Russia did to her.

China is also constrained by her discontented minorities—Uighurs in the west, Tibetans in the south, Mongols in the north—and also by her neighbors: the Vietnamese fought a war with China in 1979. The Burmese suspect the ties of their secessionist tribes to China. The Taiwanese have not been ruled from Beijing for a century and cherish their independence. The Chinese in Hong Kong are fearful of the embrace of the motherland.

Perhaps the most powerful attraction of the United States to Asia is an awareness that America, executing a long retreat from that continent and from its commitments of the twentieth century, represents no threat, while the same cannot be said with the same assurance of Beijing.

There is yet another crisis confronting China: a growing dependence on imported food as her water tables diminish and arable land disappears. Writes Lester Brown of Earth Policy Institute:

> Since 1950, some 24,000 villages in the northwestern part of the country have been totally or partially abandoned as sand dunes encroach on cropland. And with millions of Chinese farmers drilling wells to expand their harvests, water tables are falling under much of the North China Plain, which produces half of the nation's wheat and a third of its corn.
>
> Chinese agriculture is also losing irrigation water to cities

and factories. Cropland is being sacrificed for residential and industrial construction....[27]

As Britain and Japan can testify, nations that cannot feed themselves and rely on fleets of merchant ships for survival are vulnerable nations.

SOUTH KOREA AND JAPAN

Fifty-seven years after the armistice that ended the Korean war, a U.S. carrier task force steamed into the Yellow Sea in a show of force after North Korea fired artillery shells into a South Korean village.

We will stand by our allies, said President Obama. And with our security treaty and 28,000 U.S. troops there, many on the DMZ, we could do nothing else. But why, sixty years after the first Korean War began, should Americans be among the first to die in a second Korean war?

Why cannot South Korea defend herself?

Unlike 1950, South Korea is no longer an impoverished ex-colony of Japan. She is the largest of the Asian tigers, a nation with twice the population of the North and an economy forty times as large. Seoul had just hosted the G-20 economic summit. There is no Maoist China with a million "volunteers" in North Korea. There is no Stalinist Soviet Union equipping Pyongyang's armies. The U.S.-built planes, guns, and tanks of the South are far superior in quality.

Why, then, are we still in Korea? Why is every quarrel with the North our quarrel? Why is a second Korean war, should it come, America's war? Why do we retain tens of thousands of U.S. soldiers on the DMZ facing 11,000 artillery pieces and hundreds of thousands of North Korean troops? The U.S. force is too small to advance into North Korea, and South Korea could conscript the soldiers to take their place. Why, then, are the Americans still there?

The answer: our soldiers are there to ensure that Americans die in the first hours of fighting. Thus bloodied, the United States will then send an army like the third of a million men we sent in the 1950s. The U.S. troop presence on the DMZ strips the United States of its freedom to decide whether we wish to fight a second war on the peninsula and leaves that decision to the North Korean dictator. Our troops in Korea are hostages.

While the United States has been a loyal ally for six decades, the U.S.–Republic of Korea security treaty should be renegotiated and all U.S. troops pulled off the peninsula. For a second Korean war, terrible as it would be, would not involve an interest of the United States sufficient to justify sending tens of thousands of Americans to fight. The decision as to whether we fight another Korean war should be left to leaders elected by this generation, not determined by a 1953 treaty agreed to by the Eisenhower administration and President Syngman Rhee.

The same holds for Japan. Under the existing security pact, we are obligated to come to the defense of Japan, but Japan is not obligated to come to the defense of the United States. Why should this be so in 2011?

Japan is not the destroyed nation of 1945, when she became a U.S. protectorate. We are almost as far away in time from the day General MacArthur took the Japanese surrender on the USS *Missouri* as the attack on Pearl Harbor was from Appomattox. Japan's economy is nearly as large as and is more technologically advanced than China's, and Japan has the capacity to build the air, missile, and naval forces needed to deter China or any other nation. Russia may still hold the southern Kuril Islands taken as spoils after World War II, but Russia represents no strategic threat. Indeed, Tokyo is helping to develop Russia's resources in Siberia.

The rebuttal: America alone possesses the weapons to threaten atomic retaliation on North Korea, or China, should Beijing threaten Japan with nuclear weapons. But that begs the question: why should America remain forever at risk of nuclear war when the free nations we defend are capable of developing their own nuclear deterrents?

British and French development of nuclear weapons did not weaken America. It complicated the war planning of the Kremlin. South Korean nuclear weapons would cancel out any strategic advantage Pyongyang has gained from testing two crude bombs and would become North Korea's worry, not ours. Japan's possession of atomic weapons would be a threat only to those who threaten or attack Japan. That list does not include the United States.

In the negotiations to convince Kim Jong-il to give up his nuclear weapons, Beijing—the indispensable party, as she alone has economic and political leverage over Pyongyang—has been singularly unhelpful. The prospect of Seoul and Tokyo acquiring nuclear weapons might focus the Chinese mind on solving the problem on the Korean peninsula.

The Japanese and Korean security pacts should be renegotiated to restore America's freedom to act in her own best interests. U.S. forces should be withdrawn from Korea, the home islands of Japan, and Okinawa, where their presence exacerbates tensions. Japan and South Korea could build or buy from the United States the weapons necessary for their own defense, which has to be more important to them than it is to us.

From 1941 to 1989, America played a great role as the defender of freedom, sacrificing and serving mankind, a role of which we can be proud. But having won that epochal struggle, we found ourselves in a world for which we were unprepared. Like an aging athlete, we keep trying to relive the glory days when all the world looked upon us. Being the world's champion of freedom became part of our national identity. We can't let go, because we do not know what else to do. As our rivals look to tomorrow, we live in yesterday.

AFGHANISTAN SOUTH

On the last day of August in 2010, a front-page story in the *Washington Times* began thus:

> The federal government has posted signs along a major interstate highway in Arizona, more than 100 miles north of the

U.S.-Mexico border, warning travelers the area is unsafe because of drug and alien smugglers, and a local sheriff says Mexican drug cartels now control some parts of the state.[28]

This raises a question. Are vital U.S. interests more imperiled by what happens in Iraq where we have 50,000 troops, or Afghanistan where we have 100,000, or South Korea where we have 28,000—or by what is happening on our border with Mexico?

In his 1994 memoir, *Around the Cragged Hill,* the legendary U.S. diplomat and Cold War geostrategist George Kennan wondered about his nation's understanding of what was critical and what was not: "[T]he U.S. Government, while not loath to putting half a million armed troops in the Middle East to expel the armed Iraqis from Kuwait, confesses itself unable to defend its own southwestern border from illegal immigration."[29]

What does it profit America if we save Anbar and lose Arizona?

"Mexican drug cartels literally control parts of Arizona," said Pinal County Sheriff Paul Babeu.

They literally have scouts on the high points in the mountains and in the hills and they literally control movement. They have radios, they have optics, they have night-vision goggles as good as anything law enforcement has. This is going on here in Arizona. This is 60 miles from the border—30 miles from the fifth-largest city in the United States.[30]

Sheriff Babeu asked President Obama for three thousand National Guard troops. He got fifteen road signs. Prediction: After all U.S. troops in Iraq, Afghanistan, and Korea are home, a U.S. army will be on the Mexican border. For this is where the fate of the republic will be decided, as the fate of Europe will be decided by the millions streaming in from the Maghreb, the Middle East, South Asia, and sub-Saharan Africa.

Six thousand Mexicans died in drug-related killings in 2008 in a war where cartel tactics include massacre, kidnapping, and beheadings.

Sixteen hundred died in Juárez alone, just across the Rio Grande from El Paso. Thousands of federal troops are now in Juárez, where gun battles occur daily. Fifty thousand troops are now committed to this war that Mexico is not winning, as the Pentagon estimates the cartels field 100,000 foot soldiers, a force almost equal to the Mexican army.[31]

After a cartel threatened to kill a police officer every forty-eight hours if he did not resign, the chief of police of Juárez quit. To show its seriousness, the cartel had murdered four cops, including the chief's deputy. In 2008, fifty Juárez police officers were murdered. "The decision I am taking ... is one of life over death," said Chief Roberto Orduna Cruz.[32] He would seem to have a point. A colleague's head was found in an ice cooler outside a police station. The mayor of Juárez kept his family in El Paso. They, too, had been threatened with decapitation.

"Corruption throughout Mexico's public institutions remains a key impediment to curtailing the power of the drug cartels," said the U.S. State Department.[33] President Felipe Calderón retorted that while the murders may be committed in Mexico, the cash and the guns come from the United States.

The drug war is killing our neighbor. While remittances from Mexican workers in the United States are down, U.S. tourism in Mexico has also begun to suffer. Beheadings around Acapulco have not helped. Warnings have been issued to U.S. college students to avoid Mexico, as kidnappings for ransom are common. Restaurants and bars in Juárez that catered to soldiers from Fort Bliss and folks from El Paso are shutting down. In Cancún, a retired army general sent to create an elite anti-crime unit was kidnapped, tortured, and executed. Mexican troops swiftly raided the Cancún police headquarters and arrested the chief and dozens of officers in connection with the murder.

So menacing have the cartels become that Freedom House, in its 2010 annual rankings, dropped Mexico from the list of free nations to only "partly free" as the state is failing in its duty to "protect ordinary citizens, journalists, and elected officials from organized crime."[34]

Mexico is at risk of becoming a failed state, a narco-state of 110 million with a border with the United States stretching two thousand miles from San Diego to the Gulf of Mexico. In the January 2009 threat assessment given to President Obama, the U.S. Joint Forces Command wrote, "In terms of worst-case scenarios for the Joint Force and indeed the world, two large and important states bear consideration for a rapid and sudden collapse: Pakistan and Mexico."[35]

How can Mexico win a drug war when millions of Americans who use recreational drugs are clients of the Mexican cartels that are bribing, murdering, and beheading to keep our self-indulgent young supplied?

There are two ways to end this war swiftly—Mao's way or Milton's way: victory, whatever the cost in blood, or surrender. Mao's Communists killed users and suppliers alike as social parasites. Milton Friedman's way is to decriminalize all drugs and call off the war. When Nixon declared the War on Drugs in 1972, Friedman spoke out in *Newsweek:*

> On ethical grounds, do we have the right to use the machinery of government to prevent an individual from becoming an alcoholic or a drug addict? For children, almost everyone would answer at least a qualified yes. But for responsible adults, I, for one, would answer no. Reason with the potential addict, yes. Tell him the consequences, yes. Pray for and with him, yes. But I believe that we have no right to use force, directly or indirectly, to prevent a fellow man from committing suicide, let alone from drinking alcohol or taking drugs.[36]

Americans are never going to adopt Mao's solution. For the drug users are often classmates, colleagues, friends, even family. Our three most recent presidents did not deny using drugs. Nor are we going to raise the white flag of surrender, as Milton Friedman urged us to do.

It has been argued that we once outlawed homosexuality, abortion, alcohol, loan-sharking, and gambling as criminal vice. Homosexuality and abortion are now constitutional rights. Gambling and booze are sources of government revenue. Loan-sharking is done by American Express, VISA, and bank-owned credit card companies, not just Don Corleone and his family.

While the libertarianism of Milton Friedman is making converts, as long as we remain a predominantly Christian country, legalizing narcotics is off the table. But the consequence of our decision to soldier on in the drug war may be a failed state of 110 million dominated by drug cartels on America's border.

THE RETURN OF THE NATIONALIST

Which way is history marching?

At the end of the Cold War, globalism seemed the inevitable future of mankind. Everywhere countries were coming together in common purpose. West Germany reached out to embrace East Germany. The EU, the model for a world government, began to lead the liberated nations of Eastern Europe into the tent, doubling its membership. A single currency, the euro, was created. NATO expanded to take in all of Eastern Europe and the Baltic republics.

The North American Free Trade Agreement brought the United States, Canada, and Mexico together in a common market George W. Bush predicted would encompass the hemisphere from Prudhoe Bay to Patagonia.

Globalization was the word, the wave, and the way of the future. A World Trade Organization was formed in 1994 to police the rules of global trade. Vice President Gore brought home the Kyoto Protocol establishing a global regime to control the greenhouse gases that produce global warming. An International Criminal Court, modeled on the Nuremberg tribunals that dealt with Nazi war crimes, was established to deal with genocide and crimes against humanity not prosecuted by nation-states. International acceptance of the doctrine of limited sovereignty had made a great leap forward.

Supporting the drive toward the One World envisioned by Kant and

Woodrow Wilson were thousands of nongovernmental organizations, scores of thousands of international civil servants, and the transnational corporations that represent half of all the world's largest economic entities.

Where Fukuyama had written of the end of history and the triumph of liberal democracy as the final form of government, Thomas Friedman's *The World Is Flat* saw a planet brought together by American ideas and ideals, principles, products, and power. Interdependence had replaced independence as the ideal of the statesman.

Yet, the seemingly inexorable move toward global unity and global governance did not go unresisted. The American establishment was united behind NAFTA, GATT, and the WTO. The American people never were. French and Dutch voted down a European constitution that would have moved the continent toward an EU superstate. The Irish rejected a revised constitution, the Lisbon Treaty. They were made to vote a second time. The British would have killed both constitutions. They were not permitted to vote. The eastward expansion of NATO halted. Ukraine and Georgia will not now be admitted. Nor will Turkey be admitted to the EU anytime soon.

The follow-up summits to Kyoto, Copenhagen in 2009 and Cancún in 2010, were failures. Global warming is on a back burner now. China, India, and Brazil refuse to accept Western-dictated limits on carbon emissions.

Globalism has lost its luster. Few American children today go "trick or treating for UNICEF." The Doha Round of world trade negotiations long ago passed its deadline uncompleted. Czech president Václav Klaus openly calls the EU a prison house of nations. When the Lisbon Treaty was ratified, Klaus declared, "The Czech Republic will cease to be a sovereign state."[37]

When world leaders gathered at Turtle Bay in 2010, Swiss President Joseph Deiss called on the United Nations to "comprehensively fulfill its global governance role." Klaus took the podium to reject global governance and say the time had come for the UN and all international organizations to "reduce their expenditures, make their administrations thinner, and leave the solutions to the governments of member states."[38]

When the financial crisis broke, the Irish, British, and Germans bailed out their own banks, as did the Americans, who inserted a "Buy American" provision in the $787 stimulus bill. The *Economist* was close to hysterical.

"The Return of Economic Nationalism," bawled the headline on the cover, which depicted an arm thrusting out of a darkened grave, the headstones on which read, "Here Lies Protectionism," and "R. Smoot, W. G. Hawley," architects of the tariff act of 1930.[39] "[T]he globalised economy is under threat," exclaimed the *Economist:*

> [T]he re-emergence of a spectre from the darkest period of modern history argues for a...strident response. Economic nationalism—the urge to keep jobs and capital at home—is both turning the economic crisis into a political one and threatening the world with depression. If it is not buried again forthwith, the consequences will be dire.[40]

When Germany showed a reluctance to bail out Greece, whose safety net was more generous than her own, commentators saw the end of the EU. "Berlin's recent reluctance to rescue Greece during its financial tailspin—Chancellor Merkel resisted the bailout for months—breached the spirit of common welfare that is the hallmark of a collective Europe," wrote Charles Kupchan, of the Council on Foreign Relations.[41]

> The European Union is dying.... From London to Berlin to Warsaw, Europe is experiencing a renationalization of political life, with countries clawing back the sovereignty they once willingly sacrificed in the pursuit of a collective ideal.[42]

By 2011, the global moment had passed. The unipolar world of 1991, the new world order of George H. W. Bush, the flat world of Tom Friedman, and Francis Fukuyama's end of history—were all history. What brought it all to an end? Nationalism. Taking different forms in different countries, a common denominator of the new nationalism was resistance to the globalist vision and the global hegemony of the United States.

When Churchill rendered his famous description of Soviet foreign policy as "a puzzle inside a riddle wrapped in an enigma," he added, "the key is Russian nationalism."

Believing America took advantage of her after the breakup of the Soviet Union, Russia formed a partnership with China; began to carve out a new sphere of influence in the old Soviet republics; invaded and chastised Georgia, an American client, and strengthened ties to regimes America regards as hostile, such as Venezuela and Iran.

Chinese nationalism has taken the form of defiance of U.S. goals, from a refusal to revalue her currency to reduce the trade surpluses she has run at America's expense, to resistance to U.S. efforts to isolate North Korea and Iran, to deepening ties to rogue states like Sudan and Myanmar.

Israel rejected U.S. demands for a halt to new settlements in East Jerusalem and on the West Bank. Iran defies U.S. demands to stop enriching uranium, supports Hamas and Hezbollah, and calls for the end of the Jewish state in the Middle East. Turkey has gone her own way: refused to allow the United States to use her territory to invade Iraq; established warm relations with Iran; backed the flotilla that sought to break Israel's blockade of Gaza; and worked with Brazil to negotiate a deal with Iran to avert further UN sanctions.

Brazil, seeing herself as a hemispheric rival to the United States and a rising power in her own right, has pursued an independent line, maintaining warm relations with Venezuela, working with Turkey to end the isolation of Iran, and granting diplomatic recognition to Palestine.

Nations everywhere are putting their own interests first, which some of us predicted decades ago. For globalization's fatal deficiency is that it does not engage the heart. It has never won over peoples for whom love and loyalty go no higher than their own country. It never will. No one will fight and die for some vague new world order.

"One cannot be a citizen of an international cosmopolitan world order. Identity is specific, rooted in soil, custom, and religious tradition," writes Jude Dougherty, former dean of philosophy at Catholic University in his essay "National Identity."[43]

> One cannot be a citizen of the world. Identity is local; it is the characteristic of a people who have inhabited a land over a period of time, who have developed certain collective habits, evident in their manners, their dress, the feasts they collectively enjoy, their religious bonds, the premium they put on education.[44]

As Rudyard Kipling wrote,

> *God gave all men all earth to love,*
> *But, since our hearts are small*
> *Ordained for each one spot should prove*
> *Beloved over all …* [45]

In the new post–post Cold War world, with nationalism returning and ethnonationalism surging, America needs to look beyond the ideas and institutions of globalist ideology and start looking out again, as we should have done, two decades ago, for our own country and our own people first.

11

THE LAST CHANCE

Are the good times really over for good?
—MERLE HAGGARD, 1981

During the Glenn Beck rally at Lincoln Memorial on the anniversary of Dr. King's speech, Sarah Palin emitted a cry from the heart. In retort to Obama's expressed desire to be a "transformational" president, Palin told the throng, "We must not fundamentally transform America, as some would want; we must restore America."[1]

Can we restore America? Or has the America we grew up in already been transformed into another country?

It is a contention of this book that America has been changed in our lifetimes, that a revolution has taken place, that though we appear to the world the same country, we are a different nation on a course far off the one our fathers set.

Adams, Jefferson, Madison, and Hamilton disbelieved in "one-man, one-vote" democracy. We worship it. They believed in a Creator. We have exiled him from our schools and replaced him with evolution. They believed all men had a God-given and inalienable right to life. With *Roe v. Wade* we canceled that right for the unborn, fifty million of whom have since perished. For 250 years after the settlers came to Jamestown, our fathers sought to build a Protestant and British country. From the Irish immigration of the 1840s to the first Irish Catholic president in 1960, the

United States sought to maintain its character and identity as a Christian and European nation. To assert that as an ideal today would constitute a hate crime.

THE GREAT EXPERIMENT

Our intellectual, cultural, and political elites are today engaged in one of the most audacious and ambitious experiments in history. They are trying to transform a Western Christian republic into an egalitarian democracy made up of all the tribes, races, creeds, and cultures of planet Earth. They have dethroned our God, purged our cradle faith from public life, and repudiated the Judeo-Christian moral code by which previous generations sought to live.

They have declared men and women to be basically the same, that all voluntary sexual relations are morally equal, that the traditional family is but one social option, that men can marry men and women can marry women, that race is a social construct invented by bigots bent on repressing others, that all are endowed with the intelligence and ability to succeed in the most competitive society on earth. All religions and all "lifestyles" are equal and all are to be equally respected. These elites will fight to ensure that a mosque is built at Ground Zero with the same ferocity as they will to ensure that no Nativity scene ever appears on the National Mall. If there is an inequality of rewards in society, they believe, this is the residue of a reactionary America, the fruit of societal injustice, and it is the moral duty of our modern state to rectify that injustice and mandate equality. Those who reject these truths are benighted or bigoted.

Our secular elites believe in this revolution. The people never did. Middle America detests it. Thus it has had to be imposed from above, by judges, bureaucrats, professors, and those who control the content of our culture. One part of America believes we are headed for a wonderful new age. The silent majority thinks the country has lost its mind. For, as

Professor Williams, author of *Trousered Apes,* wrote, at the beginning of the great experiment:

> [V]arious practical attempts (in the Soviet Union and China for example) have been made to establish [equality] as a basis for society. All such efforts either have failed or must fail because no stable society can be built upon a theory which runs counter to reality. The harsh but unavoidable fact is that men are unequal in terms of hereditary abilities. Some are born with a greater degree of intelligence, a greater capacity for sympathy, a greater ability to succeed than others.

"The persistence of this myth" of equality, wrote Williams, "and the frustrations which its advocates experience … constitute a grave psychological and political problem."[2] This is what they call an understatement.

The experiment is failing and will continue to fail. For it is based on a "theory which runs counter to reality," an ideology whose tenets are at war with the laws of nature. Like the Marxists who were going to create a new man and a new society, our establishment is attempting the impossible.

"To create a concept is to leave reality behind," wrote the Spanish philosopher Ortega y Gasset.[3] Our elites have created a concept of the ideal nation—the most egalitarian, diverse, democratic, and liberated that ever existed. And they have mobilized the vast power of government and law to force America to conform to that concept. They will fail, and this great and good country will die of their experiment.

"Some men see things as they are and say, why. I dream things that never were and say, why not," said Robert F. Kennedy in the campaign that cost him his life.[4] But there is a reason why things are as they are, and why some dreams never come true: unalterable human nature, the unconquerable and eternal enemy of all utopians.

"We have it in our power to begin the world over again," wrote the idealist of 1776, Thomas Paine, who would barely escape the guillotine in the Revolution of 1789 that arose on the promise to begin the world over again.

In 1991, author Claes Ryn called this messianic compulsion to re-shape America and the world *The New Jacobinism*, as it recalled the intellectuals who worshipped Rousseau, made the French revolution, and sought to force France and Europe, at a legendary cost in blood, to conform to their ideals.[5]

Republicans, as Lewis Carroll's White Queen said, also manage to believe "six impossible things before breakfast." They have declared that "deficits don't matter," that America grew into a mighty industrial power through free trade, that it is within our power to democratize mankind and "end tyranny in our world."

As the melting pot turned millions of children and grandchildren of European immigrants into Americans, Republicans assert, we can bring in countless millions more from every country and culture and create a stronger, better, happier, more united nation than the America of 1960. But where in history has such diversity led to anything but cacophony and chaos?

Racially, culturally, ethnically, politically, America is disintegrating. For the third consecutive year the deficit is at a peacetime record of 10 percent of GDP. The trade deficit is returning to the heights of 2007–08. U.S. dependence on foreign nations for the needs of our national life and the loans to pay for them has never been greater. We are mired in two wars with no end in sight. If America is not to end up with all the other great nations and empires on the ash heap of history, we need to shed our illusions and to see the world as it is.

Among the leaders of the twentieth century, Deng Xiaoping is re-garded as a wise man. For he saw that Marxism and Maoism were at war with human nature, that a great nation could not be built to endure on such principles, that China was in danger of going down. And he acted on those convictions. Without renouncing Marx or Mao, Deng put the world revolution on a shelf and embraced state capitalism. What difference does it make if the cat is black or white, Deng said, as long as it catches mice. Ideology was the poison, reason the antidote. So Deng did what Lenin did with his New Economic Policy; he adopted the enemy's ideas to save his regime.

But, astonishingly, even as the Marxists were abandoning Communism as a failed experiment, the pragmatic Americans who won the Cold War were being converted to a utopian ideology. We are trying to create a nation that has never before existed, of all the races, tribes, cultures, and creeds of Earth, in which all are equal. In pursuit of the perfect society of our dreams we are killing the country we inherited—the best and greatest on earth.

THE REVOLUTION WAS

In the depth of the Depression, in his first inaugural address, FDR said, "our common difficulties.... concern, thank God, only material things."

Our generation is not so fortunate. For our difficulties go not just to the material but to the moral, to clashing beliefs about the most fundamental and critical of questions. Who are we? What constitutes a good society? What is good and what is evil? What kind of country should America be?

What took place in our recent past was a true revolution, a series of allied rebellions to overthrow the old order that came together to reach critical mass in the 1960s.

First was the sexual revolution, an in-your-face rejection of the moral code of Christianity on matters from promiscuity to fidelity to homosexuality to abortion. Your God is dead, said the rebels, take your morality and shove it.

The feminist movement, with its mockery of marriage and demands for absolute sexual freedom for women, unrestricted abortion rights, no-fault divorce, gender preferences, and mandated equality of men and women, was a frontal assault on the meritocracy and the traditional family.

The gay rights movement, beginning with the Stonewall riot in 1969, sought repudiation of the Judeo-Christian moral order and the overturning, by judicial decree, of all laws rooted in that moral order. After thirty years, the Supreme Court imposed the movement's agenda on America by striking down state laws punishing homosexuality and declaring homosexual acts to be the exercise of a constitutional right.

The sexual revolution is but one Supreme Court ruling away from a judicial mandate that same-sex marriages must be recognized in law as fully equal to traditional marriages, with all the same rights and privileges.

That voters in thirty-one states have rejected same-sex marriage makes no difference to our courts. For, in America today, we do not have government of the people, by the people, and for the people. We often have government against the people. The state is at war with the nation.

Second was an antiwar movement that was more than a protest of Vietnam. At its heart lay the rejection of an anticommunist foreign policy and of the idea that America was a good country and beneficent force in the world. Many of the militants in the antiwar movement accepted the Third World's indictment of the West for five hundred years of slavery, colonialism, capitalist exploitation, and imperialism.

Third was a civil rights revolution that began with a legitimate demand for equality of rights and an end to state-imposed segregation but became a vehicle for assailing America as irredeemably racist. The year he received his Nobel Prize, Martin Luther King declared in Berlin that the Goldwater campaign bore "dangerous signs of Hitlerism."[6] Three years later, King charged his country with killing a million Vietnamese, "mostly children," and being the "greatest purveyor of violence in the world today."[7]

America forgets. It was JFK who ordered the wiretaps on King, because of his association with Communists, his brother Robert Kennedy who saw to it that the FBI carried out the order, and Lyndon Johnson's White House that distributed the fruits of the FBI surveillance to the press to discredit and destroy King. Conservatives may claim him, but the Martin Luther King some of us knew was no conservative.

In the middle of these allied rebellions, LBJ made a great leap forward, joined the revolution, and declared that America's goal was no longer equality of rights but equality of results. Over half a century, an immense edifice of state power has been erected to bring about that egalitarian socialist ideal. While the nation will never attain that ideal, the old republic will die from the experiment.

The revolution was. It cannot be undone. While routed in its first national political expression, the McGovern presidential campaign, and in its second, the feminist campaign to add an Equal Rights Amendment to the Constitution, that revolution has sunk permanent roots. It is dominant in the culture, the arts, the academy, and the media. The Fifth Column of the cultural revolution is entrenched in the courts where judges and justices routinely discover that the constitutions they are sworn to uphold mandate the revolution they seek to bring about. As legal scholar Raoul Berger wrote of the legendary liberal activist Justice William Brennan, he had a "penchant for identifying his personal predilections with constitutional dogma."[8]

The avatar of this revolution is Obama. Pro-gay rights, pro-choice, pro-amnesty, pro–affirmative action, one foot firmly planted in the Third World, he campaigned on raising taxes on the rich and redistributing the wealth.

The ideals embraced in *Dreams from My Father: A Story of Race and Inheritance* are those of Barack Hussein Obama Sr., an Afro-nationalist. The Christianity Obama embraced for twenty years was that of Rev. Jeremiah Wright, who preached liberation theology and ranted against America. Obama was at home at Trinity United and had Rev. Wright marry him and Michelle and baptize his daughters, Sasha and Malia. Obama does not hate white people. But he does believe they have much to answer for, and in his reaction in the Sergeant Crowley–Professor Gates affair he revealed his race consciousness and reflexive bias.

The real Obama was captured at that closed-door gathering in San Francisco when he explained to the *bien-pensants* why he was failing to connect with Pennsylvanians in the industrial cities and small towns.

History has passed these people by, Barack explained:

"They get bitter, they cling to guns or religion or antipathy to people who aren't like them or anti-immigrant sentiment or anti-trade sentiment as a way to explain their frustrations."[9] Middle Pennsylvanians do not reason, Obama was saying; they react according to their biblical beliefs, backward culture, and the bigotries they imbibed with their mother's milk.

They can't really help themselves, Barack was saying. Thus, they recoil from the progressive change that has come and is yet to come via globalization and immigration. In the passage below from his Philadelphia speech on Rev. Wright and civil rights, Obama reveals how he views the grievances of black Americans and white Americans in a different light:

> Most working- and middle-class white Americans *don't feel* that they have been particularly privileged by their race.... *as far as they're concerned,* no one's handed them anything.... They...*feel* their dreams slipping away...opportunity *comes to be seen* as a zero sum game, in which your dreams come at my expense.
>
> Anger over welfare and affirmative action helped forge the Reagan Coalition. Politicians routinely *exploited fears of crime* for their own electoral ends. Talk show hosts and conservative commentators built entire careers unmasking *bogus claims of racism* while dismissing *legitimate discussions of racial injustice and inequality* as mere political correctness or reverse racism.[10] (Emphasis added.)

In Obama's mind, black anger at "racial injustice and inequality" is "legitimate." White anger and resentment over affirmative action, crime, and welfare abuse is not. Why not? Although whites may "feel" they are victims of racial injustice, this feeling is not rooted in reality, but is only an irrational emotion that is being "exploited" by conservative opportunists.

This passage reveals the great blindness and great dilemma of the left. It cannot admit that the anger of white America is legitimate. Obama cannot concede that injustice is being done to white people, because they are white, for he would then have to ask himself: Who is inflicting this injustice?

For the Left to concede that white anger is a legitimate response to racial injustices done to white people would be to concede that the Left is guilty of the very sin of which it accuses the right.

Obama's contrast of black America's legitimate anger with white America's manipulated feelings recalls Murray Rothbard's insight:

> Anger by the good guys, the accredited victim groups, is designated as "rage," which is somehow noble.... On the other hand, anger by designated oppressor groups is not called "rage," but "resentment": which conjures up evil little figures, envious of their betters, skulking around the edges of the night.[11]

Obama's ideology was manifest in the Ground Zero mosque dispute. Many intellectuals denied that there could be anything motivating opponents of the mosque other than ignorance or prejudice. Wrote Michael Kinsley: "Is there any reason to oppose the mosque that isn't bigoted, or demagogic, or unconstitutional? None that I've heard or read."[12]

Obama initially and instinctively took that side. But so stunned was he by the reaction he said the following day he was not endorsing the wisdom of putting the mosque at Grand Zero, only the imam's right to do so.

If Obama is the personification of the revolution, Palin was its antithesis. A pro-life Christian mother of five who celebrates the "Real America," Palin became an icon for people repelled by Obama. The two are the antipodes of the culture war.

Herein lies Obama's dilemma. Millions of Democrats who revere the memory of FDR, Truman, and JFK never cottoned to the 1960s revolutions, never accepted those values. They do not believe Vietnam was an immoral war. They do not believe all religions or all lifestyles are equal. They do not believe America is a racist country. They believe her to be the best country in the history of man. They love her. And, yes, they cling to their Bibles, beliefs, and guns, and resent the hell out of being called bigots.

Many names have been given to the revolution begun in the 1960s— radical liberalism, secular humanism, cultural Marxism, the Gramscian revolution. But a crucial point is this: while it changed the way millions of Americans think, it never captured the heart of America, nor is it predestined to triumph. Half a century on, most Americans reject and despise its values.

Sixty-two percent of Americans believe abortions should be more tightly restricted, or outlawed. Ward Connerly's campaign to abolish affirmative action has won in Michigan, California, Washington, and in Arizona, where it garnered 60 percent of the vote in the fall of 2010. Propositions calling for making English the official language have rarely failed. Same-sex marriage has been rejected every time it has been on a ballot. Even Obama declines to endorse it. And as Congress and Obama impose the values of Fire Island on Parris Island, he will feel the force of the counterrevolution. The culture war is not over. The culture war is never over. As it is rooted in colliding beliefs about right and wrong, God and country, good and evil, the culture war will be with us forever.

"[A]dvanced liberalism," writes Chilton Williamson Jr., has "divided the United States between the New and the Old America, a division that is unlikely to be resolved in the foreseeable future, but is becoming rather more fixed and rigid":

> Liberalism in the era of Obama represents for the Old American culture what Islam does for the culture of Old Europe....
>
> The battle lines have been drawn. America is fated to remain a house divided against herself for many generations,

and afterward to share the inevitable fate of all divided houses which are by nature ungovernable, and hence unlivable.[13]

Americans face a "real civil war, a war among citizens that cannot be settled by the physical separation of the adherents of the two sides, who are integrated one with the other across an entire continent."[14] Black columnist Carl Rowan came to a darker conclusion in his 1996 *The Coming Race War in America.*

As the revolutionaries and radicals of the 1960s did not want to live in Eisenhower's America, traditionalists do not want to live in their America. Social peace would seem to require separation.

Vanderbilt University law professor Carol Swain sees America "increasingly at risk of large-scale racial conflict unprecedented in our nation's history." The risk is growing, she writes, because of the

> changing demographics, the continued existence of racial preference policies, the rising expectations of ethnic minorities, the continued existence of liberal immigration policies, growing concerns about job losses associated with globalization, the demand for multiculturalism, and the internet's ability to enable like-minded individuals to identify each other and share mutual concerns and strategies for impacting the political system.[15]

Swain identifies what divides us. But these forces need not lead to violence. Despite threats of "a long hot summer" if Nixon did not capitulate to "non-negotiable demands," the urban riots stopped after 1968. Campus violence dissipated after the draft was ended. Violent crime leveled off when the Baby Boomers moved out of the high-crime age bracket and violent criminals were locked up in the millions. Rowan's prediction in the aftermath of Oklahoma City never came to pass.

The likelihood is far greater that this unhappy family is headed for an acrimonious coexistence. What Bill Bishop, Rich Benjamin, and

Orlando Patterson observed will continue: self-segregation and the withdrawal of Americans into ethnocultural enclaves of their own kind will become the natural and normal responses to diversity. America is a huge land. If we cannot live together, then let us live apart.

"How small of all that human hearts endure/That part which laws or kings can cause or cure," said Dr. Johnson. After Nanking and Nagasaki, there appears quite a bit of heartache modern kings can cause. But cure? Dr. Johnson's point remains valid.

THE FIRST IMPERATIVE

The first duty of a president would appear to be to put the nation's house in order before America suffers the disaster and disgrace of a default on the national debt, a run on the dollar, or an inflation that ravages the savings of her people. That is the immediate peril. And as interest on the debt must be paid, there are only two places where substantial cuts can be made. The first is the entitlement programs—Medicare, Medicaid, Social Security, and related social spending for unemployment insurance, Earned Income Tax Credits, veterans' benefits, and food stamps. The second is the national security state: over $1 trillion and counting spent on two wars, an archipelago of 700 to 1,000 bases in 130 countries, our imperial embassies, foreign aid, the military-industrial complex at home, and the hidden billions spread through the government for intelligence work and nuclear weapons.

With federal spending for the third year running at 25 percent of GDP, while taxes produce only 15 percent of GDP, deep cuts must come in both the welfare and the warfare state.

DISMANTLING THE EMPIRE

It is absurd that the United States, stumbling toward a debt default, must borrow from Japan to defend Japan, borrow from Europe to defend Europe, and borrow from the Persian Gulf to defend the Persian Gulf. How did we get to this point?

When Kennedy became president, fifty years ago, General Douglas MacArthur counseled him not to put his foot soldiers into Southeast Asia. General Eisenhower urged him to bring home the 300,000 troops in Europe, lest Europe become a dependency. Instead, Kennedy, setting out for his New Frontier, declared in his inaugural: "Let every nation know, whether it wishes us well or ill, that we shall pay any price, bear any burden, meet any hardship, support any friend, oppose any foe, in order to assure the survival and the success of liberty. This much we pledge—and more."

The result: at the end of what would have been Kennedy's second term, 525,000 U.S. troops were in Vietnam and 31,000 were dead. When the nation elected Richard Nixon to end the war, it turned away from interventionism. In his "Silent Majority" address on November 3, 1969, Nixon restated the new policy he had declared in July on Guam.

> First, the United States will keep all of its treaty commitments.
>
> Second, we shall provide a shield if a nuclear power threatens the freedom of a nation allied with us or of a nation whose survival we consider vital to our security.
>
> Third, in cases involving other types of aggression, we shall furnish military and economic assistance when requested in accordance with our treaty commitments. But we shall look to the nation directly threatened to assume the primary responsibility of providing the manpower for its defense.[16]

MacArthur, Eisenhower, and Nixon were not isolationists. But all three recognized the limits of American power and were determined to put U.S. vital interests ahead of any crusading or ideological agenda. Two generations later, let us finally reconsider what these wise men advocated.

Why are scores of thousands of U.S. troops still stationed in Europe when "the evil empire" against which they were to defend Europe collapsed twenty years ago? Why can't Europe defend itself from a Russia whose army is but a fraction of the Red Army of 1990 and whose western border is hundreds of miles east of where it was under Nicholas II? Between Russia and Central Europe lies a buffer zone of nations—Lithuania, Latvia, Estonia, Belarus, and Ukraine—that were part of the Russian Empire when the twentieth century began. How long must 310 million Americans defend 500 million rich Europeans from 140 million Russians whose numbers are shrinking every year? To shock the European Union into manning up to its responsibilities, the United States should declare its intent to withdraw from NATO, transfer leadership of the alliance to the Europeans, and begin to vacate air and naval bases.

"We've got too many daggone bases," says U.S. air commander in Europe General Roger Brady. There's "big money" to be saved in shutting them down and averting cuts in aircraft. "We really need to look at the real estate question again.... I don't think we can afford not to."[17]

The general is correct. Our strongest NATO allies are Britain and France, nuclear powers both, and Germany, which has the fourth largest economy on earth. With Poland, they can defend themselves and Central Europe as well. As for the Baltic states, America is not going to war if some Muscovite militarist marches into Tallinn. No vital U.S. interest could justify so insane a war. Our response would have to be restricted to the political, diplomatic, and economic.

The United States should also renegotiate its security treaties with South Korea and Japan and remove U.S. ground troops from both countries. We are not going to fight another land war with China or North Korea. No vital interest could justify such a war, and the American people would not support sending an army to Korea like the 330,000 soldiers we sent in the 1950s.

The European and Asian defense pacts negotiated by secretaries of state Dean Acheson and John Foster Dulles were relevant to that time. But that time is gone. And as our situation is new, so we must think and act anew. If America is to fight again in the Pacific or in East Asia, the decision should not be made by statesmen who died half a century ago but by the generations that must fight now.

When one looks at America's alliances, the war guarantees we have issued, the commitments we have made to fight other countries' wars, many dating to the 1950s, one is reminded of Lord Salisbury's insight: "[T]he commonest error in politics is sticking to the carcass of dead policies." It was an 1838 treaty to secure the neutrality of Belgium that brought Britain into the Great War of 1914–1918, which led to World War II, the bankruptcy of Britain, and the end of the empire.

The United States must bring an end to its wars in Afghanistan and Iraq. They have bled us for a decade and done less to make us safe than to inflame the Islamic world against us. And once the troops are home, the U.S. bases in Central Asia should be closed. This region is fated to be a theater of rivalry among its ethnic groups, and China and Russia. U.S. interests in Central Asia are economic and commercial, not strategic.

The immediate goal must be to derail the War Party campaign to have America launch a preemptive strike on Iran's nuclear facilities that would trigger acts of terror against U.S. soldiers and civilians from Baghdad to Beirut. An early result of such a war could be the closing of the Persian Gulf, crippling the U.S. and world economies.

And what would be the justification for such an attack? Iran has enough low-enriched uranium for one nuclear test and one bomb. That uranium is under UN watch at Natanz. Were it to be moved to a site to be enriched to weapons grade, we would have a year's notice before Iran could test a device. The Stuxnet virus, a cyber weapon likely introduced by Israel and the United States, has damaged Iran's centrifuges and set her enrichment program back two years.[18] Moreover, our sixteen intelligence agencies have never rescinded their 2007 conclusion that Iran is not actively seeking a nuclear weapon. Again, what is the justification for the new war the neocons seek?

Despite alarms about Ahmadinejad being the new Hitler, Iran has not started a war in living memory. Shia and Persian, Iran swims in a vast sea of Sunni Arabs, Sunni Turks, and Sunni Afghans. Half her people are Azeri, Arab, Kurd, and Baluch. National dissolution along tribal and ethnic lines is a permanent threat. Her economy moves at a crawl. Her population, part of which is pro-American, is fed up with mullah rule. Elections come in less than two years. Even if Iran had a nuclear bomb, would she give it to terrorists to use and thereby insure her annihilation? As Bismarck said, preemptive war is like committing suicide out of a fear of death.

If America could deter the Russia of Stalin and the China of Mao, who declared himself willing to lose three hundred million Chinese, why can't we deter an Iran that has no bomb and no missile to deliver it? As for nuclear blackmail, Kim Jong-il has atom bombs. Has he intimidated the United States?

Robert Gates, Hillary Clinton, and Admiral Mullen, Chairman of the Joint Chiefs of Staff, have all called our deficit-debt crisis the principal threat to national security. Downsizing the empire, ending our wars, and reducing our commitments to fight new wars that have nothing to do with vital interests, have become strategic imperatives.

Resistance will be intense—from diplomats and domestic agents of foreign powers, from the military-industrial complex and the lobbyists it deploys, from journalists, think tank scholars, and professors who have built careers as the acolytes of empire. But if we do not do this rationally and methodically, it will be done for us the way it was done for the British and French, through humiliation and defeat.

Troop withdrawals and a reduction in foreign bases can be made more palatable by a rise in military sales to nations that would now be undertaking their own defense. And the money saved could be used to restore the military to the condition it was in before our decade of war. The more we shrink our defense perimeter the greater the gain in national unity behind our foreign policy.

DOWNSIZING THE STATE

For three years, the U.S. government has been spending five dollars for every three it collects in taxes. This explains the surge in both the national debt and the public debt that is held by citizens, corporations, and foreign countries. To balance the budget by cuts alone, spending would have to fall 40 percent. Were tax increases alone to be used to balance the budget, the tax load on corporations and citizens would have to rise by 67 percent.

Not since World War II have we seen such deficits. But World War II was a temporary emergency. We knew that when the war came to an end, the twelve million in the armed forces would return to civilian life and spending on tanks, trucks, ships, guns, shells, and planes would abruptly halt. Then we could begin to pay down the debt.

Today that prospect does not exist. And with Republican resistance to tax hikes and Democratic determination to defend social programs, the odds of any great compromise that produces serious deficit reduction are slim. The probability is that the march of the deficits continues until the world realizes America will never repay her debts in dollars of the same value as the ones she borrowed. Then the crisis will come.

"The difference between an optimist and a pessimist," said journalist Clare Boothe Luce, "is that the pessimist is usually better informed." While it is difficult to see how our political class summons the courage to impose the necessary sacrifices upon its constituents, here are ideas for budget cuts based on two principles. The public sector must shrink and the productive sector grow, and all should sacrifice something:

- A two-year freeze on all federal salaries, including "in-step" pay raises, and including the military.
- A two-year suspension of all cost-of-living adjustments in all entitlement programs from Social Security to veterans' benefits to federal pensions.

- Social Security annual cost-of-living adjustments, or COLAs, should then be tied strictly to the consumer price index, i.e., inflation.
- A gradual rise in the retirement age for Social Security and Medicare benefits to at least sixty-four for early retirement and sixty-eight for full benefits.
- A hiring freeze in the federal work force where only three of every four retiring or departing employees is replaced.
- A Gramm-Rudman-Hollings law imposing an across-the-board freeze on all federal departments, including defense.
- No bailout of state governments, which should use their own tax revenue to meet their obligations to balance their budgets.
- A halt to foreign aid unrelated to national security. It is absurd that we borrow from China to send billions directly or through the World Bank to regimes that vote with China in the UN.

On the revenue side, the deduction for mortgage interest and state income and property taxes and even charitable contributions could be capped or eliminated in return for rate reductions, following the Reagan principle. While a low capital gains tax rate on long-term investments for retirement and for new stock issues that provide the seed corn for new and expanding companies could be retained, the tax for turnaround trades in stocks or commodities could be raised to the same level as taxes on other forms of gambling.

Every program has a constituency and any cuts will bring into play clashing interests and ideologies. Still, these suggestions, which butcher no one's sacred cow, but give every federal employee and beneficiary a haircut, would seem to be the easiest path to budget reduction. As Reagan said, "There are simple answers, just no easy answers."

As for federal agencies, departments, and programs, some should be reduced, others abolished as luxuries in an age of austerity. Do we really need a National Endowment for the Arts when its patrons are the richest Americans or a Corporation for Public Broadcasting when we have five hundred cable channels or a U.S. Commission on Civil Rights half a century after all the civil rights laws have been enacted?

Our parents made the sacrifices necessary to bring us through a Depression, a world war, and a forty-year Cold War. If we cannot manage this, we are not the people our parents were and our children will not know the life we did.

ECONOMIC PATRIOTISM

"Who won the war?" asked the posting on FreeRepublic.com. Below the question were pictures—of Hiroshima in 1945, ashes and ruins, and of Detroit in 1945, mightiest industrial hub on earth. Then came photos of Hiroshima, sixty-five years later, a gleaming city, and Detroit in 2010, a burned-out shell. Who won the war? We won the world war and the Cold War, but we lost the post–Cold War and are losing the future.

From 2000 to 2010, America saw 50,000 factories close and 6 million manufacturing jobs disappear. China, Japan, the EU, Canada, and even Mexico ran up hundreds of billions or trillions of dollars in trade surpluses with the United States. Is this because their workers are more capable and efficient?

No. Worker for worker, Americans are the best. Why, then, are we losing? Because China, Japan, and Germany are trade predators not trade partners. They look on trade the way Vince Lombardi looked on football: "Winning isn't everything; it's the only thing."

Germany, Japan, and China recite the catechism of free trade—and practice economic nationalism. Their tax and trade policies, from currency manipulation to value-added taxes (VAT) on imports and rebates for exports, to subsidies for national champions, to nontariff barriers on U.S. goods, discriminate in favor of their products in their market and in our market. We talk about a "level playing field." But they landscape the field to win.

The success of economic nationalism may be seen in the shifting balance of power. China is the world's rising power and America is everywhere seen as the declining power. Yet, while the Chinese and German economies are but one-third the size of ours, both export more than we do.

How? The game is rigged and we need to walk away from the table. For if we do not cure ourselves of this obsession with free trade, the industrial evisceration of the United States will continue until we make nothing the world wants but Hollywood movies.

Ralph Gomory, a former IBM senior vice president for science and technology, relates what the naïveté of the free-traders and the greed of our corporate elite are doing to our country.

> We have too many people today who see in the destruction of our key industries by well-organized and highly subsidized actions from abroad nothing more than the effect of free trade and the operations of a perfectly free market. This is a delusion and a dangerous one. We also have an elite industrial leadership that too often sees itself with no other duty than maximizing the price of their company's stock, even if that means offshoring the capabilities and know-how for advanced production to other nations that have no free markets themselves.[19]

"[T]he heart of the problem," writes Gomory, is "lack of leadership from our own government," which must realize that the "fundamental goals of the country and of our companies have diverged."[20] What's good for General Motors is not good for America if General Motors is shifting plants and production to Asia to build and export cars to America.

America has been running the largest trade deficits in history for decades. But a U-turn could be effected by adopting tax and trade policies that set as our national goals—the reindustrialization of America; the recapture of that huge slice of the U.S. market lost to foreign producers;

and the substitution of U.S.-made goods for foreign goods until America is a self-sufficient nation again as she was from Lincoln's time to JFK's.

To reduce our dependence on goods made abroad and grow our dependence on goods made in the United States, we should impose tariffs on all imports and use every dollar of tariff revenue to reduce taxes on U.S. producers. If the United States imports $2.5 trillion in manufactures, food, and fibers, and imposes a 25 percent tariff, that would yield close to $600 billion to virtually eliminate corporate taxation in this country.

What would such a tariff accomplish?

First, a reduction of imports (as their prices would rise), and a concomitant increase in orders to U.S. factories and farms.

Second, as the profits of U.S. factories and farms surged, Americans would be hired to meet the new demand. The income and payroll taxes of those new workers would replace sinking tariff revenue from falling imports.

Third, with corporate taxes cut to nothing, U.S. companies could cut prices on goods produced here, making U.S. goods more competitive both here and abroad. As foreign companies realized that the U.S. corporate tax rate was the lowest in the free world, they would relocate here.

Fourth, as the price of imports rose 10, 20, or 30 percent, foreign companies would realize that to hold their share of the world's largest market, the $15 trillion U.S. market, they would have to shift production here to compete with U.S. companies. Companies like Mercedes, BMW, Toyota, and Honda would not only assemble cars here but would build plants here to make their batteries, tires, motors, and frames. The tide of capital investment rolling into China would shift and begin surging back to the United States.

That would be our message to the world: every company and all products are welcome here. But if you want to sell here, you produce here, or you pay a stiff cover charge to get in. Would China, Europe, and Japan threaten retaliation? Perhaps. But we should tell Beijing, Brussels, and

Tokyo we will accept a combined VAT-tariff on U.S. products entering their markets equal to our tariff on their goods, but no more. Equality and reciprocity, not globalization and free trade, should dictate the terms of trade. And would China, Japan, or Europe risk a trade war with the United States when all three run huge annual trade surpluses with the United States?

Every year, Beijing exports to us six or seven times the dollar volume of goods we export to China. If the United States lost 100 percent of the world's markets we now have, but recaptured 100 percent of our own, we would be half a trillion in the black, for that is the size of our trade deficit with the world. We have nothing to lose but our trade deficits. We have a self-reliant republic to regain.

Economists would cry, "Protectionism! We can't turn our backs on the world." But no one is turning his back on the world. The goal is not to freeze out foreign goods but force foreign goods to carry the same share of the U.S. tax load as goods made in the USA. A tariff so high as to lock out foreign goods produces no revenue. What is proposed here is not a protective tariff to keep out foreign goods but a revenue tariff, with the rate set at a level to maximize revenue for the Treasury and maximize tax cuts for U.S. producers.

What is urged here is that we do to the VAT nations what they do to us. Pleas, protests, and threats to take Beijing to the WTO have not persuaded the Chinese to let their currency rise. Let us accept that reality, cease whining, stop hectoring, and act.

We need to bring manufacturing back and relearn truths taught centuries ago by Hamilton. Manufacturing is the muscle of a nation, vital to its defense and the securing of sovereignty. It is the magnet for research and development. It is organic. It grows. Around the factory form other businesses. Towns develop. Manufacturing workers average twice the wage of service workers.

We need to change the way we think. Production must come before consumption. We cannot consume if we do not produce. We must start making things again. We must reduce our dependence on foreign nations for our national necessities and the loans to pay for them. If it can be made here, it should be made here. We need to start relying on one another and stop listening to the "sophisters, economists, and calculators" who gutted the greatest manufacturing nation the world had ever seen. Our problem lies not in ourselves but in policies imposed by politicians in the hire of corporatists whose loyalties rise no higher than the bottom line on a balance sheet.

A MORATORIUM ON IMMIGRATION

"If destruction be our lot, we must ourselves be its author and finisher. As a nation of freemen, we must live through all time, or die by suicide," said the young Lincoln in 1838.[21] He was right. While threats to the United States from abroad still exist—a series of 9/11-scale terrorist attacks or a nuclear attack—the threats from within are more immediate.

There is the possibility of a run on the dollar, a default on the debt, and a depression. There is the danger of a sustained decline in our living standards, the end of the American Dream, and the social crisis that would come with it. And there is the possibility of a total disintegration of the nation into ethnic, class, and cultural enclaves distant from and distrustful of one another.

If America is not to disintegrate, if she is to regain the "out of many, one," unity we knew in the Eisenhower-Kennedy era, the first imperative is to readopt the immigration policy that produced that era of good feeling, so that the melting pot, fractured though it is, can begin again to do its work.

Elements of that policy would include:

- A moratorium on new immigration until unemployment falls to 6 percent. To bring in foreign workers when 23 million Americans are still underemployed or out of work is to put corporate profits ahead of country.
- Reform of our immigration laws to give preference to those

from countries that have historically provided most of our immigrants, who share our values, speak English, have college or advanced degrees, bring special skills, and can be easily assimilated. We need more taxpayers and fewer tax-consumers.

- The border fence should be completed.
- The next president should declare that there will be no amnesty for those here illegally, that illegal aliens must return to the countries from which they came. The first to be deported should be those convicted of crimes, including drunk driving.
- The erroneous interpretation of the Fourteenth Amendment that any child born to an illegal alien is automatically a U.S. citizen should be corrected by Congress via a provision attached to the law that it is not subject to review by any federal court, including or the U.S. Supreme Court.
- The U.S. government should undertake a series of high-profile raids on businesses that have hired large numbers of illegal aliens. Punishment of corporate scofflaws is the best prevention of this unpatriotic practice.
- Congress should enact a constitutional amendment and send it to the states making English the official language of the United States.

The issues addressed by these proposals are becoming a matter of national survival.

And if nothing is done to halt mass immigration, which now comes almost wholly from Third World countries, the Republican Party as we know it is history.

In 2010 James Gimpel measured the correlation between immigration and voting patterns between 1980, when Reagan won 51 percent and 2008, when McCain won 45 percent. The correlations are devastating. Between 1980 and 2008, Los Angeles County, the nation's largest, added

2.5 million people. The immigrant share of the population rose from 22 to 41 percent, and the Republican share of the vote fell from 50 to 29 percent. In Cook County, Chicago, the nation's second largest, the immigrant share of the population doubled to 25 percent and the Republican share of the Cook County vote fell from 40 to 23 percent.[22]

So it went with virtually all of the top twenty-five of the nation's counties. Increases in the immigrant share of the population were matched by plunges in the GOP share of the vote: San Diego, Riverside, San Bernardino, Santa Clara, and Alameda counties in California; Kings and Queens in New York; Dade and Broward in Florida; Dallas and Harris in Texas all followed the pattern. In Manhattan, the immigrant share of the population rose from 24 to 34 percent, and the GOP share of the vote was cut in half to 13.5 percent.[23]

Either the Republican Party puts an end to mass immigration, or mass immigration will put an end to the Republican Party. As Barry Goldwater used to say, "It's as simple as that."

Barack Obama's decision in 2011—to scrap even a virtual fence on the U.S. border with Mexico—suggests that the Democratic Party is not unaware of the fate that will befall the Republican Party if illegal immigration continues, and the illegals are put on a path to citizenship.

THE CULTURE WAR

As a consequence of the cultural revolution, America has become two countries. The differences between us are wide, deep, and enduring. Less and less often do we take the trouble to find common ground with people unlike us in views and values. Rather we secede into enclaves of people like ourselves. Cable, with its hundreds of channels, and the Internet, with its millions of websites, enable us to create worlds of our own to go to when the day's work is done. Perhaps some of us misremember the past. But the racial, religious, cultural, social, political, and economic divides today seem greater than they seemed even in the segregated cities some of us grew up in.

Back then, black and white lived apart, went to different schools and churches, played on different playgrounds, and went to different restaurants, bars, theaters, and soda fountains. But we shared a country and a culture. We were one nation. We were Americans. We spoke the same language, learned the same history, celebrated the same heroes, observed the same holy days and holidays, went to the same films, rooted for the same teams, read the same newspapers, watched the same TV shows on the same three channels, danced to the same music, ate the same foods, recited the same prayers at church and the same pledge of allegiance at school, and were taught the same truths about right and wrong, good and evil, God and country. We were a people then.

That America is gone. Many grieve her passing. Many rejoice. But we are not a people anymore. We do not share a common faith or culture or common vision of what our country is or ought to be. "We do not consider ourselves a Christian nation or a Jewish nation or a Muslim nation," said Obama, which tells you who we are not, not who we are.[24] He went on, "We consider ourselves a nation of citizens who are bound by ideals and a set of values." But what set of values binds us together when we cannot even agree on what a marriage is?

Traditionalists need to understand how we lost. In some ways, there was nothing we could do. The social, moral, and cultural revolution had been a light in the minds of men for generations, its ideas traceable to the French Revolution and the Enlightenment. Some even trace the roots back to the sundering of Christendom during the Reformation.

Some trace the seeds of this revolution back to the Garden of Eden temptation of "Ye shall be as Gods"; others even further to Lucifer's rebellion against God. As Dr. Johnson mused, "The first Whig was the Devil."

Whatever the roots, it was in the 1960s that the revolution, with its repudiation of Christian morality and embrace of secularism and egalitarian ideology, reached critical mass, as the Baby Boomers arrived to double the population on America's campuses. This revolution divided families and generations and rocked the New Deal coalition, enabling

Nixon to stitch together a New Majority that defined itself by opposition to the revolution. In 1972, Nixon crushed the first national political expression of the '60s revolution: the McGovern campaign.

Indeed, Senator Tom Eagleton, McGovern's first choice for vice president, confided to columnist Robert Novak that the McGovern campaign could be summed up as standing for "amnesty, abortion and acid."[25]

While the revolution captured many among the young, it was a revolt of the privileged, not a rising of the people. Eventually, it had to be imposed by a Supreme Court that read its own values into the Constitution, de-Christianized America, elevated secularism to a state religion, and enthroned group rights. Prayer, the Bible, and the Ten Commandments were expelled from the schools, Nativity scenes purged from public squares. Abortion and homosexuality were declared constitutional rights. Children were ordered bussed across cities to achieve the courts' concept of an ideal racial balance.

What astonishes, even now, was the lack of resistance. There were protests, and Republicans ran campaigns decrying judicial activism and the Warren Court. Once elected, however, Republicans made only futile attempts to enact constitutional amendments to overturn decisions that had no basis in the Constitution. The weapon the Founding Fathers had wisely put in the Constitution, authorizing Congress to restrict the jurisdiction of the federal courts, rested and rusted in the scabbard. With the Norris-LaGuardia Act, a Depression-era Congress had stripped courts of the power to issue injunctions in labor cases. Sens. William Jenner and Jesse Helms both proposed legislative restrictions on the court, but they failed to win passage.[26] Lately, however, Congress has acted as though the Supreme Court is the supreme branch of government, having the last word, and against whose judgments the elective branches have no appeal.

The revolution triumphed because Americans are a constitution-loving people. If the court said it, they accepted it. From Nixon to Reagan to Bush 1, Republican presidents sought to nominate justices who would return the court to constitutionalism. Only in the administration of George W. Bush did they begin to succeed. By then, however, the revolution was written into precedent, and conservatives respect precedent.

In the conflicts that come out of our clashing beliefs, conservatives should work to re-empower Congress and corral the Court. Given the current balance, with four constitutionalists (Scalia, Thomas, Roberts, and Alito) and four liberals (Ginsburg, Breyer, Sotomayor, and Kagan), Republicans should block any liberal activist Obama sends up, even if that leaves a vacancy on the Court until the next president.

Congress should also append to every law dealing with social policy, such as the Defense of Marriage Act, a rider that this law is not subject to judicial review. The Founding Fathers never intended that judges should be making the decisions they are making today.

Jefferson declared the Alien and Sedition Acts null and void. Jackson said of the Chief Justice, "John Marshall has made his decision; now, let him enforce it." The Founding Fathers of the Democratic Party would never have accepted judicial supremacy. Nor would the father of the Republican Party, Abraham Lincoln, who declared, in his first inaugural address:

> [I]f the policy of the Government upon vital questions affecting the whole people is to be irrevocably fixed by decisions of the Supreme Court...the people will have ceased to be their own rulers, having to that extent practically resigned their Government into the hands of that eminent tribunal.

As racial discrimination is still among the most divisive issues polarizing our country, Congress should settle the question with finality by enacting into law Ward Connerly's Civil Rights Initiative, which has won the support of the electorate in every state but one where it has been on the ballot: "The state shall not grant preferential treatment to or discriminate against any individual or group on the basis of race, sex, color, ethnicity or national origin in the operation of public employment, public education or public contracting." Three dozen words, written into the Constitution or federal law, would bring down the evil empire of reverse discrimination, while conforming to the letter and spirit of the Civil Rights Act of 1964. Americans supported that act because this is what they thought it said, and this is what Hubert Humphrey said it said.

With judges ignoring written constitutions to declare their opinions to be law—it was the Massachusetts Supreme Court that imposed same-sex marriage on the state—governors need to begin challenging court usurpations by defying court decisions. Had Governor Romney told the Massachusetts Supreme Court that he, too, took an oath to defend the state constitution and same-sex marriage is nowhere mandated in that constitution, and had he refused to issue the marriage licenses, he would have been the Republican nominee in 2008.

As Martin Luther King wrote, in "Letter from a Birmingham Jail," "one has a moral responsibility to disobey unjust law," for, as St. Augustine said, "an unjust law is no law at all."

> How does one determine whether a law is just or unjust? A just law is a man made code that squares with the moral law or the law of God. An unjust law is a code that is out of harmony with the moral law. To put it in the terms of St. Thomas Aquinas: An unjust law is a human law that is not rooted in eternal law and natural law.[27]

In the time of Governors Faubus in Arkansas and Wallace in Alabama, states rights became a synonym for southern resistance to desegregation. It remained so for decades. This is no longer the case. State attorneys general like Ken Cuccinelli of Virginia have gone into federal court to challenge the individual mandate of Obamacare. State legislators are talking of defying federal firearms authorities who come to enforce gun laws that exceed state law. Books are being published lauding the ideas of Jefferson and Madison at the time of the Alien and Sedition Acts, when they wrote of interposition and nullification of national laws that exceeded the federal authority granted in the Constitution. In Iowa, voters dismissed three renegade judges of the state supreme court. A counter-revolution may be in the offing, and the times may call for a more radical conservatism.

Washington and Adams were conservatives in 1770, rebels in 1775, and conservatives again when they led the country as presidents. Hamilton was a teenage firebrand in the early 1770s and a conservative secretary of the treasury in the early 1790s. Jefferson and Madison, free traders as young men, became economic nationalists when British merchants began dumping goods to kill the infant industries born in the War of 1812.

The natural conservatism of the American people, their reverence for the Constitution, their respect for the Supreme Court and the rule of law, have all been exploited by judicial radicals like Earl Warren and William O. Douglas, William J. Brennan and Harry Blackmun to impose a revolution those earlier Americans abhorred. When judges become dictators, citizens become rebels.

America is entering a time of troubles. The clashes of culture and creed are intensifying and both parties are perceived to have failed the nation. Republicans were repudiated in 2006 and 2008, Democrats in 2010. And the crises that afflict us—culture wars, race division, record deficits, unpayable debt, waves of immigration, legal and illegal, of peoples never before assimilated, gridlock in the capital, and possible defeat in war—may prove too much for our democracy to cope with. They surely will, if we do not act now.

Acknowledgments

For her perseverance in getting me to complete this book, and for coming to see me in the Reagan White House to persuade me to start writing books, my eternal gratitude goes to Fredi Friedman, editor, counselor, agent, friend. To Tom Dunne, my thanks for going ahead with it. Special thanks to Marcus Epstein for the invaluable assistance and untold hours he devoted to researching ideas, issues, and anecdotes. Also, thanks to Michael Rubin for helping match footnotes to text.

—Pat Buchanan, June 2011

Notes

Introduction: Disintegrating Nation

1. Kahlil Gibran, *The Garden of the Prophet* (New York: Alfred A. Knopf, 1933).
2. Lee Congdon, *George Kennan: A Writing Life* (Wilmington, DE: ISI Books, 2008), 154.
3. David Ignatius, "An Old-School Trick: Put Country First," *Washington Post*, Sept. 16, 2010.
4. Joe Stumpe and Monica Davey, "Abortion Doctor Shot to Death in Kansas Church," *New York Times*, June 1, 2009; Mark Guarino, "Killing of Anti-Abortion Protester Has Both Sides Questioning Violence," *Christian Science Monitor*, Sept. 12, 2009.
5. William McGurn, "Harry Reid's 'Evil' Moment," *Wall Street Journal*, Aug. 18, 2009.
6. Dana Milbank, "The High Ground Feels a Little Lonely," *Washington Post*, Sept. 16, 2009.
7. Rich Benjamin, "Inside the Mind of Joe Wilson," *Salon.com*, Sept. 11, 2009.
8. Greg Bluestein, "Carter Sees Racism in Wilson's Outburst," *New York Times*, Sept. 16, 2009.
9. Ewen MacAskill, "Jimmy Carter: Animosity Towards Barack Obama Is Due to Racism," *The Guardian*, Sept. 16, 2009.
10. "MTV Awards: West Disrupts Swift's Speech; Tribute to MJ," cnn.com, Sept. 14, 2009.
11. Ronald Brownstein, "The New Color Line," *National Journal*, Oct. 10, 2009.
12. "Vast Majority Believes America Today Is Deeply Divided (10/30–11/4)," USA Network Poll, Dec. 1, 2009.
13. Ross Douthat, "Scenes from a Marriage," *New York Times*, Jan. 16, 2011.
14. Ignatius, "An Old-School Trick."
15. Gus Lubin, "Jimmy Carter Says US Is More Polarized Now Than During Civil War," *Business Insider*, Sept. 21, 2010.
16. "Jerry Brown: California, Country Facing Regime Crisis Similar to the Civil War," CBS, April 10, 2011.

17. Fred Barnes, "The Republicans' Best Weapon," *Weekly Standard*, Feb. 2, 2009.

18. "Obama: Critics Talk About Me 'Like a Dog,'" Daily Intel, *New York* magazine, Sept. 6, 2010.

19. Theodore Roosevelt, Before Knights of Columbus, New York City, Oct. 12, 1915, quote land.com/author/Theodore-Roosevelt-Quotes/120/?p=2.

20. Charles K. Rowley, "Adam Smith Would Not Be Optimistic in Today's Economic World," *Daily Telegraph*, Sept. 6, 2009.

1. The Passing of a Superpower

1. Robert A. Pape, "First Draft of History: Empire Falls," *National Interest*, Jan./Feb. 2009, 21.

2. Leslie H. Gelb, "Necessity, Choice and Common Sense: A Policy for a Bewildering World," *Foreign Affairs*, May/June 2009, 56.

3. Ben Geman, "Obama Defends Escalation of Afghan War in Address to 2010 West Point Class," *The Hill*, May 22, 2010.

4. Michael Settle, "If Money Isn't Loosened Up, This Sucker Is Going to Go Down," *Herald Scotland*, Dec. 30, 2009.

5. Lawrence Kudlow, "Bush Boom Continues," *Human Events*, Dec. 11, 2007.

6. "'We're Greece' in a Few Years: Sen. Gregg," cnbc.com, Nov. 3, 2010.

7. David Malpass, "Near Zero Rates Are Hurting the Economy," *Wall Street Journal*, Dec. 4, 2009.

8. Gelb, "Necessity, Choice and Common Sense," 58.

9. Pape, "First Draft of History," 21.

10. Ibid., 27.

11. Neil Irwin, "Aughts Were a Lost Decade for U.S. Economy, Workers," *Washington Post*, Jan. 2, 2010.

12. Harold Meyerson, "Why Germany and China Are Winning," *Washington Post*, July 1, 2010.

13. Patrick J. Buchanan, "The Metrics of National Decline," Feb. 17, 2009, msnbc.com (Source: Charles W. McMillion, MBG Information Services).

14. "Fox News Poll: 57% Think Next Generation Will Be Worse Off," foxnews.com, Apr. 9, 2010.

15. David M. Dickson, "Volcker Blames Recession on Trade Imbalances," *Washington Times*, Feb. 5, 2009.

16. Buchanan, "The Metrics of National Decline."

17. Mark Drajem, "China's Trade Gap with U.S. Climbs to Record, Fueling Yuan Tension," bloomberg.com, Oct. 14, 2010.

18. Ibid.

19. Ibid.

20. "Persons Obtaining Legal Permanent Resident Status: Fiscal Years 1820–2009," Department of Homeland Security, dhs.gov; "Persons Obtaining Legal Permanent Resident Status by Gender, Age, Marital Status and Occupation: Fiscal Year 2009," Department of Homeland Security, dhs.gov.

21. "New Data Shows China Responsible for 78.5 Percent of U.S. Trade Deficit in

Manufactured Goods in 2009; Figure Up from 27.3 Percent in 2001," press statement, American Manufacturing Trade Action Coalition, Washington, DC, Aug. 18, 2009.

22. Senator Fritz Hollings, "Fifth Column: The Enemy Within the Trade War," *huffington post.com,* Oct. 16, 2009.

23. Charles W. McMillion, "Globalization and America's Lost Decade," MBG Information Services, March 2010, 1, 40; "Lost Manufacturing Jobs in Decade," MBG Information Services, Jan. 2011, mbginfosvcs.com.

24. James R. Hagerty, "U.S. Factories Buck Decline," *Wall Street Journal,* Jan. 19, 2011.

25. Stephen Moore, "We've Become a Nation of Takers, Not Makers," *Wall Street Journal,* Apr. 1, 2011.

26. Warren E. Buffett and Carol Loomis, "America's Growing Trade Deficit Is Selling the Nation Out from Under Us. Here's a Way to Fix the Problem and We Need to Do It Now," *Fortune,* Nov. 10, 2003, cnnmoney.com.

27. David S. Heidler and Jeanne T. Heidler, *Henry Clay: The Essential American* (New York: Random House, 2010), 240.

28. Dan Molinski and John Lyons, "China's $20 Billion Bolsters Chavez," *Wall Street Journal,* Apr. 18, 2010.

29. John Pomfret, "More Political Ads Portray China as Benefiting from Weak U.S. Economy," *Washington Post,* Oct. 28, 2010.

30. Peter Whoriskey, "As Cheaper Chinese Tires Roll In, Obama Faces an Early Trade Test," *Washington Post,* Sept. 8, 2009.

31. Larry Elder, "The Soft Bigotry of President Bush," *Jewish World Review,* July 4, 2002.

32. Ibid.

33. Ibid.

34. Betty Liu and Matthew Leising, "U.S. to Lose $400 Billion on Fannie, Freddie, Wallison Says," bloomberg.com, Dec. 31, 2009.

35. John Weicher, "Closing the Gap: The Quiet Success of the Bush Administration's Push for Minority Homeownership," *Weekly Standard,* Oct. 11, 2006.

36. Karen Kwiatkowski, "An American Tale," lewrockwell.com, Dec. 16, 2003.

37. "The Coming Debt Panic," *Washington Post,* Dec. 14, 2009.

38. David M. Walker, Rosenthal Lecture, Institute of Medicine, Nov. 9, 2009, pgpf.org; Dennis Cauchon, "U.S. Owes $62 Trillion," *USA Today,* June 7, 2011.

39. Ben Pershing, "Democrats Clear Spending Bill in Senate," *Washington Post,* Dec. 14, 2009.

40. Patrick J. Buchanan, "Fat City," townhall.com, Dec. 15, 2009.

41. Pershing, "Democrats Clear Spending Bill."

42. Jeff Zeleny, "Obama Weighs Quick Undoing of Bush Policy," *New York Times,* Nov. 9, 2008.

43. "FY10 Omnibus Disclosed Earmark Numbers," Taxpayers for Common Sense, Dec. 10, 2009, taxpayer.net.

44. Andrew G. Biggs and Jason Richwine, "Those Underpaid Government Workers," *American Spectator,* September 2010, 14.

45. Ibid.

46. Dennis Cauchon, "For Feds, More Get 6-Figure Salaries," *USA Today,* Dec. 11, 2009.

47. Ibid.

48. Dennis Cauchon, "More Fed Workers Pay Tops $150K: Number Doubled Under Obama," *USA Today,* Nov. 10, 2010.

49. Lena H. Sun, "D.C. Area Tops in Well-being Survey," *Washington Post,* Nov. 10, 2010.

50. Dennis Cauchon, "Federal Pay Tops Private Workers: Compensation Gap Doubled in Decade," *USA Today,* Aug. 10, 2010.

51. Dennis Cauchon, "Obama's Pay Freeze for Federal Workers Only Limits Raises," *USA Today,* Dec. 1, 2010.

52. Garet Garrett, *The People's Pottage* (Caldwell, ID: Caxton Printers, 1958), 1.

53. Andy Soltis, "Tax Refugees Staging Escape from New York," *New York Post,* Oct. 27, 2009.

54. Kenneth Lovett, "New Yorkers Under 30 Plan to Flee City; Cite High Taxes, Few Jobs as Reasons," *nydailynews.com,* May 13, 2011.

55. Gerald Prante, "Summary of Latest Federal Income Tax Data," Tax Foundation, July 30, 2009, taxfoundation.org.

56. "Policy Basics: The Earned Income Tax Credit," Center on Budget and Policy Priorities, Dec. 4, 2009, cbpp.org.

57. Edwin S. Rubenstein, "The Earned Income Tax Credit and Illegal Immigration: A Study in Fraud, Abuse and Liberal Activism," *Social Contract,* Spring 2009, 3.

58. Stephen Ohlemacher, "Nearly Half of U.S. Households Escape Fed Income Tax," Associated Press, April 7, 2010, finance.yahoo.com.

59. John D. McKinnon, "High-Earning Households Pay Growing Share of Taxes," wsj.com, May 3, 2011.

60. Barack Obama, Reclaiming the American Dream Speech, Bettendorf [IA], Nov. 7, 2007, "Barack Obama and Joe Biden: Making College Affordable for Everyone," barackobama.com.

61. Lawrence W. Reed, "A Subtle Destroyer," Mackinac Center for Public Policy, April 8, 2005, mackinac.org.

62. "Food Stamp Rolls Continue to Rise," *Wall Street Journal,* Dec. 8, 2010.

63. Anemona Hartocollis, "New York Asks to Bar Use of Food Stamps to Buy Sodas," *New York Times,* Oct. 6, 2010.

64. Christine Armario and Dorie Turner, "Nearly 1 in 4 Fails Military Entrance Exam," *Washington Examiner,* Dec. 22, 2010.

65. John Maynard Keynes, *The Economic Consequences of the Peace* (London: Macmillan, 1919), 220.

66. "Cheap Cigarettes from Cigarettes Below Cost," cigarettes-below-cost.com.

67. Thomas E. Woods, *Meltdown: A Free-Market Look at Why the Stock Market Collapsed, the Economy Tanked, and Government Bailouts Will Make Things Worse* (Washington, D.C.: Regnery, 2009), 1.

68. Lawrence W. Reed, "The Greatest Spending Administration in All of History," Mackinac Center for Public Policy, Jan. 1, 1998, mackinac.org.

69. Paul Krugman, "Franklin Delano Obama," *New York Times,* Nov. 10, 2008.

70. Woods, *Meltdown,* 103.

71. Robert Dell, "What Fiscal Pain? Budget-Cutting Misery Is More Imagined Than Real," *Washington Times,* Apr. 29, 2011.

72. Woods, *Meltdown,* 26.

73. Thomas Jefferson, Kentucky Resolutions, 1798, etext.virginia.edu.

74. Ernest Hemingway quotes, thinkexist.com; "Hemingway on the Costs of War," Ludwig von Mises Institute, blog.mises.org.

75. Elizabeth MacDonald, "Bernanke Re-ignites Inflation-Deflation Debate," foxbusiness .com, Oct. 15, 2010.

76. Brady Dennis, "In Capitol Hill Hearing, Bankers Remain Torn on Their Role in Crisis," *Washington Post,* Jan. 14, 2010.

77. Jackie Calmes, "Party Gridlock in Washington Feeds Fear of a Debt Crisis," *New York Times,* Feb. 16, 2010.

78. John Adams quotes, brainyquote.com.

79. "Quotes on Liberty and Virtue," complied and edited by J. David Gowdy, president, The Washington, Jefferson and Madison Institute, liberty1.org/virtue.

80. Tom Piatak, "The Necessity of Christianity," *Chronicles,* October 2009, 39; George Washington, Farewell Address, Rediscovering George Washington, Claremont Institute, 2002.

81. Piatek, "The Necessity of Christianity," 40.

82. "Quotes on Liberty and Virtue."

2. The Death of Christian America

1. James C. Russell, *Breach of Faith: American Churches and the Immigration Crisis* (Raleigh, NC: Representative Government Press, 2004), 10.

2. Carl Pearlston, "Is America a Christian Nation?" Catholic Education Resource Center, catholiceducation.org.

3. Toby Harnden, "Barack Obama in Turkey: U.S. 'Will Never Be at War with Islam,'" *Telegraph,* April 6, 2009.

4. Rick Warren's Inaugural Invocation, christianitytoday.com, Jan. 20, 2009.

5. President Barack Obama's Inaugural Address, The White House Blog, Jan. 21, 2010, whitehouse.gov.

6. *Church of the Holy Trinity v. the United States,* 143 U.S. 457, 1892, wikipedia.org.

7. "Rev. Joseph Lowery Delivers Benediction at Inaugural Ceremony," CNN, Jan. 20, 2009, politicalticker.blog.cnn.com.

8. "Harmonies of Liberty," Rev. Dr. Sharon E. Watkins, National Prayer Service, Jan. 21, 2009, nationalcathedral.org.

9. Ibid.

10. Ibid.

11. Julia Dunn, "Obama to Be Prayer Day No-Show," *Washington Times,* May 6, 2009.

12. "Obama Ends Bush-Era National Prayer Day at the White House," Top of the Ticket: Politics Coast to Coast with the *L.A. Times,* May 7, 2009, latimesblogs.latimes.com.

13. Terence P. Jeffrey, "Belief That Religion Is Losing Its Influence on American Life Hit 50-Year Peak After Inauguration of Obama, Says Gallup Data," Conservative News Service, Dec. 29, 2010, cnsnews.com.

14. Summary of Key Findings, U.S. Religious Landscape Survey, Pew Forum on Religion and Public Life, 2008.

15. Michelle Boorstein, "15 Percent of Americans Have No Religion," *Washington Post,* March 9, 2009.

16. Ibid.

17. Robert D. Putnam and David E. Campbell, "Walking Away from Church," *Los Angeles Times,* Oct. 19, 2010.

18. Ibid.

19. Ibid.; Barry A. Kosmin and Ariela Keysar, *American Religious Identification Survey 2008,* News, Office of Communications, Trinity College, Hartford, CT; Rachel Zoll, "More Americans Say They Have No Religion," AP, March 9, 2009.

20. Kosmin and Keysar, *American Religious Identification Survey 2008.*

21. Jon Meacham, "The End of Christian America," *Newsweek,* April 13, 2009.

22. Putnam and Campbell, "Walking Away from Church."

23. U.S. Religious Landscape Survey; Timothy Samuel Shah, "Born Again in the U.S.A.: The Enduring Power of American Evangelicalism," *Foreign Affairs,* Sept./Oct. 2009, 143.

24. Boorstein, "15 Percent"; Zoll, "More Americans."

25. Ibid.; Kosmin and Keysar, *American Religious Identification Survey 2008.*

26. Steven Waldman, "Fastest Growing Religion = No Religion (New Religious Identification Survey)," beliefnet.com, March 9, 2009.

27. "Catholics on the Move, Non-religious on the Rise," Trinity News, March 9, 2009, trincoll.edu.

28. "Abortion a More Powerful Issue for Women," Pew Research Center for People and the Press, April 23, 2004, people-press.org.

29. Kosmin and Keysar, *American Religious Identification Survey 2008.*

30. Michael Felsen, "Obama's Faith in 'Non-Believers,'" *The Forward,* Feb. 27, 2009.

31. "Faith on the Hill: The Religious Affiliations of Members of Congress," *Congressional Quarterly,* Dec. 19, 2008.

32. Kosmin and Keysar, *American Religious Identification Survey 2008.*

33. U.S. Religious Landscape Survey.

34. Eric Kaufmann, "Breeding for God," *Prospect,* November 2006, prospectmagazine.co.uk.

35. Kosmin and Keysar, *American Religious Identification Survey 2008;* "Catholics on the Move."

36. "Remarks by the President on a New Beginning," White House, Office of the Press Secretary, June 4, 2009, whitehouse.gov.

37. William Wan, "Abundant Faith, Shrinking Space," *Washington Post,* Aug. 22, 2009.

38. Carl Bialik, "Estimates of Religious Populations Require a Bit of Faith," *Wall Street Journal,* Aug. 14–15, 2010.

39. U.S. Religious Landscape Survey.

40. Ibid.

41. Ibid.

42. Michael Spencer, "The Coming Evangelical Collapse," *Christian Science Monitor,* March 10, 2009.

43. Ibid.

44. Ibid.

45. Ibid.

46. John Micklethwait and Adrian Wooldridge, "God Still Isn't Dead," *Wall Street Journal,* Apr. 7, 2009.

47. Ibid.

48. Russell D. Moore, "Where Have All the Presbyterians Gone?" *Wall Street Journal*, Feb. 4, 2011.

49. Spencer, "The Coming Evangelical Collapse."

50. Shah, "Born Again in the U.S.A.," 144–45.

51. "National Statistics on Belonging and Belief," ARIS, 2008.

52. Harold Meyerson, "Episcopalians Against Equality," *Washington Post*, Dec. 20, 2006.

53. Ibid.

54. Ibid.

55. Gillian Gaynair, "D.C. Board Rejects Gay Marriage Referendum Effort," *Chicago Tribune*, June 15, 2009.

56. Scott Lamb, "The Decline and Fall of Christian America (Jon Meacham)," *St. Louis Today*, special to the *Post-Dispatch*, April 8, 2009, interact.stltoday.com.

57. Julia Duin, "Catholics, Southern Baptists Losing Members," *Washington Times*, Feb. 25, 2009.

58. Ibid.

59. Ibid.

60. John Allen, "Religion in Europe: Christianity on the Defensive/Christianity Under Siege," *National Catholic Reporter*, June 13, 2008.

61. Ibid.

62. William Murchison, "Mainline Marital Melange," *Chronicles*, April 17, 2009, chroniclesmagazine.org.

63. Ibid.

64. Julia Duin, "Lutherans Second Church to Split Over Gays," *Washington Times*, Nov. 19, 2009.

65. Laurie Goodstein, "First Openly Gay Episcopal Bishop to Retire in 2013," *New York Times*, Nov. 7, 2010.

66. Edward Short, "Winston Churchill and the Old Cause," *Crisis*, Dec. 2005, 27.

67. Eugene G. Windchy, *The End of Darwinism: And How a Flawed and Disastrous Theory Was Stolen and Sold* (Arlington, VA: Eugene Windchy, 2009), 168.

68. Ibid.

69. Ibid., 40.

70. Albert Speer, *Inside the Third Reich* (New York: Simon & Schuster, 1970), 96.

71. Adolf Hitler, *Mein Kampf* (Los Angeles: Hurst & Blackett, 1939), 225.

72. Ibid.

73. Hilaire Belloc, *The Great Heresies* (Salem, NH: Ayer Company, 1985), 10.

74. Ibid.

75. Meacham, "End of Christian America."

76. Sharon Jayson, "CDC Study: Birthrates Decline Overall," *USA Today*, Dec. 22, 2010; Rob Stein and Donna St. George, "Number of Unwed Mothers Has Risen Sharply in U.S.," *Washington Post*, May 14, 2009.

77. Heather Mac Donald, "Nation of Cowards," *City Journal*, Feb. 19, 2008, city-journal.org; Brady Hamilton, Steven Malanga, "Bad Choices, Not a Bad Economy, Are to Blame," *Chicago Sun-Times*, Feb. 4, 2007, manhattan-institute.org; Walter Williams, "Victimhood: Rhetoric or Reality," *Jewish World Review*, June 8, 2005.

78. South Dakota E-Labor Bulletin, Labor Information Center, South Dakota Department of Labor, Dec. 2007.

79. "Suicides in the U.S.: Statistics and Prevention," National Institute of Mental Health, nimh.nih.gov.

80. William Bennett, *The Index of Leading Cultural Indicators* (New York: Simon & Schuster, 1994), 22.

81. "Public Safety, Public Spending: Forecasting America's Prison Population 2007–2011," Pew Charitable Trusts, Feb. 14, 2007.

82. Jeffrey Kuhner, "Hollywood's Culture of Death," *Washington Times,* Feb. 22, 2009.

83. Ibid.

84. Duncan Williams, *Trousered Apes: Sick Literature in a Sick Society* (New Rochelle, NY: Arlington House, 1991), 152; Philip Yancey, "T. S. Eliot's Christian Society: Still Relevant Today?" *Christian Century,* Nov. 19, 1986, religion-online.org.

85. Tom Wolfe, "The Meaning of Freedom," *Parameters,* March 1988, 14.

86. Aleksandr Solzhenitsyn, Harvard Address, June 8, 1978, columbia.edu/cu.

87. Angus MacDonald, "Our Christian Faith," *St. Croix Review,* December 2010, p. 2; George Grant, "Election Day Meditations," Grantian Florilegium, Aug. 3, 2006.

88. Piatak, "The Necessity of Christianity," 41.

89. Ibid., 42.

90. Ibid.

91. Ibid.

92. Tom Piatak, "Decline and Fall," *Chronicles,* August 2009, 30.

93. Ibid.

94. Ibid.

95. John Xiros Cooper, *T. S. Eliot and the Ideology of the Four Quartets* (Cambridge: Cambridge University Press, 1995), 127.

96. Williams, *Trousered Apes,* 152; Edmund Burke, "Letter to a Member of the National Assembly," 1791, *The Works of the Right Honorable Edmund Burke* (1899), vol. 4, 51–52, bartleby.com.

97. Dermot Quinn, "Dawson's Creed," *The American Conservative,* Feb. 2010, 19.

98. "Giorgio Vasari—Founder of the History of Art," Info Barrel, Apr. 6, 2009, infobarrel.com.

99. Francis Fukuyama, "A Philosophy in Context," *New York Times Book Review,* May 9, 2010, 12.

100. Ibid.

101. Naomi Schaefer Riley, "The Fate of the Spirit: The Wobbly Religious Lives of Young People Emerging into Adulthood," *Wall Street Journal,* Oct. 2, 2009.

102. Ibid.

103. Ibid.

104. Russell Kirk, "Civilization Without Religion?" American Orthodox Institute, Sept. 12, 2009, aoiusa.org.

105. Christopher Dawson, *Progress and Religion: An Historical Enquiry* (New York: Sheed and Ward, 1934), 232–33.

106. U.S. Religious Landscape Survey, 128, 136.

107. Matthew Arnold, "Dover Beach," 1867, eecs.harvard.edu.

108. Jude Dougherty, "National Identity," *Nationale und kulturelle Identität im Zeitalter der*

Globalisierung, ed. Anton Rauscher, vol. 18 of the series *Soziale Orientierung* (Berlin: Duncker & Humblot, 2006), 13.

109. James K. Robinson and Walter K. Rideout, *A College Book of Modern Verse* (Evanston, IL: Row, Peterson, 1960), 65.

110. Hilaire Belloc, *Europe and the Faith* (New York: CosmoClassics, 2007), 184.

111. Belloc, *The Great Heresies*, 132.

112. Archbishop Charles Chaput, "Living Within the Truth," *Catalyst*, Jan.–Feb. 2011, 8.

113. Denis Diderot quotes, thinkexist.com.

114. Will Durant, *The Story of Philosophy* (New York: Washington Square Press, 1961), 236.

115. Aleksandr Solzhenitsyn, "Men Have Forgotten God," Templeton Address, 1983, Orthodox America, roca.org/OA.

116. Ibid.

117. Ibid.

118. Ibid.

119. Ibid.

120. Ibid.

121. Shah, "Born Again in the U.S.A.," 139.

122. Geoffrey Wheatcroft, "Continental Drifts," *The National Interest*, March/April 2009, 39.

123. Ibid., 46.

124. Stephen Adams, "Pope's Good Friday Message Warns of a Drift into a 'Desert of Godlessness,'" *Telegraph*, April 10, 2009.

125. Chris Caldwell, "Born Again Anti-Catholicism," *Financial Times*, Sept. 17, 2010.

126. Ibid.

127. Mark Tidd, "Idolatry and the Battle for the Heart," *Reformed Worship*, Dec. 1995, reformedworship.org.

128. Meacham, "The End of Christian America."

129. Stephen Beale, "T. S. Eliot and the Idea of a Christian Society," May 4, 2009, the brownspectator.

130. Wayne Allensworth, "Who Won the Cold War?" *Chronicles*, July 2010, 24.

131. Ibid., 25.

132. Psalm 96: 5, The Holy Bible, Douay-Rheims Version (Rockford, IL: Tan Books and Publishers, 1999), 621.

133. Quinn, "Dawson's Creed," 20.

134. David Priestland, *The Red Flag: A History of Communism* (New York: Grove Press, 2010), cited by Allensworth, "Who Won the Cold War?" 25.

135. Robert Nisbet, *Prejudices: A Philosophical Dictionary* (Cambridge: Harvard University Press, 1982), 101.

136. Belloc, *The Great Heresies*, 132.

137. Ron Dreher, "Bill Maher and the Gods That Failed," CrunchyCon: Conservative Politics and Religion with Ron Dreher, *Episcopalian*, Feb. 23, 2009, episcopalian.worldpress.com.

138. Ibid.

139. Ibid.

140. Ibid.

141. Belloc, *The Great Heresies*, 127.

142. Ibid., 132–33.

143. Ibid., 93.

144. Fouad Ajami, "From Berlin to Baghdad," *Wall Street Journal,* Nov. 9, 2009.

145. "1.5 Billion Muslims in World," *Gulf Daily News,* Oct. 9, 2009.

146. Adrian Michaels, "A Fifth of European Union Will Be Muslim by 2050," *Telegraph,* Aug. 8, 2009.

147. "An Analysis of the World Muslim Population by Country/Region," CIA World Factbook, 2009, factbook.net.

148. Belloc, *The Great Heresies,* 128.

149. Kuhner, "Hollywood's Culture of Death."

150. Williams, *Trousered Apes,* 9.

151. "Afghan Christian Convert Flees to Italy," AP, March 29, 2006, foxnews.com.

152. Patrick Goodenough, "Swiss Vote to Ban Minarets Viewed by Some as Human Rights Violation, by Others as Catalyst for Muslim Assimilation," cnsnews.com, Nov. 30, 2009.

153. James Joyner, "French Burqa Ban Widely Supported in Europe," Atlantic Council, March 1, 2010, acus.org.

154. "Sharia Law for UK Is 'Unavoidable,'" BBC News, Feb. 7, 2008.

155. Ibid.

156. Ibid.

157. Paul Belien, "Islamic Immigration and Murder Among the Tulips," vdare.com, Nov. 3, 2004.

158. Ibid.

159. "John Paul II in His Own Words," BBC News, Oct. 14, 2003, news.bbc.co.uk.

160. State of the World Report, 2005–2006, Human Life International.

161. Dale Hurd, "Europe Forsakes Christianity for Islam," CBN News, Sept. 5, 2006, propheticnews.net.

162. Allen, "Religion in Europe."

163. Hurd, "Europe Forsakes Christianity for Islam."

164. Fr. John McCloskey, "The Clash of Civilizations and the Remaking of World Order," *L'Osservatore Romano,* English edition, July 27, 1997, CatholiCity.com.

165. Ibid.

166. Ibid.

3. The Crisis of Catholicism

1. Kenneth C. Jones, *Index of Leading Catholic Indicators: The Church Since Vatican II* (St. Louis: Oriens Publishing, 2003), 7.

2. Ibid.

3. Ibid., 7–11.

4. Laurie Goodstein, "U.S. Nuns Facing Vatican Scrutiny," *New York Times,* July 2, 2009.

5. Dale McDonald and Margaret M. Schultz, "United States Catholic Elementary and Secondary Schools 2009–2010," National Catholic Education Association.

6. Fr. Joseph A. Sirba, "U.S. Catholics Leaving the Church in Droves: What Can Be Done?" AD2000, May 2009, 8, ad2000.com.au.

7. Ibid.; "FACTBOX: America's Roman Catholic Population," Reuters.com, April 10, 2008.

8. Fr. Joseph A. Sirba, "The U.S. Religious Landscape Survey," *Homiletic & Pastoral Review,* January 2009, 21.

9. Ibid.

10. "A Portrait of American Catholics on the Eve of Pope Benedict's Visit," Pew Research Center Publications, March 27, 2008, pewresearch.org.

11. "Gomez Vows to Be an Advocate for L.A.'s Immigrants, the Less Fortunate," *Los Angeles Times,* April 6, 2010, latimesblogs.latimes.com/lanow/jose-gomez.

12. "The Ethnic Church," *Changing Faiths: Latinos and the Transformation of American Religion,* Pew Hispanic Center and Pew Forum on Religion & Public Life, April 25, 2007, 50.

13. Jones, *Index of Leading Catholic Indicators,* 71.

14. Ibid., 9; Nancy Frazier O'Brien, "Survey Assesses Catholic Beliefs on Mass, Sacraments," Catholic News Service, April 11, 2008, catholicnews.com.

15. Jones, *Index of Leading Catholic Indicators,* 10.

16. Ibid.

17. O'Brien, "Survey Assesses Catholic Beliefs"; "Catholics Approve of Pope Benedict, but Don't Attend Mass," Catholic News Agency, April 17, 2008, catholicnewsagency .com; "Sacraments Today: Belief and Practice Among U.S. Catholics," Feb. 2008, cara .georgetown.edu.

18. O'Brien, "Survey Assesses Catholic Beliefs."

19. Jones, *Index of Leading Catholic Indicators,* 10; Peter Steinfels, "Future of Faith Worries Catholic Leaders," *New York Times,* June 1, 1994.

20. Malachi Martin, *The Jesuits: The Society of Jesus and the Betrayal of the Roman Catholic Church* (New York: Simon & Schuster, 1987), 321; Russell, *Breach of Faith,* 45.

21. F. N. Robinson, ed., *The Works of Geoffrey Chaucer,* 2nd ed. (Boston: Houghton Mifflin, 1957), 22.

22. Matthew 18:6, King James Bible.

23. "Archbishop Chaput Hits Catholics' Complacency," *Wanderer,* April 2, 2009, 7; "Catholic 'Complacency' Shares Blame for Country's," catholicnewsagency.com.

24. "Faith on the Hill: The Religious Affiliations of Members of Congress," Dec. 19, 2008, pewforum.org.

25. Lance Morrow, "The Rise and Fall of Anti-Catholicism," *Time,* Oct. 15, 1979.

26. Archbishop Timothy M. Dolan, "Foul Ball: Anti-Catholicism Is the Nation's Other Pastime," foxnews.com, Oct. 30, 2009.

27. "The Arts," Catholic League for Religious and Civil Rights, 2007, catholic-league.ws.

28. Ibid.; Amy S. Clark, "Holy Week Angst over Naked Chocolate Jesus," AP, cbsnews .com, March 29, 2007.

29. Bill Donahue, "Virgin Mary Defiled on 'South Park,'" *Free Republic,* Dec. 8, 2005.

30. "Larry David Blasted for 'Curb' Episode Where He Urinates on Jesus Painting," foxnews.com, Oct. 28, 2009.

31. Ibid.

32. Ibid.

33. "Colorado Museum Under Fire; Vile Jesus Art Smashed," *Catalyst,* November 2010, 1.

34. David Itzkoff, "'South Park' Episode Altered After Muslim Group's Warning," *New York Times,* April 23, 2010.

35. Morrow, "Rise and Fall of Anti-Catholicism."

36. Tamara Barak Aparton, "Church Defaced by 'Hate Crime,'" *San Francisco Examiner,* Jan. 5, 2009.

37. Ben Child, "Emmerich Reveals Fear of Fatwa Axed 2012 Scene," *Guardian,* Nov. 3, 2009.

38. Penny Starr, "Smithsonian Christmas-Season Exhibit Features Ant-Covered Jesus, Naked Brothers Kissing, Genitalia, and Ellen DeGeneres Grabbing Her Breasts," cnsnews.com, Nov. 29, 2010.

39. Ibid.

40. Dolan, "Foul Ball."

41. Kathleen Gilbert, "Notre Dame Faces Groundswell of Outrage After Announcing Plan to Honor Obama," lifesitenews.com, March 23, 2009; Ralph McInerny, "Is Obama Worth a Mass?" assentingcatholic.blogspot.com, March 24, 2009.

42. Ibid.

43. Gilbert, "Notre Dame."

44. "Bishop to Skip Notre Dame Graduation over Obama's Views," cnnpolitics.com, May 14, 2009.

45. "Address of His Holiness Benedict XVI," Catholic University of America, April 17, 2008.

46. Chaz Muth, "Despite Criticism, Notre Dame Firm on Obama as Commencement Speaker," Catholic News Service, March 24, 2009.

47. Julia Duin, "Notre Dame Feels Heat Again: Funding of Gay March Attendees Is at Issue," *Washington Times,* Oct. 16, 2009.

48. "Jesuit Universities Criticized for 'Obscene' Events Promoting Sexual Ideologies," Catholic News Agency, March 2, 2009.

49. Ibid.

50. Ibid.

51. Ibid.

52. Joseph Bottum, "Bottum: Georgetown Catholic Again?" firstthings.com, Aug. 28, 2006.

53. "Georgetown Jesuit: 'Our Job Is Not to Bring People to God,'" Campus Notes, Cardinal Newman Society, February 2011, 4.

54. Irving Kristol, "Family Values: Not a Political Issue," *Wall Street Journal,* Dec. 7, 1992.

55. T. S. Eliot, *Christianity and Culture: The Idea of a Christian Society and Notes Toward the Definition of Culture* (New York: Harcourt Brace Jovanovich, 1968), 200.

56. "Jesuit Universities Criticized."

57. Ibid.

58. Ibid.

59. Stephen Adams, "Pope's Good Friday Message Warns of Drift into a 'Desert of Godlessness,'" *Telegraph,* April 11, 2009.

60. Ibid.

61. Ibid.

62. Dan Bilefsky, "Uphill Fight for Pope Among Secular Czechs," *New York Times,* Sept. 27, 2009.

63. Ibid.

64. Jason Palmer, "Religion May Become Extinct in Nine Nations, Study Says," BBC News, March 22, 2011.

65. Jonathan Capehart, "Catholics Lead the Way on Same-Sex Marriage," PostPartisan, March 21, 2011.

66. Richard Owen, "Dismay as Pope Welcomes Back Holocaust Bishop Richard William-son," *London Times,* Jan. 26, 2009.

67. "Pope in Bid to Dampen Bishop Row," *BBC News,* Jan. 29, 2009.

68. Peter Steinfels, "The Holocaust Furor and the U.S. Bishops," *New York Times,* Jan. 31, 2009.

69. "Calls for Pope to Step Down over Holocaust Denier," Agence France Presse, Feb. 2, 2009, google.com.

70. Richard Owen, "Angela Merkel Rebukes Pope in Holocaust," *London Times,* Feb. 4, 2009.

71. Julia Duin, "Cardinal Sees Duty to Play Role in Health Care Debate," *Washington Times,* Nov. 17, 2001.

72. Ray Henry, "Patrick Kennedy Banned from Receiving Communion by Bishop Thomas Tobin," huffingtonpost.com, Nov. 23, 2009.

73. Ray Henry, "Cleric to Kennedy: Forgo Communion," *Washington Times,* Nov. 23, 2009; Bishop Thomas J. Tobin, "Letter to Congressman Patrick Kennedy," Nov. 12, 2009, thericatholic.com.

74. Dolan, "Foul Ball."

75. Ibid.; Dan Mangan, "Archbishop's Blog Slams Gray Lady's," *New York Post,* Nov. 3, 2009.

76. Julia Duin, "Archbishop Rips Sebelius Appointment," *Washington Times,* May 9, 2009.

77. Laurie Goodstein, "Catholic Bishops Pick New Yorker as Their Leader," *New York Times,* Nov. 17, 2010.

78. Russell Shaw, "Notre Dame and the Americanist Impulse," *Arlington Catholic Herald,* April 16–22, 2009, 10.

79. Laurie Goodstein, "Christian Leaders Unite on Political Issues," *New York Times,* Nov. 20, 2009.

80. Ibid.

81. John S. Reist, Jr., "Vile Bodies," *The University Bookman,* Spring 2003, 28.

82. Hilaire Belloc, *Europe and the Faith* (New York: Cosimo, 2007), 20.

83. Aamir Latif, "Pakistan Christians, Muslims United Against Violence," islamonline.net, Aug. 4, 2009.

84. Michael Gerson, "A Blow to Religious Freedom," *Washington Post,* March 8, 2011, p. A15; Matthew Green, "Anger and Grief as Pakistan's Christians Fear for Future," *Financial Times,* March 5–6, 2011, 4.

85. Rhys Blakely, "Christians in India Face Prospect of More Attacks by Extremists," timesonline.co.uk, Sept. 11, 2008.

86. Alex Crawford, "Orgy of Violence Against Christians," Sky News, Oct. 15, 2008.

87. Ibid.

88. Tom A. Peter, "Three Malaysia Churches Firebombed as 'Allah' Use Tension Mounts," *Christian Science Monitor,* Jan. 8, 2010.

89. "Bishops: Middle East May Soon Be Empty of Christians," *Catholic Herald* (UK), March 6, 2009, catholicherald.co.uk

90. "Christians and Muslims in Egypt Trade Attacks After Fatal Shootings," *New York Times International,* Jan. 10, 2010; "Egypt Clashes After Copt Killings," BBC News, Jan. 7, 2010.

91. Ernesto Londono and Aziz Alwan, "Iraqi Worshipers, Troops Killed in Church Take-over," *Washington Post,* Nov. 1, 2010; "Priests Among 58 Killed During Terror Siege at Iraqi Church," *USA Today,* Nov. 2, 2010; Anthony Shadid, "Deadly Attack on a Catholic Church in Baghdad Is Seen as a Strike at Iraq's Core," *New York Times,* Nov. 2, 2010.

92. Anwar Faruqi, "Fearful Iraqi Christians Face Fresh Qaeda Threats," Agence France Presse, Nov. 3, 2010, yahoo.com.

93. Steven Lee Myers, "More Christians Flee Iraq After New Violence," *New York Times,* Dec. 12, 2010.

94. Kareem Fahim and Liam Stack, "Fatal Bomb Hits Church in Egypt," *New York Times,* Jan. 2, 2011.

95. Diane Macedo, "Thousands of Christians Displaced in Ethiopia After Muslim Extremists Torch Churches, Homes," foxnews.com, March 24, 2011.

96. Paul Marshall, "God Looked East: The Disappearance of Christianity in Its Homeland," *Weekly Standard,* April 13, 2009, 36.

97. "Christians in Middle East Are Ignored, Vatican Claims," *Telegraph,* June 6, 2010; Ed West, "Time to Stop the Christian Exodus from the Middle East, Says Vatican," *Catholic Herald,* June 11, 2010, catholicherald.co.uk.

98. Robert Fisk, "Exodus: The Changing Map of the Middle East," *The Independent,* Oct. 26, 2010.

99. Doug Bandow, "Whoever Loses His Life for My Sake...," *Townhall Magazine,* April 2010, cato.org.

100. Marshall, "God Looked East," 36.

101. *Catholic Eye,* Nov. 30, 2009, 2.

102. Philip Jenkins, "Passions of Pope Victor," review of John L. Allen's *The Future Church: How Ten Trends Are Revolutionizing the Catholic Church* (2009), *The National Interest,* Jan./Feb. 2010, 65.

103. Ibid.

104. Ibid., 71.

105. Ibid., 72.

106. William Wan, "Enrollment of Muslim Students Is Growing at Catholic Colleges in U.S.," *Washington Post,* Dec. 20, 2010.

107. Ibid.

4. The End of White America

1. John Hope Franklin, Speech to a Freshman Symposium, Duke University, *Duke University Alumni Magazine.*

2. Joe Klein, "Obama's Victory Ushers in a New America," *Time,* Nov. 5, 2008.

3. Gary Younge, "Obama and the Decline of White America," *The Nation,* Oct. 9, 2009.

4. Hua Hsu, "The End of White America?" *Atlantic Monthly,* Jan./Feb. 2009.

5. Ibid.

6. Edwin Black, *War Against the Weak: Eugenics and America's Campaign to Create a Master Race* (New York: Thunder's Mouth Press, 2003), p. 6.

7. Hua Hsu, "The End of White America?"

8. "Lothrop Stoddard: Biography," wikipedia.com.

9. Hua Hsu, "The End of White America?"

10. Sam Roberts, "A Generation Away, Minorities May Become the Majority in U.S.," *New York Times*, Aug. 14, 2008; Paul Overberg and Emily Bazar, "America's Face Evolves, Blurs, Ages," *USA Today*, Aug. 14, 2008.

11. Sabrina Tavernise, "Numbers of Children of Whites Falling Fast," *New York Times*, Apr. 6, 2011.

12. Hua Hsu, "The End of White America?"

13. Ibid.

14. "Larry King Live," cnn.com, Jan. 21, 2009, 14; "Larry King on Barack Obama: 'Black Is In…My Eight-Year-Old Son Wishes He Were Black,'" *Telegraph*, Jan. 22, 2009.

15. Timothy Homan, "Diversity on Rise in U.S.," *Charleston Daily Mail*, Dec. 23, 2010.

16. Hua Hsu, "The End of White America?"

17. Ibid.

18. Rich Benjamin, "Inside the Mind of Joe Wilson," salon.com, Sept. 11, 2009.

19. Frank Rich, "Small Beer, Big Hangover," *New York Times*, Aug. 2, 2009.

20. Frank Rich, "The Rage Is Not About Health Care," *New York Times*, March 28, 2010.

21. Tim Wise, "The Last Gasp of Aging White Power: But Time Is Not on Your Side," AlterNet, Nov. 5, 2010.

22. Hua Hsu, "The End of White America?" Hsu quotes from Baldwin's "Down at the Cross," published in *The Fire Next Time* (NY: Dial Press, 1963).

23. Hua Hsu, "The End of White America?"

24. Ibid.

25. Mark J. Perry, "The Great Man-Cession of 2008–2009 Continues," *Carpe Diem*, June 5, 2009, mjperry.blogspot.com.

26. Jeffrey Passel, "A Portrait of Unauthorized Immigrants in the United States," Pew Hispanic Center, April 14, 2009, pewresearch.org.

27. Shankar Vedantam, "Report Points to Faster Recovery in Jobs for Immigrants," *Washington Post*, Oct. 30, 2010.

28. Ibid.

29. Passel, "Portrait of Unauthorized Immigrants."

30. David Paul Kuhn, "Revenge of the White Men," *Los Angeles Times*, March 22, 2010.

31. "Rightward, March," *New York Times*, Nov. 7, 2010.

32. Jon Cohen and Dan Balz, "Non-College Whites Gloomy About Economy," *Washington Post*, Feb. 22, 2011.

33. Kelefa Sanneh, "Beyond the Pale," *New Yorker*, April 12, 2010.

34. Ibid.

35. "What They're Saying About the 8/28 Rally," dailycaller.com, Aug. 29, 2010; Nathan Burchfiel, "Overwhelmingly White Media Criticize Conservative Rallies as 'Overwhelmingly White,'" newsbusters.org, Aug. 31, 2010.

36. Ibid.

37. Shelby Steele, "Yo, Howard! Why Did Dean Have to Embrace the Confederate Flag?" *Wall Street Journal*, Nov. 13, 2003.

38. Garance Franke-Ruta, "9/12: Race, the Tea Party Protesters and a Battle of Interpretations," *Washington Post*, Sept. 13, 2009.

39. Ibid.

40. "NAACP Delegates Unanimously Pass Tea Party Amendment," NAACP, July 13, 2010, naacp.org.

41. Conor Dougherty, "Nonwhites to Be Majority in U.S. by 2042," *Wall Street Journal*, Aug. 14, 2008; Emily Bazar and Paul Overberg, "Census Projects More Diversity in Workforce," *USA Today*, Aug. 14, 2008.

42. Sudeep Reddy, "Latinos Fuel Growth in Decade," *Wall Street Journal*, March 25, 2011, 2.

43. Ibid.

44. "Texas Demographer: 'It's Basically Over for Anglos,'" Texas Politics, Feb. 24, 2011.

45. Ibid.

46. Suzanne Gamboa, "Almost 1 of 2 Americans Was Latino," Yahoo! News, April 7, 2009; Juan Castillo, "Nearly Half of New Citizens Were Hispanic," Somos Austin, April 7, 2009, statesman.com.

47. Sabrina Tavernise, "Number of White Children Falling Fast," *New York Times*, Apr. 6, 2011, A14.

48. Roberts, "A Generation Away, Minorities May Become the Majority"; Hope Yen, "White Americans' Majority to End by Mid-Century," Associated Press, Dec. 16, 2009. google.com.

49. Michael Gerson, "The GOP's Harsh Immigration Stance Will Cost It," *Washington Post*, May 14, 2010, p. A17.

50. "Hispanics Now Majority in Texas Public Schools," AP, March 23, 2011.

51. "Hispanics, Asians," *Migration News*, September 1998, vol. 5, no. 9, migration.ucdavis.ed; Patrick J. Buchanan, "Who Voted for Clinton's Revolution?" July 1, 1997, buchanan.org.

52. Hua Hsu, "The End of White America?"; "President Clinton's Speech on Diversity," Portland State University, June 13, 1998, *Social Contract*, Summer 1998.

53. Susan Sontag, *Partisan Review*, Winter 1967, 57.

54. Arthur M. Schlesinger, Jr., *The Disuniting of America* (New York: W. W. Norton, 1992), 47–48.

55. Anthony Pagden, "Of Skulls and Buttocks," *The National Interest*, March/April 2010, 95.

56. Thomas Aquinas, *Summa Theologica*, translated by the Fathers of the English Dominican Province, Benziger Bros. ed., 1947. http://dhspriory.org/thomas/summa. Second Part, q. 27, a. 3.

57. Steve Sailer, "Demography Is Destiny, and Our Destiny (Courtesy of Immigration Policy) Is Disastrous," vdare.com, March 22, 2009.

58. Heather Mac Donald, "The Hispanic Family: The Case for National Action," *National Review*, April 14, 2008.

59. William Bennett, *The Index of Leading Cultural Indicators* (New York: Simon & Schuster, 1994), 48.

60. Ann Coulter, "Murder Spree by People Who Refuse to Ask for Directions," *Human Events*, Jan. 14, 2009.

61. Leila Darabi, "Despite Being Largely Illegal, Abortion in Mexico Is Far More Prevalent Than in the United States," News Release, Guttmacher Institute, Feb. 2, 2009.

62. Mac Donald, "The Hispanic Family."

63. Steve Sailer, "Diversity Is Strength! It's Also...2006's Demographic Death Spiral," vdare.com, Dec. 9, 2007.

64. Miriam Jordan, "Latino Aging Stumps Experts," *Wall Street Journal,* Oct. 16, 2010.

65. Ruy Teixeira, "Demographic Change and the Future of the Parties," Center for American Progress, June 2010, 8.

66. Patrick J. Buchanan, "Buenas Noches, America!" *American Cause,* Sept. 7, 2007.

67. John Fonte, "Dual Allegiance: A Challenge to Immigration Reform and Patriotic Assimilation," Center for Immigration Studies, November 2005, cis.org.

68. Ibid.

69. Buchanan, "Buenas Noches."

70. Ibid.

71. Schlesinger, *The Disuniting of America,* 16.

72. Mark Krikorian, "Mexico First?" *National Review,* Jan. 28, 2008.

73. Fonte, "Dual Allegiance," 14.

74. Steven A. Camarota, "Public Opinion in Mexico on U.S. Immigration," Backgrounder, Center for Immigration Studies, October 2009, 1.

75. Buchanan, "Buenas Noches."

76. Ibid.

77. Fonte, "Dual Allegiance."

78. Steven A. Camarota, "100 Million More: Projecting the Impact of Immigration on the U.S. Population, 2007–2060," Center for Immigration Studies, August 2007, 1.

79. Ewen MacAskill, "Mexico's Felipe Calderon Says Arizona Laws Breed Hate and Intolerance," *Guardian,* April 27, 2010.

80. "White House, Democrats Applaud Mexican President Slamming Arizona Law," foxnews.com, May 20, 2010.

81. Joel Gerstein, "DOJ Sues over Arizona Immigration Law," *Politico,* July 8, 2010.

82. Jon Dougherty, "Mexicans: Southwest U.S. Is Ours," WorldNetDaily, June 13, 2002.

83. "Between Two Worlds: How Young Latinos Come of Age in America," Pew Hispanic Center, Dec. 11, 2009, 22.

84. John Judis, "End State: Is California Finished?" *The New Republic,* Nov. 4, 2009, 16, 22.

85. Ibid.

86. Will Kane, "Latino Kids Now Majority in State's Public Schools," *San Francisco Chronicle,* Nov. 13, 2010.

87. Sailer, "Demography Is Destiny."

88. Michael R. Blood, "Californians Looking for the Exit," *Arizona Republic,* Feb. 1, 2009, 4.

89. "California Sales Tax Rate Increase," California Business Law Blog: Law Office of Jonas M. Grant, April 9, 2009.

90. Robert Samuelson, "California's Reckoning—and Ours," *Washington Post,* Aug. 2, 2009.

91. David Brooks, "Tom Joad Gave Up," *New York Times,* Sept. 28, 2010.

92. "Best and Worst States for Business in 2010," *Chief Executive,* May/June 2010.

93. Ibid.

94. Ibid.

95. "No Gold in State: Voters Reject a Ballot They Could Not Comprehend," *The Economist,* May 21, 2009.

96. Terry Jeffrey, "Government Killed California," cnsnews.com, Dec. 29, 2010.

97. Passel, "Portrait of Unauthorized Immigrants"; Sam Roberts, "Census Finds Rise in Foreign Workers," *New York Times,* Dec. 8, 2009.

98. Jack Martin and Eric A. Ruark, "The Fiscal Burden of Illegal Immigration on United States Taxpayers," Federation for American Immigration Reform, July 2010, fairus.org.

99. "Chicano Nationalism, Revanchism and the Aztlan Myth," Federation for American Immigration Reform, Jan. 2005, fairus.org; James Lubinskas, "Expressions of Ethnic Animosity," frontpagemagazine.com, Nov. 24, 1999.

100. Ibid.

101. Meredith May, "Hispanics Expected to be State's Majority by 2042," *San Francisco Chronicle,* July 10, 2007.

102. Sailer, "Demography Is Destiny."

103. Jennifer Smith Richards, "Reading Rate Dismal," *Columbus Dispatch,* Jan. 9, 2009.

104. Will Kane, "Latino Kids Now Majority in State's Public Schools," *San Francisco Chronicle,* Nov. 13, 2010.

105. Solomon Moore, "Hundreds Hurt in California Prison Riot," *New York Times,* Aug. 10, 2009.

106. Lee Baca, "In L.A., Race Kills," *Los Angeles Times,* June 12, 2008.

107. "Hate Crime Report 2008," Los Angeles County Commission on Human Relations, Nov. 2009, 19.

108. Erik Eckholm, "Gang Violence Grows on an Indian Reservation," *New York Times,* Dec. 14, 2009.

109. Ibid.

110. Jim Rutenberg, "Black Radio on Obama Is Left's Answer to Limbaugh," *New York Times,* July 27, 2008.

111. Ibid.

112. Jesse Washington, "Can Minority Journalists Resist Applauding Obama?" realclear politics.com, July 26, 2008.

113. "Aim of New UNITY Initiative Is More Diversity in Top Media Management," press release, UNITY: Journalists of Color, July 22, 2008, unityjournalists.org.

114. Ibid.

115. Ibid.

116. Amanda Carpenter, "'Diversity Czar' Takes Heat over Remarks," *Washington Times,* Sept. 23, 2009.

117. Ibid.

118. Ibid.

119. Ibid.

120. "House Apologizes for Slavery and Jim Crow: Resolution Does Not Mention Reparations, Commits to Rectifying Misdeed," AP, msnbc.msn.com, July 29, 2008.

121. Josephine Hearn, "Black Caucus: Whites Not Allowed," *Politico,* Jan. 22, 2007, dyn. politico.com.

122. Ben Pershing, "Tennessee Primary Gets Nasty," Capitol Briefing, *Washington Post,* Aug. 7, 2008; Darryl Fears, "Tennessee Defies Cliches on Race and Politics," *Washington Post,* Aug. 10, 2008.

123. Adam Nossiter, "Race Takes Central Role in a Memphis Primary," *New York Times,* Aug. 7, 2008.

124. Ibid.

125. "False Allegations of White Racism Are Widespread While Black Racism Is Tolerated: It's Time to End the Double Standard," *Lincoln Review,* vol. 13, no. 5, Sept.–Oct. 2009, 2.

126. Amos Maki, "Memphis Mayor Willie Herenton Forming Committee to Study Run for Congress," *Memphis Commercial-Appeal,* April 21, 2009.

127. Woody Baird, "White U.S. Rep. in Black Tenn. District Faces Fight," Associated Press, June 18, 2009, breitbart.com.

128. Robbie Brown, "Ex-Mayor of Memphis Starts Bid for Congress, Invoking Race in Campaign," *New York Times,* Sept. 14, 2009.

129. Ibid.; "False Allegations," *Lincoln Review.*

130. Hearn, "Black Caucus."

131. David Knowles, "John Lewis Switches to Obama," politicsdaily.com, Feb. 27, 2008; "Congressman John Lewis," Southern Freedom Fighter Museum, May 21, 2008, southernfreedomfighter.blogspot.com.

132. Michael Saul, "Geraldine Ferraro Resigns Clinton Post Amidst Furor over Obama Comments," *New York Daily News,* March 12, 2008.

133. Orlando Patterson, "The Red Phone in Black and White," *New York Times,* Mar. 11, 2008.

134. Mike Allen and Jonathan Martin, "Powell Endorses Obama," *Politico,* Oct. 19, 2008, dyn.politico.com; Lynn Sweet, "Colin Powell Endorses Barack Obama on NBC's 'Meet the Press.' Turned Off by McCain's Focus on Ayers," *Chicago Sun-Times,* Oct. 19, 2008.

135. Peter Wallsten, "Wall Divides Republican Party Factions," *Seattle Times,* June 3, 2007.

136. Sailer, "Diversity Is Strength!"

137. Charlie Savage, "Videos Shed New Light on Sotomayor's Positions," *New York Times,* June 11, 2009.

138. David D. Kirkpatrick, "Sotomayor's Focus on Race Issues May Be Hurdle," *New York Times,* May 30, 2009.

139. "The Franchise for Felons," *Washington Times,* May 29, 2009.

140. Charlie Savage, "A Judge's View of Judging Is on the Record," *New York Times,* May 15, 2009.

141. Ibid.

142. Edward A. Adams, "Race and Gender of Judges Make Enormous Differences in Rulings, Studies Find," *ABA Journal,* Feb. 6, 2010.

143. "Aloha, Segregation," *Wall Street Journal,* Dec. 17, 2009.

144. "Sen. Akaka on Native Hawaiian Government Reorganization Act," Feb. 23, 2010, allamericanpatriots.com

145. "Britain Nixes Iroquois Team's Passports," AP, *Washington Times,* July 15, 2010.

146. Paul Krugman, "The Town Hall Mob," *New York Times,* Aug. 6, 2009.

147. Ibid.

148. Mark Finkelstein, "Cynthia Tucker: 45–65% of Town-Hall Protesters Are Racists," NewsBusters.org, Aug. 7, 2009.

149. Susan Davis, "WSJ/NBC News Poll: Tea Party Tops Democrats and Republicans," *Wall Street Journal,* Dec. 16, 2009.

150. David Zinczenko, "Decline of the American Male," *USA Today,* June 17, 2009.

151. Edwin S. Rubenstein, "July Jobs: Americans Are the Biggest—and Only—Losers. Moratorium Now!" vdare.com, Aug. 6, 2010.

152. Edwin S. Rubenstein, "July Jobs: Displacement Returns with a Vengeance," vdare
     .com, Aug. 7, 2009.

5. Demographic Winter

1. John Feffer, "New Neighbors, New Economy," *Epoch Times,* Nov. 17, 2009; "A Migration Summit to Address Shrinking Birth Rates," huffingtonpost.com, Nov. 10, 2009.
2. Pierre Eugène Marcelin Berthelot, *Dictionary of Science Quotations,* quoted in R. Desper,
   The Human Side of Scientists, 1975.
3. Comprehensive Tables, *World Population Statistics: The 2008 Revision,* vol. 1 (New York:
   United Nations, 2009), 86, 142, 248, 390, 406, 476, 228, 306, 316, 162, 404, 84, 102, 48,
   62, 114, 166, 210, 264, 312, 368, 474.
4. Jack Goldstone, "The New Population Bomb: The Four Megatrends That Will
   Change the World," *Foreign Affairs,* Jan./Feb. 2010, 32–33.
5. Phillip Longman, "Think Again: Global Aging," *Foreign Policy,* November 2010, 54.
6. Edward Bernard Glick, "Who Will Be on Top at the End of the Century?" *American
   Thinker,* Dec. 27, 2010.
7. Comprehensive Tables, *World Population Statistics: The 2006 Revision,* vol. 1 (New York:
   United Nations, 2007), 5.
8. "Can Policies Boost Birth Rates?" policy brief, Organization for Economic Cooperation and Development, November 2007, 1.
9. Ibid., 2.
10. Ibid.
11. *World Population Statistics: The 2008 Revision,* 292.
12. Lisa Twaronit, "Japan's Low Birth Rate Poses Demographic Dilemma," MarketWatch,
    March 18, 2010.
13. Joel Kotkin, "The Kid Issue," forbes.com, Sept. 8, 2009.
14. Nicholas Eberstadt, "The Demographic Future: What Population Growth—and
    Decline—Means for the Global Economy," *Foreign Affairs,* Nov.–Dec. 2010, 61.
15. Frank Zeller, "Baby Shortage Is an Economic Time Bomb," *Vancouver Sun,* Dec. 29, 2010.
16. Blaine Harden, "For Young Japanese, U.S. Degrees Lose Lure," *Washington Post,* April
    11, 2010.
17. Hiroko Tabuchi, "China's Day Arriving Sooner than Japan Expected," *New York Times,*
    Oct. 2, 2009.
18. Ibid.
19. Ibid.
20. *World Population Statistics: The 2008 Revision,* 398.
21. Ibid.
22. "S. Korea Urges Lights Out to Boost Birthrate," AFP, Jan. 20, 2008, breitbart.com.
23. Goldstone, "The New Population Bomb," 34.
24. Longman, "Think Again," 55.
25. Zeller, "Baby Shortage Is an Economic Time Bomb."
26. Henry A. Kissinger, *Diplomacy* (New York: Simon & Schuster, 1994), 134.
27. Reiner Klingholz, "Europe's Real Demographic Challenge," *Policy Review,* Oct.–Nov.
    2009, 63.

28. Ibid.

29. Ibid., 66.

30. "Birth Control Pill Inventor Laments Demographic 'Catastrophe,'" catholicnewsagency .com, Jan. 11, 2009.

31. Russell Shorto, "No Babies," *New York Times Magazine,* June 29, 2008, 71.

32. Longman, "Think Again," 58.

33. *World Population Statistics: The 2008 Revision,* 480.

34. Cal Thomas, "Invasion by Immigration," Tribune Media Services, Aug. 12, 2009, calthomas.com.

35. Ibid.

36. Ibid.

37. Graeme Wilson, "White Britons a Minority by 2066," *The Sun,* Nov. 18, 2010; "White Britons a Minority by 2066," *The Independent,* Nov. 18, 2010, belfasttelegraph.co.uk.

38. Fouad Ajami, "Strangers in the Land," *New York Times Book Review,* Aug. 2, 2009, 7.

39. Ibid.

40. Tom Whitehead, "Labor Wanted Mass Immigration to Make UK More Multicultural, Says Former Adviser," *Telegraph,* Oct. 23, 2009.

41. Ibid.

42. Richard Kerbaj, "Muslin Population 'Rising 10 Times Faster Than Rest of Population,'" *London Times,* Jan. 30, 2009; "Hinduism in the United Kingdom" and "Black British," wikipedia.com.

43. Alexi Mostrous and Christine Seib, "Tide Turns as Poles End Great Migration," *Sunday Times,* Feb. 16, 2008.

44. Charles Krauthammer, "Never Again?" *Washington Post,* May 5, 2006.

45. Leon Cohen, "Jewish Pro-Life Activist Medved Says Children Are 'A Gift, Not a Choice,'" *Wisconsin Jewish Chronicle,* May 7, 2004, jewishchronicle.org.

46. Philip Roth, *The Counterlife* (New York: Farrar, Straus, 1986), 103.

47. Stephen Steinlight, "The Jewish Stake in America's Changing Demography: Reconsidering a Misguided Immigration Policy," Center for Immigration Studies, October 2001.

48. Ibid.

49. Isabel Kershner, "Some Israelis Question Benefits for Ultra-Religious," *New York Times,* Dec. 28, 2010.

50. "Shall the Religious Inherit the Earth?: Demography and Politics in the Twenty-first Century," Introduction, Eric Kaufmann, Belfer Center, Harvard University/Birkbeck College, University of London, p. 7.

51. John Mearsheimer, "Saving Israel from Itself," *American Conservative,* May 18, 2009.

52. Guy Lieberman, "Housing Minister: Spread of Arab Population Must Be Stopped," *haaretz.com,* Feb. 7, 2009.

53. Ibid.

54. Yair Lapid, "What Demographic Problem?" YNET, July 7, 2009, ynetnews.com.

55. Mearsheimer, "Saving Israel from Itself."

56. Rory McCarthy, "Olmert: Israel Must Hand Back Land for Peace with Palestinians and Syria," *Guardian,* Sept. 29, 2008.

57. John Lynn, "Ehud Barak Defies Benjamin Netanyahu on Threat to Israel," *The Australian,* Jan. 28, 2010.

58. John Mearsheimer, "Sinking Ship," *The American Conservative,* Aug. 2010, 11.

59. Alan Dershowitz, "Palestinians and the 'Right of Return,'" *Christian Science Monitor,* April 16, 2007.

60. Goldstone, "The New Population Bomb," 37.

61. *World Population Statistics: The 2008 Revision,* 406.

62. Casimir Dadak, "A New 'Cold War'?" *Independent Review,* Summer 2010, 95.

63. Martin Walker, "The World's New Numbers," *Wilson Quarterly,* Spring 2009.

64. Nicholas Eberstadt, "Drunken Nation: Russia's Depopulation Bomb," *World Affairs,* Spring 2009.

65. Ibid.

66. Ibid.

67. Richard Fairbanks and Paul Hewitt, "Demography vs. an Imperial Impulse," *Washington Times,* Sept. 17, 2008.

68. William Hawkins, "U.S. Need Not Decline," *Washington Times,* Dec. 4, 2008.

69. Bill Gertz, "Hayden Warns of Russian Unrest," *Washington Times,* May 1, 2008.

70. "Russia's Exploding Muslim Population," foreignpolicy.com, Jan. 16, 2007.

71. Clifford J. Levy, "Its Population Falling, Russia Beckons Its Children Home," *New York Times,* March 22, 2009.

72. "Rivalries of the Bear and Dragon," *Financial Times,* Oct. 15, 2009, 10.

73. Dadak, "A New 'Cold War'?" 95.

74. Kotkin, "The Kid Issue."

75. Feffer, "New Neighbors, New Economy."

76. Ibid.

77. Ibid.

78. Ariana Eunjung Cha, "In Aging China, a Change of Course," *Washington Post,* Dec. 12, 2009.

79. Ibid.

80. Peter Hitchens, "Gendercide: China's Shameful Massacre of Unborn Girls Means There Will Soon Be 30M More Men Than Women," *Daily Mail,* April 10, 2010, dailymail.co.uk.

81. Longman, "Think Again," 55.

82. Eberstadt, "Demographic Future," 57.

83. Cha, "In Aging China, a Change of Course."

84. "Taiwan Seeks Baby-Boosting Slogan," BBC News, March 16, 2010.

85. Edwin Mora, "NYT Environment Reporter Floats Idea: Give Carbon Credits to Couples That Limit Themselves to One Child," cnsnews.com, Oct. 19, 2009.

6. Equality vs. Freedom?

1. James Fenimore Cooper, *On the Disadvantages of a Monarchy,* wikiquote.org.

2. Will and Ariel Durant, *The Lessons of History* (New York: MJF Books, 1968), 20.

3. Murray Rothbard, "Egalitarianism as a Revolt Against Nature," *Modern Age,* Fall 1973, lewrockwell.com.

4. President Barack Obama, Inaugural Address, Jan. 20, 2009, abcnews.go.com.

5. Irving Kristol, "The Neoconservative Persuasion," *Weekly Standard,* Aug. 25, 2003.

6. Kevin Phillips, *The Cousins' War: Religion, Politics, Civil Warfare, and the Triumph of Anglo-America* (New York: Basic Books, 1999).

7. "An Excerpt of Query XIV from the Notes on the State of Virginia (1781)," *The Atlantic,* October 1996.

8. Thomas Jefferson, "Letter to John Adams, Oct. 28, 1813," The Founders Constitution, press-pubs.uchicago.edu/founders.

9. Thomas Jefferson, "Letter to Lafayette, Feb. 14, 1815," etext.virginia.edu.

10. Thomas Jefferson, *Autobiography,* 1821, etext.virginia.edu.

11. Bertrand Russell, famous-proverbs.com.

12. Willmoore Kendall, *Contra Mundum* (New York: Arlington House, 1971), 351–52.

13. Ibid., 352.

14. Roy P. Basler, ed., *The Collected Works of Abraham Lincoln,* vol. 3 (New Brunswick, NJ: Rutgers University Press, 1953), 145–46.

15. Roy P. Basler, ed., *The Collected Works of Abraham Lincoln,* vol. 2 (New Brunswick, NJ: Rutgers University Press, 1953), 255–56.

16. Ibid.

17. "Abraham Lincoln's Speech on the Dred Scott Decision," June 26, 1857, The Freeman Institute, freemaninstitute.com/lincoln.htm.

18. Roy P. Basler, ed., *The Collected Works of Abraham Lincoln,* vol. 5 (New Brunswick, NJ: Rutgers University Press, 1953), 388.

19. Kendall, *Contra Mundum,* 354.

20. Thomas E. Woods Jr. and Kevin Gutzman, "*Brown vs Board* vs the U.S. Constitution," vdare.com, July 25, 2008.

21. Ibid.

22. Ibid.

23. Martin Luther King, "I Have a Dream," Washington, D.C., Aug. 28, 1963, american rhetoric.com.

24. Ibid.

25. "Moving Toward a Genuinely Color-Blind Society," *Lincoln Review Letter Digest,* May–June 2009, 2.

26. Lyndon B. Johnson, "To Fulfill These Rights," Commencement Address at Howard University, June 4, 1965, lbjlib.utexas.edu.

27. Ibid.

28. Ibid.

29. Ibid.

30. William J. Quirk and Randall J. Bridwell, *Judicial Dictatorship* (New Brunswick: Transaction, 1995), 21.

31. James Fenimore Cooper, *On the Disadvantages of a Monarchy.*

32. Quirk and Bridwell, *Judicial Dictatorship,* 23.

33. Lyndon B. Johnson, "To Fulfill These Rights."

34. Rothbard, "Egalitarianism as a Revolt Against Nature."

35. Will and Ariel Durant, *Lessons of History,* 19.

36. Ibid., 19–20.

37. Ibid., 20.

38. Ibid.

39. Jude P. Dougherty, "Two Treatises on the Acquisition and Use of Power," *Modern Age,* Spring 2010, 110–11.

40. Pierre Thomas and Jason Ryan, "U.S. Prison Population Hits All-Time High: 2.3 Million Incarcerated," ABC News, June 6, 2008.

41. Duncan Williams, *Trousered Apes: Sick Literature in a Sick Society* (New Rochelle, NY: Arlington House, 1991), 131.

42. Lewis Carroll, *Alice's Adventures in Wonderland* (New York: Avenel Books, Crown Publishing), 33, 34.

43. Gillis J. Harp, "Are We All Ideologues Now?" *St. Croix Review,* Oct. 2010, 56.

44. Ibid.

45. Will and Ariel Durant, *Lessons of History,* 20.

46. W. E. B. DuBois, "The Talented Tenth," September 1903, teachingamericanhistory.org.

47. Sarah O'Connor, "Men Bear the Brunt of US Jobs Lost," *Financial Times,* April 19, 2009; Gabriella Boston, "Recession Slams Blue-Collar Workers," *Washington Times,* March 26, 2009; Mark J. Perry, "The Man-Cession Continues," *Carpe Diem,* March 9, 2009; Catherine Rampell, "As Layoffs Surge, Women May Pass Men in Job Force," *New York Times,* Feb. 6, 2009.

48. Rothbard, "Egalitarianism as a Revolt Against Nature."

49. Leo Congdon, *George Kennan: A Writing Life* (Wilmington, DE.: Intercollegiate Studies Institute, 2008), 145.

50. Ibid., 143.

51. Monica Gabriel, "Former Bush Solicitor General Ted Olson Files Suit Claiming Same-Sex Marriage Is Constitutional Right," cnsnews.com, June 23, 2009.

52. Thomas Jefferson, "A Bill for Proportioning Crimes and Punishments," 1778, Amendment VIII, The Founders Constitution, press-pubs.uchicago.edu/founders.

53. Charles Murray, *Real Education: Four Simple Truths for Bringing America's Schools Back to Reality* (New York: Crown Forum, 2008), 58.

54. Daniel Goleman, "Richard Hernnstein Dies; Backed Nature over Nurture," *New York Times,* Sept. 16, 1994.

55. Murray, *Real Education,* 60, 62, 66.

56. Heather Mac Donald, "Nation of Cowards?" *City Journal,* Feb. 19, 2009.

57. Sewell Chan, "The Highest Per-Pupil Spending in the U.S.," *New York Times,* May 24, 2007.

58. Stacy Teicher Kadaroo, "Graduation Rate for U.S. High Schoolers Falls for Second Straight Year," *Christian Science Monitor,* June 10, 2010.

59. Joel Schectman and Rachel Monahan, "Cuny's Got Math Problem: Report Shows Many Freshmen from City HS Fail at Basic Algebra," *New York Daily News,* Nov. 12, 2009.

60. Sharon Otterman and Robert Gebeloff, "Triumph Fades on Racial Gap in City Schools," *New York Times,* Aug. 15, 2010.

61. Meredith Kolodner, Rachel Monahan, and Adam Lisberg, "Just Who Is Cathie Black?" *New York Daily News,* Nov. 10, 2010.

62. Trip Gabriel, "Proficiency of Black Students Is Found to Be Far Lower Than Expected," *New York Times,* Nov. 9, 2010.

63. Ibid.

64. Ibid.

65. Robert Weissberg, *Bad Students, Not Bad Schools* (New Brunswick: Transaction Publishers, 2010), 7.

66. Ibid.

67. Sam Dillon, "Top Test Scores from Shanghai Stun Educators," *New York Times*, Dec. 7, 2010; Christine Armario, "'Wake-Up Call: U.S. Students Trail Global Leaders," AP, Dec. 7, 2010, msnbc.com.

68. Ibid.

69. Steve Sailer, "PISA Scores Show Demography Is Destiny in Education, Too—But Washington Doesn't Want You to Know," vdare.com, Dec.19, 2010.

70. Jason Richwine, "The Myth of Racial Disparities in Public School Funding," Backgrounder, Heritage Foundation, April 20, 2011, 1.

71. Weissberg, *Bad Students, Not Bad Schools*, vii.

72. Michelle Rhee, "New York Needs Its Best Teachers in the Classroom," *Wall Street Journal*, March 11, 2011.

73. Jonah Lehrer, "Why Rich Parents Don't Matter," *Wall Street Journal*, Jan. 22, 2011.

74. Justin Pope, "Transcript Shows Harvard Professor Arguing Differences Between Genders Play a Role in Science Careers," *Seattle Times*, Feb. 17, 2005; Patrick D. Healy and Sara Rimer, "Furor Lingers as Harvard Chief Gives Details of Talk on Women," *New York Times*, Feb. 18, 2005; Leonard Fein, "The 'Availability' of Aptitude," *Jewish Daily Forward*, Feb. 25, 2006.

75. Sam Dillon, "Harvard Chief Defends His Talk on Women," *New York Times*, Jan. 18, 2005; Marcella Bombardieri, "Summers' Remarks on Women Draw Fire," *Boston Globe*, Jan. 17, 2005; Christina Hoff Sommers and Sally Satel, "Where Were You on 1/14?" American Enterprise Institute, Aug. 14, 2005, aei.org.

76. Cahal Milmo, "Fury at DNA Pioneer's Theory: Africans Are Less Intelligent Than Westerners," *The Independent*, Oct. 17, 2007.

77. Ibid.

78. Charles Murray, *Human Accomplishment: The Pursuit of Excellence in the Arts and Sciences, 800 B.C. to 1950* (New York: Cox and Murray, 2003).

79. Charles Murray, "Intelligence and College," *National Affairs*, Fall 2009, 96.

80. Charles Murray, "The Inequality Taboo," *Commentary*, September 2005, bibleresearcher.com.

81. Williams, *Trousered Apes*, 139.

82. Samuel Francis, *Beautiful Losers: Essays on the Failure of American Conservatism* (Columbia, MO: University of Missouri Press, 1993), 209.

83. Alexis de Tocqueville, *Democracy in America*, translated by Henry Reeve, vol. 2 (New Rochelle, NY: Arlington House, 2003), 320–21.

84. Dougherty, "Two Treatises on the Acquisition and Use of Power."

85. Francis, *Beautiful Losers*, 209.

7. The Diversity Cult

1. Ann Coulter, "At the End of the Day, Diversity Has Jumped the Shark," *Human Events*, Nov. 18, 2009.

2. Peter Skerry, "Beyond Sushiology: Does Diversity Work?" Brookings Institution, Winter 2002.

3. "Brigadier General Pinckney to Head New Diversity Task Force," Army News Service, Dec. 3, 2007.

4. Ben Wattenberg, *The Good News Is the Bad News Is Wrong* (Washington, D.C.: AEI Press, 1984), 84.

5. John Derbyshire, "Ethnomasochism: The Musical," Cultural Caviar, Nov. 10, 2010, takimag.com.

6. Ibid.

7. Christopher Lydon, "Carter Defends All-White Areas: Says Government Shouldn't Try to End 'Ethnic Purity' of Some Neighborhoods," *New York Times,* April 6, 1976.

8. Ibid.

9. Dan Quayle, "Murphy Brown Speech," Commonwealth Club, San Francisco, May 19, 1992, commonwealthclub.org.

10. Peter Wood, *Diversity: The Invention of a Concept* (San Francisco: Encounter, 2003), 5.

11. Ibid., 5–6.

12. Ibid.

13. Ibid., 6.

14. John Derbyshire, *We Are Doomed: Reclaiming Conservative Pessimism* (New York: Crown Forum, 2009), 22.

15. Bill Clinton, "Transcript of Clinton's 1997 State of the Union—Jan. 21, 1997," cnn.com.

16. Steve Sailer, "The Michigan Mess: On Cognitive Dissonance About Quotas—and the Need for a Constitutional Amendment," vdare.com, June 29, 2003.

17. Wesley Clark, Amicus Brief to the United States Supreme Court, Feb. 19, 2003, Issue Briefs—Affirmative Action, Clark 04, texasforclark.com.

18. Wood, *Diversity,* 81.

19. Ben Franklin, "Letter to Peter Collinson," May 9, 1753, *The Writings of Benjamin Franklin, Philadelphia, 1726–1757,* historycarper.com; "Ben Franklin on 'Stupid, Swarthy Germans,'" dialoginternational.com.

20. John Jay, Federalist No. 2, "Concerning Dangers from Foreign Force and Influence," Oct. 31, 1787, *Independent Journal,* americanconservativedaily.com.

21. Ibid.

22. Peter Brimelow, *Alien Nation: Common Sense About America's Immigration Disaster* (New York: Random House, 1995), 76–77.

23. Ibid., 77.

24. Hua Hsu, "The End of White America?" *The Atlantic,* Jan.–Feb. 2009.

25. Skerry, "Beyond Sushiology."

26. Orlando Patterson, "Equality," *Democracy: A Journal of Ideas,* Winter 2009, 9, democracyjournal.org.

27. "Remarks as Prepared for Delivery by Attorney General Eric Holder at the Department of Justice African American History Month Program," Department of Justice, Feb. 18, 2008, doj.gov.

28. Orlando Patterson, "Race and Diversity in the Age of Obama," *New York Times,* Aug. 16, 2009.

29. Ibid.

30. Mireya Navarro, "National Parks Reach Out to Blacks Who Aren't Visiting," *New York Times,* Nov. 2, 2010.

31. Amanda Paulson, "Resegregation of American Schools Deepening," *Christian Science Monitor,* Jan. 25, 2008.

32. Ibid.

33. Bill Bishop, "An Election Story for Those Who Like to Watch," slate.com, Oct. 21, 2008.

34. Robert J. Samuelson, "Political Perils of a 'Big Sort,'" *Washington Post,* Aug. 6, 2008.

35. *The Autobiography of Malcolm X: As Told to Alex Haley* (New York: Ballantine, 1964), 348; Edward Banfield, *The Unheavenly City: The Nature and Future of Our Urban Crisis* (Boston: Little, Brown, 1970), 67; Patrick J. Buchanan, *Conservative Votes, Liberal Victories: Why the Right Has Failed* (New York: Quadrangle, 1975), 67.

36. Scott Stossel, "Subdivided We Fall," *New York Times,* May 18, 2008.

37. Ibid.

38. Rich Benjamin, *Searching for Whitopia: An Improbable Journey to the Heart of White America* (New York: Hyperion, 2009), p. 6.

39. Alan Ehrenhalt, "Like-Minded, Living Nearby," *Wall Street Journal,* April 22, 2008.

40. Jennifer Harper, "Immigration, Loss of Culture Worry Nations," *Washington Times,* Oct. 5, 2007.

41. David Gauvey Herbert, "Americans Divided Along Race, Class Lines," nationaljournal.com, Dec. 1, 2009.

42. U.S. Department of Justice, Bureau of Justice Statistics, *Criminal Victimization in the United States, Statistical Tables, 2007* (Washington, DC, 2010), Table 42.

43. Heather Mac Donald, "Nation of Cowards?" *City Journal,* Feb. 19, 2009.

44. Walter Williams, "Is Racial Profiling Racist?" townhall.com, Aug. 19, 2009.

45. "Racial Profiling of Taxi Passengers," My Fox New York, Dec. 8, 2010, myfoxny.com; Bryce Watkins, "Un-fare: New York Taxi Driver Rep Endorses Racial Profiling," *Atlanta Post,* Dec. 7, 2010.

46. Ibid.; Walter Williams, "Is Profiling Racist?" lewrockwell.com, Aug. 3, 2010.

47. "Jesse Jackson's Car Stolen in Detroit," *Chicago Sun-Times,* Sept. 4, 2010.

48. "Resegregation Now," *New York Times,* June 29, 2007.

49. "Black Sorority Protests 'Old South' Days," AP, *Montgomery Advertiser,* April 30, 2009.

50. Ibid.

51. Katherine Kington, "Kappa Alpha's 'Old South Week' Bans Confederate Uniforms," wtvm.com, April 23, 2010.

52. Skerry, "Beyond Sushiology."

53. Ryan O'Donnell, "The Corporate Diversity Scam," frontpagemagazine.com, Jan. 27, 2003.

54. Barbara Barrett, "Black Farmers to Share in Settlement," *Washington Post,* Dec. 12, 2010.

55. "Federal Government Offers Payouts to Hispanic, Female Farmers," aberdeennews.com, May 13, 2011; Mary Clare Jalonick, "USDA Offers Settlements to Women, Hispanic Farmers," washingtonpost.com, Feb. 25, 2011.

56. Ibid.

57. Derbyshire, *We Are Doomed,* 23.

58. Fay Hansen, "Diversity's Business Case Doesn't Add Up," workforce.com, April 2003.

59. Hans Bader, "Diversity Training Backfires," openmarket.org, Dec. 26, 2007.

60. Roland S. Martin, "Commentary: Obama's Press Office Needs Diversity," cnnpolitics .com, Feb. 4, 2009.

61. "Blacks Equaled or Exceeded Their Relevant Civilian Labor Force Representation in 17 of 18 Executive Departments [and]...All 24 Independent Agencies," FY 2008 FEORP, U.S. Office of Personnel Management.

62. Danielle Douglas, "Winding Down Fannie and Freddie Could Put Minority Careers at Risk," *Washington Post*, Feb. 22, 2011; Chris Isidore, "Fannie, Freddie Bailout: $153 Billion...and Counting," cnnmoney.com, Feb. 11, 2011.

63. Richard Slimbach, "The Transcultural Journey," *Frontiers: The Interdisciplinary Journal of Study Abroad*, vol. 11, 2005.

64. Richard Garnett, "The Minority Court," *Wall Street Journal*, April 17, 2010.

65. Noah Feldman, "The Triumphant Decline of the WASP," *New York Times*, June 27, 2010.

66. Ibid.

67. James A. Barnes, "Obama's Team: The Face of Diversity," *National Journal*, June 20, 2009.

68. Daniel de Vise, "Naval Academy Professor Challenges Rising Diversity," *Washington Post*, July 3, 2009.

69. Ibid.

70. Bruce Fleming, "The Cost of a Diverse Naval Academy," *The Capital*, June 14, 2009, hometownannapolis.com.

71. Ibid.

72. Daniel de Vise, "Naval Academy Defends Move to Adjust Image on National TV," *Washington Post*, Nov. 11, 2009.

73. Fleming, "The Cost of a Diverse Naval Academy."

74. De Vise, "Naval Academy Defends Move."

75. Admiral Gary Roughead, USN, "Shaping the Navy," interview by Gina DiNicolo, *Military Officer*, October 2009, 73.

76. De Vise, "Naval Academy Professor Challenges Rising Diversity."

77. Fleming, "The Cost of a Diverse Naval Academy."

78. "High Seas Segregation: The Navy Is Listing Dangerously in Politically Correct Waters," *Washington Times*, July 30, 2010.

79. Ron K. Unz, "Some Minorities Are More Minor Than Others," *Wall Street Journal*, Nov. 16, 1998, onenation.org.

80. "Record Retrospective: Obama on Affirmative Action," *Harvard Law Record*, Oct. 30, 2008; *Harvard Law Record*, vol. 91, no. 7, Nov. 16, 1990.

81. Unz, "Some Minorities Are More Minor Than Others."

82. Patrick J. Buchanan, "Our Self-Selecting Elite," Jan. 1, 1999, buchanan.org.

83. Russell K. Nieli, "How Diversity Punishes Asians, Poor Whites and Lots of Others," mindingthecampus.com, July 12, 2010.

84. Ibid.

85. Ibid.

86. Ibid.

87. James Webb, "Diversity and the Myth of White Privilege," *Wall Street Journal*, July 23, 2010.

88. "Harvard Tries to Diversify Portraits on Campus," whdh.com, Nov. 7, 2010.

89. Alexis de Tocqueville, *Democracy in America,* trans. Henry Reeve, vol. 2 (New Rochelle, NY: Arlington House), 114.

90. Ibid., p. 115.

91. Jason Richwine, "A Smart Solution to the Diversity Dilemma," *The American,* Aug. 12, 2009.

92. Ibid.

93. Ibid.

94. John Leo, "Bowling with Our Own," *City Journal,* June 25, 2007.

95. John Lloyd, "Study Paints Bleak Picture of Ethnic Diversity," *Financial Times,* Oct. 8, 2006.

96. Ibid.

97. Leo, "Bowling with Our Own."

98. Ibid.

99. Eduardo Porter, "Race and the Social Contract," *New York Times,* March 31, 2009.

100. Ibid.

101. Ibid.

102. Skerry, "Beyond Sushiology."

103. Ibid.

104. Schlesinger, 10.

105. Richwine, "A Smart Solution to the Diversity Dilemma."

106. Ibid.

107. Paul Gottfried, "Multiculturalist International," *Orbis,* 2002, fpri.org/orbis.

108. Samuel Francis, "The Other Face of Multiculturalism," *Chronicles,* April 1998.

109. Ibid.

110. H. A. Scott Trask, "The Whale in Times Square," *Chronicles,* May 2011, 30.

111. Ibid.

112. Nick Allen, "Fort Hood Gunman Had Told U.S. Military Colleagues That Infidels Should Have Their Throats Cut," *Telegraph,* Nov. 8, 2009.

113. Dorothy Rabinowitz, "Dr. Phil and the Fort Hood Killer," *Wall Street Journal,* Nov. 10, 2008.

114. Bryan Bender, "Ft. Hood Suspect Was Army Dilemma: His Extreme Views Possibly Overlooked in Favor of Diversity," *Boston Globe,* Feb. 22, 2010.

115. Peter Baker and Clifford Krauss, "President, at Service, Hails Fort Hood's Fallen," *New York Times,* Nov. 11, 2009.

116. Radio Derb, Transcript, Nov. 13, 2009, johnderbyshire.com.

117. "Police: Gunman in Binghamton, N.Y., Immigration Center Massacre Was a Coward," foxnews.com, April 4, 2009.

118. Michael Vlahos, *Fighting Identity: Sacred War and World Change* (Westport, CT.: Praeger Security International, 2009), 34–35.

119. Rabinowitz, "Dr. Phil and the Fort Hood Killer."

8. The Triumph of Tribalism

1. "Remarks by the President at the Acceptance of the Nobel Peace Prize," Dec. 10, 2009, whitehouse.gov.

2. Christopher Meyer, "A Return to 1815 Is the Way Forward for Europe," *London Times*, Sept. 2, 2008.

3. Arthur Schlesinger Jr., *The Disuniting of America*, 10.

4. Nathan Gardels, "Two Concepts of Nationalism: An Interview with Isaiah Berlin," *New York Review of Books*, Nov. 21, 1991.

5. Jerry Z. Muller, "Us and Them: The Enduring Power of Ethnic Nationalism," *Foreign Affairs*, March–April 2008.

6. Ibid., 19.

7. Ibid., 28.

8. Ibid., 19–20, 18.

9. Daniel Patrick Moynihan, *Pandaemonium: Ethnicity in International Politics* (London: Oxford University Press, 1994), 10.

10. Ibid., 11.

11. Lord Byron, "The Isles of Greece," *The Oxford Book of English Verse*, Sir Arthur Quiller-Couch, ed. (New York: Oxford University Press, 1955), 708.

12. Jasper Ridley, *Mussolini: A Biography* (New York: St. Martin's Press, 1997), 66.

13. Roy Denman, *Missed Chances: Britain and Europe in the Twentieth Century* (London: Indigo, 1997), 30; Ralph Raico, "World War I: The Turning Point," in *The Costs of War: America's Pyrrhic Victories*, John Denson, ed. (New Brunswick, NJ; Transaction, 1999), 240.

14. Moynihan, *Pandaemonium*, 83.

15. Wenzel Jaksch, *Europe's Road to Potsdam* (New York: Praeger, 1963), 276–77.

16. H. G. Wells, *The Outline of History*, vol. 2 (Garden City, NY: Doubleday, 1971), 795.

17. Ibid.

18. Ibid., 793.

19. Benjamin Disraeli, *The Oxford Dictionary of Quotations*, rev. ed. (New York: Oxford University Press, 1966), 182.

20. Thomas Cahill, *How the Irish Saved Civilization* (New York: Doubleday, 1995), 6.

21. Sean Clarke, "Am I a Horse," *Guardian*, March 17, 2008.

22. Anthony Pagdon, "Of Skulls and Buttocks," *National Interest*, March/April 2010, 90.

23. James K. Robinson and Walter B. Rideout, eds., *A College Book of Modern Verse* (Evanston, IL: Row, Peterson, 1960), 62–63.

24. Ibid., 65.

25. Albert Einstein, thinkexist.com.

26. Andrew Roberts, *Eminent Churchillians* (New York: Simon & Schuster, 1994), 211.

27. Ilya Ehrenburg, "Vojna (Moscow: 1942–43)," wikipedia.org; Alfred-Maurice de Zayas, *The German Expellees: Victims in War and Peace* (New York: St. Martin's Press, 1986), 34.

28. Jonathan Yardley, "A Distinguished Philosopher Asks If Killing Innocents Is Ever Justifiable," *Book World, Washington Post*, April 9, 2006.

29. Ho Chi Minh, thinkexist.com.

30. Meyer, "A Return to 1815."

31. Clifford J. Levy, "President of Ingushetia Is Wounded in Suicide Bombing," *New York Times*, June 23, 2009.

32. "Opposition Activist Shot Dead in Ingushetia," *Guardian*, Oct. 25, 2009.

33. Charles Clover, "Changing Face of Terror in Russia," *Financial Times*, Apr. 3–4, 2010, 2.

34. "Suicide Bomber Kills 16 in North Caucasus," *Washington Post*, Sept. 10, 2010.

35. Leon Aron, "Vladimir Putin Charts His Return," *Washington Post,* Oct. 16, 2010.

36. "Islamist Rebel Urges 'Total War' with Russia," AFP, Breitbart.Com March 3, 2011.

37. Shaun Walker, "Russians Name Muslim Convert as Prime Suspect for Airport Bombing," *Independent,* Jan. 28, 2011.

38. Elena Milashina, "The Roots of Moscow's Chechen Problem," *Wall Street Journal,* Feb. 2, 2011.

39. Charles King and Rajan Menon, "Prisoners of the Caucasus: Russia's Invisible Civil War," *Foreign Affairs,* July/Aug. 2010, 22.

40. Ibid.

41. Ellen Barry, "Russian Protests Erupt over Soccer Fan's Killing," *New York Times,* Dec. 13, 2010; Charles Clover, "Racists Battle Riot Police in Moscow Streets," *Financial Times,* Dec. 14, 2010.

42. Ibid.

43. Gregory L. White, "Russia Vows Action After Riots," *Wall Street Journal,* Dec. 14, 2010.

44. Charles Clover, "'Managed Nationalism' Turns Nasty for Putin," *Financial Times,* Dec. 24, 2010.

45. Kadyr Toktogulov and Alan Cullison, "Ethnic Clashes Rekindle Kyrgyz Strife," *Wall Street Journal,* June 12, 2010.

46. Sarah Lyall, "Rule, Britannia, But Maybe Not over Scotland," *New York Times,* July 18, 2008.

47. Victor Mallet, "Catalonia Pays Homage to Independence," *Financial Times,* Oct. 7, 2009.

48. "Catalans Turn Out for Greater Autonomy," *Washington Post,* July 11, 2010.

49. Alessandra Galloni, "An Italian Fringe Firebrand Gains Votes, Power in Crisis," *Wall Street Journal,* Dec. 13, 2010.

50. "Europe's Backlash Against Immigrants," *Financial Times,* April 5, 2010.

51. Ibid.

52. Tony Paterson, "Far-Right Leader Claims He Is 'Real Victor' in Austria," *Independent,* Sept. 30, 2008.

53. James Blitz, "Five European States Back Burka Ban," *Financial Times,* March 1, 2010; James Blitz, "FT Poll Shows Support for Burka Ban," *Financial Times,* March 2, 2010.

54. "Hungarian Demons," *Financial Times,* April 12, 2010.

55. Charles Kupchan, "The European Union, Going Its Separate Ways," *Washington Post,* Aug. 29, 2010.

56. John F. Burns, "Rightist on BBC Panel Draws Protests and Viewers," *New York Times,* Oct. 24, 2009.

57. "Court Ruling Puts Future of Belgian Far-Right Party in Doubt," *International Herald Tribune,* April 23, 2004, hartford-hwp.com.

58. Burns, "Rightist on BBC Panel Draws Protests and Viewers."

59. Diana West, "Free Susanne Winter," April 3, 2008, dianawest.net.

60. Paul Belien, "Appeasing the Islamists: Geert Wilders's Ordeal and the Lessons of the Past," *Washington Times,* March 26, 2008.

61. "Dutch Election: Liberals Take One-Seat Lead As Far-Right Party Gains in Influence," *Telegraph,* June 10, 2010.

62. Ben Berkowitz, "Muslim Cleric Calls for Beheading of Dutch Politician," Reuters, Sept. 3, 2010, news.yahoo.com.

63. Steve Erlanger, "Racial Tinge Stains World Cup Exit in France," *New York Times,* June 23, 2010.

64. Ibid.

65. Ben Hall, "Sarkozy Comes Out Fighting After Rampage in Grenoble," *Financial Times,* Aug. 14–15, 2010.

66. Stanley Pignal and Peggy Hollinger, "Sarkozy Rages at EU 'Humiliation,'" *Financial Times,* Sept. 16, 2010; Ben Hall and Peggy Hollinger, "Divisive and Defiant," *Financial Times,* Sept. 18–19, 2010.

67. "Marine Le Pen Poll Rating Shock for French Politics," BBC News, March 6, 2011.

68. Anthony Faiola, "Italy Closes the Door on Gypsies," *Washington Post,* Oct. 11, 2010.

69. Anthony Faiola, "Official's Views on Muslim Immigration Divide Germans," *Washington Post,* Sept. 10, 2010.

70. Nicholas Kulish, "Long Dormant, Ethnic Pride Blinks and Stirs," *New York Times,* Sept. 11, 2010.

71. Ibid.

72. "Merkel Says German Multicultural Society Has Failed," BBC News, Oct. 16, 2010, bbc.co.uk.

73. Matt Falloon, "Multiculturalism Has Failed in Britain—Cameron," Reuters, Feb. 5, 2011.

74. "Greece Follows U.S. Example by Building Giant Border Wall to Keep Out Illegal Immigrants," *Daily Mail,* Jan. 4, 2011.

75. Michael Kimmelman, "With Flemish Nationalism on the Rise, Belgium Teeters on the Edge," *New York Times,* Aug. 4, 2008.

76. Muller, "Us and Them," 19.

77. Bret Stephens, "Europe Needs a Tea Party," *Wall Street Journal,* Dec. 13, 2010.

78. Carl Gershman, "China's Invisible Atrocity: Who Will Stand Up for Uighur Rights?" *Washington Post,* July 5, 2010.

79. Edward Wong, "China's Money and Migrants Pour into Tibet," *New York Times,* July 28, 2010.

80. Michael Wines, "On a Day for Chinese Pride, Little Interest in Ideology," *New York Times,* Oct. 1, 2009.

81. Ibid.

82. Ibid.

83. Akash Kapur, "Growing Yes, but India Has Reasons to Worry," *New York Times,* Nov. 29, 2009.

84. Krishna Pokharel, "Maoist Rebels Ambush Indian Troops, Kill 76," *Wall Street Journal,* Apr. 7, 2010.

85. "India Is 'Losing Maoist Battle,'" BBC News, Sept. 15, 2009, newsvote.bbc.co.uk.

86. Thomas Fuller, "Fleeing Battle, Myanmar Refugees Head to China," *New York Times,* Aug. 29, 2009; Michael Wines, "China Fails to Prevent Myanmar's Ethnic Clashes," *New York Times,* Sept. 4, 2009.

87. Tim Johnston, "Renegade Soldiers Seize Burma Town," *Financial Times,* Nov. 9, 2010.

88. Cassie Fleming, "Thailand: Ethnic Violence Spreads: Muslims, Buddhists Fight in South," *Washington Times,* July 24, 2009.

89. Seth Mydans, "Churches Attacked Amid Furor in Malaysia," *New York Times,* Jan. 11, 2010.

90. Ibid.

91. Norimitsu Onishi, "In Philippine Strife, Uprooting Is a Constant," *New York Times,* Nov. 23, 2009.

92. Pia Lee Brago, "UN, EU, US Condemn Maguindanao Massacre," *Philippine Star,* Nov. 26, 2009.

93. Jim Gomez, "At Least 21 Killed in Attack on Journalists and Supporters of Philippine Politician," *Washington Post,* Nov. 24, 2009.

94. "Remarks by the President at the Acceptance of the Nobel Peace Prize, Dec. 10, 2009," whitehouse.gov.

95. Meyer, "A Return to 1815."

96. Ishaan Tharoor, "Pakistan's Other Problem Area: Baluchistan," *Time,* Nov. 1, 2009.

97. "Barzani Says Kurdistan Nation Should Have Its Own State—Paper," Aswat al-Iraq, July 16, 2010, en.aswataliraq.info.

98. Pamela Constable, "In Afghanistan, Shifting Political Fortunes," *Washington Post,* Dec. 24, 2010.

99. Ibid.

100. Jeffrey Gettleman, "Violence Grips Southern Sudan as Vote on Independence Nears," *New York Times,* Dec. 12, 2009.

101. Hamza Hendawi, "Sudanese Split May Set Risky Precedent," *Washington Times,* Jan. 24, 2011.

102. Laura Kasinof, "Yemen Used Lethal Force to Quell Southern Secession Protests, Says Report," *Christian Science Monitor,* Dec. 15, 2009.

103. Moynihan, *Pandaemonium,* 11.

104. "Gadaffi Tells Palestinians: Revolt Against Israel," Reuters, Feb. 13, 2011.

105. "Survey: Arabs to Form Majority in Historic Palestine After 2014," Agence France Presse, *Daily Star,* Dec. 31, 2010.

106. Spencer Ackerman, "So About Israel," *American Prospect,* Oct. 1, 2006.

107. Peter Beinert, "The Failure of the American Jewish Establishment," *New York Review of Books,* June 10, 2010.

108. Glenn Kessler, "'Jewish State' Concept Could Pose Another Hurdle in Peace Deal," *Washington Post,* Oct. 3, 2010.

109. Martin Arostegui, "Vote Reflects Racial Divide," *Washington Times,* Jan. 27, 2009.

110. "A Passport to Utopia: Evo Morales Campaigns for a Great Leap Forward. Or Back, Say Some," *Economist,* Jan. 24, 2009.

111. Arostegui, "Vote Reflects Racial Divide."

112. Joshua Partlow, "Bolivian Referendum Points Up Clashing Visions," *Washington Post,* Aug. 6, 2008.

113. Ibid.

114. John Zmirak, "Should We Tolerate Intolerance?" insidecatholic.com, Aug. 11, 2010, catholicity.com.

115. Amy Chua, *World on Fire: How Exporting Free Market Democracy Breeds Ethnic Hatred and Global Instability* (New York: Doubleday, 2003), 6; "Albion's Seedlings," March 14, 2006, anglosphere.com.

116. Amy Chua, "A World on the Edge," foster.20megsfree.com; Emily Eakin, "On the Dark Side of Democracy," *New York Times,* Jan. 31, 2004.

117. Chua, *World on Fire,* 136.

118. Ibid., 270.

119. Thomas Fuller, "Malaysia to End Quotas That Favor Ethnic Malays," *New York Times*, July 1, 2009.

120. Chua, *World on Fire*, 112.

121. Joshua Hammer, "(Almost) Out of Africa: The White Tribes," *World Affairs*, May/June 2010, 38.

122. "Zuma Must Bury Terre'Blanche," *Financial Times*, April 7, 2010.

123. Ibid.; Chris Makhaye and Terna Gyuse, "White Supremacist's Death Highlights Post-Apartheid Tensions," *The Final Call*, April 12, 2010.

124. Dan McDougall, "Jacob Zuma Warns ANC to Halt Racial Anger," *Sunday Times*, April 11, 2010.

125. Robert Guest, "The World's Most Extreme Affirmative Action Program," WSJ Opinion Archives, Dec. 26, 2004.

126. Simon Wood, "Race Against Time," *The Observer*, Jan. 22, 2006.

127. Frank Salter, "The Misguided Advocates of Open Borders," Quadrant Online, June 2010, quadrant.org.au.

128. Ying Lowrey, "Race/Ethnicity and Establishment Dynamics, 2002–2006," Office of Advocacy, Small Business Administration, census.gov/econ/sbo/02/asiansof_korean,html.

129. "Black Korea," Ice Cube lyrics, azlyrics.com.

130. "Andrew Young Resigns from Wal-Mart Group," AP, Aug. 18, 2006, msnbc.msn.com.

131. R. Asmerom, "Why Do Koreans Own the Black Beauty Supply Business?" *Atlanta Post*, Sept. 27, 2010.

132. Chua, *World on Fire*, 142.

133. Simon Romero, "Dueling Beauty Pageants Put Income Gap on View," *New York Times*, Dec. 1, 2010.

134. Ibid.

135. Jonathan Wheatley, "Brazil's Leader Blames White People for Crisis," *Financial Times*, March 27, 2009; Gary Duffy, "Brazil's Lula Raps 'White' Crisis," BBC News, March 27, 2009.

136. Orlando Patterson, "Jamaica's Bloody Democracy," *New York Times*, May 29, 2010.

137. Ibid.

138. Andrew Higgins, "As China Finds Bigger Place in World Affairs, Its Wealth Breeds Hostility," *Washington Post*, Sept. 8, 2010.

139. Ibid.

140. Chua, *World on Fire*, 143.

141. "Interview with Dmitry Rogozin," *Russia Today*, Nov. 18, 2008.

142. Aleksandr Solzhenitsyn, Nobel Lecture, 1970, nobelprize.org.

143. Muller, "Us and Them," 18.

9. "The White Party"

1. Soledad O'Brien, CNN Transcripts, Nov. 4, 2008.

2. CNN Transcripts, Nov. 4, 2008.

3. "Howard Dean Shares Plan to Unite Dems," interview by Michel Martin, NPR, Aug. 15, 2008.

4. Bruce Bartlett, *Wrong on Race: The Democratic Party's Buried Past* (New York: Palgrave Macmillan, 2008), 55.

5. Ibid., 57–58.

6. Adam Liptak, "Stevens, the Only Protestant on the Supreme Court," *New York Times,* April 9, 2010.

7. Greg Garrison, "1921 Slaying of Catholic Priest Gets Renewed Interest," Religion New Service, May 27, 2010, religionnews.com; Bartlett, *Wrong on Race,* 120–21.

8. Bartlett, *Wrong on Race.*

9. Robert George, "Back in Black," *National Review,* July 12, 2000.

10. Richard Nixon, "Statement on Signing the Voting Rights Act Amendments of 1970, June 22, 1970," John T. Woolley and Gerhard Peters, The American Presidency Project, presidency.ucsb.edu.

11. Zoltan Hajinal, "The GOP's Racial Challenge," *New York Times,* Nov. 10, 2010.

12. Amy Chozick and Laura Meckler, "Race Re-Enters the Spotlight As Candidates Turn Negative," *Wall Street Journal,* Aug. 6, 2008.

13. Kelefa Sanneh, "Beyond the Pale: Is White the New Black?" *New Yorker,* Apr. 12, 2010.

14. Norman Podhoretz, "Why Are Jews Liberal?" *Wall Street Journal,* Sept. 10, 2009.

15. Chuck Todd and Sheldon Gawiser, *How Barack Obama Won: A State-by-State Guide to the Historic 2008 Election* (New York: Vintage Books, 2009), 31.

16. Thomas Edsall, "For the Modern GOP, It's a Return to the 'White Voter Strategy,'" HuffingtonPost.com, Aug. 4, 2009.

17. Bill Greener, "My GOP: Too Old, Too White to Win," salon.com, July 20, 2009.

18. Ibid.

19. Ron Brownstein, "Obama's White-Out," *National Journal,* Jan. 20, 2010.

20. Michael Moore, "17 Reasons Not to Slit Your Wrists," *Mike's Letter,* Nov. 5, 2004, michaelmoore.com.

21. Frank Rich, "The Pit Bull in the China Shop," *New York Times,* Nov. 22, 2009.

22. Ruy Teixeira, "Demographic Change and the Future of the Parties," Center for American Progress, June 2010.

23. "Rightward March," *New York Times,* Nov. 7, 2010.

24. Campbell Robertson, "White Democrats Lose More Ground in South," *New York Times,* Nov. 7, 2010.

25. Ben Evans, "White Southern Democrats Nearly Wiped Out After Mid-term Elections," AP, Nov. 5, 2010, ljworld.com.

26. Ronald Brownstein, "White Flight," *National Journal,* Jan. 7, 2011.

27. Ibid.

28. Ronald Brownstein, "Dems Find Electoral Safety Behind a Wall of Blue," *National Journal,* Jan. 17, 2009, rbrownstein@nationaljournal.com.

29. Jeff Jacoby, "Cradle of Democracy?" *Boston Globe,* March 18, 2009, jeffjacoby.com.

30. Cathleen Decker, "For the GOP, California Is a Deep Blue Hole," *Los Angeles Times,* Nov. 19, 2010.

31. Michael Blood, "California Avoids GOP Wave," *Washington Times,* Dec. 1, 2010.

32. Ronald Brownstein, "The March of Diversity," *National Journal,* Dec. 19, 2009.

33. Teixeira, "Demographic Change and the Future of Parties," 9.

34. Adam Nagourney, "Orange County Is No Longer Nixon Country," *New York Times,* Aug. 30, 2010.

35. Gustavo Arellano, "Loretta Sanchez on Univision: 'Vietnamese' Trying to Take Her Congressional Seat Away from Democrats," Sept. 20, 2010, blogs.ocweekly.com.

36. Nagourney, "Orange County Is No Longer Nixon Country."

37. John C. Calhoun, *Disquisition on Government,* The Online Library of Liberty, oll.liberty fund.org.

38. Ibid.

39. Sara Murray, "Obstacle to Deficit Cutting: A Nation on Entitlements," *Wall Street Journal,* Sept. 15, 2010.

40. Ibid.

41. James Bovard, "The Food-Stamp Crime Wave," *Wall Street Journal,* June 23, 2011, A17.

42. "U.S. Vote Rate Dips in '08, Older Whites Sit Out," *USA Today,* July 20, 2009.

43. Frank Rich, "She Broke the G.O.P., and Now She Owns It," *New York Times,* July 11, 2009.

44. Ibid.

45. Katharine O. Seelye and Jeff Zeleny, "On the Defensive, Obama Calls His Words Ill-Chosen," *New York Times,* April 13, 2008.

46. Mike Allen, "Bill Clinton: Right Wing Is Weaker," *Politico,* Sept. 27, 2009.

47. Richard Benedetto, "GOP: We Were Wrong to Play Racial Politics," *USA Today,* July 14, 2005.

48. Ben Wattenberg, "Winner for the Harshest Political Rhetoric of the Year," *Jewish World Review,* Aug. 3, 2001.

49. Kathy Kiely and Jill Lawrence, "Clinton Makes Case for Wide Appeal," *USA Today,* May 7, 2008.

50. Joan Walsh, "The Brazile-Begala Smackdown," salon.com, May 7, 2008.

51. Frank Rich. "She Broke the G.O.P."

52. Jacob Weisberg, "The Lou Dobbs Democrats: Say Hello to the New Economic Nationalists," slate.com, Nov. 8, 2006.

53. Todd and Gawiser, *How Barack Obama Won,* 39.

54. Karl Vick and Ashley Surdin, "Most of California's Black Voters Backed Gay Marriage Ban," *Washington Post,* Nov. 6, 2008.

55. "Teaching the Bible," CBS News Poll, April 16, 2006, cbsnews.com.

56. "Religion a Strength and Weakness for Both Parties: Public Divides on Origin of Life," PEW Forum on Religion & Public Life: Summary of Findings, Aug. 30, 2005, people-press.org.

57. Ibid.

58. Scott Keeter, "On Darwin's 200th Birthday, Americans Still Divided About Evolution," Pew Research Center Publications, Feb. 5, 2009, pewresearch.org.

59. "Religion a Strength and Weakness."

60. Anthony York, "The GOP's Latino Strategy," salon.com, Jan. 13, 2000.

61. Justin Ewers, "Republicans and Latino Voters: Has the GOP Shifted on Immigration Reform?" *U.S. News & World Report,* Jan. 30, 2009; "Meet the Press Transcript for Nov. 9, 2008," msnbc.msn.com.

62. "87% Say English Should Be U.S. Official Language," Rasmussen Reports, May 11, 2010, rasmussenreports.com.

63. "Poll Shows Support for Official English at New High," Zogby International, U.S. Newswire, March 21, 2006; Edward Rothstein, "In the U.S. and Europe, Tensions Between a National and Minority Languages," *New York Times,* May 29, 2006.

64. "77% Oppose Driver's Licenses for Undocumented Immigrants," Rasmussen Reports, Nov. 6, 2007, rasmussenreports.com; Bonnie Erbe, "Poll: Immigration Amnesty Is Unpopular Outside the Beltway, Pols Remain Clueless," *U.S. News & World Report,* April 16, 2009.

65. N. C. Aizenman, "Economy, Not Immigration, a Main Worry of Hispanics," *Washington Post,* Jan. 16, 2010.

66. "April 2006 Field Poll (Blacks Sampled)," Public Opinion Polls, numbersusa.com.

67. "Mass Migration vs. Black Americans," numbersusa.com.

68. Ralph Z. Hallow, "Steele: GOP Needs 'Hip-Hop' Makeover," *Washington Times,* Feb. 19, 2009.

69. "The 14th Biannual Youth Survey on Politics and Public Service," Institute of Politics, Harvard University, Spring 2008, 12.

70. "Executive Summary: The 14th Biannual Youth Survey on Politics and Public Service," Institute of Politics, Harvard University, April 2008.

71. Philip Rucker, "As Fla. Tea Party's Rubio Surges, Crist and Meek Turn Firepower on Each Other," *Washington Post,* Oct. 1, 2010.

72. "Carol Moseley Braun: Clinton Endorsement of Rahm 'A Betrayal,'" huffingtonpost.com Jan. 19, 2011.

73. "Danny Davis Tells Clinton to Back Off as Racial Tension Grows in Mayor's Race," huffingtonpost.com, Dec. 28, 2010.

10. The Long Retreat

1. Englishforums.com.

2. Andrew Bacevich, "American Triumphalism: A Postmortem," *Commonweal,* Jan. 30, 2009.

3. Anne Applebaum, "The Slowly Vanishing NATO," *Washington Post,* Oct. 20, 2009.

4. Garet Garrett, *The People's Pottage* (Caldwell, ID: Caxton Press, 1958), 158–59.

5. Ibid., 159.

6. Bacevich, "American Triumphalism."

7. Tony Smith, "It's Uphill for the Democrats," *Washington Post,* March 11, 2007.

8. Bacevich, "American Triumphalism."

9. Ibid.

10. Steven Thomma, "Americans Turning Sharply Inward Toward Isolationism," Yahoo News, Dec. 3, 2009; "Poll: America's Place in the World," Pew Research Center, Dec. 3, 2009, historynewsnetwork.org.

11. Walter Lippmann, *U.S. Foreign Policy: Shield of the Republic* (Boston: Little, Brown, 1943), 6–7, 9–10.

12. Ibid., 8

13. Amanda Bransford, "U.S. Military Spending Far Outpaces Rest of the World," antiwar.com, May 29, 2010.

14. CNN Opinion Research Poll, CNN Opinion Research Corporation, Jan. 25, 2011.

15. Laurence Vance, "Same Empire, Different Emperor," lewrockwell.com, Feb. 11, 2010.

16. Ibid.

17. John Gray, "A Shattering Moment in America's Fall from Power," *Observer,* Sept. 28, 2008.

18. Gary Hart, Joan Meyers, "The Shield and the Cloak: The Security of the Commons," Carnegie Council, March 3, 2006, cceia.org.

19. Stephen Whitfield, Synopsis, *The Culture of the Cold War (The American Moment),* powells.com.

20. Richard Lugar, "Lugar Says It's Time to Reaffirm the Fundamental Value of NATO," press release of Senator Lugar, Sept. 28, 2009, lugar.senate.gov; Richard Betts, "The Three Faces of NATO," *National Interest,* April 10, 2009.

21. "Top General: It's a Draw in Afghanistan," ABC News, May 13, 2010.

22. Steven Erlanger, "Europeans Fear Crisis Threatens Liberal Benefits," *New York Times,* May 22, 2010.

23. Ibid.

24. Geoffrey Wheatcroft, "Boxed In, the Constraints of U.S. Foreign Policy," *World Affairs,* Jan./Feb. 2010, 48–49.

25. Ibid., 49.

26. William Knowlton, "Economy Helps Make Chinese the Leaders in Optimism, 24-Nation Survey Finds," *New York Times,* July 2, 2008.

27. Lester Brown, "Can the U.S. Be China's Breadbasket?" *Washington Post,* March 13, 2011.

28. Jerry Seper and Matthew Cella, "Signs in Arizona Warn of Smuggler Dangers," *Washington Times,* Aug. 31, 2010.

29. George F. Kennan, *Around the Cragged Hill: A Personal and Political Philosophy* (New York: W. W. Norton, 1994), 154.

30. Jerry Seper and Matthew Cella, "Signs in Arizona."

31. Michael Webster, "Mexico Federal Troops and Police Rush Into Juarez to Try and Retake the City," articlesbase.com, March 4, 2009.

32. "Mexican Police Chief Quits After Officers Killed," Reuters, Feb. 20, 2009.

33. "Calderon Vows to Win Mexico's Drug 'Cancer' Fight," Agence France Presse, Feb. 27, 2009, google.com.

34. Joshua E. Keating, "Freedom Gone South," *Foreign Policy,* Jan. 13, 2001.

35. "Military Report: Mexico, Pakistan at Risk of 'Rapid and Sudden Collapse,'" foxnews.com, Jan. 14, 2009.

36. Milton Friedman, "Prohibition and Drugs," *Newsweek,* May 1, 1972.

37. "Czech President Signs Lisbon Treaty," EUBusiness, Nov. 4, 2009.

38. Louis Charbonneau, "Czech President Tells UN to Stay Out of Economics," Reuters, Sept. 25, 2010.

39. "The Return of Economic Nationalism," *The Economist,* Feb. 7–13, 2009.

40. Ibid.

41. Charles Kupchan, "As Nationalism Rises, Will the European Union Fall?" *Washington Post,* Aug. 29, 2010.

42. Ibid.

43. Jude Dougherty, "National Identity," *Nationale und kulturelle Identität im Zeitalter der Globalisierung,* ed. Anton Rauscher, vol. 18 of the series *Soziale Orientierung* (Berlin: Duncker & Humblot, 2006), 23.

44. Ibid, 19.

45. Rudyard Kipling, "Sussex," oldpoetry.com.

11. The Last Chance

1. Silla Brush and Gautham Nagesh, "Controversial Beck Rally is an Event Heavier on Religion than Politics," thehill.com Aug. 28, 2010.

2. Duncan Williams, *Trousered Apes: Sick Literature in a Sick Society* (New Rochelle, NY: Arlington House, 1991), 140.

3. Herbert London, "U.S. Endorses Tolerance of Dictators Killing Their Own," *Human Events,* March 26, 2011.

4. Edward Kennedy, "Address at the Public Memorial Service for Robert F. Kennedy," June 8, 1968, St. Patrick's Cathedral, New York, American Rhetoric, Top 100 Speeches, americanrhetoric.com.

5. Claes Ryn, *The New Jacobinism: America as Revolutionary State* (With a Major New Afterward by the Author) (Bowie, Md.: National Humanities Institute, 2011).

6. "German Lessons," German Historical Institute, Washington, DC, ghi-dc.org, reprint of *Frankfurter Allgemeine Zeitung,* Nov. 27, 2008.

7. Rev. Martin Luther King, "Beyond Vietnam: A Time to Break Silence," Riverside Church, Apr. 4, 1967, hartford-hwp.com.

8. Justin Driver, "Robust and Wide-Open," *The New Republic,* Feb. 17, 2011, 37.

9. Ed Pilkington, "Obama Angers Midwest Voters with Guns and Religion Remark," *Guardian,* April 14, 2008.

10. "A More Perfect Union," Remarks of Sen. Barack Obama, Constitution Center, Philadelphia, huffingtonpost.com, March 18, 2008.

11. Murray Rothbard, "A Strategy for the Right," *The Irrepressible Rothbard,* lewrockwell.com/rothbard/ir/Ch1.html.

12. Michael Kinsley, "Cordoba House: Charles Krauthammer, and the First Amendment," theatlanticwire.com Aug. 16, 2010.

13. Chilton Williamson, Jr., "The New American Mob," *Chronicles,* July 2010, 17.

14. Ibid., 18.

15. Carol Swain, *The New White Nationalism in America: Its Challenge to Integration* (Cambridge: Cambridge University Press, 2004), 423.

16. "President Nixon's 'Silent Majority' Speech, November 1969," vietnamwar.net.

17. "Military Needs to Close More Bases," reuters.com, Sept. 15, 2010.

18. Yaakov Katz, "Stuxnet Virus Set Back Iran's Nuclear Program by 2 Years," *Jerusalem Post,* Dec. 15, 2010.

19. Ralph Gomory, "A Time for Action: Jobs, Prosperity and National Goals," huffingtonpost.com, Jan. 25, 2010.

20. Ibid.

21. Abraham Lincoln, "The Perpetuation of Our Political Institutions," Lyceum Address, Jan. 27, 1838, Speeches and Writings, Abraham Lincoln Online, showcase.netins.net.

22. James Gimpel, "Immigration, Political Realignment, and the Demise of Republican Political Prospects," backgrounder, Center for Immigration Studies, Feb. 2010, 5.

23. Ibid.

24. Toby Hamden, "Barack Obama in Turkey: US 'Will Never Be at War With Islam,'" *The Telegraph,* April 6, 2009.

25. "Novak's Secret Source Revealed: Former Sen. Tom Eagleton Labeled '72 Dem Nominee as Candidate of 'Amnesty, Abortion and Acid,'" Crown Forum, July 10, 2007, yubanet.com.

26. David Gordon, "Courts and Congress: America's Unwritten Constitution," *The Mises Review,* April 2008, mises.org.

27. "Letter from a Birmingham Jail [King Jr.]," African Studies Center, University of Pennsylvania, africa.upenn.edu.

Index